Introducing Autodesk® Inventor® 2009 and Autodesk® Inventor LT™ 2009

Introducing Autodesk® Inventor® 2009 and Autodesk® Inventor LT™ 2009

THOM TREMBLAY

WILEY

Wiley Publishing, Inc.

Acquisitions Editor: WILLEM KNIBBE

Development Editor: PETE GAUGHAN

Technical Editor: STEVE WARREN

Production Editors: MELISSA LOPEZ, LAUREL IBEY, AND ERIC CHARBONNEAU

Copy Editor: LIZ WELCH

Production Manager: TIM TATE

Vice President and Executive Group Publisher: RICHARD SWADLEY

Vice President and Executive Publisher: JOSEPH B. WIKERT

Vice President and Publisher: NEIL EDDE

Book Designer: CARYL GORSKA

Compositor: CHRIS GILLESPIE, HAPPENSTANCE TYPE-O-RAMA

Proofreader: JEN LARSEN, WORD ONE

Indexer: JACK LEWIS

Cover Designer: RYAN SNEED

Cover Images: THOM TREMBLAY (TOP IMAGE), ISTOCKPHOTO (BOTTOM ROW)

Dear Reader,

Thank you for choosing *Introducing Autodesk Inventor 2009 and Autodesk Inventor LT 2009*. This book is part of a family of premium quality Sybex books, all written by outstanding authors who combine practical experience with a gift for teaching.

Sybex was founded in 1976. More than thirty years later, we're still committed to producing consistently exceptional books. With each of our titles we're working hard to set a new standard for the industry. From the paper we print on, to the authors we work with, our goal is to bring you the best books available.

I hope you see all that reflected in these pages. I'd be very interested to hear your comments and get your feedback on how we're doing. Feel free to let me know what you think about this or any other Sybex book by sending me an email at nedde@wiley.com, or if you think you've found a technical error in this book, please visit http://sybex.custhelp.com. Customer feedback is critical to our efforts at Sybex.

Best regards,

Neil Edde
Vice President and Publisher
Sybex, an Imprint of Wiley

Dedication

To Tony Fox, a true friend who is the epitome of what it means to be an Inventor.

Acknowledgments

I would first and foremost like to thank my wife Nancy for convincing me that I was capable of writing this book, then putting up with me while I did it. I hope that everyone who reads this has someone like her to lean on. ▪ I'd like to thank tech editor Steve Warren for all of his hard work and expertise, along with his willingness to put in the overtime. Thanks also to my good friends Mick Fears and Don Strimbu, who were the first to recognize that my passion for these technologies had other uses and encouraged me to find out all that I was capable of. ▪ I'm working on a new word to describe my gratitude for the Sybex team who endured my learning curve: Willem Knibbe, Jim Compton, Melissa Lopez, Eric Charbonneau, Laurel Ibey, Sandy Jaffe-Belanger, Janet Chang, Pete Gaughan, Liz Welch, and the others whose names that I don't know but whose professionalism (and patience) was beyond compare. ▪ I also want to extend my sincere thanks to Lynn Allen, Alan Jacobs, and all of the Autodesk family who supported and encouraged me during this effort. ▪ Many thanks to Mr. Jay Tedeschi, a good friend whose fantastic Helicopter Rotor Head is featured on the front cover and is just one example of what can be done with Inventor and a creative mind.

About the Author

Thom Tremblay supports the Autodesk Worldwide Education group as a technical specialist on Inventor and AutoCAD Electrical. In his first seven years with Autodesk, Thom supported the Autodesk Inventor commercial sales group, working with customers to understand and improve their processes using Inventor and other technologies.

Thom's professional experience includes working in the design of facilities, plastics, electronics, ship building, and commercial air conditioning. Early in his career he realized the benefits of using 3D geometry to create the 2D drawings that are so critical to create the products of the vast majority of companies around the world.

CONTENTS AT A GLANCE

Introduction ■ **xiii**

Chapter 1 ■ Inventor Face to Face **1**

Chapter 2 ■ Creating 2D Drawings from 3D Data **37**

Chapter 3 ■ Introducing Part Modeling **81**

Chapter 4 ■ Putting It All Together with Assemblies **137**

Chapter 5 ■ Standards and Styles **169**

Chapter 6 ■ Advanced Annotation: Drawing Views and Detailing **195**

Chapter 7 ■ Getting in Shape: Advanced Part Modeling **229**

Chapter 8 ■ Advanced Assembly Tools **293**

Chapter 9 ■ Introducing Sheet Metal Parts **341**

Chapter 10 ■ Introducing Inventor Studio **369**

Appendix A ■ Keyboard Shortcut Guide **393**

Appendix B ■ Import and Export File Formats **397**

Appendix C ■ Additional Resources **399**

Index ■ **401**

Contents

Introduction   xiii

Chapter 1 ▪ Inventor Face to Face   **1**

Learning to Use the Dialog Boxes   2

The Open Dialog Box   3

The New File Dialog Box   7

Navigating Inventor's User Interface   8

Make Yourself at Home:
Customizing Inventor   18

Project Files   28

Using the Help System   34

Summary   36

Chapter 2 ▪ Creating 2D Drawings from 3D Data   **37**

Drawing Views of a Part   38

Creating Base Views   40

Detailing Drawing Views   55

Adding Dimensions in Inventor   59

Associativity   71

Assembly Drawings   74

Detail Views   75

Presentation Views   77

Summary   79

Chapter 3 ▪ Introducing Part Modeling   **81**

The Concept of Parametric Modeling   82

Sketch Constraints   87

The Extrude Tool   104

The Fillet Tool   108

The Hole Feature   113

Work Features   120

The Revolve Tool   129

Feature Libraries   134

Summary   136

Chapter 4 ■ Putting It All Together with Assemblies   137

The Assembly Modeling Concept   138

Creating Assembly Constraints   138

Representations   153

Enabled Parts   156

Working with Standard Parts   157

Summary   167

Chapter 5 ■ Standards and Styles   169

Styles and Standards   170

Drawing Templates   185

Summary   193

Chapter 6 ■ Advanced Annotation:
Drawing Views and Detailing   195

Moving Beyond the Basic View   196

Expanded Dimensioning Options   210

Summary   227

Chapter 7 ■ Getting in Shape: Advanced Part Modeling   229

A Feature-Rich Application   230

Beginning a New Part   230

The Thread Tool   232

The Split Tool   238

The Emboss Tool   240

Rectangular and Circular Patterns   244

More Sketching Tools   245

The Loft Tool   250

The Sculpt Tool   256

The Shell Tool   262

The Rib and Web Tools   266

The Sweep Tool   268

The Coil Tool   274

The Mirror Tool   278

The Thicken/Offset Tool   284

iParts   286

Summary   292

Chapter 8 ■ Advanced Assembly Tools   **293**

An Assembly-centric Application   294

Design Accelerators   294

Derived Parts   319

Component Move and Rotate   322

iAssembly   323

Animation within the Assembly   328

Presentation Files   331

Positional Representation   336

Weldments   339

Summary   340

Chapter 9 ■ Introducing Sheet Metal Parts   **341**

A Manufacturing-Focused Toolset   342

Sheet Metal Rules   342

Making Sheet Metal Parts   350

Sheet Metal Detailing   367

Summary   368

Chapter 10 ■ Introducing Inventor Studio   **369**

Enhancing Your Design   370

Creating a Rendering   370

Working with Animation   383

Summary   389

Appendix A ◼ **Keyboard Shortcut Guide**   393

Appendix B ◼ **Import and Export File Formats**   397

Appendix C ◼ **Additional Resources**   399

                          Index   401

Introduction

In the spring of 1998 I was working for an Autodesk reseller at an event that we hosted. I was shown a preview of a yet-to-be-released technology that would eventually be known as Autodesk Inventor. It was simple and quick, and looked like it would be effortless to learn. I was hooked.

Ten years later Autodesk Inventor is the world's largest-selling 3D mechanical design application. Its capabilities are branching into areas that until now were exclusive to applications that cost nearly ten times the price. With these capabilities comes the potential for complexity, but Inventor looks and behaves remarkably like it did when it was first released in the fall of 1999.

When the opportunity to write a book introducing people to Inventor came about, I was thrilled because I have seen how it has helped so many people. I immediately decided that I wanted to try to structure the book for the working designer and engineer who wants to learn Inventor but has very little time. I also wanted to change the order in which Inventor is usually taught, and the process for learning it, with the working professional in mind.

Traditionally, learning a 3D-based system begins with you constructing models, then learning how to assemble those models together, and finally (after many, many hours) creating a drawing. In my experience the people who would benefit most from Inventor are those who are spending much, if not most, of their time making 2D drawings. So why not begin the hands-on work with Inventor by working with 2D drawings and seeing just how easily they're made and how powerful they are?

The next decision was to introduce these processes in stages. I wanted you to be able to spend time with the most fundamental tools and focus on getting comfortable with them before learning the more advanced tools in each of the main portions of the program. I also think moving more quickly through the fundamentals will expose the consistency in the Inventor approach and build your confidence and comfort level as you see that the dialog boxes and other elements for each tool have something in common with the tools you've already learned. In fact, one of the greatest challenges was paring down what to include, because an advanced feature is usually only a click or two away from the most basic tools.

Finally the use of the individual tools is also meant to be absorbed in stages. First I will try to walk you through the use of a particular tool; when you use the tool later you may be reminded of where to find it or a required step, and then later you will just be asked to use the tool as part of learning another topic. Hopefully this will build your confidence while allowing you to focus on new tools rather than ones you've used repeatedly.

Who Should Buy This Book

This book is not intended as a text on creating engineering drawings or to teach engineering or design philosophy. This book assumes that you are:

- A working professional with design and drafting experience
- Familiar with basic Microsoft Windows functions
- Familiar with drafting and design terminology

For example, this book will discuss how to create orthographic projections in a drawing but will not discuss what an orthographic projection is.

Given that, I don't assume readers have 3D solid modeling or even experience with a computer-aided design (CAD) program. If this book encourages people who've never used 3D or even CAD to try Inventor, then I will consider it an unqualified success.

The exercises in this book will focus on how Autodesk Inventor and Autodesk Inventor LT can be used as a tool to carry out design work for a production environment.

System Requirements

The basic system requirements for Autodesk Inventor Suite and LT 2009 are as follows:

Operating systems

- Windows© XP Professional, Home, XP Professional x64 SP2
- Windows© Vista (32-bit or 64-bit)

Hardware

- Intel © Pentium © 4 or AMD® Athlon® 64 or later. 2GHz or faster processor.
- 512MB of RAM (minimum); >1GB recommended
- >1.5GB free disk space for Inventor LT and >3GB for Inventor Suite with Content Center
- Direct3D 9 or 10 Graphics support with >64MB of RAM

What's Inside

Here is a preview of each chapter.

Chapter 1: Inventor Face to Face This chapter presents the interface and working environment of Autodesk Inventor.

Chapter 2: Creating 2D Drawings from 3D Data Creating production drawings is critical for most designers. This chapter introduces the primary tools used by Inventor to create 2D drawings.

Chapter 3: Introducing Part Modeling The fundamentals of building 3D parts are the focus of this chapter. Understanding sketching and the application of parametric dimensions and constraining the movement of sketch elements are a big part of the exercises.

Chapter 4: Pulling It All Together with Assemblies* Building assemblies out of individual parts is an important part of developing products using Autodesk Inventor. This chapter takes you through the process of making common assembly models.

Chapter 5: Standards and Styles Creating parts and drawings consistently is important, and using the same layers, dimensions, and other styles makes it much easier to do.

Chapter 6: Advanced Annotation: Drawing Views and Detailing* Continuing the topics introduced in Chapter 2, this chapter works with additional drawing view creation and annotation tools.

Chapter 7: Getting in Shape: Advanced Part Modeling In this chapter you will work with tools not covered in Chapter 3. These tools will include special editing tools, advanced sketching techniques, and family parts.

Chapter 8: Advanced Assembly Tools* Additional tools for building assemblies are just a part of this chapter. Learn about Inventor's true design capabilities using Design Accelerators and families of assemblies.

Chapter 9: Introducing Sheet Metal Parts* Tools are available for sheet metal parts. This chapter will take you through the basics of creating these specialized parts.

Chapter 10: Introducing Inventor Studio Inventor Studio is an environment inside Inventor that allows you to create photo-realistic renderings and animations from 3D models.

* Topics covered include functionality not available in Autodesk Inventor LT 2009.

You will need to download data for some exercises from www.sybex.com/go/ introducinginventor2009. The files will be contained in a zip file and downloading the data beforehand will save time.

How to Contact the Author

I appreciate your interest in this book and in Inventor. If you would like to share your feedback or stories about how this book may have helped, I would love to hear from you.

You can reach me at thom.tremblay@yahoo.com

Sybex strives to keep you supplied with the latest tools and information you need for your work. Please check the website at www.sybex.com, where we'll post additional content and updates that supplement this book should the need arise. Enter **Introducing Autodesk Inventor** in the Search box (or type the book's ISBN: 9780470375525), and click Go to get to the book's update page.

Now let's begin exploring Inventor, and hopefully you'll have some fun along the way.

CHAPTER 1

Inventor Face to Face

This chapter focuses on the Autodesk Inventor Suite's 2009 interface and the fundamental tools for accessing files, working with the tools of Inventor, and getting additional information.

One of the greatest barriers that I've found to learning new software (or learning any new task) is the feeling that you have no control over the environment you are working in. In this chapter we'll look at ways to modify the look and feel of Inventor so that you feel more comfortable and learn where things are. A thorough understanding of the interface may not seem exciting, but getting comfortable with the interface and knowing where to look for help is the foundation for everything else that you will learn in this book.

- Opening existing files

- Understanding Inventor's Interface behavior

- Modifying the look and feel of Inventor

- Managing file locations

- Accessing the Help system

Learning to Use the Dialog Boxes

One thing that makes Inventor easy to use is a kind of "graphical language" common to all the dialog boxes. These are items that behave consistently wherever they appear. As you use Inventor, working with these items will become second nature. As you're getting started, knowing what to look for will make it easy to understand what Inventor needs from you in order to accomplish your task.

Buttons

The following buttons and button states have the same effect no matter where you encounter them in Inventor's interface:

A button with a red arrow indicates that Inventor needs you to select something. Text may appear next to the arrow, identifying the type of input that Inventor is looking for.

A button with a white arrow means that Inventor has been given the information that it needs.

The OK button will be grayed out until Inventor has the necessary user input to execute an operation. Clicking OK initiates the command or function and closes the dialog box.

The Apply button will also be grayed out until Inventor has the necessary user input to execute an operation. Clicking the Apply button initiates the command or function but it will not close the dialog box. This allows you to execute the function and start using it again immediately.

The Cancel button closes the dialog box without executing any operation.

The More button exposes additional options for a dialog box. Once those options become visible, the arrows then point to the left so you can hide the options again.

Any button with an ellipsis after the name launches another dialog box or selection window when clicked.

Tabs

Another element of the common graphical language is the way dialog boxes are organized. Many dialog boxes have tabs across the top, with each tab offering additional options. Though most common functions are contained on the first tab, when you begin working with a new dialog box, it is worth taking a few moments to explore what options are on the other tabs. For example, in the Extrude dialog box illustrated here, the Shape tab offers the basic options to select the shape and define the distance it will be extruded, while the More tab offers options to apply taper or draft to the shape.

Context Menus

You can access a large number of Inventor's tools by clicking your secondary mouse button—typically the right button—at different places on your screen. As in other Windows software, right-clicking displays a *context menu* of options that are relevant to what you're doing at the time. For example, as you'll learn in Chapter 5, right-clicking a drawing's border in the Browser displays a menu that lets you delete the border or add a new one. In the exercises and examples in this book, I'll often instruct you to right-click and select the next operation from a context menu.

The Open Dialog Box

Each time you start Inventor you will be presented with the Open dialog box (see Figure 1.1) to select the file(s) you want to work on.

Inventor LT users will see a slightly different Open dialog box. Inventor LT does not have assembly capabilities, so there are elements that are not necessary to have. It will still be beneficial for the LT user to understand the capabilities of Inventor Suite or Professional 2009 in case they use it in the future.

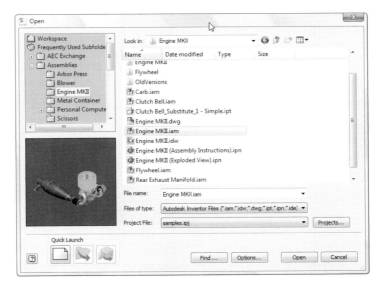

Figure 1.1

File list displaying small icons

As in any contemporary software, this dialog box allows you to select a file or files to open in Inventor. If you're accustomed to Microsoft Windows Explorer and some of its viewing options, this dialog box will seem familiar. Using it should be comfortable for you right away. There are several components to the dialog box, and it is important to understand what these parts are and what they will do for you.

It is possible to resize the dialog box by clicking and dragging the corners in order to allow easy viewing of the information it displays.

Shortcuts and the File List

In the upper left of the dialog box is an area with a list of shortcuts to Frequently Used Subfolders (Figure 1.2). You can customize this pane to create shortcuts to folders that you'd like to access quickly. You can even set up subreferences and have a structure that replicates the folder structure on your hard drive.

Figure 1.2

Frequently Used Subfolders list

Centered in the dialog box and making up the bulk of it is the File list, where the files are displayed. What files are listed is controlled by the File Of Type option, described shortly. You can open a file (or files) from here by selecting the filename(s) and clicking OK or by double-clicking on the filename.

At the top of the dialog box is the Look In field. This displays the name of the folder whose files are currently displayed below it in the File list. The arrow to the right allows you cascade the folder structure or to begin browsing for other folders.

Navigation Controls

To the right of the Look In field are four icons that allow you to navigate easily and to control how you view the files that you're looking for.

These tools share icons and functions with many standard Windows icons and tools.

You will find commonality in the controls between Inventor and many Microsoft applications. This is done so that you don't have to learn every aspect of the user interface from scratch.

Go To Last Folder Visited The first button has an arrow pointing left. This button allows you to navigate back to the previous folder(s) you were browsing in. It works on the same principle as the Back button in a web browser. When you've just begun a session, the arrow will be grayed out, as you don't have any browsing history to recall.

Up One Level The next icon looks like a folder with a green arrow pointing up. This takes you up a level in your folder structure from wherever you are currently browsing.

Create New Folder The third icon allows you to create a new folder in the folder that you are currently browsing in.

The View Menu The icon on the right is a flyout tool that allows you to change the way the files that you're browsing will be displayed. Depending on the operating system you're using, you will see different options ranging from a detailed listing of dates and file size to thumbnail previews of the files in the display area. In Figure 1.3 you can see the same folder as in Figure 1.1 being browsed with the Thumbnail display option.

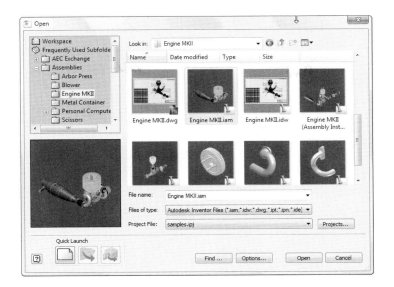

Figure 1.3
**File list showing
Thumbnail view**

File Display Options

Immediately below the File list are three selection pull-down lists that control the file display options.

File Name This pull-down displays the full name of the selected file(s). If you click the arrow to the right, it opens a list of recently open files.

Files Of Type This option is very important. Clicking the arrow to the right lets you choose from a list of file types that Inventor can open. It's important to filter the file types displayed because of the broad array of types.

Project File This flyout allows you to select from a list of project files that have been used in the past. The active or current project file is shown any time the Open dialog box is brought up. To the right of the pull-down is a button marked Projects, which launches the Project File editor, which in turn allows you to select project files that have not been used previously, edit existing project files, or create a new project file. We'll take a look at the Project File dialog box later in this chapter in the Project Files section.

To the left of File Display Options is the File Preview pane. As you select a file in the File list, a preview of that file appears in this area. Not all files have a preview to display.

At the lower left of the Open dialog box you'll find three icons under the heading Quick Launch.

At least one of these icons will not be available at any given time. If you're in the Open dialog box, the first icon will be available; it switches you from Open to the New dialog box. The middle icon switches you back to Open from New. The third icon is for opening files from the Vault, a great data management system that I highly recommend install-

Figure 1.4

The Find *tool* dialog box

ing. (The Vault comes with Inventor so there's no additional cost but there are great benefits that I will talk about briefly in Appendix C.) This icon will be available only if the project file that is active has the Vault enabled.

In the lower right you'll see the Find button. Clicking it displays a Find *tool* dialog box (Figure 1.4) that can execute simple or complex searches. You can search for file properties, creation dates, or strings of text, and you can even save your searches to be reused in the future.

Other Controls

Three more options complete the Open dialog box:

Options Available only when you import, export, or open a file that can have additional settings applied to it. For example, if you want to export a DWG file for use with AutoCAD, you can select which version of AutoCAD can open the file, back to AutoCAD 2000.

Open Executes the opening of the selected file or files. You can open multiple files at the same time by holding the Ctrl key to select multiple individual files or by holding Shift to click a range of files. You can also open multiple files by dragging a file or files from Windows Explorer onto the title bar of Autodesk Inventor.

Cancel Exits the attempt to open a file and returns you to Inventor.

Opening a File

Now that you have had an overview of the parts and functions of the Open dialog box, let's put what you've learned to use. (Some options will not be available to Inventor LT users; again, LT cannot work with assemblies.)

1. If the Samples project isn't displayed as the active project, use the pull-down list to select it. It should be on the short Project File list. If it doesn't appear on the list, open the Project File dialog box as described earlier, select Samples from the list, and click Open. This should set that project to be active and return you to the Open dialog box.

2. Use the Frequently Used Subfolders list to find the Assemblies\Engine MKII\Engine MKII.iam assembly file. Inventor LT users should select a part file of their choosing to review changes. You can find samples files to choose from at C:\Program Files\ Autodesk\Inventor LT Technology Preview\Samples.

3. Once you have found the file, you can select it with a single mouse click and click OK, or you can double-click on the file in the window. Once the file is open, you should see something like Figure 1.5.

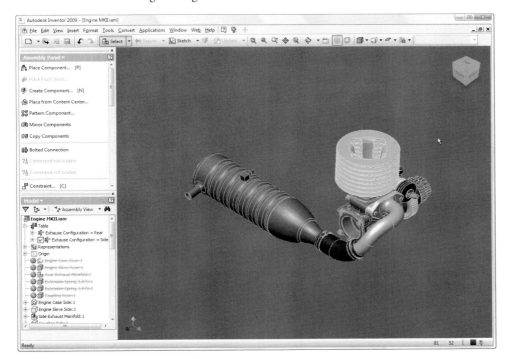

Figure 1.5

The Engine MkII assembly in the Design window

The New File Dialog Box

The New File dialog box (Figure 1.6) is much simpler than the Open dialog box. Like the Open dialog box, it has a Quick Launch section that allows you to switch to the Open dialog box, and where you can set the active project file.

Every new drawing you create in Inventor is based on a template, which provides information such as borers, title blocks, layer colors, and the standard dimension style. These templates can be customized, and Inventor comes with a sizable selection to give you a head start. It is also possible to convert existing AutoCAD drawings to Inventor templates.

In the New File dialog box, Inventor's collection of built-in templates is categorized in tabs across the top. There are templates for Default, English, and Metric measurements.

Figure 1.6

**The New File dialog
box showing Metric
templates**

Navigating Inventor's User Interface

With Inventor open and a file loaded, it is time to get familiar with the component of
Inventor that you will use every time you start the program; the graphical user interface
(GUI). Figure 1.7 shows the main components.

Figure 1.7

**The parts of the
Inventor GUI**

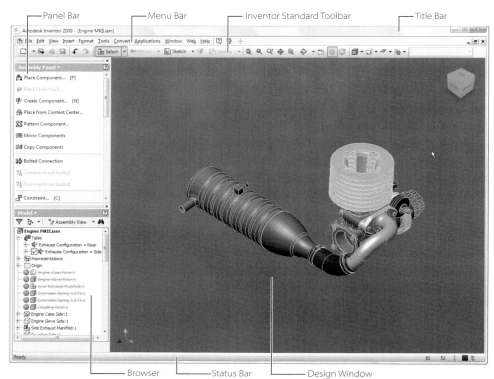

If you're used to the look and feel of Microsoft Word (prior to 2007) and Microsoft Internet Explorer, you should find a lot of similarities to many of the standard tools in Inventor. If you are experienced with recent versions of AutoCAD, you will find a lot of similarities with the drawing and sketching tool icons in Inventor.

Across the top of the Inventor application is the title bar. It will remind you that you are in Autodesk Inventor and tell you what version you are using. It will also tell you the name of the file that you are currently editing if that file is in its maximized view. If the Inventor file is in a floating window, then each window's title bar will display the filename.

Just below that is the menu bar, a collection of tools is organized in pull-down menus. These menus contain valuable tools for everything from an alternative way of opening files to measuring geometry on the screen. You can even launch a website containing components manufactured by other Inventor users that you can download into your designs. The names, content, and number of these menus will vary depending on whether you have a file open and what type of file it is.

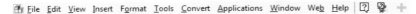

Over the course of the book we will examine some of the tools in the menu bar pull-downs as needed. A majority of the tools in the menu bar establish how you are working with Inventor rather than containing the tools that you would use for modeling or drawing.

Immediately below the menu bar is the Inventor Standard toolbar. This is where a lot of the basic file and view manipulation tools can be accessed easily. The toolbar is a collection of groups of different types of tools. The tools available depend on the type of file you're editing at the time. Most of the differences will be found on the right end of the toolbar. The first three groups of tools are consistent regardless of the type of file you're editing.

Since you have the assembly loaded, let's use it to explore how you will interact with Inventor and take a closer look at some of the elements of the interface that we just touched on.

Let's begin with an in-depth look at the Inventor Standard toolbar. Most of the other elements of the interface will be used as part of exercises, but the Standard toolbar contains tools that are used to control and better understand the model that you're creating. These tools do not create geometry, but they make it easy to do so.

On the left you may recognize the standard icons for New, Open, and Save. The third icon may not be immediately recognized; it is Open From Vault. This is the same tool that you saw in the overview of the Open dialog box.

The next section has to do with working in the context of parts and assemblies. The first two icons are our old friends Undo and Redo. If you make a mistake, Inventor will allow up to 30 steps of Undo and Redo. A great feature is that changes to the model view (zooming, panning, etc.) do not use Undo steps. You can even undo the creation or opening of a file.

Immediately to the right of those tools is the selection Filters list. Filters are a tool for focusing or streamlining selections. They can limit or enhance the selection of certain types of entities in parts, assemblies, or drawings. The use of filters is a great thing to learn and explore. Many experienced Inventor users are missing out by not becoming more comfortable with them.

You will use the Return button frequently. This tool moves you from one editing state to the one above it. Its importance will become clear as we start working in Inventor.

Several toolbar buttons have a down arrow next to them. This indicates that an additional option or options are under the primary command. For example, the Sketch icon, which allows you to create or edit sketches, has a 3D Sketch button under it.

If Inventor is unsure that what it is displaying is the most current information, the Update button becomes available and allows you to update the data that is on the screen.

The third portion controls how you look at the file you are editing. Many of the icons will be familiar. They are commonly used tools, so take a moment to practice using them in context. Begin on the left and work your way across.

The first icon is Zoom All. No matter what your point of view, clicking this icon frames your model evenly in the Design window, which is where you are currently seeing the engine assembly.

Zoom Window allows you to zoom in on a specific area by creating a "window" frame around the area that you want larger. To create the frame, you select the tool, click where you want one corner, and while continuing to hold the button down, drag the size of the frame. When you've encompassed the area you want to make larger, release the mouse button. Figure 1.8 shows the zoom area being framed, and Figure 1.9 shows the result. Try enlarging your view of a portion of the assembly using the Zoom Window tool. You can also access Zoom Window by pressing the Z key on your keyboard.

Figure 1.8

Framing the area to zoom in on

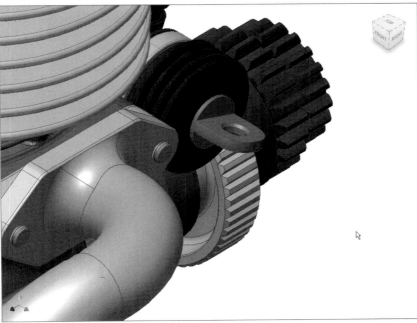

Figure 1.9

The result of zooming

Click the Zoom icon. You'll notice the onscreen pointer changes its shape to two arrows: a small arrow pointing up and a large arrow pointing down. Click and drag anywhere in the Design window, and note that as you drag up, the model gets smaller and, as you drag down, the model gets larger. If you drag as far as you can in the Design window but want to continue to zoom, release the mouse button, move the cursor, and click to start zooming again. To stop the Zoom command, press your Esc key or right-click on the screen and select Done [Esc]. You can also access the Zoom command by pressing and holding the F3 key. Releasing the key ends the command. If you're not convinced that it's easy enough to access the Zoom command, there's one more option. If you have a wheel mouse, try rolling it. If you roll the mouse away from you, the model gets smaller. If you roll the wheel toward you, it gets larger.

In AutoCAD you get the exact opposite zooming with a wheel mouse. This is because Auto-CAD's zoom is based on the idea of moving a camera and Inventor's is based on moving the object that you're looking at. If you absolutely need to have Inventor to zoom in the Auto-CAD fashion, you can change a setting in the application options, which we'll review later in this chapter.

 Next try the Pan command. Panning is sliding the image on the plane of the screen without changing its size or the point of view that you have of it. As with Zoom, it is a click-and-drag tool. You can also release and restart panning while staying in the command. Pan is also available by pressing the F2 key or by pressing and holding the wheel or the middle mouse button.

The keyboard shortcut appears in brackets on the menu. For a complete listing of keyboard shortcuts, refer to Appendix A.

 Zoom Selected centers and enlarges any face of any part that you select. After you have started the command, you can move your screen pointer over any part of an assembly or any face of a part. As you do so, you'll also notice yellow or green dots appear as you move over points. If you select one of the points, the view will not enlarge but will center on the selected point.

 The next tool is the Free Orbit tool (commonly referred to simply as the Orbit tool). Until the introduction of the ViewCube (see the ViewCube section later in this chapter), it was the primary way users could quickly rotate a model to view it from other directions. It is valuable to learn about this tool, but I expect most new users to become as dependent on the ViewCube as I have in the short time that I've been using it.

When the Orbit tool is running, a circle with four rays will appear. This is known as the *Reticle*. The horizontal and vertical lines represent the X and Y axes of the screen. As you near them, the cursor changes to an arrow in a loop. Clicking and dragging at that time rotates the object about the axis of the screen. When you move your mouse outside the circle but away from the axes, the cursor changes to an arrow in a circle. Clicking and dragging at that time causes the model to rotate about the Z axis of the screen. If you move away from the center of the screen, you see yet another cursor: this one takes the shape of the arrow on an Enter key. Clicking with this arrow displayed is a shortcut out of the Orbit tool.

Now move the cursor inside the circle, where it will look similar to the toolbar button you selected in the first place. Clicking and dragging inside the Reticle causes the model to tumble about the center point of the screen. You can change what portion of the model is centered on the screen by hovering over a point and double-clicking the primary mouse button. This causes the model to shift position similar to clicking a point using the Zoom Selected tool.

The Constrained Orbit tool is basically the same as Free Orbit but designed to pivot around the axes of the model.

After the ViewCube (discussed next), the Look At tool is the one that I use the most. Once you've selected the tool, it highlights planar faces and edges as you move your cursor over the model. If you select an edge, it rotates the view of the model so that the edge that you selected is centered and horizontal. If you select a face, it rotates the view so that you are looking directly at the face, and it centers the face in the view as well. This is a great tool to get yourself reoriented if you become confused about what you are looking at. You can also access the tool through the Home key.

The next two items are toggles to control the visibility of the ViewCube and the Steering Wheels, so I'll briefly explain those important features.

The ViewCube

When you click the ViewCube toolbar button, the ViewCube appears in the upper-right corner of the Design window. The ViewCube allows you to click the named faces of the cube and have the part orient itself to match the cube's new orientation. You can also rotate the part about its center by clicking the cube and dragging it while holding down the mouse button. Other features include the ability to select corners and edges of the cube to rotate the part. There are also two curved arrows that appear when you're looking directly at a standard view. These arrows allow you to spin the part about the axis of the screen. It is the same effect as if you pressed a finger into the center of a piece of paper and rotated the sheet under your finger. As you near the ViewCube, another icon appears in the upper left; it looks like a house. Clicking this returns your model to the Home view. You can also return to the Home view at any time by pressing the F6 key. You'll work with the ViewCube throughout this book.

The Steering Wheels

The Steering Wheels (plural because there are a few different versions) allow "heads up" access to the Zoom, Orbit, and Pan tools as well as several other features. The ViewCube and Steering Wheels can be found not only in Inventor but other Autodesk products as well, such as AutoCAD. Because of this, some of the tools on the Steering Wheels are not specifically built for Inventor. Walk, Look, and Up/Down may be useful for showing someone how to navigate through a large assembly, but I suspect that other tools will be more useful to you.

The Rewind Tool

The Rewind tool (Figure 1.10) is particularly valuable. As I mentioned earlier, the Undo function does not record or effect changes to Zoom. Rewind shows you a "film reel"–style list of previous views, and as you move through them you see the model move back to previous points of view. This is a double benefit because the "film reel" allows you to move quickly to an approximate view that you want to recall, but the onscreen display gives you the full view immediately so you can be sure you are getting what you want. In case you're wondering, there's also a keystroke that can recall previous views, but it does not offer the "film reel" view. Pressing the F5 key recalls the previous view. If you press F5 again, it goes back again. Holding the F5 key automatically cycles back through previous views until you release it.

Figure 1.10

The Rewind tool

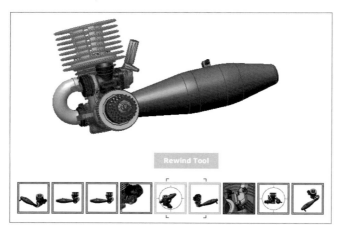

Display Options

The last four icons on the Inventor Standard toolbar deal strictly with the appearance of the model.

The first flyout button allows the 3D model to be displayed as a Shaded Display, Hidden Edge Display, or Wireframe Display. Figure 1.11 illustrates the three modes.

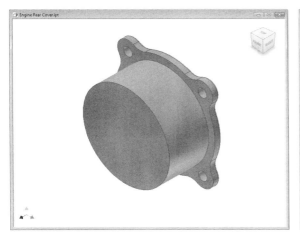

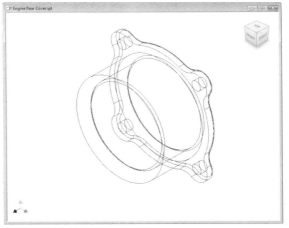

Figure 1.11

3D display modes. Shaded Display (left) is the most realistic; Hidden Edge Display (right) shows the edges on the back of the shaded model; and Wireframe Display (bottom) allows you to see all of a part's features.

The next flyout button controls whether the model will be viewed in Perspective. You can even alter the lens length of the perspective view to give a different effect. Do this by selecting the Zoom command and then holding the Alt and Shift keys at the same time. This changes the apparent focal length of the perspective view "lens." Holding the Alt key and pressing the Shift key while rolling a mouse wheel also works.

As you can see in Figure 1.12, displaying a shadow of the model can sometimes help you keep your orientation. The display of the two types of shadow is controlled by the flyout to the right of the Perspective button. Ground Shadow casts a shadow of the overall shape of the part or assembly as though there were a light above it, and X-Ray Ground Shadow shows more of the internal characteristics of a part and casts individual shadows for the parts of an assembly.

Figure 1.12

Displaying a shadow can help maintain perspective.

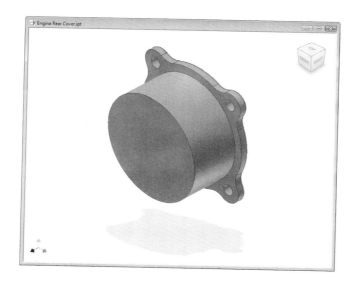

The final button is only available in the assembly. It is a flyout that controls whether other parts of an assembly dim or become transparent when you activate a part in the assembly to edit it. It is not available to Inventor LT users.

If Component Opacity is left on (the default), only the part being edited in the context of an assembly will be of a solid color. All of the other parts will change in some way. I highly recommend working in this way as it helps you to keep track of whether you are in the assembly or are editing a part in the assembly.

To demonstrate this, hover over the muffler (Tuned Pipe) of the assembly and notice that it highlights. Once it has become highlighted, double-click it quickly. After it has been made "active," your display should look something like Figure 1.13.

Figure 1.13

Using the Component Opacity option

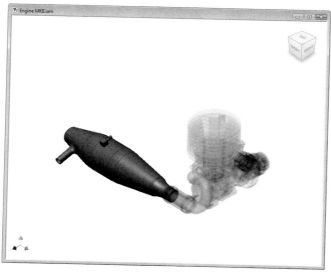

Additional buttons and flyouts appear on the Inventor Standard toolbar (usually at the right end of the toolbar) as you work with different files. Like the tools that you just reviewed, these additional tools provide some great options and additional capabilities. We'll cover these in future exercises so that you learn each one in its most relevant context.

The Panel Bars

The vast majority of the tools that you use day to day with Inventor can be found in the Panel bars. By default the Panel bars are located in the upper left of the display and display their tools with an icon and descriptive text.

Panel bars can be thought of as smart toolbars. I prefer to think of them as toolbars that are "contextual." They understand what tools are needed based on whether you are sketching 2D elements, putting 3D features on a part, or creating drawings. They adjust to provide you with these tools automatically. There are two major benefits to this. First, you don't need to have screen space occupied by toolbars that are not relevant to what you are doing. For example, why have a dimension tool taking up screen space when you are attaching parts to one another in an assembly? Second, it provides feedback about what Inventor thinks you're trying to do. For example, suppose I am in a part model and make an errant mouse click, thinking that I have asked to create a new sketch. If the sketch tools do not automatically appear, I can instantly recognize that I must have made a mistake in my request.

The Browser Bar

In the default display, the Browser bar is positioned directly below the Panel bar. The Browser bar displays a list of features or relationships that reflect how the file that you are working in was built. Regardless of the type of Inventor file, critical information on how it was constructed can be easily reviewed. This is particularly important when you are working on a file that you did not create or last edit.

As you create and edit 3D and 2D files in later chapters, you will do quite a bit of work with the Browser, and you'll see some capabilities that any user can take advantage of.

The Design Window

The Design window is where the file that you're editing is displayed. Along with the display of drawings and geometry, this window has a couple of special elements worth noting that appear by default. The 3D indicator shows what orientation the part or assembly file has to the X, Y, and Z axes. For the sake of clarity, the X axis is red, the Y axis is green, and the Z axis is blue. Although it is not always critical to orient parts in a particular direction, doing so can be useful for understanding how a part is constructed and for sketching a horizontal or vertical relationship between points.

The Status Bar

The final major screen element that I'd like to review before you begin working in Inventor is the status bar. This term refers to the display along the bottom edge of the Inventor window. It has multiple functions, but most of them are for delivering information.

If you're an AutoCAD user, you probably noticed that there is no "command line" in Inventor. However, when you're in a command if you become unsure of what is expected, you can look at the lower-left corner of the Inventor window and on the status bar will be a prompt describing what is expected of you.

While you are creating geometry, the right side of the status bar displays feedback on that geometry. For example, while you're drawing a line, the status bar tells you the position of your endpoint, along with the line's length and direction. This helps you to approximate the size of the geometry you're creating.

The status bar has a couple of other important capabilities. At the far right you'll find two numbers and a rectangular black box that may have one or more portions colored in. The first of the two numbers represents Total Occurrences In Active Document, which is the number of parts being shown on screen. The second number represents the Open Documents In Session, which is the number of files being accessed by Inventor.

For example, an assembly that has five copies of one part file in it may display the numbers 5 and 2 because you are displaying five components on screen that reside in two files—one part file and an assembly file. The Engine MkII.iam that you have loaded shows that there are 83 total occurrences and 54 active files in Inventor. The bar represents the amount of memory that Inventor is using. On 32-bit operating systems (Windows XP, Windows 2000), the bar starts out green, and as memory consumption increases, it changes to yellow and eventually red. On 64-bit systems (Windows XP 64, Vista 64-bit), a second bar shows the total system consumption of RAM. On my system I was happy to see how little RAM Inventor was using but alarmed to see how little was left by other programs running.

The last item in the status bar looks like a satellite dish. This is your Communication Center. You can use the Communication Center to look for updates periodically to the software. You can establish other settings, such as alerts for online tutorials or even notifications of when a new hot fix or service pack is available. This is another functionality shared with many Autodesk applications.

Make Yourself at Home: Customizing Inventor

Now that you have a basic feel for some of the tools that you will use most frequently, it's time for you to make yourself at home. You've already seen examples of customizing Inventor in some of the previous images, where you may have noticed that the background of the Design window changed colors. I made this change for clarity in the printed images; you can also make changes to tailor Inventor to your needs. Inventor can be customized at several levels. In this section, I'll detail a few of the options and even show you how to save the way you've configured Inventor for future use.

Changing coloring of Inventor's work environment and sketching elements can make it easy to see what you're working on. Some users like to reposition or resize the tools to give themselves more room to work or to make the tools easier to find. Most of these settings you will experiment with once or twice, but once you are comfortable you may not want to change them again.

Some of the options in these exercises are unique to assemblies and drawings of assemblies, so they will not appear in Inventor LT.

Application Options

Let's start with the Application Options dialog box (Figure 1.14). This is the central repository for your personal settings. These are the settings that control how Inventor looks to you and what options you want to use. These tools do not affect settings that are local to models and drawings. To access the Application Options dialog box, choose Tools → Application Options.

Figure 1.14

The Application Options dialog box, with the General tab displayed

Notice the Import and Export buttons at the bottom of the window. These two tools allow you to save the settings that you prefer or even transfer them to other users or other systems where you will be using Inventor. Your settings are saved as XML files.

The `AutoCAD_Related_Options.xml` file will change the help system to AutoCAD-related settings, reverse mouse wheel zoom direction, and change the background to black. If you installed Inventor with AutoCAD preferences, you may have some of the same settings already active. The `Inventor_Default_Options.xml` file restores Inventor's default settings.

As with other dialog boxes, there is a Help button in the lower left with specific help for the tool you are working with. Clicking Help lists the specific portions of the tab that you have active.

Let's walk through the dialog box tab by tab. We won't cover absolutely everything, but there are some items that can make major changes to Inventor's look, feel, and behavior. There will be some items not covered at this time that I'll discuss when they become more relevant later on in the book.

Each tab has several subsections that have a border around groups of check boxes, radio buttons, and pull-downs lists. Each section has a header that makes it easy to figure out what all of those devices will affect. The following comments will be organized by tab and subsection to make navigation as painless as possible.

The General Tab

Tools on the General tab (see Figure 1.14) tell Inventor how you want the program to start, what name you want recorded as the author for files that you create, and other basics.

Start-up The Show Help Focused On option may be useful if you're an experienced Auto-CAD user; you may want to consider switching the focus of the help system to the one for AutoCAD users.

Start-up Action The Open dialog box allows you to switch to the New dialog box, but in this section you can change whether Inventor starts with Open or New. You can also have Inventor begin a new file based on a specific template, or by deselecting the check box at the top of the section, you can have Inventor just open without creating or editing a file.

ToolTip Appearance This is an interesting set of options. The first option will allow the "in command" tips that normally appear on the status bar to appear near your cursor to guide you through command options. This can be a great option particularly for new users to get additional help in a more "heads up" fashion.

Selection The Enable Optimized Selection option may be useful if you're using Inventor on a system with limited graphics performance. It sets the selection and highlighting to initially only highlight the parts that are closest to the front in the display.

The Colors Tab

To change the overall look of Inventor, the Colors tab (see Figure 1.15) has the tools for the job. Many users simply change the color scheme, but there are several other options that can be useful.

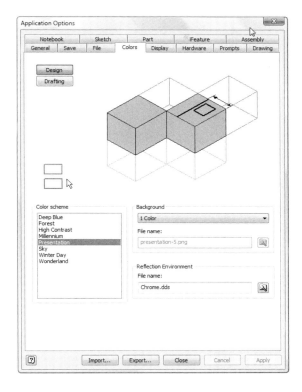

Figure 1.15

The Colors tab in the Application Options dialog box

Color Scheme Inventor has several standard color schemes that control the color of the graphics window background, highlighted elements, and sketch elements.

Background Inventor can use a single color, a gradient of colors, or any standard raster image as a background for the graphics window. It comes with a library already installed.

Reflection Environment Inventor comes with several image files that surround the model you're working on, so that if you have reflective colors on parts such as chrome, you will see this image "reflected" on those parts.

The Display Tab

This is the tab for Inventor Suite 2009 users where they can do the most tailoring of how Inventor will respond to specific actions. Looking at Figure 1.16, you can see just how many options there are, and many of them can have a noticeable effect on how Inventor looks.

Figure 1.16

**The Display tab in
the Application
Options dialog box**

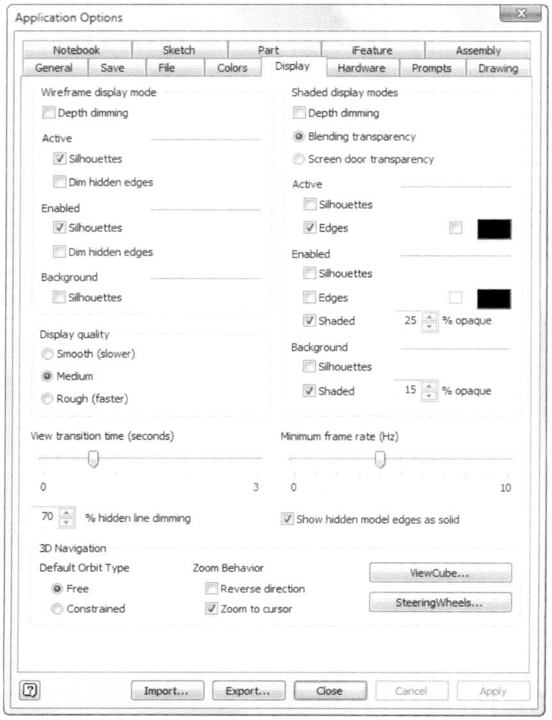

Wireframe display mode When you're in Wireframe mode, choosing Active → Dim Hidden Edges enables the model edges in the background to appear darker than edges in the foreground. The amount of dimming is controlled by the % Hidden Line Dimming value near the bottom of the Display tab.

Shaded display modes There are a lot of interesting ways to work with these options. Experiment—you can't hurt anything. In an exercise later in this chapter, you will change a couple of the settings and see an effect in which rather than parts fading when you activate a single component, the parts that you are not editing will go to wireframe display.

Enabled Confusingly, this setting affects the display of parts that will be *inactive* in the assembly when you've activated another part. For example, when you double-clicked on the muffler earlier in the chapter, you activated that part. The other parts appeared dimmed but still shaded. If you had Shaded deselected in this tab, those inactive parts would have appeared as wireframe.

Display quality When there is limited graphic or system memory capacity, Inventor may degrade the quality of the model image while rotating or zooming. These settings will affect how quickly Inventor begins to degrade the display quality. If you have a high-performance system, you may want to click the Smooth setting to keep rounded edges and faces smoother longer.

Show hidden model edges as solid Deselecting this checkbox changes the display of hidden edges in the wireframe view from solid lines to hidden lines.

3D Navigation The Reverse Direction option under Zoom Behavior controls the direction of the wheel button zoom. This option was added for AutoCAD users who prefer the effect of moving the camera as mentioned earlier.

The Hardware Tab

If you are using Windows 2000 or XP, you can use this tab to select whether the graphics engine in Inventor will be based on OpenGL or Direct3D. Vista users will see that there is no OpenGL option.

Notice the Use Software Graphics option. If you experience frequent crashes, try running with this setting for a while. Your performance will be greatly limited, but if you find that your system is more stable that way, it means you need to find an approved driver for your graphics card or update your graphic hardware. You can find more information on graphics drivers under the Help flyout menu under the heading Additional Resources.

The Drawing Tab

Notable here is the Default Drawing File Type option. Beginning with Inventor 2008, you can create your 2D drawings as native DWG files, which are compatible with AutoCAD. The original IDW file format of Autodesk Inventor is still a valid and reliable file, but the strength of having fully native 2D data that can be shared with AutoCAD is very useful.

The Sketch Tab

Figure 1.17 shows the Sketch tab. The settings on this tab tend to be personal. Just the Display group with its grids and axes are often set differently from user to user in a company, which is why the options are available.

Overconstrained dimensions When we discuss applying dimensions and constraints to sketches in Chapter 3, you will learn that Inventor will not allow a sketch to be "overconstrained." Constraining a sketch means that you apply controls to the movement of points in a sketch and to the size of a sketch. When Inventor detects a redundant or unnecessary constraint, this option defines whether Inventor automatically places a "reference" dimension or prompts you for what to do.

Figure 1.17

The Sketch tab in the Application Options dialog box

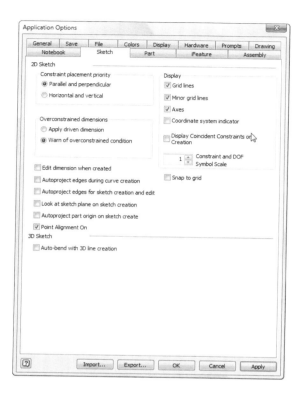

Display When beginning a new sketch, you may or may not want to see a grid. Some users feel the grid helps them keep the proportions of the sketch more accurately. Minor gridlines are smaller gridlines that appear between the primary ones. The axes are thicker lines that cross through the center of the sketch on the X and Y axis.

Edit dimension when created Selecting this checkbox causes Inventor to prompt you for the value of a dimension as soon as it is placed it in a sketch. This can be helpful for remembering to apply the values for the dimension as you place them.

Autoproject edges for sketch creation and edit When you create a new sketch on a part or assembly face with this option selected, the edges that are coplanar with that sketch are copied into the sketch. This can be handy for locating new features, but I find that many of these projected edges aren't used as a reference and can also cause errors downstream. Autodesk has improved the robustness of this feature, but it is an option that I often remove.

Look at sketch plane on sketch creation When you create a new sketch on a face in an isometric view of a part, Inventor's default is not to change your view orientation. With this option selected, the display will behave like the Look At zooming tool and bring your focus perpendicular to your new sketching plane.

Autoproject part origin on sketch create This option will cause Inventor to project the location of the "zero" or "origin" of the part into every new sketch. Having this geometry projected does not mean that you have to use the geometry or constrain geometry to it.

The Part Tab

The option you may want to customize here is Sketch On New Part Creation. This allows you to choose what your "default" sketching plane is. It is a purely subjective preference, but many people find that they think about parts they are designing in either a profile or an overhead view. This option allows you to choose how a part is oriented when it is first created.

The Assembly Tab

The noteworthy option here is Constraint Audio Notification. By default, when a constraint is placed in Inventor, the sound of a cowbell is played. When you're starting out, this is a handy feature for confirming that a constraint was placed. After you hear the cowbell a couple of hundred times per day, you can come here to disable the audio cue.

Creating a New Work Environment

I know that some of this can be hard to digest, so let's do some hands-on work. Let's create a new work environment. We will keep the changes limited to the visual elements for now. After you are finished, you can make other changes at any time.

Some steps will not be applicable to Inventor LT users.

1. If you still have Tuned Pipe (muffler) active from the previous action, you are all set. If not, double-click on the muffler in the Design window to activate it. Another alternative is to double-click Tuned Pipe in the Browser or to right-click Tuned Pipe and select Edit.

2. Open the Application Options dialog box by selecting Tools → Application Options.

3. Select the Colors tab.

4. Under Color Scheme, choose Wonderland and watch the preview change at the top. Note that most of the elements of the screen change. Click the Apply button in the lower right, and you will see the change take effect on the Design window in the background.

5. In the upper left of the preview pane are Design and Drafting buttons that show the effect of the color scheme in the 3D and 2D environments. Click the Drafting button and then click the Design button.

6. In the Background area, change the style from 1 Color to Gradient and note the effect.

7. Select the Presentation Color scheme and click Apply.

8. Now change the Background option to a Background Image. Although there is a file that is the default for each color scheme, after you make this change you can select any BMP, JPG, PNG, GIF, or TIF for use as a background. After switching to the Background Image, click Apply again to see the effect.

9. Switch the Background option back to Gradient. A Gradient background will offer better performance than a Background image for lower-powered systems.

> For clarity in print, screen images captured for this book are created with the Presentation Color scheme and the 1 Color option. This is a great setup if you need to create printable images from your models.

10. Switch to the Display tab.

11. Under the Wireframe display mode, select Dim Hidden Edges under the Active group.

12. Under Shaded display modes in the Enabled group, deselect Shaded and select Silhouettes.

13. Under Shaded Display Modes in the Active group, deselect Edges and select Silhouettes.

14. Update your display by clicking Apply. Tuned Pipe should be the only shaded component on the screen.

15. In the Display tab, deselect the Show Hidden Model Edges As Solid option.

16. Now let's save it all. Click the Export button at the bottom of the dialog box. The Export dialog box opens to the default location for the profile, but you can save your settings to any location. Name your file **Test settings.xml**.

17. Your screen should look something like Figure 1.18.

18. Click the Return button to return to the assembly environment.

You've done it. You've made Inventor look and behave differently than it did when it was installed. For your own use you may choose different settings, but it is critical that you are comfortable with making changes to Inventor so that it suits you and the interface is not a distraction from working. There are a few more changes that can be made to suit your needs.

The Panel bar displays both the icon and the name of tools that it contains. As you become more comfortable with Inventor, you may want to display only the icons. Keep in mind that a tooltip will still be displayed if you hold your cursor over an icon even if you no longer display the command name.

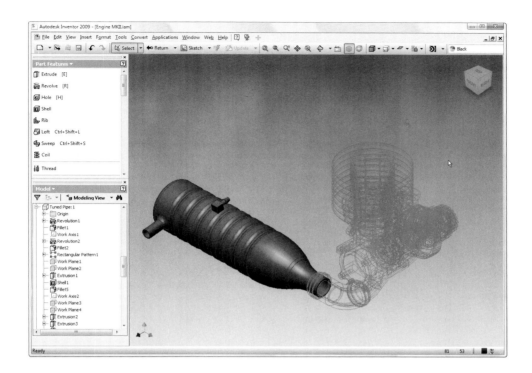

Figure 1.18

The Inventor display is flexible and can be modified to suit your taste.

You can change your Panel bar to no longer display the command name. To do this, right-click in an open part of the Panel bar or click the flyout arrow next to Assembly Panel and deselect the checkmark next to Display Text with Icons.

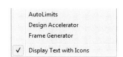

When you do this, the scrollbar (which was previously necessary to view all the commands) disappears because all the commands now fit in a small area. Many users prefer this as a way to maximize screen space and avoid having to scroll to find some tools. I want to stress that I do not recommend working with icons only while you are beginning to use Inventor.

Depending on the version of Windows that you're using, you may see two horizontal bars at the top of the Browser and at the top of the Panel bar. If you click and drag on this area, you can move the components around, or "undock" them from the side of the Inventor window so that they are "floating." Once you are comfortable enough to work with only the icons, you can dock the Panel bar next to the Browser and then narrow the Panel bar to show one vertical column of icons. The result looks something like Figure 1.19.

Figure 1.19

Alternate Panel bar and Browser arrangement

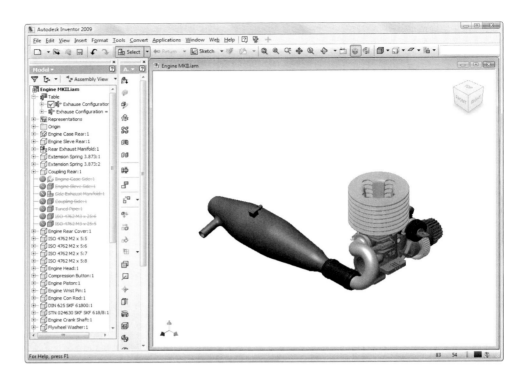

At this point, if you've changed your interface it may be best to put the Panel bar and Browser back in their default location.

One last thing that you need to know about the Panel bar, the Browser, and the Inventor Standard toolbar is that their display can be turned off if you want to show your model in a maximum screen mode. You can do this from the menu bar: choose View → Toolbar and deselect any of the tools that you do not want displayed. You can use the same method to reselect them if they somehow get turned off.

Project Files

Inventor is normally a breeze to work with. There are only a handful of ways to make it difficult. One common bad habit is not properly controlling where files are kept. Inventor keeps track of where things are supposed to be using a *project file*.

As an old friend of mine so perfectly put it: "A project file is a text file that tells Inventor where to put stuff"—and that's all there is to it. The project file allows you to control where Inventor looks for templates, what styles are available, and where Inventor stores files, including standard parts like bolts. This opens up a lot of possibilities, such as using different project files to switch templates with different title blocks when you work on jobs for multiple customers. Over time, more and more Inventor users establish one project file and sort jobs as folders under that project file. In an earlier example, in the Open

File dialog box you used the Frequently Used Subfolders list to find the assembly of the engine. The Samples.ipj project file that you selected is a great example of a project file that is used to organize many different datasets with many different types of design. Figure 1.20 shows what Samples.ipj looks like if you open it in the Project File editor.

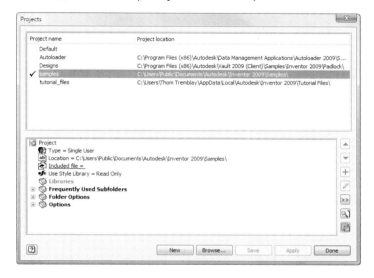

Figure 1.20

The Project File editor

The Project File editor is a fairly simple tool. It has a list of project files that have been used at the top in the Select Project pane, a display of the paths and properties of the highlighted project file in the bottom in the Edit Project pane, and a handful of tools on the right for modifying the project file. There are a few rules for project files:

• You cannot change the active project file when a file is open.

• You cannot add a Frequently Used Subfolders shortcut to a folder that is not "under" the location of the project file.

• To edit a project file, you must have read/write access to the file or folder that it is in.

As you select different options, buttons on the right change to show that they are available or unavailable. As you read through the descriptions of what the sections of the project file do, try selecting them and note which buttons become available. As you explore, continue to use the Samples.ipj project file that you made active previously. Here are some of the elements of the project file:

Type You will work with two primary types of project file. The Type option allows you to select between them:

Single User For the stand-alone user who will not be sharing data with other users simultaneously.

Vault Only available if you have installed the Vault, Autodesk's file management tool that comes with Inventor. It enables simultaneous sharing with multiple users.

Two other types of Project file allow multiple users to access data, but I cannot recommend strongly enough that you use the Vault if you intend to share data in a network environment. The Vault is free and provides additional tools to make your work easier.

Location This setting tells Inventor where the file is installed and also establishes a "relative path" that the other search paths will use to shorten their own searches for files. The project file may be in `C:\Users\Public\Documents\Autodesk\Inventor 2009\Samples\` but in its search Inventor will skip all of the previous directories and begin searching for files under the `\Samples` folder. This may not seem important, but it can greatly improve performance.

Use Style Library Only users with the proper permissions can control the value of this setting. This setting controls whether a user can edit, use, or even access style libraries (see Chapter 5).

Libraries In addition to the Content Center libraries that ship with Autodesk Inventor, users can declare that files in specific folders be treated as library files. These files cannot be edited while you are using a project file that defines them as a library. It's also important that you not allow these files to be edited by people who don't consider them a library.

Frequently Used Subfolders As you saw earlier in this chapter, you can define shortcuts that take you to folders that are relevant to the work you need to get done. Creating a path to a folder and another path to another folder under it replicates the structure on the disk. These shortcuts can be given any name, and you should name them in a way that is clear to you. For example, a disk path of `C:\Data\Components\support structure components` could have a shortcut of Brackets.

Folder Options This area allows you to establish paths to styles and templates that are in locations other than the ones that Inventor uses when it is installed. This is important in a network environment where you may want to have everyone accessing the same templates from a central source. The Content Center Files path tells Inventor where to put the "local" copies of standard content used by the files that you'll be working with. This too is an important consideration for a network environment so that you don't, for example, have multiple people keeping individual copies of the same standard bolt on their own computers.

Options The group contains a couple of interesting items, but most of them are less frequently modified than other parts of the project file. The Old Versions To Keep On Save value controls the number of versions of the file that will be saved to an Oldversions directory in the file path. These older files can be restored as a new file or over the current version of the file. It's important to note that if you restore over the current version, all changes made since the old version was saved will be lost.

The Oldversions directory can hold multiple versions of a file, created each time the file is saved. It's like having multiple BAK files that can be restored.

Project File Manager Buttons

The buttons on the right side of the editor not only help you edit the file but also, by being available or being grayed out, offer visual cues for whether you can make certain changes.

The arrow buttons are available where there are lists of folders that you may want to sort for priority or convenience.

The Add button appears when you have selected a category where a path or other information can be added.

Edit will be active when a value can be edited.

Clicking this button expands options for the project workspace or for establishing a workgroup. Note that workgroups are not used with single-user or Vault-oriented project files. When this (and any other) dialog is expanded, the arrows point to the left to show that the dialog can also be collapsed.

Clicking this button generates a list of duplicate files in the project. You can use the list to compare files and choose how to treat them. If two unique parts have the same name, you can modify one of them to avoid confusion downstream. If there are two instances of an identical file, you should remove one of them and allow Inventor to seek out the remaining instance so there is no risk of having the incorrect version of a part in the assembly.

The Content Center can have many types of standard content (nuts, bolts, etc.), and you may not use all of them in a project. This button allows you to limit the standards that are used by the project itself.

Creating a Project File

Now that you have a basic overview of the project file, it is time to make one of your own that you will use for future exercises.

1. Close any files that you have open in Inventor. Don't save changes to the Engine MkII. iam file if you are prompted to do so.

2. On the main menu, choose File → Projects.

3. Click the New button at the bottom of the dialog box. This will open a Wizard that will help you step through creating a new Project file.

   If you have Autodesk Vault installed, you have the option to choose to create a new Vault project or a new single-user project, as shown in Figure 1.21. If you do not have the Vault installed, you will not be offered the Vault project option.

4. Select the radio button next to New Single User Project and click the Next button at the bottom.

Figure 1.21

**Defining the type
of new project**

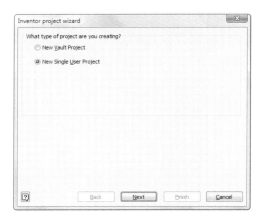

On the next screen, you can name the file and set up its location. Keep in mind that you are not only establishing the location of a file but also establishing the root folder for the models that you will be creating.

5. Start by typing **Introducing Inventor** in the Name text box.

6. On the next line, the default path that Inventor uses will be listed. Click the ellipsis icon to the right to begin browsing to a different folder. Figure 1.22 shows the Browse For Folder dialog box. In this case we want to create a new folder. Do not create the folder in the location initially offered. Instead, scroll to your C drive, select the root of the C drive, and click the Make New Folder button. This creates a new folder on the C drive and allow you to rename it. Name the new folder **Data**, and click OK to close the Browse For Folder dialog box.

7. When you return to the Inventor Project Wizard, you should see the path C:\Data under Project (Workspace) Folder and a text string showing C:\Data\Introducing Inventor.ipj under Project File To Be Created (Figure 1.23).

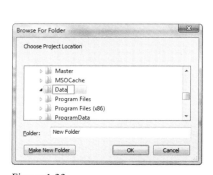

Figure 1.22

Creating a new folder

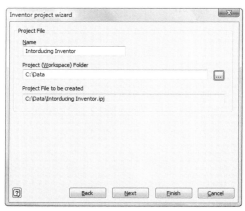

Figure 1.23

The new project name and path

8. Click Finish.

9. When you return to the Projects dialog box (Figure 1.24), your new project file will not automatically become the active project file. Do *not* change the active project file at this time. When you do wish to make you new project active, you must highlight it and click the Apply button or double-click on the filename in the Select Project pane.

Figure 1.24

Introducing Inventor added to the list of project files

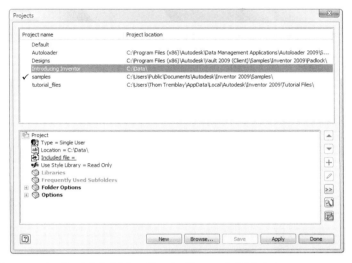

10. You will see that the Frequently Used Subfolders line is dimmed. This is because no shortcuts are currently listed. In some cases you will add a new shortcut that leads to an existing path. We will create a shortcut and the path it leads to in one sequence.

11. Select the Frequently Used Subfolders line in the Edit Project pane. When you do so, you the Add button becomes available. Click that button and two boxes appear. The first is for the name of the shortcut that you want to add; the second is for the path. Next to the Path button is a folder search icon that you can click to select an existing folder or create a new one.

12. Change the Shortcut name to **Parts**.

13. In our case we are adding a new folder to the path, so we can just simply add a Parts folder after Data in the path and press Enter.

14. You can click the folder search icon and a file dialog box will appear, Choose Or Add A Path For The Project File, appears with one important difference. Clicking the Make New Folder button automatically creates a new folder under the workspace folder you defined when you created the new project file. Inventor should create a new folder and highlight the name for renaming. If Inventor does not offer you a chance to rename the folder to Parts, you can do so using Windows Explorer.

15. After you have added this new path, save the change by clicking the Save button at the bottom of the dialog box.

Defining a project file is not a difficult process, but it is an important one. It is a good idea to decide how you want to share data with others and review how you currently sort your design data to help define how your project file should be arranged. It is possible to change your file structure after the fact if necessary, and Inventor is able to help you find the files it needs—but it is worth some extra time to think about how you want to sort your data.

Inventor must know where files are to work effectively. Failing to control your file locations can inhibit the program's performance—and having to tell Inventor where to find files will cause you undue stress.

Using the Help System

While any software can be improved, I find the Help system in Inventor to be very good. It even comes in different flavors. There is the help that is oriented toward existing Inventor users and those who have used other 3D design programs, or if you are an experienced AutoCAD user, you can have the help system compare Inventor to AutoCAD to help you relate a little more easily. Regardless of how you use it, I encourage you to take advantage of the Help system as an additional resource.

To access the primary Help system, from the main menu select the icon with the question mark, or click Help → Help Topics. Alternatively, you can press the F1 key as in most Windows-compatible programs. In the resulting Help window (Figure 1.25), you can access the contents, which will show categorized help topics in a book- and chapter-like format. Index narrows topic titles as you type a keyword. Search looks through the titles and contents of help topics.

Next to the Help icon on the main menu is the icon for the Visual Syllabus. The Visual Syllabus (Figure 1.26) is a direct access to the Show Me Animations portion of the Help system. This is a collection of animations that show how to use various tools and perform tasks. These animations can be used as a way to introduce yourself to new topics or refresh your memory on items that you don't use frequently.

The final icon is Recover, which will normally appear gray. When it is red, this indicates an error that Inventor's Design Doctor wants to assist you with.

The Design Doctor (Figure 1.27) lists any errors and allows you to select which one you want to fix first in the Select screen. On the Examine screen, it offers a solution, and the Treat screen allows you to select what treatment method you want to use.

Another important thing to know about the Design Doctor is that you do not have to respond immediately. You can do most things in Inventor while there is a problem unresolved. In fact, you may do something that you know will cause a problem, and when you're finished, the problem will resolve itself. This is the kind of flexibility that has made Inventor popular.

Figure 1.25

The primary Help window

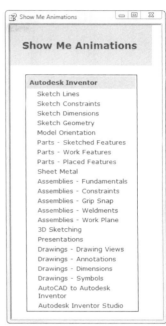

Figure 1.26

The Visual Syllabus

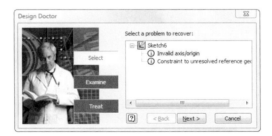

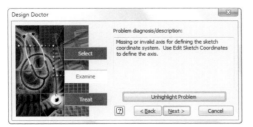

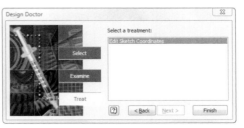

Figure 1.27

The Design Doctor

Summary

Inventor's user interface is as flexible as it is simple. Learning where to find tools and recognizing what Inventor's tools are asking of you are the first steps. Making yourself comfortable allows you to be more efficient with Inventor and makes the overall experience more enjoyable.

The Inventor development team has put a lot of work into trying to make tools consistent. As we go forward, many of the fundamentals that you've learned in this chapter will be reused every step of the way. If you are using a tool and it is not offering you Open or Apply, take a look for any red arrows or scan the status bar to see what Inventor is looking for.

Finally, never be afraid to ask Inventor for help. The Help system is a great resource that is often overlooked.

CHAPTER 2

Creating 2D Drawings from 3D Data

Two-dimensional (2D) drawings are certainly an effective way of communicating information. How many centuries have people been producing sketches in 2D form on cave walls, animal hides, and anything that would hold an image long enough to produce the idea?

When I started working in the design and engineering field, I was taught on the drafting board. This was a good tool, but making even the most basic changes proved difficult. I never pursued many ideas for product improvement, simply because of the time and effort it would take to change all of my drawings and the risk that the idea would have no benefit.

Moving to 2D computer-aided design was a huge breakthrough. Being able to use tools like AutoCAD's Stretch, Move, and Array made editing a drawing much faster. Creating the original drawing wasn't much faster, though, and you still had to be careful about aligning and producing all of the features in each drawing view.

Many of you reading this book probably make your living producing 2D drawings. By the end of this chapter, my goal is for you to be excited and convinced that moving to a 3D system is worth it if for no other reason than this: you will be making the best 2D drawings that you've ever made and it will be easier than it has ever been before. I hope you'll agree with me that one of the best reasons to move to 3D is 2D.

- **2D Drawing View Creation**

- **Drawing Views of Parts**

- **Detailing Basics**

- **Automatic View Updates**

- **Drawing Views of Assemblies**

- **Drawing Views of Presentation Files**

Drawing Views of a Part

The 2D drawing creation environment is essentially the same as all of the other working environments in Inventor. If you worked through the exercises in Chapter 1, you already have an understanding of the fundamentals to begin the next phase of using the product to create something. Let's begin by creating a 2D drawing of a part and applying some dimensions.

Beginning a New Drawing from a Template

Every new drawing begins with one of Inventor's templates. In this exercise, we'll be using an ANSI template that anticipates working with a metric part. Because it's an ANSI template, it creates third-angle view projections, although that is not the standard for much of the world. For future reference, using a DIN, ISO, or many other standards automatically projects in the first angle.

1. Make sure that *Samples.ipj* is the active project file. If you've closed the `Engine MkII` `.iam` file, reopen it.

2. In the folder that contains the `Engine MkII.iam` file, a subfolder named Components contains a part file named `Carb Intake Plate.ipt`, shown in Figure 2.1. Open that file now.

3. Autodesk Inventor LT users need to download the `Carb Intake Plate.ipt` file from `www.sybex.com/go/introducinginventor2009` and place it in the Samples folder. The typical path for this folder will be `c:\program files\autodesk\Inventor LT 2009\Samples`.

Figure 2.1

Selecting Carb Intake Plate.ipt **from the Open dialog box**

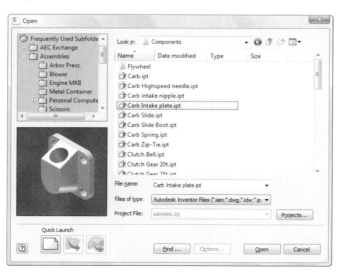

It is not necessary to have a file open in Inventor to create a 2D drawing of it, but for our purposes it will make things a little more convenient.

4. Using either File → New or the New File button on the Inventor Standard toolbar, open the New File dialog box. This dialog box has three tabs, offering the Default templates, as well as common templates in English and Metric units for creating new files.

5. Find the ANSI (mm).dwg template on the Metric tab (Figure 2.2). Double-click on the template or select it and click OK to create a new drawing file based on that template.

Figure 2.2

Selecting ANSI (mm).dwg **in the Metric tab**

You have now created a new, blank drawing. Next you'll fill in some of the blank space.

Your Inventor session should now have three floating windows containing three different files. To make the view of the drawing page as large as possible in the Design window, click the Maximize button in the upper right of the window displaying the new drawing. Figure 2.3 shows the result. You can switch between files to choose which one to display by selecting the filename on the flyout of the Window menu on the main menu or by holding down the Ctrl key and pressing Tab until the file that you want is displayed.

Along with the new file, you should also see that the tools in the Panel bar have changed. The default Panel bar for a new drawing is the Drawing Views panel. This Panel bar contains tools for creating different types of drawing views.

Now I'll show you some of the tools for creating 2D drawings. We'll explore a series of exercises that will walk through the process of creating a basic 2D drawing of a 3D model. As we use each new tool, I'll describe its function and any alternate ways to access that tool.

Figure 2.3

**A new drawing
sheet in a "maxi-
mized" state**

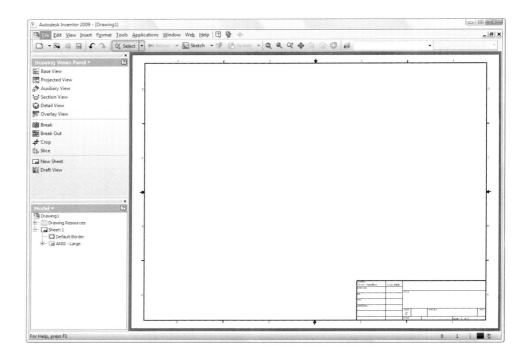

Creating Base Views

Detail drawings frequently require multiple views to describe the geometry properly. Because of this need, Inventor allows you to create a *base* view and project views from it.

The first view that you place on a drawing must be a base view regardless of its orientation. You can have multiple base views on each drawing. The base view acts as a *parent view* and establish initial scaling and other view properties for *child views*. You will create child views later and project them from the base view.

Figure 2.4

**Right-click in an
empty part of the
screen and choose
New Sheet from the
list to create a new
base view.**

To create a base view, you can select the Base View tool from the Panel bar or right-click a blank portion of the drawing sheet in the Design window and choose Base View. Figure 2.4 shows the context menu that appears when you right-click in an empty portion of the screen. In the coming pages, you'll find that the right-click menus contain a sizable percentage of the most common tools that Inventor users need the most. There is a phrase that is often used among experienced Inventor users: "When in doubt, right-click."

Once you initiate creating a Base View, the Drawing View dialog box shown in Figure 2.5 appears. This dialog box is your toolkit for setting up different views of your drawing. In addition to its options and tool groups, notice the Component, Model State, and Display Options tabs; each offers various settings that control the display of geometry in the view.

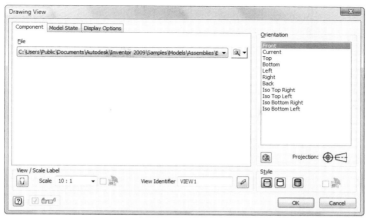

Figure 2.5

The Drawing View dialog box is your starting point for defining a base view.

Component The Component tab allows you to select from a list of files that are currently open in Inventor or browse for other files on your computer or network using the icon to the right of the file list flyout. If you are using a Vault project, you can also browse the Vault for a file.

Model State Some files can be presented in different conditions or "states" in a drawing. This tab controls what form of the geometry will be displayed in the drawing view.

Display Options This tab controls how the geometry will be represented in the drawing view. Selecting different standard views (Top, Front, Iso Top Right, etc.) from the list on the right changes the drawing view preview that appears when you start the Base View command.

On the upper-right side of this dialog box is the Orientation group. This is a listing of standard viewpoints that corresponds with the names on the ViewCube. Selecting different standard views from the list changes the drawing view preview that appears when you start the Base View command.

If none of the predefined views are suitable or you would like to place a perspective view on a drawing, you can click the Change View Orientation icon below the list of standard orientations. This switches your view to the model with an abbreviated Standard toolbar showing only view manipulation tools. Once you've found the point of view that you want to use, select the green checkmark on the left to return to the Base View dialog box. The Base View tool will now consider the view position changes to be your current view.

In the lower left, you'll find the Scale control and display. The icon with a lightbulb determines whether the view's scale and label are to be displayed. The Scale flyout allows you to select the scale for the view. You can choose from a list of standard scale ratios or simply type in the value that you would like. As you change the scale value, the drawing view preview also changes size, allowing you to more easily select a scale that you like. Parts and assemblies are always created in full scale, so it is this value that controls their apparent size on the drawing. Dimensions applied to the view will always be accurate to the model, so use of nonstandard scales is allowable.

To the right of the Scale control and display is the View Identifier field. If you would like to give the view a specific name, such as Front, you can enter it in this field. The value you enter appears in the Browser as the name of the view and, if you choose to make the scale and label visible, this value is then also the name displayed with the view.

In the lower right, you'll see the Style group. These three buttons can make things very interesting. Hidden Lines generates line objects for edges that are not visible from the point of view selected. Hidden Lines Removed won't generate those lines. One of these two buttons will always be used as long as the Style group is available. In the exercises for this chapter, you'll learn to make them accessible if you choose to. The third button, Shaded, is optional for any view. It generates a shaded view of model geometry in the drawing view.

Defining the Base View

Defining the base view is always the first step, but it is also important to think about what the base view should be. Apply the same methodology you would use with any drawing and choose the most descriptive point of view to define your base view.

1. Start the Base View command.

2. Select Carb Intake Plate.ipt from the File flyout to identify what part we wish to make a base view of.

3. Try a few different orientations but settle on the Front view orientation.

4. From the Scale flyout, select a scale of 5:1.

5. The Style settings should have Hidden Lines selected, but not Shaded.

6. Roughly position the view preview in the center of the drawing sheet and click to place the view. It is not necessary to be perfect when placing the drawing view. You may have to move the Base View dialog box to the side to see the center of the sheet depending on your screen resolution.

7. Your drawing should now look something like Figure 2.6.

If you look at the Browser, you'll see that the same icon that is used next to the Base View command now appears next to the name *View1: Carb Intake plate.ipt*. This is simply documenting that it is the first view placed in your drawing and what file it is based on. The second piece of information can be useful as Inventor allows you to create any number of drawing views from any number of files all on the same drawing sheet. You can change the name of a view to something different by slowly clicking twice on the name in the Browser or by editing the view and changing the View label.

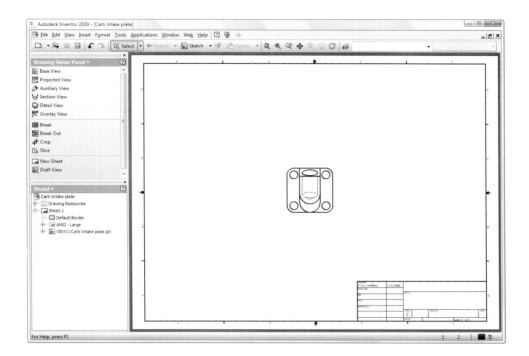

Figure 2.6

The base view placed on the drawing

Saving a Drawing File

The only time Inventor forces you to save a file is before you can create a drawing of it. It is a good idea to save your work anytime you complete something that you're sure you want to keep.

When you tell Inventor to save this drawing, it will want to place the drawing at the root of the Workspace, which is a couple of levels above the model files in this case.

1. From the main menu, choose File → Save (take care not to click Save As) or click the Save icon to begin saving your new file.

2. Navigate back to the level where you opened the assembly (or for LT users, where you placed the part).

3. Use the Create New Folder tool in the upper-right corner to create a new folder at this level and name that folder **Drawings**.

4. Double-click on the Drawings folder to open it. Tip: Pressing your Enter key after typing the name opens the Drawings folder automatically.

5. Save your file as `Carb Intake plate.dwg`. You are prompted with a dialog box that allows you to save changes to related files at the time you save the active file (Figure 2.7). Click OK to save the new file.

Figure 2.7

When saving a new file, you'll also see the state of related files.

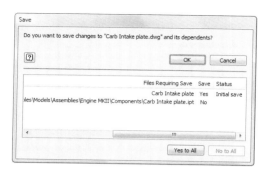

Note that the option to save the part file (`Carb Intake plate.ipt`) was set to No. This is because the part file was not modified and therefore does not need to be saved. This is also the first indication of the dynamic relationship between the 3D models and the 2D drawings, which we'll explore as we progress.

That's all it takes. Really.

Zoom in on the drawing view and observe how the hidden lines were generated and are even displayed with a different line weight than the object lines.

Now it is time for some real fun. In the next sections you'll learn how to create Inventor's four different types of child views from the parent base view: a projected view, an auxiliary view, a section view, and a rotate view.

Creating a Projected View

A projected view can be a standard orthographic projection or it can also be an isometric view of just about any kind of parent view. Any drawing sheet can have more than one base view from which to project child views, and you can also create a projected view from another projected view.

Selecting the Projected View tool in the Drawing Views panel does not launch a dialog box. Instead, the cursor changes to a special character or "glyph," and on the status bar you'll be prompted with Select A View. This will be the parent view, to which the view that you'll now create will belong.

There is also a context menu option for this tool. As with the other context menu options (and there are many), it has more of a "hands-on" feel. To access it, you must right-click over an existing view or you'll only get the pop-up menu that was shown in Figure 2.4. If you right-click over the existing view, you'll get a much broader set of tools, including Create View, which displays a list of different types of drawing views if you move your mouse cursor over it (Figure 2.8).

Inventor displays a dashed rectangular line around the view extents to verify that the view is selected.

Once you have selected your parent view, you'll see a line showing the direction the view will be projecting. You should also see a pre-view of the item in its position. This helps you confirm that you are getting the view you want in the position on the sheet that you want. Once you select the position for a new view, the tool offers you the opportunity to place additional views. After you click to place a view, a frame appears, showing the perimeter of the new view. When you are done placing views from this parent view, you can right-click and click Create to generate the new drawing views.

Figure 2.8

The context menu from an existing view

Defining Projected Views

Projecting a new drawing view from an existing one is where many new Inventor users begin to see the real potential of using 3D to create drawing views.

1. Use the Projected View tool to create new views above, to the left of, and below the base view that you created in the previous exercise. (Create them in that order to aid with future exercises.) Position them similar to Figure 2.9. Be sure to click Create to generate the views.

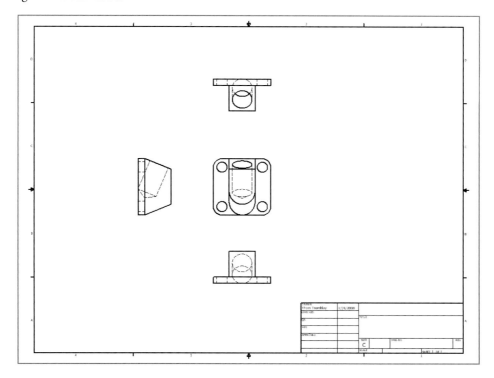

Figure 2.9

Adding projected views to the drawing

When you place the views, they appear in the Browser with the icon next to the Projected View tool. They also appear "indented," or underneath the view they were projected from. This is a helpful visual cue to keep track of the relationships within the file.

2. Save the drawing.

3. Restart the projected view from your original base view again and create an isometric view in the upper right of the sheet by moving your cursor toward the corner. The preview shows you when you transition from an orthographic view to an isometric view.

> You can restart any command in Inventor by pressing the Enter key or the spacebar, or by right-clicking and choosing the top item on the context menu, which will always be Repeat (last command).

4. Place the view. Your result should be similar to Figure 2.10.

5. Just to be safe, save your drawing again.

Figure 2.10

Creating an isometric projection

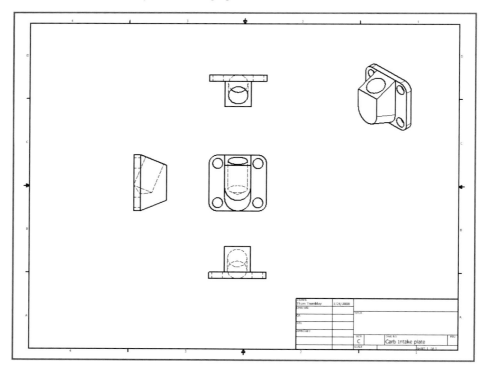

6. The next projected view you'll create will be based on the view you placed to the left of the original base view (View3 in the Browser). Place the new projected view to the left of that view to get a result similar to Figure 2.11.

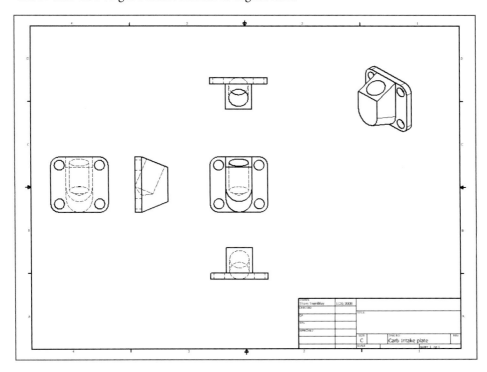

Figure 2.11

Adding more value by projecting a view from an existing projected view

If you don't like the spacing between your views, you can easily change it by clicking a view and dragging its location. By default, orthographic projections are aligned with the parent view. You'll know when Inventor is ready for you to click or right-click in a view when the boundary for that view highlights.

7. Move the views on your page around to see how they remain aligned and to get more even spacing. You'll likely need to do this more than once as you add additional views and dimensions to maintain the clarity of your drawing. Figure 2.12 shows how I arranged mine.

Take a minute and look at the drawing that you have made. Try to imagine creating that drawing using any 2D-based CAD system, or if you did board drafting in the past, think about how long it would take you to make this very basic layout of views.

Figure 2.12

Arranging multiple views of a drawing for clarity

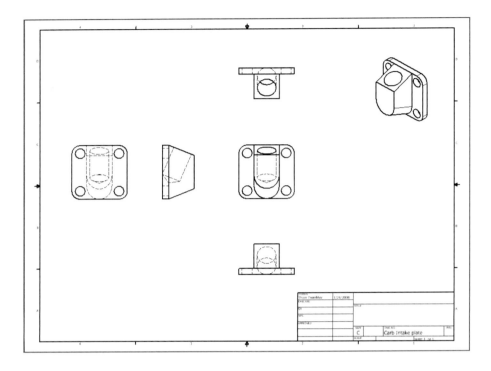

Figure 2.12

Arranging multiple views of a drawing for clarity

Creating an Auxiliary View

The Auxiliary View tool creates a projected view that is initially aligned perpendicular to an edge you select in its parent view.

Auxiliary views are created in much the same way as a projected view. You are asked to define a parent view to base the new view on. Once you have selected it, a dialog box appears, where you can name the view and choose whether or not it will be labeled. The settings of the parent view are adopted by default, but you also have the opportunity to set a different scale than the parent view, and you can even modify the style of the view. Once you have set up how the view will appear, you need to select an edge to project the

view from. The edge you select must be a line. It cannot be a curve in the parent view. Usable edges will highlight as you pass over them. As soon as you do this, you'll get the same type of preview that the Projected View tool offered, and you can place the view in the same way.

The Definition in Base View option adds a section line external to the model body to show what orientation the view is based on. You can select whether to use this depending on the drafting standards and practices that you use.

You can access the Auxiliary View tool through the right-click option in the same way as the Projected View tool. You'll find all of the view creation options under the Create View flyout.

Defining an Auxiliary View

Many drafters and designers find auxiliary views very challenging, especially when working with parts that contain oblique planes or a large number of holes. The power of the computer can really prevent some headaches when creating these views.

1. Begin an auxiliary view and base it on the same view (View3) as the last projected view using the long, angled edge at the top of the part as the projection edge, as shown in Figure 2.13. Position the new view above and to the right of the parent.

2. Place the new view as shown in Figure 2.14.

Take a look at the Browser. The new items in the Browser have the same icon as the command. Are you seeing a pattern here? Nice, isn't it?

In many cases, you'll leave an auxiliary view aligned to the parent view to maintain the relationship and the proper orientation. In our example, however, the auxiliary view exists to make it easier to document the placement of a feature, so alignment to the parent view is not the primary concern. In the next section, you rotate the view so that its edges are aligned vertically and horizontally on the sheet, and you also change the appearance of the view for better clarity.

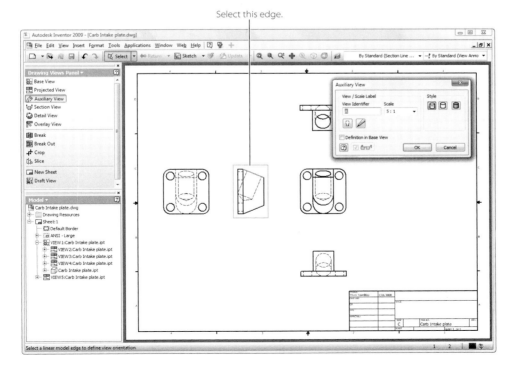

Figure 2.13

Choosing the edge from which to project the auxiliary view

Figure 2.14

Placing the new auxiliary projection

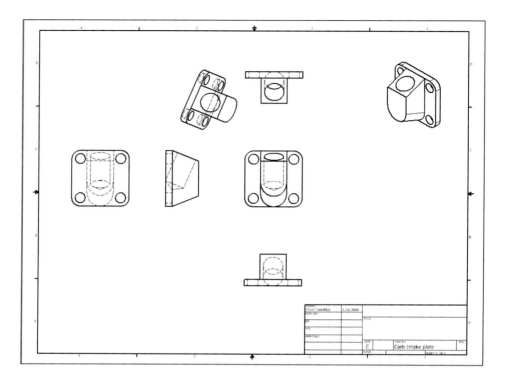

Editing drawing views in Inventor is very easy. You can right-click the view listed in the Browser or right-click the highlighted view and select Edit from the list of options.

If you know that you want to edit the view and forgo the list of options, you can just double-click a view on the drawing sheet and the editing dialog box appears. In most cases, it is essentially the same dialog box that you used to create the view.

Rotating a View

Another option that appears on the right-click menu is Rotate. This tool allows you to change the orientation of the drawing view on the sheet.

In the Rotate View dialog box (Figure 2.15) is a pull-down list that allows you to establish what method you want to use. Absolute Angle sets the angle the view appears on the sheet, Relative Angle rotates the view further in the direction that you select, and the Edge option allows you to select an edge in the drawing view and make it vertical or horizontal by rotating the view in the direction that you have selected. Rotating a view breaks its alignment to the parent view, but it doesn't limit the view's ability to update if the model changes. The two circular arrows set the direction you want to rotate the view: clockwise or counterclockwise.

Figure 2.15

Rotate View options: Edge (left), Absolute Angle (middle), Relative Angle (right)

Defining a Rotated View

Any view can be rotated for clarity. Doing this breaks the positional alignment with the parent view but can make things much easier to understand.

1. Use the Rotate tool to turn the auxiliary view so that the long edges are horizontal and toward the bottom of the view. If the view rotates so that the long edges are at the top of the view, select the same edge again and it rotates the view 180 degrees.

2. Move the drawing view to the lower-left portion of the drawing sheet so that there is more room around it for detailing.

3. Edit the view and change its style to Hidden Lines Removed. To do this, you have to break the link between the view and the style of the parent view. Just deselect the checkbox in the lower right near the icon that resembles a chain link near the drawing view icon. When this is done, you will be able to select the buttons in the Style group. Refer to Figure 2.16 as an example.

Figure 2.16

The auxiliary view rotated and repositioned

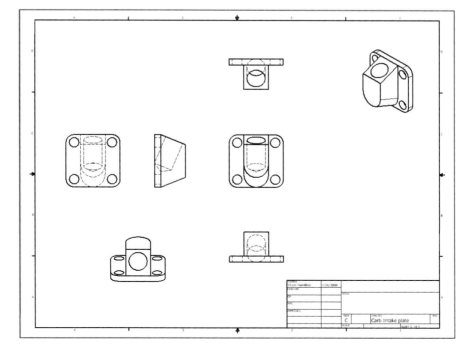

4. Now change the view to the far left (View6) to Hidden Lines Removed as well. Figure 2.17 shows the result. Since it is an orthographic view, its appearance is linked to the parent view and the Style link will have to be broken. Breaking the Style link does not affect the alignment to the parent view.

5. Edit the isometric view (View5). Isometric views are created with hidden lines removed by default and only share the scale of the parent view upon creation, though there is no link to maintain the same scale once the view is created. Change the scale to 4:1, select the Shaded style option, and under the Display Options tab deselect Tangent Edges. Your drawing should appear similar to Figure 2.18.

6. Save your drawing.

All of these drawing views are good at describing the outside of the part, but what if you require more detail of the inside? Then you'll use a *section view*.

Figure 2.17

Changing the hidden line display of a view

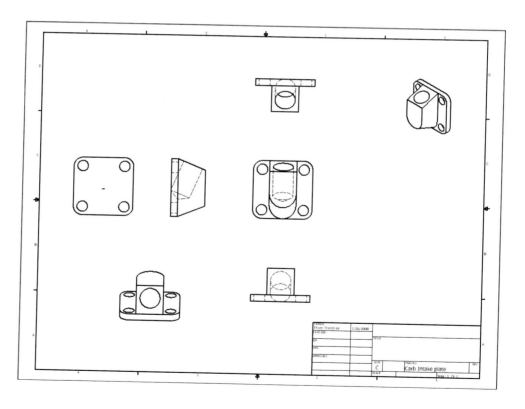

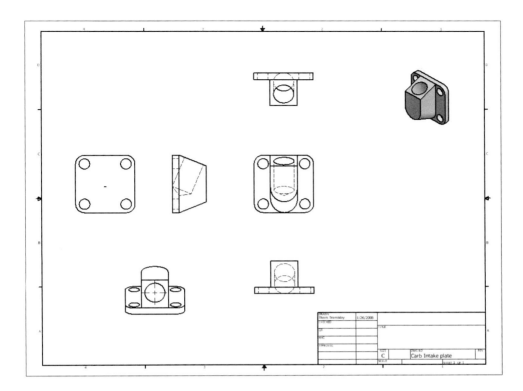

Figure 2.18

**Changing the iso-
metric view to make
it more descriptive**

Creating Section Views

Section views are essential for many kinds of drafting and design. The Section View tool
in Inventor allows you to define your section view using one or more straight segments
that pass through the part. The *section line* can be defined to have a relationship with
geometry in the drawing view, or as you'll learn a little later on, you can define it using a
dimension as well. There is no limit to the number of section views that you can place on
a view, and the section does not have to pass entirely through the parent view.

The operation of the Section View tool is straightforward. It is similar to the Auxiliary
View tool, which makes sense as the auxiliary view is often viewed as an "External Section" view.

Defining the Section View

For this exercise you'll create a basic section view. Section views can also be created with
a section line in several segments.

1. Zoom into the empty space next to View1 (see Figure 2.19).

2. Select the Section View tool. If you did not have a view highlighted when you started
   the command, you'll have to select a view to use as the parent.

Figure 2.19

**Zooming into the
drawing area where
you'll create the
section view**

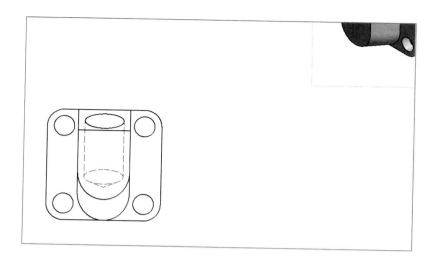

3. After you have selected the parent view, move your cursor around the view. You'll see points become highlighted and, if you move around outside the perimeter of the view, you'll see *inference* lines, showing when you are in vertical or horizontal alignment with a point in the view. Move your cursor over the center of the large hole, which appears as an ellipse, and you'll see a green dot appear at the center. Do *not* click this point. Instead, begin to move your mouse upward and you'll see the inference line indicate that you are able to create a line that passes through the center of the hole.

4. Move your cursor to a distance just outside the highlighted view boundary and click. This begins the process of creating the section line. In this case, just move straight down through the view to about the same distance below the view and click again. After you have selected these two points to define a section line, right-click and select Continue.

The Section View dialog box opens, offering you the opportunity to change the View Identifier, the Scale, and other appearance characteristics. Do not change any of these options at this point.

5. Now a preview of the section view appears, to show you the orientation of the view as you move it perpendicular to the section line's beginning or end before you place it.

6. The section reverses depending on which side of the section line you move your cursor to. Place the view to the right of the parent view as shown in Figure 2.20.

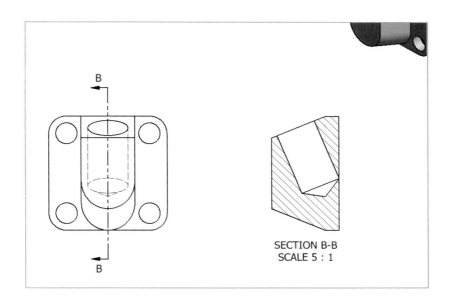

By moving the cursor over the hole and using the inference line to place the section line, you have associated the section with the center of that feature. It is not necessary to associate a section with geometry to create a section view, but most often it is best for an accurate and useful view.

Detailing Drawing Views

Now it's time to look at the other primary need for a 2D drawing: detailing and dimensioning. Since you began your new drawing, the Panel bar has been displaying the Drawing Views panel. To access the detailing and dimensioning tools, you need to change the Panel bar to the Drawing Annotation panel. Begin by selecting the down arrow on the Panel bar's title bar and select Drawing Views Panel from the flyout menu. As always, there is also a context menu option; just right-click in a blank area of the Panel bar and select the new panel.

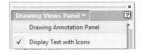

Let's begin by placing an often-overlooked but very useful detailing tool.

The Center Mark Tool

Yes, *Center Mark*. It doesn't seem like a tool that's worth describing first when it comes to detailing, but if we could harness all of the energy wasted placing individually made blocks of center marks on drawings just since the advent of 2D CAD, we could probably power a large city for years. (OK, I'm exaggerating, but only a little.) Center marks and their variations are an important detailing item in mechanical drafting, and I think you'll appreciate how easy it is to place these items.

When you look at the Center Mark tool in the Panel bar, you'll see the down arrow indicating that other options are available. We'll explore three of the four options: Center Mark, Centerline, and Centerline Bisector.

Placing a Center Mark in a View

In this exercise, you see that even when a center mark isn't perfect, there are tools to make it right.

1. Zoom in on the auxiliary view that you placed in the lower left of the drawing sheet.

2. Select the Center Mark tool. You are prompted to click on a location. As you pass over radial or circular edges in the view they highlight, indicating that a center mark can be placed there.

3. Select the edge of the large hole (circle) in the middle of the part.

   When you place the center mark, it will be rotated, reflecting the original alignment angle the view had with its parent. This is not typical but it offers us a chance to explore the tool.

4. Press the Esc key to exit the tool or right-click and select Done [Esc].

5. Place the mouse cursor over the center mark. When it highlights, right-click and select the Edit → Align to Edge tool.

6. Select a horizontal edge in the drawing view, and the center mark rotates into proper position for the view's new orientation (Figure 2.21).

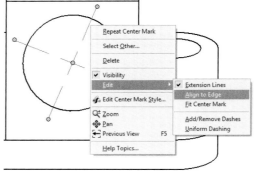

Figure 2.21

The center mark added and rotated into position

You can use this tool to align the center mark to an edge at an odd angle to establish a dimension between the hole and that edge with more clarity.

Placing a Centerline in a View

Creating a series of center marks and linking them with centerlines can be tedious with 2D CAD. Inventor has a very elegant solution.

1. Change your focus to View1, the base view that you first placed on the drawing.

2. On the Center Mark flyout, select the Centerline tool.

3. Select the bottom-left hole and notice that it first creates a center mark on the hole but then continues, extending a centerline to your cursor as you move around.

4. Select the hole on the bottom right of the view. The command continues to place center marks and extend the centerline if you have several holes in line with one another.

5. To finish placing a centerline, you must right-click and select the Create option to place the centerline on the drawing. If you end the command before telling it to create the centerline, nothing is added to the drawing.

6. End the command and you'll see that Inventor has placed a centerline between the two new center marks.

7. For further practice, add centerlines between the remaining holes, taking care to use the Create option after each *pair* of holes has been selected. If you don't, you'll discover a special capability of the Centerline tool: "chaining" holes, as demonstrated in the next exercise.

   Do not worry about making redundant center marks by selecting holes more than once. Inventor is good at keeping things clean when it comes time to print.

8. End the command when you have placed the other three centerlines in the view, and save your drawing. It should appear similar to Figure 2.22.

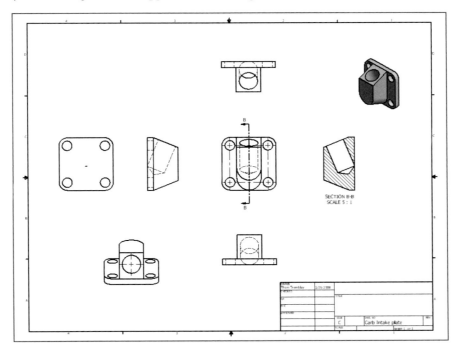

Figure 2.22

Centerlines added to all of the holes

Using Centerline to Create a Bolt Circle

As I mentioned in the previous exercise, a special capability of the Centerline tool is that you can "chain" a series of holes with it; this allows you to create a bolt circle, a common task in mechanical drafting. Let's try it out.

1. Zoom in on View6, the view placed to the far left on the drawing sheet.

2. Select the Centerline tool and select the upper-right hole.

3. Select the other holes in a clockwise or counterclockwise order. After you click the third hole, the centerline should turn into an arc.

4. After selecting the fourth hole, select the first hole again to create a complete "bolt circle." If you don't, the centerline will leave a gap between the last and first holes.

5. Create the centerline.

6. End the command. View6 should now appear similar to Figure 2.23.

7. Save the drawing.

While you are zoomed in closely to View6, make note of the small arcs near the center of the part. These arcs represent edges where the hole in the part has penetrated the

Figure 2.23

A bolt circle created using Centerline's chaining capability

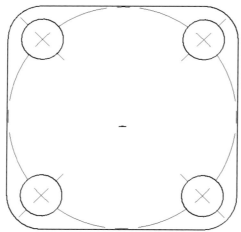

bottom of the part. If we were doing traditional 2D CAD, this might have been overlooked or ignored, but basing our 2D on 3D brings errors like this to light. We'll change this later, but it is a powerful example of the enhanced accuracy that your drawings can possess.

Change your Design window view to focus on View3, the side view of the part. We'll use this view to try out the last of the detailing tools for this chapter, the Centerline Bisector. We'll explore more detailing tools in Chapter 6.

Creating a Centerline Bisector

There are times when you need to display a centerline but do not have circles or arcs to use as a basis for the Centerline tool. You'll also often want to show a centerline down the middle of parts or features such as shafts, conical parts, slots, or the side view of a hole.

In View3 we can see the side of the hole. The Centerline tool would allow you to find the center of the hole even from the side, but the Centerline Bisector tool does this and allows you to bisect nonparallel edges as well. When you select the tool, it prompts you to click on a location like the other Center Mark tools did, but in this case it is looking for line segments, not arcs or circles.

1. Select the Centerline Bisector tool.

2. Click the edges of the hole that are displayed in the view as hidden lines. Once you click the second edge, the centerline appears. You do not need to execute a create step to keep the centerline.

3. Repeat these steps on the section view as well.

4. End the command.

5. The centerline is created to exceed the length of the edges selected to place it. In this case, the new centerline doesn't extend through the bottom of the hole as most drafting standards would demand.

6. Move your cursor to the end of the centerline at the bottom of the hole. As you near it, the centerline highlights and a green dot appears, allowing you to click the end of the centerline.

7. Click and drag the length of the centerline until you think its length is appropriate. The view should now look something like Figure 2.24.

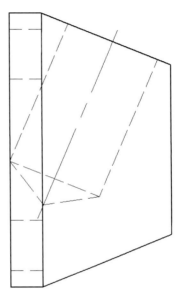

Figure 2.24

A centerline can be placed by bisecting two edges.

Adding Dimensions in Inventor

Simple tools like the Center Mark tools are necessary to create drawings correctly. You will learn other drawing tools in later chapters, but for now let's examine the important dimensioning tools.

Your approach to dimensioning will vary with the national and corporate standards that you must adhere to. The dimensioning tools in Inventor follow the standards that you select for their appearance, but the basic tools are the same regardless of what that standard is. In this chapter we'll discuss the General Dimension, Baseline Dimension, Hole/Thread Notes, Retrieve Dimension, and various dimension editing tools. Then, in Chapter 5 we will go on to discuss how to set up things like dimension or layer styles and how to establish standards for consistency.

The General Dimension Tool

Inventor has a few different tools for placing dimensions on drawing views. The one we'll work with first is the General Dimension tool. This tool allows the user to add dimensions to a drawing view one at a time, but as you will see, it is a multiple-function tool.

The single General Dimension tool can place Linear, Diameter, Radius, Aligned, and Angular dimensions based solely on the types of geometry you select while placing the dimension and a few context menu options.

To access the General Dimension command, you can click on the tool in the Drawing Annotation panel, or in most cases you can simply press the D key on your keyboard.

The General Dimension tool is *click-sensitive*. This means that depending on the type of geometry you select, you will be offered different dimension types. It is much easier to show how this works than to explain it. So in the following exercises let's try out some of the ways the General Dimension tool can be used.

> The Inventor help system for AutoCAD users shows five different AutoCAD dimensioning commands that are replaced by the single General Dimension command in Inventor. By the end of this chapter, I'm sure you won't miss any of those extra buttons.

Adding Basic Dimensions with the General Dimension Tool

This exercise is the first step in creating a complete drawing.

1. Zoom in on View3. This is a good view to demonstrate clicking options for linear and angular dimensions.

2. Select the General Dimension tool. You are prompted with Select Model Or Sketch Geometry.

3. Move your cursor over the angular line at the top of the part view. This is the same angular line that was used for the auxiliary view projection line.

4. Select the line with a single click. Take care that the entire line segment is highlighted, not an option or a point on the line.

5. Move your cursor upward, and you should see a preview of a horizontal dimension that will follow the movement of your mouse.

6. Now move your mouse to the right of the view and a vertical dimension should preview, following your mouse movements.

7. Move the mouse back near the selected edge. As you near it, you should get a preview of an aligned dimension.

As you have been moving around, you may have noticed that the dimension and extension lines will go from solid to dotted from time to time. They may even do so in increments. These highlighted positions show when the dimension is spaced away from the model edges properly based on the dimension style. If your dimension text moves as well as the line work, you'll see a dotted line appear when the text is centered between the extension lines.

8. Place the horizontal dimension at the first highlighted position above the model. Your drawing should look similar to Figure 2.25.

Figure 2.25

Adding a linear dimension by selecting an edge

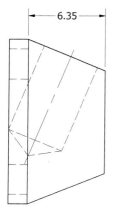

Dimensioning with More Complex Selections

If you have line segments that make up an entire model edge, the method we've just used makes things simple. Unfortunately, more often than not on a complex part what appears as a single line segment may be broken up into multiple edges. In these cases, you need to select points or combinations of points and edges. Depending on what you click, the options presented can be very different. It will take time to get comfortable with all of the options and which ones you prefer. Let's do another exercise to show how what you click can limit you from getting what you want.

The goal for this exercise is to dimension the distance between the lower-right corner of the part and the edge of the hole to show how much material is left.

1. Continuing to use View3, select the General Dimension tool.

2. As shown in Figure 2.26, carefully select the lower-right corner (Point A) of the part where the bottom angular edge meets the vertical edge on the right. This is your first point.

3. Again you see previews of the dimension types available, including an aligned dimension between the points. Place this dimension on your drawing as shown in Figure 2.27.

4. This dimension looks good but does not give us the correct value. We need the distance to the edge of the hole to know what the minimum distance would be if we continued to drill the hole deeper.

5. Restart the General Dimension tool.

6. This time click Point A again, but instead of clicking Point B, select the edge of the hole that ends at Point B.

7. Now you will only be offered one dimension preview. You can change its location but there is only one valid dimension that can be placed.

8. Position this dimension on your drawing and note the difference in the values of the two dimensions. Your drawing should appear similar to Figure 2.28.

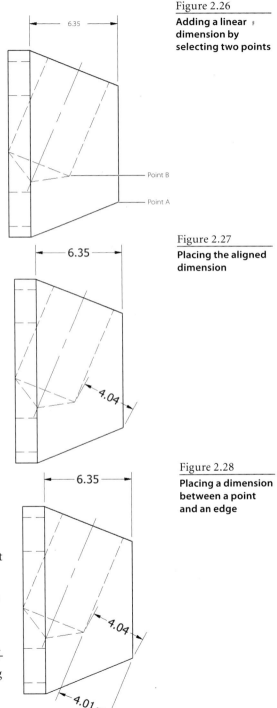

Figure 2.26

Adding a linear dimension by selecting two points

Figure 2.27

Placing the aligned dimension

Figure 2.28

Placing a dimension between a point and an edge

Adding an Angular Dimension

Selecting a line segment while placing a dimension limits the options that can be used. At times this can save you a lot of mouse gesturing to get the dimension that you want. Again, knowing which option is right will come with time and experience.

You can also limit what points are available for selection. While you are in the General Dimension tool, the context menu will have a flyout called Snap Settings that allows you to choose what points can be selected for dimension placement.

Just as selecting two points, or a point and an edge, can give you different options, selecting two edges can give you a completely different type of dimension. Selecting two parallel edges gives you a dimension that tells you the distance between the edges. If you select an edge and move to select another edge that is not parallel with it, the glyph near the cursor changes from a linear dimension to an angular dimension. Selecting the second nonparallel edge gives you an angular dimension.

You say you want to try it? I thought you would never ask.

Figure 2.29

Adding an angular dimension

1. Still working in View3, restart the General Dimension tool.

2. Select the short horizontal edge in the upper left of the part.

3. Now move your cursor to the angled line that you used to place your first dimension.

4. After you've seen the Angular Dimension glyph appear, select the edge and a preview of an angular dimension appears and follows your cursor. If you move out of the primary placement angle, you may see opposite angular dimensions offered. Also notice that the dimension highlights at recommended placement points, as the linear dimensions do.

5. Place the dimension so that it is similar to Figure 2.29.

6. Save your drawing.

Continuing with the General Dimension tool, let's move on to the nonlinear dimension types.

Adding Diameter and Radius Dimensions

In this exercise, you will find that the General Dimension tool isn't just for straight edges.

1. Zoom to View1 and select the General Dimension tool.

2. Move your cursor over one of the holes in the view and then over one of the radii on the corners of the part. The glyph near the cursor changes to indicate whether a radial or diametric dimension would be placed if you selected that edge.

3. Select the radius in the upper right of the part. As with linear dimensions, the dimension will "snap" into preset locations. As you move the dimension, it snaps

into an angle every 15 degrees. If you move your cursor into the model, you see that the text can be placed inside the model view with the leader still going to the arc. You can even move the text so that an arced dimension line appears to extend a short arc for proper dimensioning.

4. Place the dimension on the snap that is 30 degrees from vertical with roughly the same distance from the part, as shown in Figure 2.30.

5. Now click on the hole in the upper right.

6. Move the cursor around to see what display options exist for this type of dimension. Some additional options can be found by passing the cursor back over the dimension to flip the leader and arrow inside or outside of itself. If you are having too much fun and find you can't get back to the dimension look that you want, you can always cancel and start over. Inventor won't mind or tell anyone.

7. Place your diameter dimension at the 45-degree snap similar to Figure 2.31.

8. Press Esc to close the tool, and save your work.

There is another option for the Radius and Diameter dimensions: manual override.

In the context menu under Dimension Type you can override whether a dimension will be a radius or diameter while placing the dimension. Generally, Inventor will choose what it thinks is best, but no CAD program can possibly anticipate when you may need to call out a hole by its Radius. This is another example of flexibility and the level of control you can keep over your drawings.

Now you know just how easily you can apply dimensions and how easy it is to move from one type of dimension to another without even having to learn more than one command or tool.

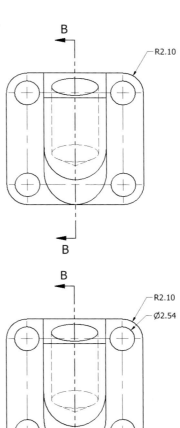

Figure 2.30

Adding a radius dimension

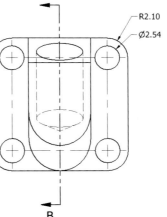

Figure 2.31

Add a diameter dimension to the drawing

The Baseline Dimension Tool

Placing dimensions one at a time is effective, and the tools Inventor has to assist with proper spacing of the dimension are helpful, but they're no match for placing multiple dimensions simultaneously. The need for placing multiple dimensions spaced properly from a baseline is a basic one for mechanical drafting.

The Baseline Dimension tool allows you to place multiple individual dimensions at once. Once you start the command, you can select the geometry that you want, right-click, and select Continue. This gives you a preview of the dimensions that will be placed. It is important to note that the first geometry you select is going to be used as the base or *origin* of all of the dimensions. Once you place the dimensions that you initially selected, you can select other geometry and add the the new dimension to the group in its proper position. When you have finished placing the dimensions, you must tell Inventor that you are done selecting geometry by right-clicking and selecting the Create option.

Before you select the Create option, you can change your origin by moving over the extension line of the dimension, opening the context menu, and selecting Make Origin. This immediately rebuilds the dimension group. You cannot change the origin of the dimensions created by this tool once the dimensions have been placed. These dimensions will not preview suggested placements with dotted geometry, but if you move your cursor slowly the tool pauses when it finds strategic placements.

The Baseline Dimension Set tool allows you to place multiple dimensions as a group so that a change to the appearance of one will affect all of them. After the group has been placed, it is possible to separate members if you want to make them unique. You can also change the origin of the group after the dimensions have been placed.

Creating a Baseline Dimension Set

Creating several properly spaced dimensions at once is a great capability. In this exercise, you'll learn how to do it in a way that is easier than you have ever done before.

1. Continuing to work with View1, select the Baseline Dimension tool.

2. Select the bottom of the part and the two holes on the left-hand side of the part. Remember to use Continue to see the dimensions.

3. Place the dimensions to the left of the view as shown in Figure 2.32. Remember to use Create to place the dimensions.

4. Select the Baseline Dimension Set tool.

5. Select the same geometry and place the dimension set to the right. Once you select Continue, you can place the dimensions. The tool closes once you click to place the dimensions. See Figure 2.32.

6. Right-click one of the dimensions that you placed with the Baseline Dimension tool. The menu displayed is the same as if you had placed that dimension using the General Dimension tool.

7. Right-click one of the dimensions created by the Baseline Dimension Set tool. The menu you see should be the same as shown in Figure 2.33. It has all of the options that the last menu did along with some additional options for modifying a baseline dimension set.

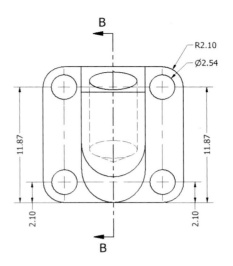

Figure 2.32

Adding baseline dimenions to your drawing view

Dimension Editing Tools

Before we move on, I want to walk through the menu in Figure 2.33 and define some of the functions. I'll focus on the group beginning with *Copy Properties*.

Copy Properties This function allows you to capture the appearance and precision information of any dimension or dimension group and transfer it directly to another dimension or dimensions in the drawing. The behavior is much like the "format painter" you will find in many Windows applications.

Options This flyout will have tools under it that are specific to the type of dimension you are editing. For example, the options for a radial dimension can force the dimension's leader to be "jogged" or force the "Arrowheads Inside." The options for a linear dimension offer the ability to disable either arrowhead or place the dimension text on a "leader" so it can be more easily read.

Precision When you place a dimension, its Precision setting is based on the active dimension style. While most of the model may have the same precision, it is often necessary to give some dimensions more or less precision than the others. This flyout allows you to override the precision of the dimension style for one that is more suitable for the geometry or process that will be used to create it.

Edit This offers several options. When the dialog box first appears, the value of the dimension will appear as a set of characters: <<>>. These characters indicate that Inventor is obtaining the value of the dimension from the model's actual geometry. If the geometry changes, this value will as well. By checking Hide Dimension Value, you can place substitute text on the dimension but its value will not change with the part. You can also add text before or after the value for annotation purposes. The other tabs in the dialog box allow you to add tolerance or fit information to your dimension, change

Figure 2.33

Context menu options for baseline dimensions

the dimension's classification (reference, basic, etc.), or declare the dimension to be an *inspection dimension*. The Edit Dimension dialog box can also be accessed by double-clicking on the dimension text.

Text This function also allows you to add text around the dimension, but it also offers the ability to change the formatting of the text appearance.

Arrange Arrange is only available if your dimension set has multiple dimensions in it. If you delete a member of the set, Arrange will allow you to quickly reposition the remaining dimensions into their proper locations.

Make Origin A baseline dimension is useful because all of the dimensions reference one origin. Make Origin changes the origin for a dimension set without having to re-create the dimension set.

Add Member After you have created a dimension set, you can use Add Member to include new geometry in the dimension set. The new dimension will automatically locate itself and rearrange other dimensions if need be.

Detach Member When you use Detach Member, you are separating one of the dimensions in the set so it can be edited as though it were placed on its own. This is very helpful if you want to create a dimension set with many members, of which a handful will need a different precision or appearance.

Delete Member This removes the dimension from the set and deletes it from the screen. The remaining dimensions do not automatically reposition themselves, so it is common to use the Arrange tool after deleting a member.

Putting the Dimension Editing Tools to Work

How about an exercise to try some of these tools?

1. Double-click the 11.87 dimension on the left to open the Edit dialog box.

2. Click the Precision and Tolerance tab and under the Tolerance Method group select Reference. Click OK and observe the change on the screen.

3. Now right-click the 2.10 dimension on the left. Once the menu is open, expand the Options flyout and select Leader.

4. When you do this, the dimension text changes position and orientation.

5. Move your cursor over the dimension text, and four arrows appear next to your cursor.

6. Click and drag the text up and to the left until it is easy to read and the leader is clear of any arrowheads.

7. Right-click one of the dimensions on the right. From the menu, select Add Member, and when prompted in the status bar, select the top edge of the part. See Figure 2.34 to check your progress.

8. The new dimension should appear outside of the existing dimensions. If your diameter dimension is too close to the extension line for the new dimension, it will automatically break the extension line to keep the value of the diameter legible. You can continue to add dimensions to the set until you close the tool by selecting Done, or simply press the Esc key to finish adding dimensions.

9. Right-click the 11.87 dimension on the right side of the part and select Delete Member. Notice that the dimensions do not rearrange themselves.

10. Right-click the dimension set and use the Arrange tool to correct the dimension placement. See Figure 2.35 for reference.

11. On the 2.10 dimension on the right, right-click the extension line that goes to the hole and select Make Origin to rearrange the dimension base on the hole. Two of the three dimensions will change value.

12. Right-click the new 11.87 dimension and choose Detach Member. This will not visibly affect the dimension, but it will no longer follow any changes we make to the dimension set it formerly belonged to.

13. Now use the Precision option on the context menu to change the dimension set's precision to a single decimal place by selecting 1.1—[1/2] from the flyout list.

14. Right-click the 11.9 dimension on the right and select Copy Properties.

15. Now select the 11.87 dimension on the left. Your drawing should appear similar to Figure 2.36.

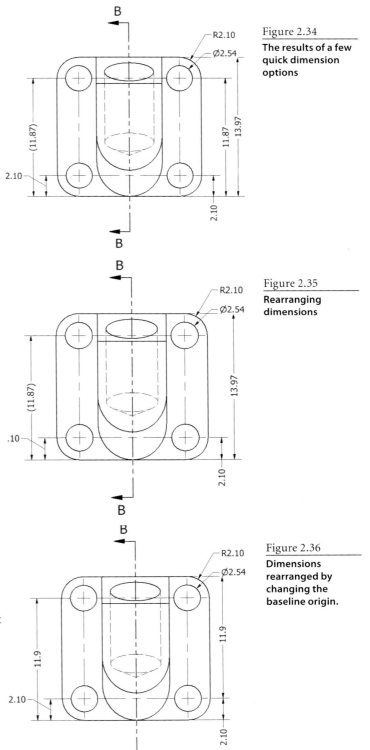

Figure 2.34

The results of a few quick dimension options

Figure 2.35

Rearranging dimensions

Figure 2.36

Dimensions rearranged by changing the baseline origin.

Hole/Thread Notes

Whereas the General Dimension tool is extremely flexible, the Hole/Thread Notes tool exchanges some flexibility for power. When you apply a Hole Note or a Thread callout to your drawing view, you will find that the only geometry that highlight are holes or external threads. This is a good thing.

Adding Hole/Thread Notes to the Drawing

The basic tool is very simple. As you would expect, it's a point, select, and place type of dimension, but there are some pretty great options that you will explore more in depth in Chapter 6. In this exercise we will stick to the basics—with one very nice exception.

1. If you have moved away from View1, return and zoom in similar to Figure 2.36.

2. Start the Hole/Thread Notes tool in the Drawing Annotation Panel bar.

3. Pass over different geometry in the view. Only five edges should highlight: the four holes in the corner and the large hole that is not aligned with this view but that can still be called out in this view.

4. Select the hole in the lower right of the part.

5. Just like the General Dimension command, the Hole/Thread Notes tool allows you to place several notes, so you will have to use the Esc key to let Inventor know that you're done.

6. Place the callout above and to the right of the hole.

   Initially the callout will look and move pretty much like the diameter dimension that you placed in the previous exercise, but the diameter is displayed based on the hole's original design, which was in Imperial units. The hole has a 0.1-inch diameter.

7. To be sure that the hole will be created properly, we need to modify this callout. This will not always be necessary, but it gives us an opportunity to learn how.

8. Edit the Hole Note by double-clicking quickly on the text or right-clicking and choosing Edit Hole Note.

9. The Edit Hole Note dialog box has a lot of options. We want to add the unit information. In the Text window, you see the standard diameter callout with the text HDIA framed by carets. This is the parameter callout that automatically extracts the value for the hole diameter. After that, the THRU value has been added automatically because the hole was made as a "through all" hole feature. Add the text **in.** after <HDIA>.

10. The special tool that I want you to learn is a very handy option. Pressing the Home key on your keyboard moves the blinking cursor to the beginning of the Hole Note text. Among the Values and Symbols buttons is one with the pound, or number, symbol. Click this button. When you do, another parameter will appear in your note. <QTYNOTE> is the parameter for the number of holes of the same size that are in the view.

11. Click OK and watch the update to your text. You should see the value 4× appear at the front of your note and "in." should be added to the diameter. Changing the number of 0.1-inch diameter holes will update the quantity value just as changing the diameter of the holes would change the size value.

    The results should look similar to Figure 2.37.

12. Be sure to save your work.

13. Change your view to the rotated auxiliary view.

14. Add a Hole Note to the large hole that is in the middle of the part.

15. This note could also be updated to reflect the units for both diameter and the depth that is called out. You can choose whether you want to do so. See Figure 2.38 to compare your results.

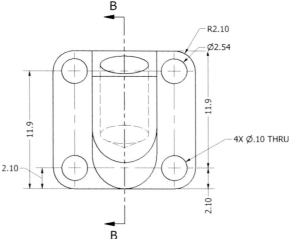

Figure 2.37

Hole notes can automaticaly count the number of holes in a view.

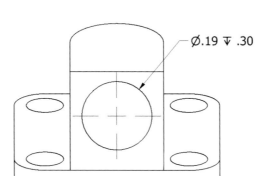

Figure 2.38

Add a Hole note to the view

The Retrieve Dimensions Tool

In this chapter you've been working with one of Inventor's built-in sample models so that you can try out the power of the drawing tools right away. In most real-world projects, of course, you'll start by creating your own models.

As you begin in the following chapters to learn how to create the 3D model you have been working with, you will be doing a lot of 2D sketching using dimensions that specify the size of various elements or features of the parts. These dimensions control the size and shape of the parts, and sometimes you'll have them placed exactly where you want to call them out in the drawing.

The Retrieve Dimensions tool allows you to bring representations of the original modeling dimensions into the drawings. Some believe that you should build a model in such a way that you'll be able to leverage this capability; I do not.

To start the Retrieve Dimensions tool, scroll to the bottom of the Drawing Annotation Panel bar and select Retrieve Dimensions, or select it by opening a context menu over the view that you want to work in.

If you select the tool from the Panel bar without having a drawing view highlighted, the Select View button will be active and no other options (except Cancel) will be available.

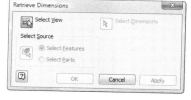

Once you select a view, the other tools will become available. Tool dialog boxes in Inventor are very straightforward. Anything that you need to select on screen has a button with a red arrow in the dialog box.

There is also a Select Source option that allows you to preselect a feature on the part or select a part in an assembly view to extract dimensions from. If you just click the Select Dimensions icon, all part dimensions that are "normal" or usable in the active view become visible. If you do this on a complex part, you will discover why the ability to preselect a particular feature is available.

Retrieving Dimensions from a View

This functionality can allow you to recycle your work in the part, but it is debatable whether it is valuable enough to build your part for this purpose.

1. Change your view so that the Auxiliary view fills your Design window.

2. For this exercise you'll use the right-click option. Right-click the auxiliary view and choose Retrieve Dimensions from the menu.

3. There aren't a lot of usable dimensions in this view but there are enough to make things confusing, so click the Select Source icon with Select Features active and select the hole in the view.

4. As soon as you select the hole, three dimensions will appear: the diameter of the circle (ignoring the hole feature at this moment) and the two linear dimensions that were used to position the hole on the face.

5. In the Retrieve Dimensions dialog box, click the icon next to Select Dimensions.

6. Select the two linear dimensions. Do not select the diameter.

7. Click OK in the dialog box, and the two selected dimensions now become part of the drawing view.

8. To edit the position of the text for the dimensions, click and drag the text for each of them, one at a time, into position. You will see the same type of highlighting and centering lines that would appear if you were placing the dimensions.

9. When you select a dimension, two pull-down menus become active in the upper right on the Inventor Standard toolbar. The first shows the layer of the selected item, and the second shows the dimension style that controls the dimension.

10. Select the 3.18 dimension and use the second flyout menu to change the dimension style for that dimension to Default—mm [in] (ANSI).

11. Adjust your dimension text to have the dimension look correct. Compare your work with Figure 2.39 and save the file.

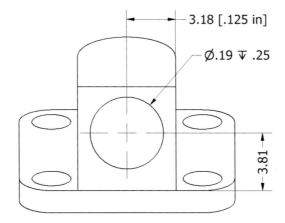

Figure 2.39

Dimensions that have been retrieved from the part can still be made appropriate for the drawing.

Associativity

The principle of associativity simply means that any change made to the part or assembly documented in your drawing will be reflected in the drawing. This is the crux of creating 2D detail drawings from 3D geometry. So far you have been able to exploit the 3D model to quickly create a drawing. Now it is time to see the payoff as you will change the 3D model and have the drawing update.

For this exercise I will be explicit in my directions since we have not begun the process of learning how to create the 3D model. Nonetheless, I'm going to ask you to change a 3D model in order to correct a problem that is visible in the drawing.

Do you remember the problem with the hole feature that has pierced the bottom of the part? Well, it's time to fix it.

Drawing View Associativity

In this exercise you will see the result of modifying a part model on the drawing.

1. Zoom into the model so that you can clearly see View3 and View6, as shown in Figure 2.40. In this view you can see the hole in View3 on the right as a hidden line that appears to extend all the way to the leftmost edge of the part. In View6 on the left, you can see that the edge of the drill point that makes the hole will break through.

2. Change your active file to Carb Intake plate.ipt. If you use the Window pull-down menu on the main menu, you will see at the bottom a list of the files that are currently open. Once this list is visible, you can click the file that you want to work in. Use Ctrl+Tab to cycle between multiple files.

3. Once the Part file is active, the Panel bar displays the Part Features tools and the Browser shows the existing features that make up the part (Figure 2.41).

4. Pass your mouse cursor over the features listed in the Browser. As you pass over features like Extrusion 1, Fillet1, and Hole2, the geometry that those features created will appear highlighted on the model. This helps you understand how the part was constructed (in case you are responsible for editing a part that you did not create).

Figure 2.40

The hole feature has penetrated the bottom of the part.

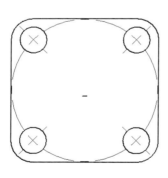

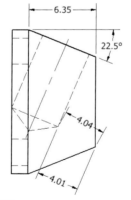

Figure 2.41

Editing a feature shows you the same dialog box used to create it.

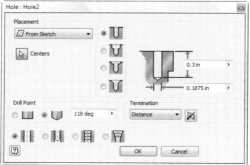

5. Double-click the icon next to Hole2. This brings up the dialog box that the part's creator used to build this solid model. The dialog box displays different types of holes as well as different ways to define holes. In the upper right, you see a preview of a hole, with a vertical dimension defining its depth and a linear dimension defining the hole's diameter.

6. Click and drag over the number 0.3 or double-click the number and its value will highlight. Once the number is highlighted, type **.25**. This part was created in English units so if the "in." disappears, it's all right. If the text turns red, that signals that something is wrong with the value.

7. Click OK once you've changed the value for the hole depth.

8. The part model will update, but with a small change like this it will be impossible to tell, especially since the change occurs inside the part.

9. Change your active file back to your drawing. The drawing may take a few seconds to update, but once it is done you should note two things: there is no longer any geometry in the middle of View6, and a visible gap exists between the major diameter of the hole and the edge of the part in View3. These changes should be noticeable in the section view of the part. The Hole Note in the auxiliary view also updates to indicate the new depth.

10. Use the Zoom All command to see the full drawing sheet and save the changes to your drawing, which should look something like Figure 2.42.

11. Please save your drawing for use in an exercise in Chapter 6.

Figure 2.42

The finished drawing

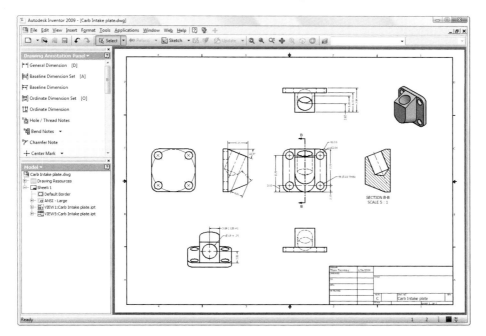

Let's move on to creating a basic drawing from an assembly and a drawing that shows how an assembly looks in an exploded view. All of the tools that you have learned so far are equally applicable to creating drawings of these files, but each of the different types of 3D model you may want to create drawings of will offer you slightly different options.

Assembly Drawings

Assembly drawings often have more variety than part drawings. Although 2D drawings of parts are most often used to create the physical component, assembly drawings can be more illustrative than highly detailed.

> Because Inventor LT cannot open assembly files, it cannot create drawing views of assemblies.

Creating a drawing view of an assembly file follows the same workflow as creating views of a part file. When the dialog box comes up, you'll see some differences. In the following exercise, you'll learn that there are a lot of options. For example, on the Component tab the Representation group offers different ways of displaying the assembly file. On the Model State tab, the Interference Edges option allows an edge to be created when there is a perfect fit or slight interference between parts.

When you have created a view from a 3D presentation file, you can show trails that trace the movement of the parts. On the Display Options tab, you can choose whether those trails will be on the drawing by selecting Show Trails. Chapter 8 shows how to create a presentation file and explains what it is commonly used for.

Creating a Simple Assembly Drawing

Let's create a simple assembly drawing using tools that you have already worked with.

1. Create a new drawing file using the same ANSI (mm).dwg template that you used for the part drawing.

2. Select the Base View tool.

3. Select Engine MkII.iam from the pull-down list of files in the Base View dialog box. Selecting an assembly file activates a number of options that you have not seen before. For now we will leave the Representation options alone.

4. Change the View Style option to Shaded.

5. In this case the standard scales do not work very well. Inventor can create a drawing view in any scale you need. Set the scale to 1.3.

6. Place the new view in the left half of the drawing sheet.

7. Created a projected isometric view in the upper right.

8. Now create a section view that passes through the center of the engine to the right side of the base view.

9. Right-click the section line that you drew through the engine.

10. Select Reverse Direction from the context menu. This creates the view that would have been created if you had placed the view to the left of the parent view.

11. Compare your drawing to Figure 2.43.

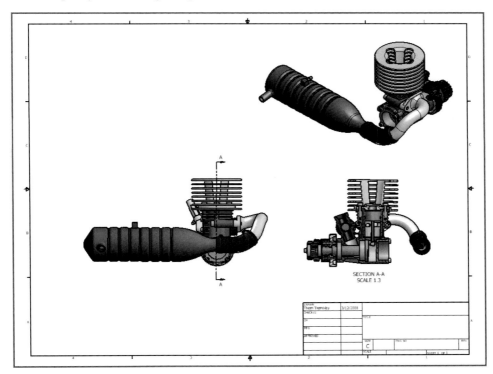

Figure 2.43

Quickly creating the basic drawing views

Zoom in and take a close look at the section. You will see that different hatch patterns have automatically been applied to the parts to make the view easier to see. Using shading and color in the view also adds to the clarity in an assembly drawing view.

Detail Views

Selecting the scale for your drawing views is important, and being able to change that scale after the fact is great as well. There are times, though, when you need a closer look at a portion of the part or assembly for clarity. You need a view with a different scale than the others. You need a *detail view*.

The Detail View tool must have a parent view selected, like the section or auxiliary view. Once that parent view is selected, the Detail View dialog box (Figure 2.44) appears. This dialog box has quite a few options, but most of them are ones you have seen before, such as the Style and View Identifier options. Other options include the following:

Scale In the Scale area, you can select a standard view scale or type in a custom setting.

Fence Shape This option defines the shape that the boundary of your detail view will have.

Cutout Shape This option specifies whether the detail view will display a smooth or a jagged edge. Selecting a smooth edge makes the Display Full Detail Boundary option available.

Figure 2.44

The Detail View dialog box

Display Full Detail Boundary This option causes the boundary for the view to be displayed in the parent view and the detail view. Selecting this option makes the Display Connection Line Option available. If you select this option, a line is drawn between the boundaries in the parent and detail views to better illustrate the source of the detail view. This setting was added to support some standards that require this additional clarity.

Creating a Detail View

Use this exercise to create a quick detail view that will help to clarify the drawing.

1. Select the Detail View tool and use the section view as the parent view.

2. Set Scale to 2:1. Set Fence Shape to Circle and Cutout Shape to Jagged.

3. Click near the center of the yellow heat sink at the top of the engine. You see a preview of the fence and the callout letter. Place the letter at the top of the circle and have the circle encompass the piston and the heat sink. Click to choose the size of the fence and place the callout.

4. Place the detail view in the upper left of the drawing sheet by clicking the sheet when the preview is in a open space; see Figure 2.45.

Looking at the section or the detail view, you may notice that some parts are not sectioned. In many standards, moving parts and purchased parts like nuts and bolts are not sectioned.

Inventor drawings can have several sheets. You can detail the same model on each sheet, different models on each sheet, or even as many different models as you can fit on one sheet.

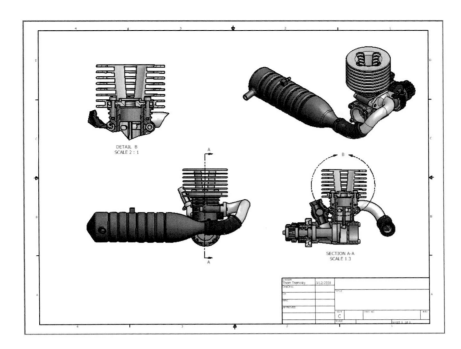

Figure 2.45

**Adding a detail view
to the drawing**

Some people prefer to separate the drawings by the model that they'll be detailing, while others collect an entire design—assembly, parts, and other information—into a single drawing file. The benefit is that you can continue to maintain your drawings the way that you have been in the past.

Presentation Views

Inventor has the ability to pull assemblies apart to show how they are constructed. We used to call these *exploded views*. When we discuss building assemblies in Chapter 4, you'll learn how to keep parts in their place. In exploded views the parts must be seen individually, so to make things easier Inventor uses a separate file for creating exploded views, called a *presentation file*. The views created from them are called *presentation views*.

Creating a drawing view of a presentation file is just like creating views of parts or assemblies. A couple of unique options are available that can make the drawing even better.

In the Drawing View dialog box, on the Component tab you can choose which presentation view you want to use. One presentation file can display the presentation view in several ways.

On the Model State tab, you can choose how reference parts will be displayed. A reference part has a distinct appearance in an assembly drawing view, but in a presentation view you may want it to be displayed the same as other parts, or not at all. When you create a presentation view in the 3D file, you can show trails that trace the movement of the parts. On the Display Options tab, you can specify whether those trails will be on the drawing by selecting Show Trails.

In this next exercise, we'll test the ability to contain multiple files that show the same geometry in different ways in the same drawing file.

Creating a View of a Presentation File

Adding a drawing view of a presentation file can help clarify how an assembly would be built.

The Browser displays all the views and even basic model information for those views. The Browser also contains other resources, such as borders and title blocks.

1. Right-click in an empty area of the Browser, and on the pop-up menu select New Sheet. You can also right-click a blank part of the drawing sheet.

2. The new drawing sheet will automatically become the active sheet. Select the Base View tool.

3. In the Drawing View dialog box, click the Browse button at the end of the file list.

4. Browse to the folder that contains Engine MKII.iam and select the Engine MKII (Assembly Instructions).ipn file. In case you can't see the file extension, presentation files display a blue icon next to the filename.

5. Set Orientation to Iso Top Right, Scale to 1:1, and Style to Shaded.

6. Place the view in the center of the sheet, as shown in Figure 2.46.

7. Save your work.

Figure 2.46

The finished exploded view

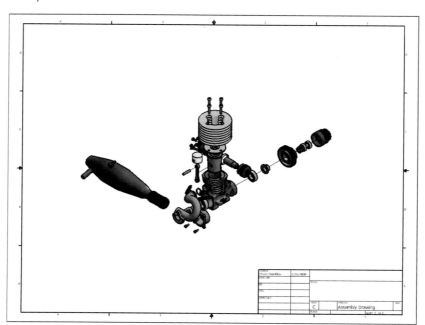

Summary

Inventor's ability to create drawings with any number of sheets and views that update automatically when the 3D model is changed is a truly wonderful thing. The ability to try new things in 3D with the security of knowing that your 2D drawings will be kept up to date allows you to be innovative with your designs.

In Chapter 6 we will return to take a more in-depth look at the drawing options and additional ways of creating views and detailing them. Some of these options may not apply to the work you need to do, but others allow you to create drawings that are easily understood and therefore improve the quality of your work.

CHAPTER 3

Introducing Part Modeling

Replicating reality on a computer is commonplace now. Sometimes it can even be hard to tell what is real and what is not. A few years ago, much of this "virtual reality" was science fiction—with one notable exception: mechanical engineering, where some people have been creating their products in 3D for over 20 years.

Early models like some of those I created in 1988 were based on primitive shapes using crude surfaces to define their physical boundaries. It was nonetheless an effective way to communicate a complex idea to people who would have had difficulty understanding a 2D drawing.

Not long after that, the first solid modeling tools emerged, with the ability to conduct Boolean operations by adding, subtracting, or intersecting basic shapes. These tools were effective at creating geometry, but it was often too difficult to edit and maintain designs as they evolved to warrant the effort. Right around the time that I was creating my primitive models, companies were developing the ancestors of today's parametric solid modeling systems.

The term *parametric* generally describes a system where the features (such as holes, fillets, and other shapes) maintain knowledge of their size and relationships to the other features they are based on. You may also hear these types of modeling systems referred to as feature-based modelers, as they maintain a history of the shapes that define the part and show how some features are built on top of other features.

- ▪ **2D Sketch Creation**

- ▪ **Dimensioning and Constraining the Sketch**

- ▪ **Making a Basic Solid Model**

- ▪ **Adding Features to a Solid Model**

- ▪ **Changing a Solid Model**

- ▪ **Alternative Creation and Editing Techniques**

The Concept of Parametric Modeling

In this chapter we'll explore parametric modeling as it applies to the single-part model. Parametric modeling revolves around *features*, which define the critical elements of the body: its shape, dimension, and order.

There are two types of features: *sketched* and *placed*. A sketched feature is the first feature that you place in a part. It is generally made up of a 2D sketch on a face or plane that you convert into a 3D shape. Examples of sketched feature tools include Extrude, Revolve, and Rib.

Placed features are, well, placed on other features. Examples of placed feature tools include Fillet, Chamfer, and Face Draft. Features that are placed or that use the faces of other features as a foundation are said to be *children* of the features they are built on, which are called *parent* features. For example, if you add a rounded edge to a cylinder and change the size of the cylinder, the rounded edge updates to follow the change to the geometry of the parent feature.

Here are some other basic considerations:

- The first shape you define in a model should make up the primary shape of the part.

- When adding dimensions, focus on what features on the part are most likely to change and how.

- While most considerations of order will be obvious, there are elements that should be added at the end to enhance the performance of the software and hardware. For example, it is common practice with most 3D systems to recommend that users add small fillets and rounds at the very end of the modeling process whenever possible.

One of the biggest hurdles to be overcome is the mental approach. Years of board drafting or using 2D CAD have trained you to draw the geometry precisely and then add dimensions to the geometry; this demonstrates that you know how to draw precisely. But when sketching for parametric models, you want to draw things close to the final size, but there is no real value in being overly accurate, because Inventor will correct the sketch to reflect the dimensions you provide. That is, when you first add a dimension to, say, an edge, it will reflect the size that you drew the edge, but changing the value of the dimension will then change the size of the geometry in the sketch.

The first time I worked with parametrically controlled sketches, I felt cheated. Where had this been all those years? Why didn't these programs start out with the concept that the dimension would change the geometry? Worse yet was the realization that all of the precise work was squandered as soon as the sketch needed changing.

Going beyond the basics, you'll discover the second value of dimension-driven geometry: you can use formulas and relationships between dimensions to modify things automatically. You'll also find that dimensions are not the only way, or even always the best way, to define relationships. Geometry can be related to other geometry directly. For example, two circles that should be the same size can have their diameters linked without using dimensions on both of them. This can be as reliable for keeping things in shape as dimensions, or more so. Parametric relationships can even exist between files so that changes made to one part can affect values in another part or assembly.

> Part modeling tools and capabilities are the same for the Autodesk Inventor Suite, Professional, and LT versions.

A Hands-On Introduction to Sketching

This exercise is the first step. Remember, you should sketch close to the correct size, but don't drive yourself crazy trying to be perfect. Perfect will come soon—but not in this step.

1. Close any files that you have open in Inventor.

2. Set your Active Project File to the Introducing Inventor.ipj that you created in Chapter 1.

3. Create a new file based on the Standard (mm).ipt template in the Metric tab on the New File dialog box.

    When Inventor is finished, you will have a new look in Inventor. The Panel bar will now display the 2D Sketch Panel, and (unless you changed it in the Application Options earlier) there will be a grid displayed on the screen. Review the tools in the Panel bar. They are in groups based on whether they create geometry, duplicate geometry, define its size, or modify it. There are also other tools that we won't use in this chapter. Let's begin by creating something very basic.

4. Select the Line tool in the Panel bar. The letter in brackets indicates the keyboard shortcut (in this case, pressing L) that you can also use to start the command.

5. Move your cursor near the center of the Design window. If you don't have a grid, that's OK. Once you have chosen your spot, click your mouse to begin creating a line. If you move your cursor straight up or down, a vertical line appears next to the end. This indicates that the line is vertical.

6. Now move your cursor to the right so that you see the glyph that shows that the line is horizontal. Look at the lower right of the screen on the status bar. Move your cursor so that your line segment is horizontal and the Length value is roughly 35mm.

7. Click to place the other end of the segment. See Figure 3.1 for reference.

Figure 3.1

Creating the initial horizontal line

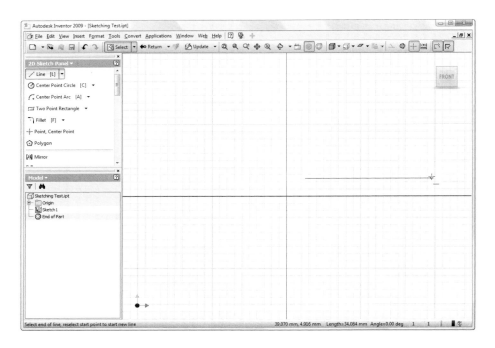

Creating a line segment will not exit the Line tool. Inventor lets you keep creating as many segments as you like. Each new segment previewed is attached to the last point that you selected. This allows you to chain segments together quickly to form a shape that Inventor can use.

8. Move your cursor upward, and Inventor indicates when the new line segment is perpendicular to the horizontal segment that you just created. Move the cursor up so the new line segment will be approximately 20mm and click to place the new segment (see Figure 3.2).

When Inventor shows that the new segment is perpendicular, it really means it. When you place that new line segment, it will be held perpendicular to the other. You cannot accidentally change it from being perpendicular. These relationships are known as "constraints" because they place rules or constraints on the possible behavior of the geometry. This is a very important element providing control of the sketch geometry.

AutoCAD's osnap options behave in a similar fashion to many of Inventor's sketch constraints, with one critical difference. If you tell AutoCAD that a line is attached to the endpoint of another line by using an osnap, it will create the new line with an endpoint that's precisely in the same position as the other point. It will not create a relationship between the points. If the first line were moved, the new line would not follow. In Inventor, the relationship is maintained until it is deliberately removed or Inventor is told that the relationship should not be created.

Figure 3.2

Relationships between geometry will define themselves while sketching.

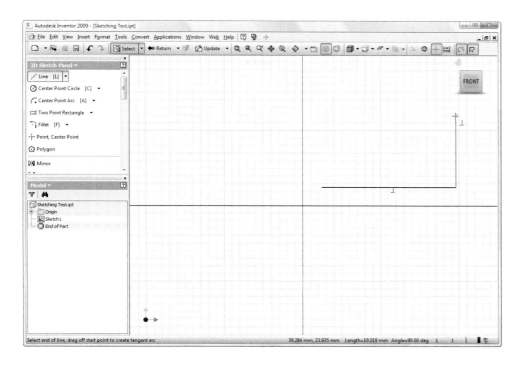

It is also possible to change the way the geometry is being constrained while you are placing the geometry.

9. Continue using the Line tool. Move to the left of the last line endpoint. You will see Inventor placing a Perpendicular constraint between the last line segment and the new one you are creating. Let's say that what you really want is your new line to be parallel to the first line you drew. In this case, that will produce the same geometry, but that won't always be so.

10. While dragging your new line endpoint, move over the horizontal line that you created first without clicking. This is called *gesturing*, and there are a number of uses for it in Inventor sketching. When you gesture or hover over the horizontal as you've just done, you tell Inventor that you intend to build a relationship between that line and your new one.

11. Now move your cursor so the line is going to the left of the last selected point again. Now the glyph near your cursor should be parallel to the first line that you drew.

12. Continue dragging the line to the left. When the new preview is nearly the same length as the first line, you will see a dotted inference line appear from the first point that you created. This indicates that there is an alignment between the points. When the inference line appears, and the line segment is parallel to the first line, click to place the new endpoint. See Figure 3.3.

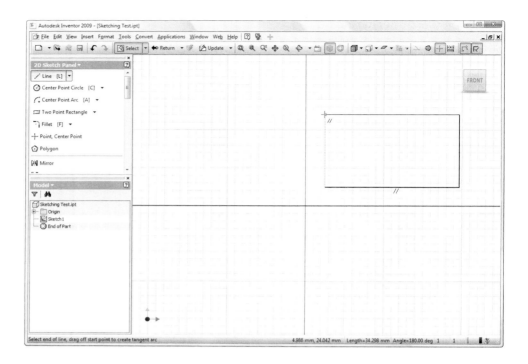

13. Now move the cursor down to the first point. Note that as you near the endpoint, the dot on your cursor changes color to show that you are on the endpoint, and a new glyph appears, displaying a point with a curved arrow going toward another point. Click the mouse so that the last endpoint is constrained "point to point" to the first point, completing the rectangle.

14. Save your work as Sketching Test.ipt. When you tell Inventor to save, you will be warned that you cannot save while in a sketch. Choose Yes to accept leaving the sketch environment and then finish saving your file into the Data folder.

As you saw, Inventor infers the automatic creation of constraints between entities in a sketch and even allows you to guide that process. Constraints can be added or removed whenever necessary. The key to working with constraints is to keep in mind what is important about this part in your project. If you intend a shape to be held in position in relation to another point, then find the easiest way to bind them together. Before we move on, let's take a closer look at the constraints and see how they can be changed after they're created if you need to.

Sketch Constraints

There are a number of types of constraint that can be placed in a sketch. Figure 3.4 shows the list of constraints available for sketching. It's worth taking a little time to review them.

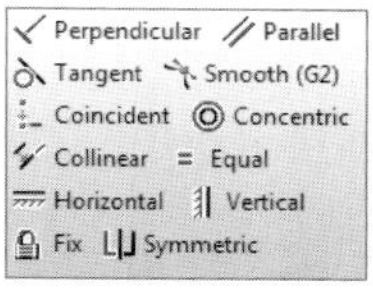

Perpendicular This constraint creates a relationship between line segments that keeps them at 90 degrees. It is commonly placed automatically while sketching.

Figure 3.4

The Sketch Constraints menu

Parallel This constraint is also commonly applied while sketching. Like all constraints, it is maintained until it is removed. If one of the members of the constraint relationship changes direction, the other will as well.

Tangent This condition can be created between lines and arcs, arcs and splines, and even circle to circle.

Smooth This constraint is similar to Tangent but with a deeper mathematical meaning. Rather than a simple relationship that affects the points where two entities meet, Smooth causes splines to change downstream from the connection point to maintain the continuity of the curve. This constraint is not placed automatically in a sketch.

Coincident This constraint is by far the most common. It can be placed between endpoints, midpoints, and even between a point and a curve. If you want a point to maintain a relationship with just about anything, coincident will do it.

Concentric For a Concentric relationship to be placed, you need to have at least one arc and one circle. Two arcs or two circles will also work. This is essentially a specialized Coincident constraint used only for the centerpoint of a radius. Since an ellipse also has a centerpoint, it will work with that shape as well.

Collinear This simply tells edges to be aligned with one another.

Equal Using the Equal constraint can create a lot of interesting relationships. You can keep any two (or more) like entities at the same value. Two lines can maintain the same length, and two (or more) arcs can maintain the same radius. This helps to reduce the number of redundant dimensions that would be placed in a sketch otherwise.

Horizontal and Vertical These two constraints can occasionally catch you off guard. It's important to remember the orientation to the coordinate system. Vertical relates to the Y axis of the active sketch and Horizontal relates to the X axis. They are used for far more than keeping lines oriented. You can constrain a point to be vertical or horizontal to another point. This can aid in aligning critical points as you develop around them.

Fix The Fix constraint enables you to hold a position on a point. It can be useful for positioning critical points while others are allowed to move freely around them.

Symmetric This constraint is often overlooked but very powerful when you're working on symmetrical sketches whose size is in flux. As with Parallel, any change made to one member affects the mirrored or symmetrical member of the constraint.

To review the constraints that exist on an entire sketch, right-click in the Design window and select Show All Constraints from the menu or press the F8 key. If you want to review the constraints placed on an individual geometry piece, select the geometry, right-click, and select Show Constraints.

Viewing Existing Constraints in a Sketch

In the previous exercise, you learned how to build a sketch that has intelligent relationships. There may come a time when you need to change how you have constrained a sketch or how someone else did. In this exercise, we'll explore how to view the existing constraints in a sketch.

1. Staying in the sketch, use the context menu or the F8 key to make all of the existing constraints visible, as shown in Figure 3.5.

2. Note that the icons for the applied constraints are the same as the tools used to apply them manually.

3. Hover over the Parallelism icon at the top of the sketch. As you do, the icon will highlight in yellow, the line beneath it will highlight in red, and the parallel line will also highlight to show you what members belong to that constraint.

Figure 3.5

Displaying the constraint icons in a sketch can help you understand how geometry relates to other geometry in the sketch.

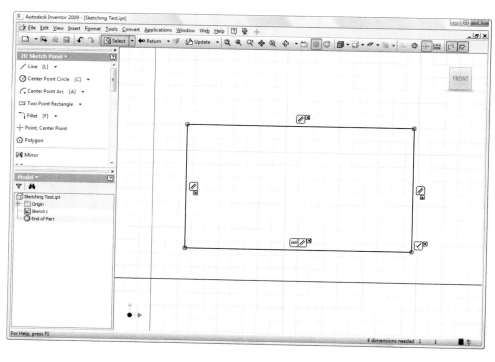

4. Try hovering over other constraints to review how the sketch is constrained.

5. In a smaller or more complicated sketch, these icons may crowd one another. You can move them away from their standard location by clicking and dragging them to an open space. You can also close an icon by clicking the small X attached to the constraint icon.

6. Coincident constraints appear in the sketch as small yellow icons on the points where they occur. Clicking them brings up icons for each of the members of the constraint set.

On the status bar in the lower right is a note that reports how many dimensions (or constraints) are needed for the sketch to be in a "fully constrained" state. Inventor does not require sketches to be fully constrained before you can use them to make a 3D model. Some older systems do require this, and it can be limiting when you are trying to rough in an idea.

7. Right-click the Parallel icon on the left edge and select Hide from the menu. Doing so removes this constraint from the visible set, including the icon on the right vertical line.

8. Hide all the icons by right-clicking on a blank part of the screen and selecting Hide All Constraints, or by pressing F9.

Nothing that you did changed the constraint system of the sketch at all. Unless you want to make a change or the sketch is not behaving the way you thought it would, you probably won't even make the constraints visible.

A new option added to Autodesk Inventor 2009 is one you may want to use frequently: the ability to display the *degrees of freedom* that remain on elements of the sketch. Degrees of freedom in the context of a sketch are a way of defining the ability of a sketch element (line, arc, and so on) to be able to move by dragging on them. As you apply constraints to a sketch to limit its flexibility, these DOF symbols provide a graphic representation of the movements that are still allowed within the sketch.

When a sketch still has degrees of freedom available, it can be edited by simply clicking and dragging elements. Depending on how it is and is not constrained, you'll be able to move elements in various ways. This is a great way to quickly "massage" a part into a new size and sometimes new shape. The next exercise will concentrate on altering constraints and will introduce the basic dragging of elements for editing.

As you add dimensions and constraints, the ability to edit elements by dragging them in certain directions will be limited because degrees of freedom will have been removed.

Sketch Dimensions

Sketch constraints create specific relationships between parts of the geometry. When you need to be able to define a relationship based on a size, that's when you need a *sketch dimension*.

Sketch dimensions have slightly fewer options than drawing dimensions but follow the same basic rules. The General Dimension tool still places several types of dimensions based on gesturing, which can speed the sketch constraining process. Inventor's sketch dimensions can also simplify creating geometry with different units. If you're working in inches but need to size something based on a known metric measurement, simply input the value and the units. If you don't specify the units, Inventor uses the default units of the template you started the part from. Inventor does the calculations for you and maintains the units that you specified in the background.

In Chapter 2 you were able to reuse sketch dimensions in the drawing. One school of thought says you should dimension the part sketches so that the dimensions can be reused. I believe you should dimension your sketches in whatever fashion allows you to change your part in a predictable way; if they happen to be reusable, great. If they can't be reused, then it's easy to create new dimensions in the drawing.

Some companies do not allow sketch dimensions to be reused in the drawing. Inventor is installed by default with the ability to update the 3D part by modifying a sketch dimension's value in the 2D drawing. This can be changed during installation, but rather than risk a mistake, many companies discourage or bar the practice of reusing sketch dimensions.

Sneaking Up on Perfection: Correcting a Sketch by Adding Dimensions

In the previous exercise, you learned to review the geometric constraints that have been applied to the sketch. Once a sketch is constrained correctly, it's time to start adding dimensions to size the sketch properly.

1. Press F8 to make the sketch constraints visible.

2. Right-click in a blank portion of the screen and select Show All Degrees Of Freedom from the context menu.

In addition to the constraint icons, you should now see a collection of arrows. The line segments have some restricted movement. The lines constrained to be horizontal can only move vertically. The opposite is true for the vertical lines. The points in the corners can move in any direction on the sketch plane. See Figure 3.6 for a reference.

3. Right-click the Parallel constraint on the left vertical line and select Delete from the context menu.

The constraint set will now change. The vertical line on the left can now be rotated so a curved arrow has been added to indicate that its angle can be changed. Also note that the number of dimensions required to fully constrain the sketch has increased to 5, as shown on the status bar.

4. Test the degrees of freedom by clicking and dragging on different points and lines. Remember to release the mouse button when you have moved a point or line into a position that you like. After experimenting, make your sketch look similar to Figure 3.7.

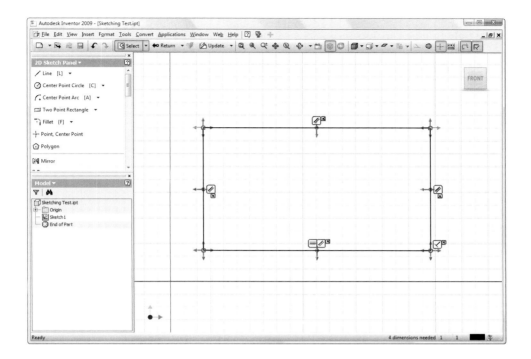

Figure 3.6

DOF symbols help you understand how applied constraints limit sketch flexibility.

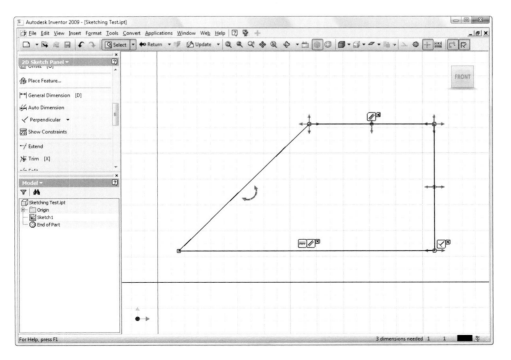

Figure 3.7

Chaining constraints changes the related DOF symbols.

5. In the 2D Sketch panel under the Perpendicular constraint flyout, select the Fix constraint. You can also find the Fix constraint via the context menu under the Create Constraint flyout.

6. With the constraint active, click the lower-left corner. Watch what happens to the constraint system of the sketch and the remaining degrees of freedom.

7. Press the Esc key to end the Fix constraint.

The point you selected can no longer be moved. The angled line can no longer slide, but it can still pivot. The bottom lines cannot be repositioned, although you can change their length by dragging the vertical line on the right.

Another change happens that is not as obvious. The bottom line has changed colors. In the Inventor sketch environment, color is a constant source of feedback. As elements become constrained, their color changes.

While in the sketch environment, the context menu holds a large number of tools. Right-click and select the General Dimension tool, select it from the 2D Sketch panel, or press the D key.

8. Place a dimension on the bottom line. To do so, select the line itself and click below the line away from the basic shape to locate the dimension.

9. Click on the dimension text and set the value to 40, then click the green check button to close the window. The line changes length, the DOF symbol on the vertical line on the right is removed, the color of that line changes, and you now only need two dimensions. See Figure 3.8.

Figure 3.8

Applying dimensions has the same effect as placing Sketch constraints.

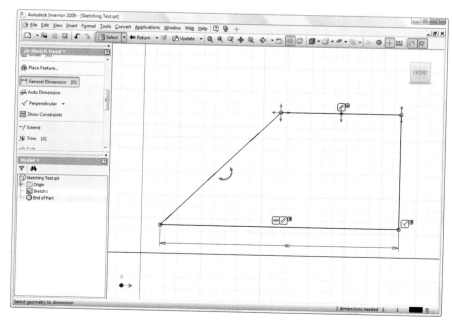

10. While the General Dimension tool is still active, select the vertical line on the right and place a dimension next to it. Set its value to 25.

   The geometry will update, colors have changed, and now there is only one dimension required for the sketch. Let's see what else we can do with it.

11. Select the dimension text again but set the value to .75in. After you click the green check button, the geometry will update. The dimension will not show .75in but instead the metric equivalent, 19.05mm.

   That is because this is a metric part; you don't have to do the math, and you don't have to reapply the dimension to change its value.

12. Select the 19.05 dimension value. Note that the dialog box is showing the value that you typed in, not the calculated value. Inventor recognizes that the value you entered takes priority.

13. Highlight the dimension value in the dialog box. Now click on the 40mm dimension and the name of the dimension appears in the dialog box.

14. Type **/2** after d0 and accept this value. Now the dimension value is set to one half of the first dimension. An *fx* symbol appears next to the dimension to indicate that it has a relationship to another dimension.

   When you place a dimension into a sketch, it is given a name—a parameter name— and the number that you enter is the value for that parameter. When you selected that dimension, it created an association between the two dimensions. Adding the /2 created a mathematical formula that stated that the second dimension was equal to the first dimension divided by 2.

15. The General Dimension tool should still be active. Select the angled line and the bottom line to place an angular dimension.

16. Place the dimension and set the value to 60. The sketch is now fully constrained, as you can see in Figure 3.9.

17. For a final item, change the bottom dimension to 35 and see the effect.

18. To clear the constraint icons, press the F9 key.

19. Save your work and compare it to Figure 3.10.

Figure 3.9

Adding an angular dimension

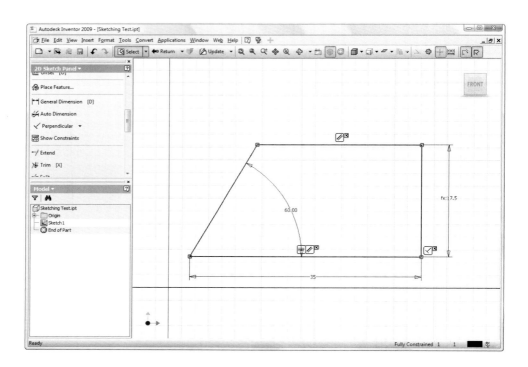

Figure 3.10

The sketch with the constraint icons hidden

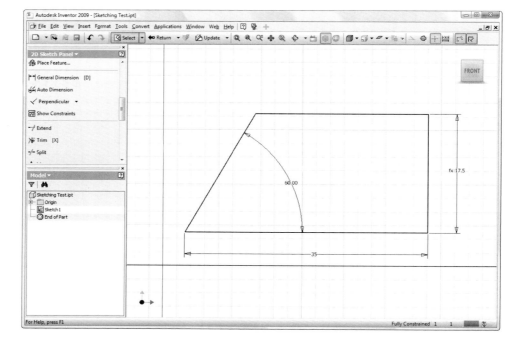

Specialized Linetypes

That was a long exercise, but look at how many tools you used. You have already learned many of the tools that you will need for beginning any model.

There are also ways to have your sketch geometry aligned or guided by other geometry without constraints being added. When working with shallow angles near horizontal or vertical, parallelism, or perpendicularity with other objects, you can skip placing constraints even momentarily. For example, if you're working with a plastic or cast part you may want to include the draft angle in the part.

When you started your new part it automatically put you into the sketch environment. The Inventor Standard toolbar looks pretty much like it did before, but as noted in Chapter 1, every environment adds a few extra tools. When sketching, you'll find six additional tools in two groups added to the end of the toolbar. These icons do not access tools but instead work as switches, enabling optional functions or disabling standard ways of working. If you select one of these options before placing sketch geometry or dimensions, the new items you place will be built based on the option. If you have created an item but want to change how it is affected by an option, select it and then change the switch, and the item takes on the new properties. This saves you from having to re-create things to give them a different function. Let's take a look at the options:

Construction When you draw in Inventor, the geometry is "normal" geometry by default. Normal geometry is intended to build shapes to make 3D features from. Construction geometry is ignored by 3D modeling tools but can be used to define the shape and location of the 2D sketch geometry.

Centerline This option can convert any normal or construction geometry to take on special properties as a centerline. Centerlines can be selected automatically for creating round or turned shapes using the Revolve tool. They can also change the behavior of dimensions, causing them to recognize a sectional profile as having its size based on a diameter rather than a linear dimension.

Center Point Any geometry placed in a sketch will have points included. These points can be selected for different functions. When the Center Point override is selected, points that are placed in a sketch are automatically selected as a place to put a hole feature.

Driven Dimension The dimensions that you placed on the sketch in the previous exercise are referred to as *parametric* dimensions. Their value will change the size of sketch geometry. There are times where you want a dimension to simply show what size something is but not be able to change the geometry. A *driven dimension* will allow this. It even displays itself in the sketch in parentheses as a reference dimension would be displayed.

> Since AutoCAD Release 9, associative dimensions have had the ability to change their values when the geometry they are tied to changes. This is how driven dimensions behave.

The final two options control how or whether constraints are placed automatically in the sketch. The default is to have both options turned on so they appear as engaged buttons.

Constraint Inference This controls whether Inventor recognizes conditions such as Parallel or Perpendicular in the sketch. With the option off, tools such as Line will still appear to follow horizontal or vertical, but no glyph is displayed. If you build a shape, any coincident constraints are automatically added to the sketch.

Constraint Persistence Turning this off prevents Inventor from capturing any conditions in the sketch. With Constraint Inference on and Constraint Persistence off, you can draw using parallelism and so forth, but when you finish your sketch there will be no actual constraints (other than coincidence) included in the sketch. You cannot have a condition where Constraint Inference is on and Constraint Persistence is off. Shutting off Inference automatically disables Persistence.

You can tell Inventor to ignore inference and persistence momentarily by holding the Ctrl key while sketching. Coincidence will still be captured, but everything else will be ignored.

Let's do one more exercise in 2D sketching before you build 3D. These options or overrides are very important as they allow you to build your 3D models with incredible control.

Not All Sketch Lines Are Created Equal: Construction Geometry

In this exercise you'll begin to work with construction geometry. This geometry allows very creative ways of creating a sketch.

1. Continue working in `Sketching Test.ipt` or reopen it.

2. Make sure that Display All Degrees Of Freedom for your sketch is still on; your context menu should show Hide All Degrees Of Freedom.

3. Select the 17.5mm dimension and click the Driven Dimensions override. The dimension loses its link to the dimension it was linked to. The top line will show that it can be moved again, and the status bar shows that you need 1 dimension again.

4. Select the Construction override and then select the Line tool.

5. Select the upper-left corner for the first point of your line. Select the lower-right corner as the second point, as shown in Figure 3.11. Close the Line tool.

6. The line that is created will be dotted. This is the visual cue that it is a construction line.

7. Select the General Dimension tool.

8. Click the new line and the bottom line, which creates an angular dimension. Place the dimension as shown in Figure 3.12 and set the value to 30 degrees.

9. Save your work and close the file.

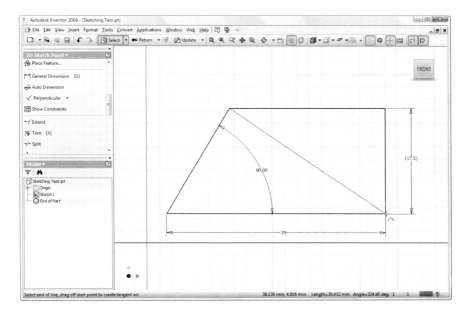

Figure 3.11

Adding a construction line to the sketch

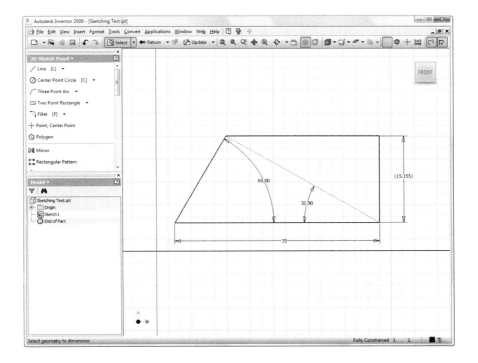

Figure 3.12

Fully constraining the sketch by dimensioning to the construction geometry

To satisfy the constraints that the 60-degree and the 30-degree angle put on the sketch, the height had to change. Changing the height dimension to a driven dimension allowed that to happen. That does not mean that a driven dimension has no value. Any relationship that you can create between one dimension and another can be made with either parametric or driven dimensions. In this book we won't use the ability to drive a parameter from the value of a driven constraint, but it is something to keep in mind as you work with Inventor going forward.

While Line is probably the most commonly used sketch tool and drawing your original rectangle the way the exercise did is perfectly fine, it is not the fastest way to do it. Sketch tools like Rectangle can shortcut the sketching process even if the final shape may be a rectangle with a corner cut off.

In 2D CAD and older 3D tools, a lot of focus is put on drawing the perimeter of the shape and much time is invested in making sure the perimeter is clean, without a lot of overlapping or segmented edges. Inventor can work with that perimeter, but it can also work with multiple shapes stacked together to form what is sometimes called a *multiloop* sketch.

In Inventor, working with a multiloop sketch opens up a lot of options. Inventor even has the ability to reuse a sketch to make several features. Although that's not always possible, it is an interesting approach and you can control many features at once.

Building a More Complex Part Model

You have built a basic sketch and controlled it. Now let's use the sketching techniques to begin building a part model. We'll use this model for the next several exercises.

1. Create a new file based on the Standard(mm).ipt template in the Metric tab in the New dialog box.

2. In the Browser, expand the Origin folder to show the standard axes and planes that exist in the part.

The standard Center Point, X, Y, and Z axes, and YZ, XZ, and XY planes exist in every 3D file in Inventor, and although it is not necessary to build your part around them, doing so can be helpful. In particular, with symmetrical or turned parts it can dramatically reduce creation and editing times.

3. In the 2D Sketch panel, select the Project Geometry tool.

4. Click the Center Point under Origin in the Browser. The point projects in the sketch but may be hard to see because of the grid displayed in the sketch. Press Esc to close the tool.

5. In the 2D Sketch panel, select the Two Point Rectangle tool.

6. Draw a rectangle similar to Figure 3.13. When you're dragging the size of a two-point rectangle, the status bar will not list the size of the rectangle; it will show the position

of the cursor. You have to approximate the size or compare the position of the first point placed to the coordinate of your cursor.

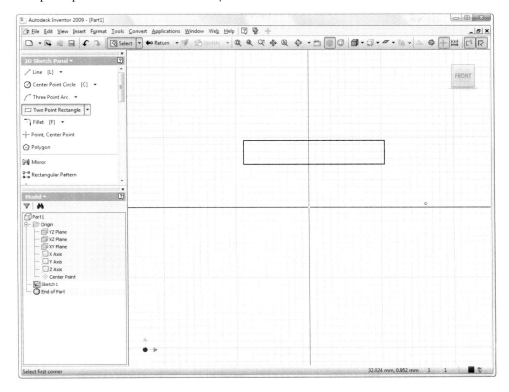

Figure 3.13

Roughing in the first rectangle

7. Draw a slightly larger rectangle, starting it in the upper-left corner of the first rectangle. When you're done, close the tool.

8. Start the Coincident constraint.

9. Move your cursor near the middle of the bottom line on the first rectangle. As you move along, a glyph appears near your cursor that looks like a point on a line. Move until you find the midpoint; it highlights with a green dot, and the glyph shows the point in the middle of a short line. Select the midpoint.

10. Select the projected center point of the sketch. When you do, the rectangles move to their new location but remain attached to one another.

11. Switch your constraint tool to Equal.

12. Select the bottom lines of each rectangle. The rectangle will now have the same exact width. Close the Equal tool and drag to move the lines around. You will see that they remain centered in the sketch.

13. Select the Circle tool and draw a circle above the rectangles.

14. Using the Vertical constraint (keyboard shortcut I), then select the sketch center point and the center of the circle. This aligns the circle directly over the center of the rectangles.

15. Close the Vertical constraint tool. The circle can still move vertically. Position it as shown in Figure 3.14.

Figure 3.14

Constraining the circle to be positioned over the center of the rectangles

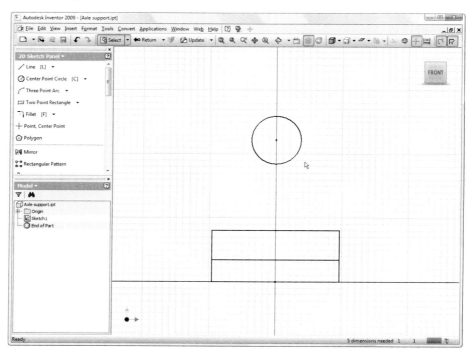

16. Start the Line command and make the origin of the new line the top left corner of the upper rectangle.

17. Drag the line to the upper left of the circle until you see a glyph that indicates that the line will be tangent. Click the mouse to create the line; see Figure 3.15.

18. The Line tool will be ready to start a new line. Hover over the top of the circle with the cursor directly over the edge of the circle. Click and hold the mouse button and drag the mouse to the right. The new line should automatically be tangent to the circle and remain so as you drag the line segment preview on the screen (see Figure 3.16).

19. Select the top-right corner of the upper rectangle to create the line.

20. End the Line command.

21. Click the Return button on the Inventor Standard toolbar to exit the sketch and save the new file to Axle support.ipt in the Parts folder.

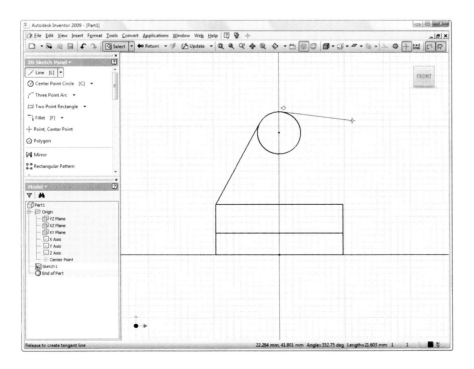

Figure 3.15

Drawing a line tangent to the circle

Figure 3.16

Gesturing over a line to be tangent from the circle

The next step is to apply the sketch dimensions.

You will want to dimension the sketch in the way that best fits the critical features of the part and what you will most likely change in the future. If down the road you decide there would've been a better way to dimension the sketch, Inventor's flexibility will make it easy to change things. So give it your best shot but don't worry if it's not perfect.

For this model the size of the circle may change and the distance from the base to the center may change as the design is refined. The size of the rectangles may also change, but changing it may not affect the position of the axle. Using those basic principles, you'll dimension the sketch.

Refining the Sketch by Adding More Dimensions

You have created a new sketch and used geometric constraints to rough in the shape. Now it is time to bring back the dimensions.

1. Start the General Dimension tool.

2. Select the vertical edge of the bottom rectangle to dimension its height.

3. Place the dimension and set its value to 10mm.

4. Place a dimension from the bottommost line to the top of the second rectangle and set its value to 20mm.

5. Set the diameter of the circle to 20mm. Use Figure 3.17 to check the last several steps.

Figure 3.17

Beginning to dimension the sketch

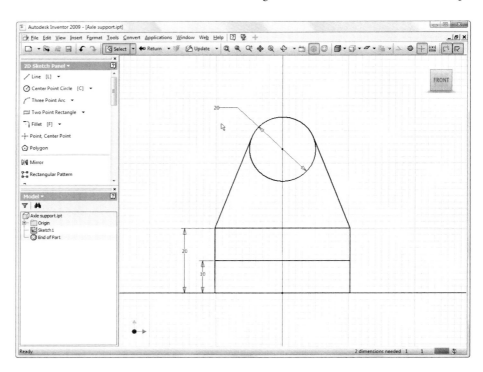

6. Move your cursor near the ViewCube and click the icon that looks like a house to reposition the model to the Home view, or press the F6 key. The dimension tool will not be interrupted by changing the view (see Figure 3.18).

7. Continue placing dimensions by dimensioning the center of the circle to be 50mm above the base.

8. Dimension the base to be 55mm wide. This will work the same in an isometric view as it does when looking directly at the sketch.

9. Use the ViewCube to reposition the view as shown in Figure 3.20.

10. Move your cursor near the ViewCube. When the Home View icon becomes visible, right-click the icon of the house.

11. In the menu under Set Current View As Home, select the Fit To View option. Doing so sets this point of view as the one that Inventor will return you to every time you invoke the Home View command.

A Home view is not restricted to an isometric view. It can be established at any point of view. Dimensions added in any point of view will be sized and positioned so that they are legible.

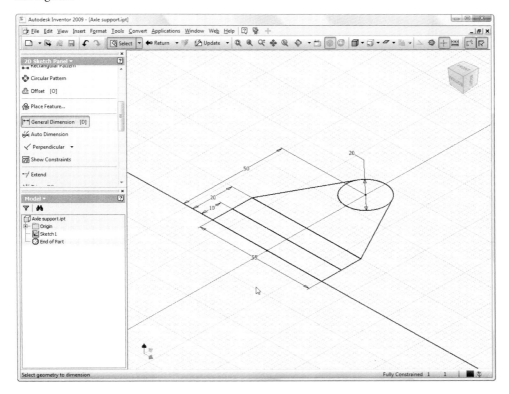

Figure 3.18

Dimensions can be added in an isometric view or from any viewpoint.

12. Click the large Return button to move from the sketch environment to the part modeling environment.

13. Save your work.

The Extrude Tool

For most parts that people create with Inventor, Extrude is far and away the most common feature for creating the initial shape.

The Extrude tool dialog box (Figure 3.19) is typical of Inventor dialog boxes.

Figure 3.19

The Extrude dialog box

The buttons and boxes on the Shape tab ask you to select a profile or profiles, select a direction for the extruded feature to be created, and define what size the feature should be. If your sketch has only one viable profile to be used for an Extrude feature, it is automatically selected and Inventor moves on to prompting for the remaining information.

Initially you are offered the Join tool, which creates a positive shape in the model. After your first or base feature is placed, additional options are made available in the dialog box:

- Cut takes the shape and removes material to a depth or through the entire model.

- The Intersect option passes the new shape through the existing shape and only the portions of the model that were common to both sketches remain.

- The More tab lets you define a taper angle, which allows the creation of a draft angle for cast or plastic parts.

Making a 3D Model

Finally, you get to do something fun. I know that you have been waiting, but everything you have learned to this point is critical to make this possible.

With this exercise we will begin to create an Axle support. Through the exercises, you will see different ways of using solid modeling tools to add features to the part.

1. Start the Extrude tool from the Panel bar or by pressing the E key. Since there is more than one viable sketch profile, Inventor will want you to select which profile you will use for a feature.

2. Select all of the profiles. As you select a profile, a preview of the finished feature appears.

3. Highlight the Distance value and enter **15**. The thickness of the feature or height that it will build to updates as you type in the number.

4. After the preview updates, move your cursor to the edge of the preview.

5. When the preview highlights and a glyph with two opposed arrows appears, you can click and drag the height of the extrusion. As you drag the value for the extrusion updates. You can even drag the preview to the opposite side of the preview.

6. After experimenting, set the extrusion height to 10mm and use the middle directional arrow below the distance value dialog box to force the extrusion to the right.

7. Compare what is on your screen to Figure 3.20. If the screens look alike, click OK to create the feature.

   Inventor will create your feature but as you can see, the sketch disappears. That's because when you create a sketched feature, the sketch will be "consumed" by the feature.

   In this case the sketch that you created is one that we will want to reuse for more than just one feature. Inventor allows you to share a sketch and make it usable for several features.

8. In the Browser, find the Extrusion1 feature. Select the + next to it to show the sketch that was consumed by the feature.

9. Right-click on the sketch and select Share Sketch from the menu.

10. The sketch now becomes visible and also appears in the Browser, listed before the feature. It can now be used again and will not be consumed by another feature.

11. Start the Extrude tool again and this time select only the bottom rectangle.

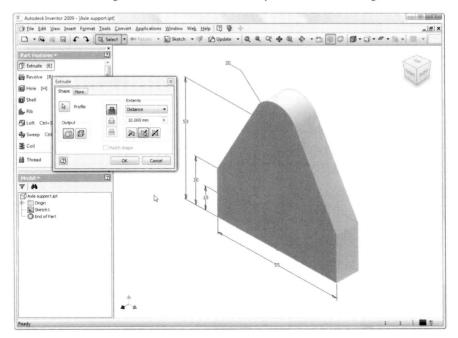

Figure 3.20

Selecting several sketch loops to create the primary face, which will be the base feature

12. Set its direction to be the same as the first feature, set its distance to 40mm, compare your result to Figure 3.21, and click OK to create Extrusion2.

13. Press the spacebar or Enter key to start the Extrude command one more time.

14. Select the circle, leave the direction at its default, and set 10 for the Distance. See the preview in Figure 3.22.

15. Click OK to create the feature and save the file.

You should now have three features created from one sketch. This is not to suggest that all of your parts should be created this way.

Instead, the purpose was to make you aware that Inventor is capable of using one or more profiles in a sketch to construct a feature. This particular part lends itself to a single sketch creating multiple features, but in most cases you will use a single sketch to create a single feature. Even then the sketch does not have to be trimmed to show only the perimeter of the sketched shape.

Your sketch is still visible even though you will not be creating more features from it. Typically you would not leave a sketch visible after you are finished creating features from it.

To edit a sketch that has been consumed, you can double-click on it in the Browser or right-click and select Edit Sketch. This causes the feature to disappear so that you can focus on the sketch edits you need to make.

Figure 3.21

Reusing a shared sketch to create the second feature, which makes the bottom of the part

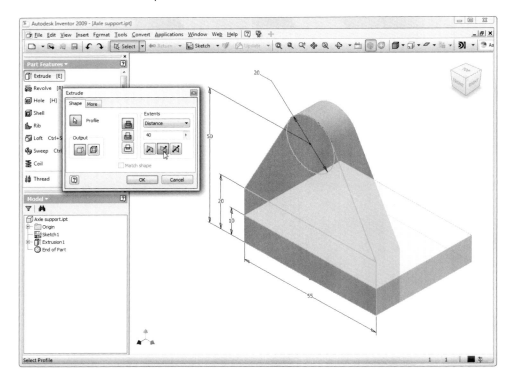

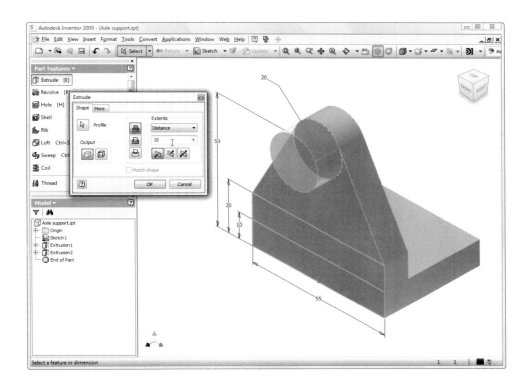

Figure 3.22

**Extruding the cylin-
drical feature**

Modifying the Part with Parametric Dimensions

This is just a short exercise, but it demonstrates how changing a parametric dimension produces a quick modification of the entire part and is typical of the type of change that needs to be made regularly.

1. Double-click the 50mm dimension and change its value to 60.

2. The sketch will change but the model will not. The Update button becomes available on the Inventor Standard toolbar.

3. Click Update to refresh the model.

4. Right-click on Sketch1 in the Browser and deselect Visibility to turn off the sketch. Your model should look like Figure 3.23.

> Pressing the F10 key can turn off any visible sketches, but this should only be done temporarily to make it easier to see the 3D model. Otherwise, you make a sketch visible to edit it, and it will not appear, possibly causing confusion.

Figure 3.23

Part after the change to the dimension

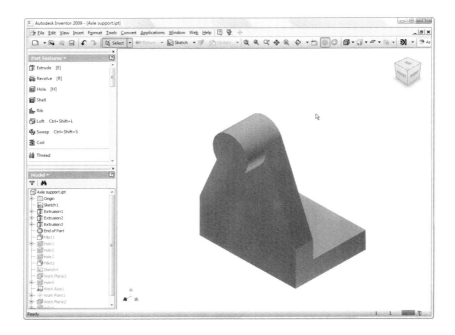

The Fillet Tool

In the chapter introduction, I noted that it is common practice to add fillets as a final step. This is true for the small fillets and rounds that remove the sharp edges on a part.

Figure 3.24

The Fillet dialog box

The Fillet tool can also be used instead of drawing fillets or rounded corners in a sketch to add major features to a part.

The Fillet tool may be the most used feature in typical part modeling, because there are so many reasons for rounding an edge on a part. The Fillet dialog box, shown in Figure 3.24, provides a large number of options for creating fillets.

On the left are the primary construction types for fillets:

Edge Fillet Works by selecting an edge or several edges and defining a radius you would like applied to the edge.

Face Fillet Allows you to place a fillet between two faces that do not need to be able to touch to place a fillet.

Full Round Allows you to place a fillet across three faces. Typically the middle planar face will be removed as the new rounded face is placed tangent with the first and last faces selected.

Also, the dialog box offers one or more tabs of options, depending on the type of fillet that has been selected.

For the Edge Fillet, you will see three tabs. The first is the Constant tab. You can select multiple edges, and by clicking Click To Add you can also place fillets with differing radii in one feature by changing the value of the radius. An additional option is defining whether the fillet will simply be tangent to adjacent faces or will continue the curvature; for the latter option, click the down arrow and select Smooth (G2). How you select edges has several options as well, and you can mix and match them. For example, the Edge option will have you select each edge to be rounded individually, while the Loop option will have you try to select multiple edges based on a face or the edges of a surface. By mixing them, you can set a fillet radius, select multiple edges using the Loop option, and select additional edges by changing your Select Mode to Edge. There will be a display showing how many edges are selected as you go. Choosing the Feature option selects all the edges of a specific feature. If you have created an extrusion with a large number of edges, you can select them all by switching to the Feature mode.

With cast or plastic parts, you may not want any sharp edges. The All Fillets and All Rounds options will do as they say and select every sharp edge that is external for all fillets and every sharp edge that is internal for all rounds.

The Variable tab allows you to place a fillet or round that changes size as it moves along the edge. You can reference points along the edge to define a different radius between the beginning and end. You can do this after you have selected the edge on which you want to place the feature by moving your cursor to the end and clicking where you want to add another radius.

Setback is a way to control the shape of a corner where several fillets meet. This allows you to soften the corner to a larger radius than is used on the edges.

The Face Fillet method only has one group of options. You can override whether the fillet will include tangent faces to the ones you selected to build the fillet between.

Optimize For Single Selection allows you to select your two faces quickly. If this option is deselected, you can build a collection of faces for Face Set 1 and another individual face or collection of faces for Face Set 2 to build a complex fillet feature. This type of fillet also needs to have a radius specified, but you can only place a fillet with one radius.

Full Round calculates the only radius it can use based on the geometry that you select. You do have the Optimize For Single Selection option as well as the Include Tangent Faces option.

The icon with the eyeglasses next to the checkbox allows you to disable a preview of the Fillet feature if the performance of your system is suffering.

You can find four other options by clicking the More button and expanding the dialog box. These options affect how the fillet or round will be generated:

Roll Along Sharp Edges When this option is selected, Inventor varies the fillet radius in order to maintain a sharp edge corner where it intersects. If this option is off (the default), Inventor maintains the radius by pulling the face it meets up into the radius. It's as if a fillet was put around an object and then part of the fillet was milled off.

Rolling Ball Where Possible   This option controls how corners are resolved where multiple edges meet at a corner. With Rolling Ball Where Possible selected, the corner shows a spherical radius that is the same as the edge radius. With the option off, Inventor enlarges the corner and extends the radius back down the edge to create a smoother appearance.

Automatic Edge Chain   Automatic Edge Chain is on by default; when it is disabled, selecting an edge will not automatically select edges that are tangent to it.

Preserve All Features   Preserve All Features takes features that are affected by the fillet into consideration for the calculation. You would use this option primarily when placing a fillet has the effect of removing another feature. For example, if you cut a notch into a face near an edge and then place a fillet that passes over the notch, the notch may disappear even though the notch is deep enough that you expected it to remain. With this option turned on, the Fillet tool recognizes that there is a cut that should not be removed and calculates its rounded face with the notch built into it.

Even with all of the options and flexibility, placing fillets and rounds on a part can be challenging to get exactly right. The order in which you place fillets, along with the numbers and combinations of edges that you select, affects how the fillets appear on the model. This takes time to master, and you have to look at the model to make sure you are getting the result you want. The good news is that if it doesn't come out right the first time, it is easy to try it another way.

Adding an Edge Fillet

In this exercise you begin working with placed features. Most of these features have names that are the same as tools used in 2D CAD, but they will have considerably more options in Inventor.

1. Use the ViewCube to take a look around the part.

2. Set the view to the corner that leaves the top, right, and back visible.

   Placing fillets modifies the mass of the part just as adding or removing any material would do to a real part. Before we begin adding features, let's establish what the part is made of.

3. Right-click on the root of the part in the Browser and select Properties. Select the Physical tab, which displays the mass, volume, and inertial properties of the part as you develop it. To calculate the mass properly, you have to select a material.

4. On the Material flyout, locate and select Cast Steel.

5. Set your Requested Accuracy value to Medium.

6. Click Apply and note the calculated mass of the part; my part reported a mass of 0.373 kg, or approximately .82 lbs. Now let's make some changes. Figure 3.25 shows the results for my model.

7. Select the Fillet tool from the Panel bar or press the F key.

8. Inventor asks you to select an edge or edges. For the first features we'll place, keep the Edge Fillet selected and set Radius to 10 by selecting the value under the word *Radius* and setting it to 10.

9. Select the two short vertical edges, as shown in Figure 3.26. A preview appears, showing how the model will be affected.

10. Below the Radius column, choose Click To Add. You will now set a new radius and select more edges to fillet. When the Fillet feature is created, all the edges and radii are included in one feature.

11. Select the horizontal edges where the part faces angle up to the cylinder. You can select the second edge through the part by moving your cursor near where the edge should be on the other side of the part and clicking it when it highlights. Set the radius of this new selection of edges to 15. Figure 3.27 shows how the edge will highlight before being selected.

Figure 3.25

Physical properties are available on demand from the 3D part.

Figure 3.26

The fillet previews when the edges are selected.

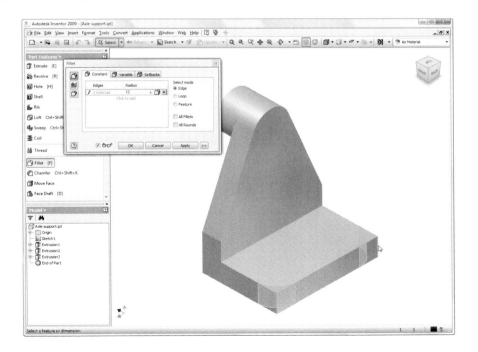

12. You should now have four edges selected with two different radii.

13. Click OK to add the fillets to the model and exit the command.

14. Save your work and compare the result to Figure 3.28.

Figure 3.27

Add two more edges using a different radius.

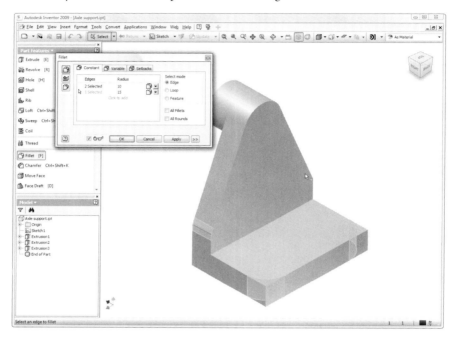

Figure 3.28

The part is really taking shape.

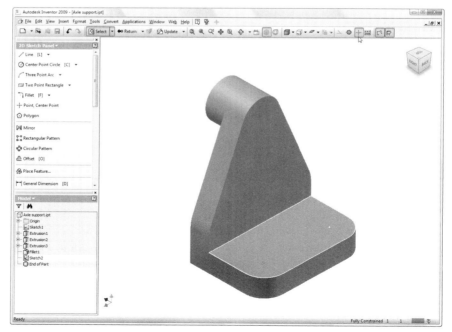

In this exercise you worked with two of the most commonly used tools for most Inventor users. If you do machine design, you will have learned nearly every tool you will use in a typical day by the end of this chapter.

The Hole Feature

The Hole dialog box, shown in Figure 3.29, is a great example of how many capabilities can be stuffed into a small, easy-to-navigate interface.

Four groups of options in this dialog box walk you through placing holes on your model.

The options in the first group, Placement, reflect which type of placement you select from the flyout menu.

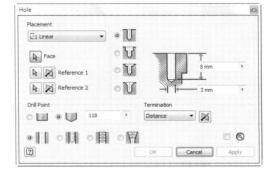

Figure 3.29

The Hole dialog box

Linear is the default placement. To use it, just select the face that you want to place the hole on, and select two edges that you want to position it from. When you select an edge, a dimension is placed showing the hole's current distance from the edge. You have to click both edges before you can change the dimension value for placing the hole. The edges do not have to be perpendicular to each other, but they cannot be parallel. The Reference buttons allow you to flip the hole to the other side of the edge that you are dimensioning from.

The From Sketch placement asks you to select points on an existing sketch to place holes on. In your sketch, if you have specified that a point is a Hole Center (by using the sketching override buttons on the Inventor Standard toolbar or by using the Center Point tool in a 2D sketch), those Hole Center points will automatically be selected for placing a hole. If a point that you don't want to use is automatically selected, you can deselect it by holding the Ctrl key and clicking on the point.

Concentric placement works by selecting a plane to place the hole on and then selecting an arc, circle, or face with a radius on which to center the Hole feature.

The last option, On Point, is similar to From Sketch, but the hole center has to be placed on a special point called a *work point*, and it allows you to select a direction vector for the hole based on a model edge, or a *work axis*.

Select the type of hole you want to create by using one of the four icons just to the right of the Placement group. To the right of the area where you select the type of hole you want to place, a graphic displays the contour of the hole and the dimensional values the hole has. You can change those values directly in the graphic when they are made available.

 Drilled This hole has one diameter from the beginning edge to the bottom of the hole.

 Counterbore This uses a drilled hole for the middle portion but creates a cylindrical relief beginning from the same plane.

 Spotface Spotface is geometrically similar to a Counterbore hole—the two could be mistaken for each other—but they are typically used for different real-world applications. A Spotface is usually used when the surface it is being placed on is unsuitable for a bolt or fitting to be tightened to. In a Spotface hole, the depth and diameter of the upper cylinder is controlled just like a Counterbore, but the depth of the drilled portion begins at the bottom of the Spotface instead of the same plane as the Counterbore. This can be seen easily by clicking back and forth between the two and watching the dimension in the graphic change.

 Countersink Countersink uses a conical relief to seat screws so their heads are flush or nearly flush with the surface the hole is placed in.

Drill Point Drill Point allows you to specify whether a hole is pointed or flat at its bottom. The pointed option even allows for the use of custom drill point angles for special applications.

The Termination group These options control how and where the end of the hole will occur.

Distance Distance uses a dimension in the graphic above it to set a value.

Through All Through All passes the hole through any feature that it encounters and is theoretically an infinitely deep hole.

To This option allows you to define a stopping face where the drill will pass through but not continue beyond.

In the bottom left are four more options that control what class of hole will be created. This area is where you can save a lot of work looking up standards.

 Simple Drill Simple Drill creates a basic, cylindrical hole that will be sized in the graphic in the dialog box.

 Clearance Hole This is a personal favorite of mine. After years of keeping a handbook or wall chart handy to be able to properly size the Counterbore for a Hex Head bolt, I enjoy being able to have the hole sized for me by simply selecting the fastener type and size.

 Tapped Hole Tapped Hole is also a simple option to use. All you do is select the thread you need, and Inventor sizes the hole based on the standard. Tapped holes do not have actual helical threads placed in the model, but they do appear threaded; Inventor uses a bitmap on the surface of the hole, and in drawings displays the major and minor diameter of the thread.

Taper Tapped Taper Tapped is the same as Tapped Hole but uses the tapered standards like NPT and ISO Taper. Because of industrial standards, you are not allowed to place a Taper Tapped hole at the bottom of a Counterbore.

Both types of threaded hole also allow you to control the depth of the threaded portion of the hole, with an option to fully thread the hole by checking Full Depth. You can also choose whether the threads are Right Hand or Left Hand.

Using the Hole Feature

The next exercise shows you how to place a few different types of Hole features. This exercise explores more than one option, which is realistic as there are times when a hole can be located in more than one way but any of the approaches are reasonable depending on the way the part may update.

1. With the model in the same orientation as shown in Figure 3.28, start a new sketch by clicking the Sketch icon on the Standard toolbar and selecting the top face of the bottom of the part.

2. When the sketch is created, your Panel bar changes, and if you are using Inventor the way it was set up in Chapter 1, the edges of the face you are sketching on will have automatically been projected to be members of the new sketch.

3. Also projected are the centerpoints of the arcs created by two of the fillets that you created.

4. Click the centerpoint of the left arc in the sketch and select the Center Point option on the Standard toolbar.

5. Use the Return button to move from the sketch back to the part features.

6. Open the Hole tool by clicking on it in the Part Features Panel bar or by pressing the H key.

   Inventor detects a visible sketch and opens with the From Sketch Placement tool active and automatically selects the hole center that you changed with the Center Point option.

7. The Hole tool will still be looking for more points to place holes on. Select the centerpoint of the other arc by clicking on its center.

8. You should now see the preview of both holes centered on fillets you placed in the corner. Figure 3.30 shows the result.

9. Change the type of hole to Counterbore.

10. Select the Clearance Hole class in the lower left of the Hole dialog box.

Figure 3.30

Preview of hole features

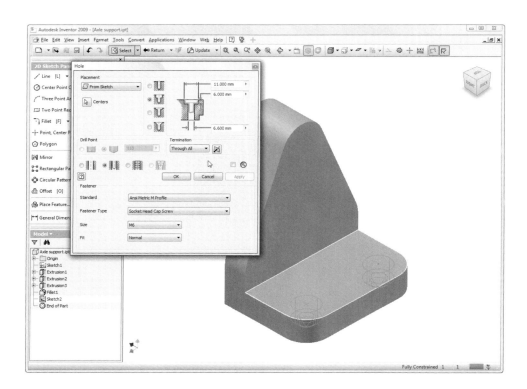

11. You will then be asked to select the type of fastener to be placed in the hole. Select ANSI Metric M Profile as the Standard, specify Socket Head Cap Screw as the Fastener Type, and set the size to M6.

12. Change the Termination to Through All.

13. It is possible to override the drill size and counterbore dimension, but the dimensions used are per the selected standard. Click OK to create both holes. See Figure 3.31 to verify your work.

    The incorporation of clearance hole standards is a simple example of what Autodesk refers to as *functional design*. The idea relates to allowing for engineering calculations to determine what parts to use or what size something should be. I think that limiting the potential for error by using documented standards is also a move toward the same goal. If nothing else, it sure makes life easier.

14. Select the Hole tool again and change your placement type to Linear and select the same face that you placed the previous holes on.

15. Be sure the hole class and other information is the same as the last two holes.

Figure 3.31

**Holes placed on
the part**

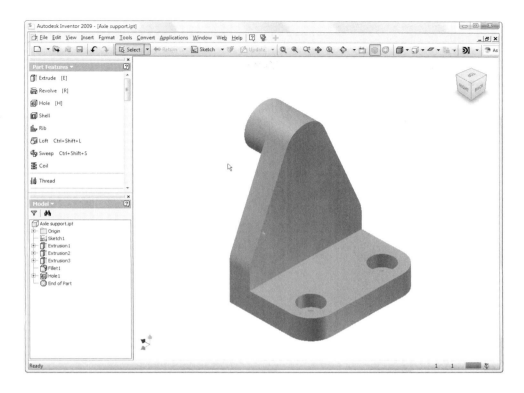

16. For Reference 1, select the long edge between the two holes that you placed.

17. For Reference 2, select one of the short edges perpendicular to the first dimension.

    Once the references are placed, dimensions are displayed so you can locate the hole from the selected edges.

18. Change the first dimension to 20mm.

19. For the second dimension, select the arrow pointing to the right next to the dimension value and select Show Dimensions, as shown in Figure 3.32.

20. When you use the Show Dimensions option, Inventor expects you to select a feature. Click the first feature that the three holes were placed in. Take care not to select the holes or the fillet. Select the 55mm dimension. The name of the dimension appears in the dimension value display. Divide this value by 2 by simply adding **/2** after the name of the 55mm dimension. This ensures that the hole is centered if the width of the bottom changes.

21. Click OK to place the holes and exit the tool (see Figure 3.33).

Figure 3.32

**Placing a hole using
a Linear placement
option**

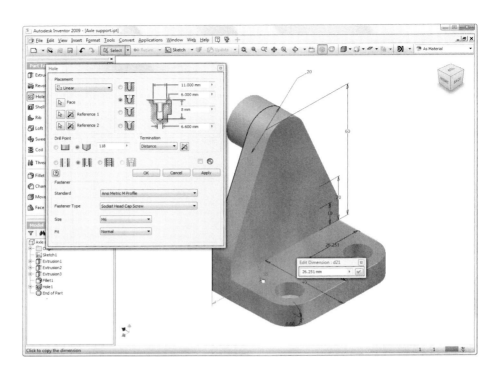

Figure 3.33

Creating a third hole

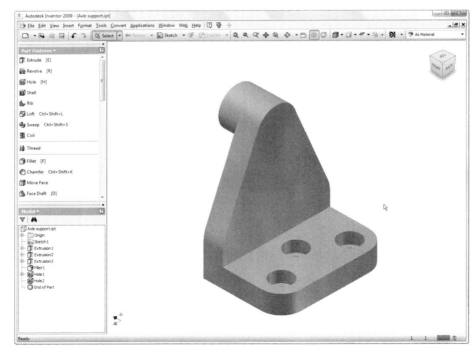

22. Change your point of view so that it's similar to Figure 3.34. Select the Hole tool again. Because there are no visible sketches, you will need to change the placement type from Linear to Concentric.

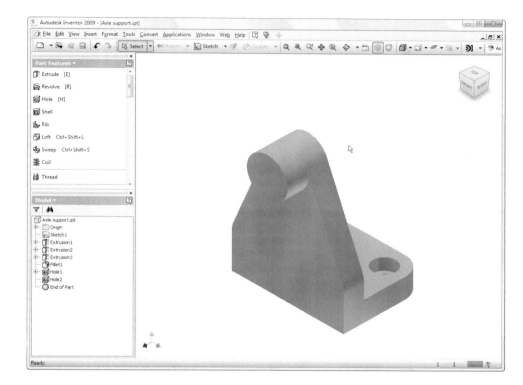

Figure 3.34

New model point of view

23. To satisfy the requirements, click the round, flat face of the cylinder for the plane and either the round edge of the face or the cylindrical face for the concentric reference.

Note that Inventor will highlight the first geometry in blue and the second geometry in green. This is a feedback system that you will find in several tools in Inventor.

24. Set the type of hole to Drilled, the class to Simple, and Termination to Through All.

25. Set the diameter in the graphic to 13mm. Double-check your settings compared to Figure 3.35 and click OK.

Figure 3.35

Placing a hole concentric to a curved face

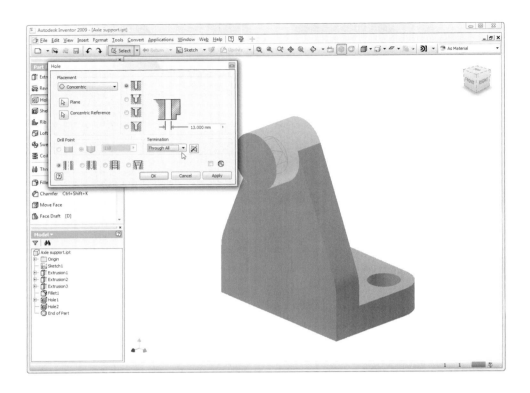

Work Features

A sketched feature is always started with a sketch on a plane or planar face. Many placed features like the hole that you just created also depend on placement using a plane or planar face. A part has three origin planes, but there are times when you need to create a sketch or place geometry for which there is no planar face available and the origin planes are not in the right place. In these instances, you can create a feature that will work as a platform, called a *work plane*.

The work plane feature is one of three work features; the work axis and work point are the others. These three features are ways to build a foundation for other features of a part. In and of themselves, they do not build the part.

A work plane can be defined in several ways. It can be offset a distance to another plane or face, or it can be created by defining a cylindrical face and either another plane, face, axis, or edge to build a plane tangent to the cylindrical face. It can be built based on two axes (or edges) that lie in the same plane, on an axis and a point, or by selecting three points. A work plane can also be placed normal to a path in a sketch by clicking the endpoint of a line or curve and then the curve. You have many ways to define a work plane, but the most important thing to keep in mind is that the work plane is associative to the geometry that you used to define it.

A work axis, like any theoretical axis, can be created by two intersecting faces or planes, by passing through two points, or by passing through a point normal to a face. Axes and planes are infinite, and another great way to build them is to be coincident with a sketched line segment to extend that piece of line beyond its normal boundaries to use to define more of the part.

⊿ Work Axis /

A work point can be defined at the intersection of an axis and a plane, but it can also be placed on top of a model point, like a corner or the midpoint of an edge, or on a point on a sketch.

✦ Work Point .

There are a hundred ways to approach building work features, but only one purpose: to allow you to construct the model the way it needs to be built. You often have a few different ways to build the same geometry as well. As with other parts of Inventor, you will be in charge of how you choose to do it.

Applying Work Features

In this exercise you will define the placement of a hole that is axial to the cylindrical face on your part. There's no effective way to create it with the current geometry of the part, so you will use a work plane to construct a solution and use sketch geometry to position the work plane. You could also use another technique that is sketch based. This exercise will incorporate all three work features.

> For image clarity I have disabled Grid Line, Minor Grid Lines, and Axes on the Sketch tab of my Application Options dialog box.

1. Let's begin by defining an axis. Start the Work Axis tool by pressing the / key. You can also scroll down the Part Features Panel bar and select it there.

2. Pass over various edges and features to see how the tool responds. Then create the axis by clicking the cylindrical face on the part. The axis will be placed and the tool will close.

3. Select the Work Point tool. You'll be placing the work point to use as a reference point.

4. Construct the work point by selecting the face at the end of the cylinder and selecting the work axis; see Figure 3.36.

5. Select the Work Plane tool to create a plane that will set the angle.

6. Select the work axis and the face with the three holes. This will open an angle input box that allows you to establish the angle the plane will be from the top. Set the value to 42.5 and click the green checkmark icon to approve. Compare to Figure 3.37 before you create the plane.

7. Now that you have a plane establishing the angle, start the Work Plane tool to create a plane by selecting the previous work plane and the cylindrical face.

Figure 3.36

Placing a work point at the intersection of a face and a work axis

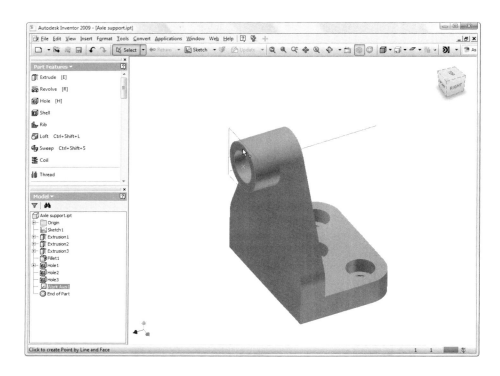

Figure 3.37

Establishing an angle for a work plane by selecting an existing face

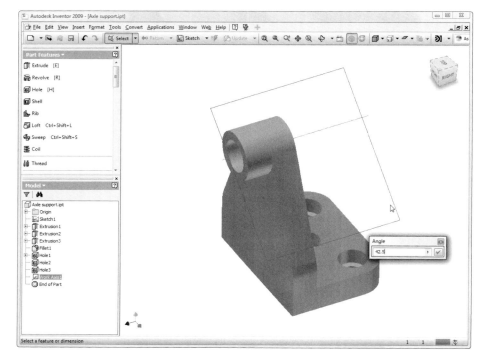

Inventor creates a parallel plane that is positioned where you need it to sketch the hole placement. The result should look like Figure 3.38.

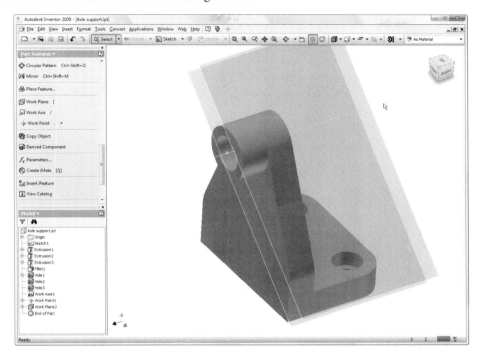

Figure 3.38

Creating a second work plane parallel to the angled work plane

8. Using the Sketch tool, select the last work plane.

9. Using the Project Geometry tool, project the location of the work point into the sketch.

10. Create a new point and centerpoint, and note the orientation of the 3D indicator.

11. Apply a Vertical constraint between the projected point and the point that you added.

12. Dimension the new point so that it is 12mm from the projected point. After you close the General Dimension tool, compare your work to Figure 3.39.

13. Select the Hole tool. If the point you added was the only one that was of the Hole Center Point style, it will automatically be selected. If not, make sure it is the only one selected.

14. Set your hole to be drilled and tapped. Set the Thread Type to ANSI Metric M Profile and set the size to 3.

15. Select To from the Termination drop-down and select the large drilled hole as the termination face (see Figure 3.40). Click OK when you are ready.

Figure 3.39

Placing a hole center on the new plane

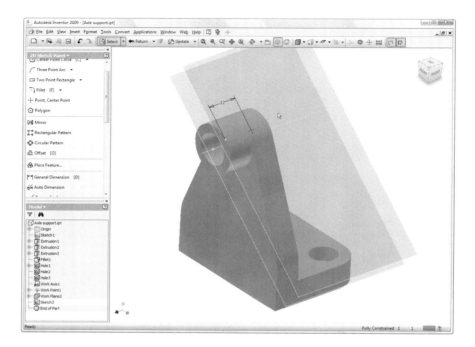

Figure 3.40

Creating a tapped hole that is axial to the cylindrical face

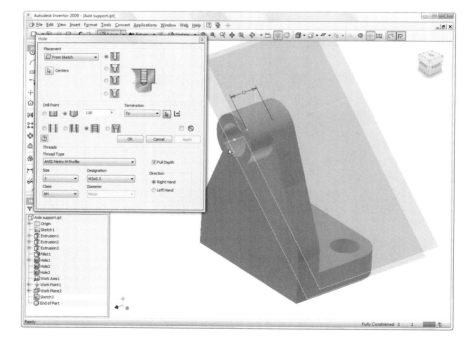

16. To turn off the visibility of the work features, select them in the Browser, right-click, and deselect Visibility. To access Work Plane1 you must expand the tree for Work Plane2 in the Browser.

17. Rotate the model to see the inside of the large hole and observe how the new hole is terminated.

18. Set your view to match Figure 3.41.

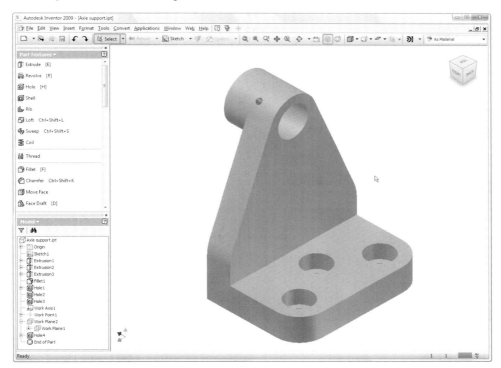

Figure 3.41

Returning to the Home view

19. Using the Fillet tool, choose a Face Fillet, and for the Face Set 1, select the face with the three holes. For Face Set 2, select the vertical face that the large hole penetrates.

    The Face Fillet tool recommends a radius that will work between the two faces.

20. Set Radius to 10mm. Click OK to place the fillet when your display matches Figure 3.42.

    For the next part of the exercise you will need the fillet that you just created to come before Work Axis1. The ability to reorder features in the part can save you from having to delete and re-create features. It can also allow you to correct a mistake when you realize that you should have created a feature before you did.

Figure 3.42

Creating a fillet between two faces

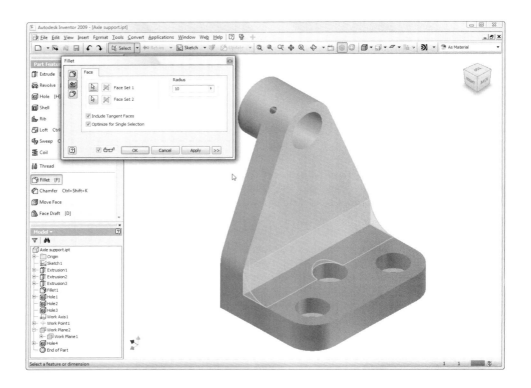

21. In the Browser, click the icon next to Fillet2 and drag it up the Browser tree above Work Axis1 (see Figure 3.43).

22. Release the feature to rearrange the order in which the features were created. This is possible as long as you do not try to drag a child feature above its parent feature.

23. Save your work.

Figure 3.43

Changing the position of the Fillet feature in the Browser

Now that you have learned how to create your model using multiple work features, you will re-create the last hole using a sketch-oriented technique. Once again, the technique that you choose is up to you, but it this is a great example of alternative options that create the identical geometry.

For this portion of the exercise, we need to pretend that you didn't create the work axis, work point, or work planes that you created before. Rather than delete the features, we will instead tell Inventor that they don't exist. To do this, we will move the End of Part icon above those features in the Browser. As far as Inventor will be concerned, they will no longer exist.

1. Click and drag the End of Part icon in the Browser above Fillet 1. When the model updates, it will look like Figure 3.44. This is a great technique if you discover that

you should have created a feature earlier in the process. Rather than deleting a lot of work, simply tell Inventor that you haven't done that work yet.

2. Now drag the End of Part icon below Fillet2 and release. Your model should look as it did before you started this exercise with the exception of Fillet2.

3. Rotate your model to match Figure 3.32 shown earlier.

4. Create a new sketch on the end of the cylinder where you placed the drilled hole.

The inner and outer diameters will be projected along with their common centerpoint.

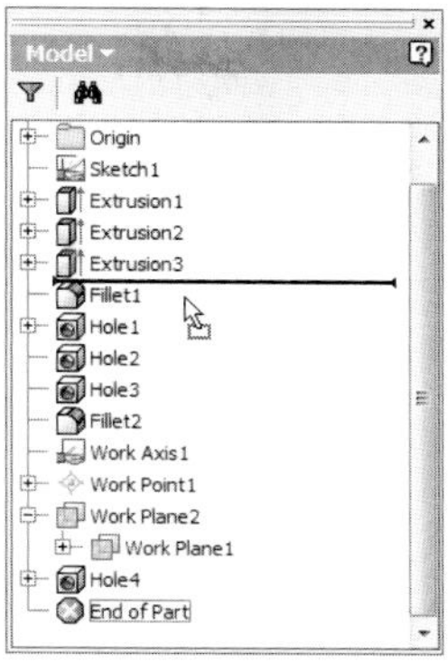

5. Draw a vertical line from that projected center; its length is not important.

6. Right-click and select Restart to draw another line. Start this line at the same point, but drag it to be coincident with the outer diameter and click on the edge to place the line (see Figure 3.45).

7. Close the Line tool.

8. Using the General Dimension tool, create an angular dimension between the two lines and set the value to 42.50 as shown in Figure 3.46. Close the General Dimension tool and press Enter to exit the sketch.

9. Select the Work Plane tool and pass over various planes and elements of the existing part to see a preview of the work planes that could be created and how much geometry can be used as a basis for a work plane.

Figure 3.44

Moving the End of Part icon removes features from the part without permanently deleting them.

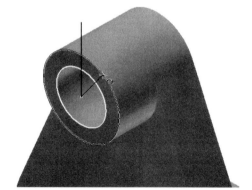

Figure 3.45

Creating a sketch to construct a location for a work plane

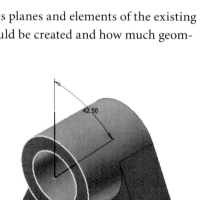

Figure 3.46

Adding an angular dimension to the sketch

10. Select the cylindrical face and the endpoint of the second line that you drew. This creates a plane that is tangent to the cylindrical face and normal to the line (see Figure 3.47).

11. Create a new sketch on the work plane you created.

12. Project the center of the circle and re-create the point and centerpoint as you did earlier in this exercise.

13. Constrain and dimension the point using a Vertical constraint and a dimension of 12mm.

14. Create the hole as shown in Figure 3.48, as you did before.

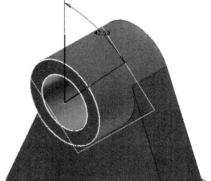

Figure 3.47

Placing a work plane normal to the end of the sketch line

15. Turn off the Visibility of Sketch4 and Work Plane3.

16. Right-click on the `Axle Support.ipt` root of the Browser.

17. Select the Physical tab and click Update to refresh the Mass Properties of the part; see Figure 3.49.

18. Save your work and close the part by choosing File → Close.

Figure 3.48

Placing the hole on the sketch

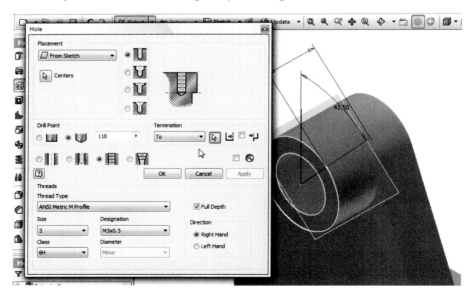

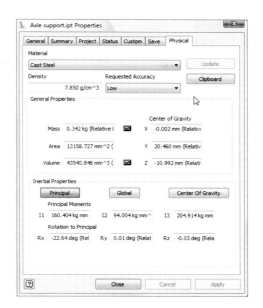

Figure 3.49

**Physical proper-
ties update with
changes to the
model**

The Revolve Tool

The second most frequently used tool for creating the base feature in a model is Revolve. Whereas the Extrude feature builds a sketch in one direction, Revolve wraps a sketch around an axis. The axis does not have to be part of the sketch or geometry that is part of the profile. This allows for the use of origin axes, and it also allows the use of an axis separate from the profile to create a hollow part.

Figure 3.50

**The Revolve
dialog box**

To revolve a sketch, you need two fundamental items: the *profile*, or shape, and the *axis* to revolve around. As with Extrude, you will initially only be able to use Join for the base feature. Cut and Intersect options are available once you have a base feature.

The Extents group allows you to select termination options for the feature. The Revolve tool's window (see Figure 3.50) includes the following options:

EXTENTS

Angle Develops the shape through the specified angle. You can change the direction from one side of the sketch to the other or make an equal division, with the sketch in the center.

To Next Revolves the profile until it intersects with the first body it intersects in the direction selected. This option is not available for creating the base feature.

To Similar to To Next but is available as a base feature. You can select a terminating plane or surface that has been created or imported.

From To Revolves the shape between two selected planes or surfaces.

Full This option revolves the sketch 360 degrees about the axis.

Using Revolve to Create a Turned Part

In this exercise you will create a simple shaft. There are more advanced technologies for creating shafts in Inventor, but in this case you will create a basic part.

1. Open the New dialog box and create a new part based on the Standard (in).ipt file in the English tab.

2. Project the model Origin Center Point into the sketch.

3. Begin creating a two-point rectangle starting with the projected point. Draw the rectangle to be approximately 0.7 in by 0.3 in. Use the status bar to estimate (see Figure 3-51).

4. Draw a second rectangle starting from the lower right of the last rectangle. Draw it up and to the right and make it roughly 1.5 in by 0.5 in.

Figure 3.51

Placing the first sketched rectangle

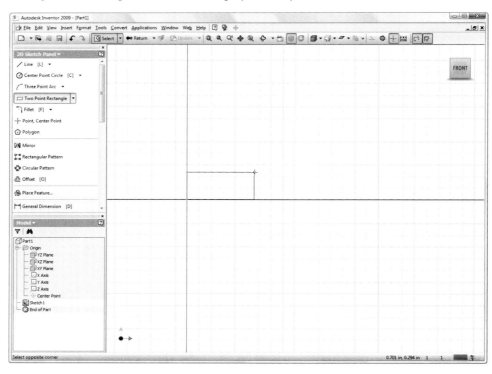

5. Draw a third rectangle around the same length as the first and use sketch inferenc-
    ing to achieve the same height as the first rectangle. Compare to Figure 3.52, and if
    things are correct, close the Rectangle tool.

6. Inventor allows you to select multiple geometry by dragging a window around the
    geometry that you would like to select. Drag a window around all of the bottom lines
    of the rectangles; see Figure 3.53.

> In AutoCAD, dragging a selection window from left to right will select geometry that is com-
> pletely encompassed by the window, and dragging from right to left will select anything
> touched by the window. Inventor drag-selection works exactly the same way.

7. Once you've made the selection, turn on the Centerline override from the Inventor
    Standard toolbar. The bottoms of the rectangle will appear like Figure 3.54 (with
    Grid and Axes off).

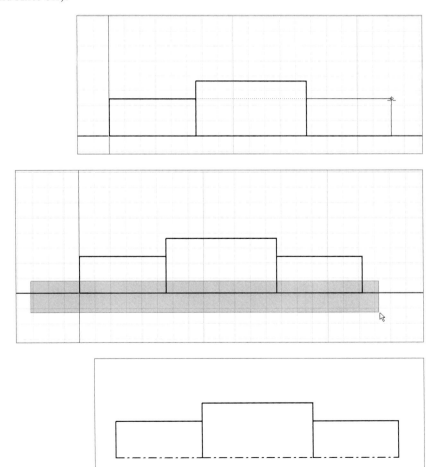

Figure 3.52

**Completing the
sketch geometry**

Figure 3.53

**Selecting geom-
etry by dragging a
window around the
desired elements**

Figure 3.54

**Changing the
selected lines to
be Centerlines
(Grid off)**

8. Using the General Dimension tool, click the bottom (centerline) first, then click the top line of the first rectangle.

9. When the dimension previews, it will be shown as a diameter, as you can see in Figure 3.55.

Figure 3.55

Using a centerline to define a dimension automatically gives you a linear diameter.

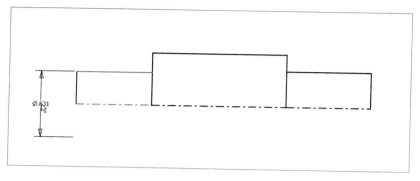

10. Set the Value to 0.5 in.

11. Apply another diameter to the bottom and top of the middle rectangle. Set its diameter to 0.7 in.

12. Apply a length to the top of the first rectangle. Make it 0.7 in.

13. Apply a length to the middle rectangle. Set its value to 1.2 in. Close the General Dimension tool.

Your sketch should look like Figure 3.56.

14. Apply a Collinear constraint between the top of the first and third rectangles.

15. Create an Equal constraint between the same two edges. Refer to Figure 3.57.

There is no set rule for whether to apply geometric constraints or dimensions first. Look for the simplest way to control the sketch, so that you are able to make modifications without having to remove dimensions and constraints at a later time.

16. Exit the sketch and launch the Revolve tool from the Part Features Panel bar. As always, the letter next to the command indicates the keyboard shortcut.

17. Press the F6 key to switch to the Home view.

18. Since more than one profile is available, select all three rectangles for the profile.

19. After you've selected the profiles, you need to tell Inventor that you are ready to choose an axis. Click the Axis button in the dialog box and select one of the bottom lines.

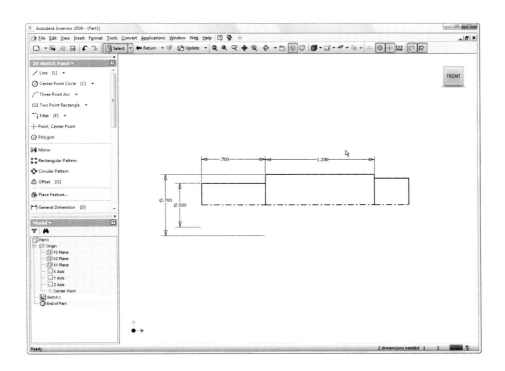

Figure 3.56

Adding dimensions to further refine the shape

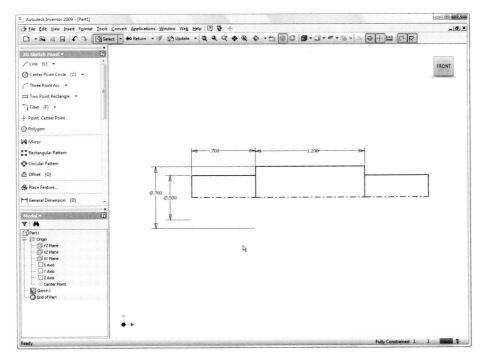

Figure 3.57

The simple shaft is complete after applying geometric constraints.

20. A preview appears. Refer to Figure 3.58 and click OK if the preview is correct.

21. Choose the Chamfer tool from the Part Features Panel bar.

22. Click the edges of the two ends of the shaft. Set the Distance value for the Chamfer tool to 0.05 in.

23. Click OK to place the chamfer and close the dialog box.

24. Set your Material to Steel, High Strength Low Alloy.

25. Save your file to the Parts folder, naming it Shaft.ipt, and close it.

Figure 3.58

The preview of the Revolve feature allows you to verify the task before accepting it.

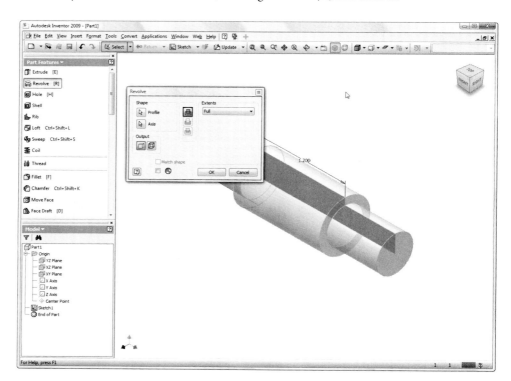

Feature Libraries

The Content Center is a library of standard components, primarily used in machine design, that that are typically bought for a project rather than built. It also contains standard steel sections and hydraulic fittings, and it also includes standard shapes.

These shapes can be used to define features in parts rather than using sketched features. Therefore, they are an excellent resource to quickly create shapes. You can also add custom shapes to allow users to drag and drop features that a company uses regularly.

Using a Library Feature

In this exercise we will use a predefined feature to build a part. While this is not a commonly used technique, it is still an option you should be aware of.

1. Start a new part file based on the `Standard (mm).ipt` file.

2. Scroll down the 2D Sketch Panel and select the Place Feature tool.

3. A dialog box appears and you should see two folders: English and Metric. Inside these folders are the standard features.

4. Double-click on the Metric folder. Inside is a wide variety of shapes.

5. Locate the Rectangle folder and open it.

6. Inside this folder and in all of the other folders, you will find two versions of each shape. One will be positive and one will be a negative or cutting feature.

7. Double-click the Rectangle tool. Doing this opens a dialog box for sizing the feature that we want to place in the model.

8. Set the values for Height to 15, Length to 150, and Width to 70.

9. Click OK to see a preview of the model. Switch to the Home view to get a better view. The model will show the dimensions that are built into the model (see Figure 3.59).

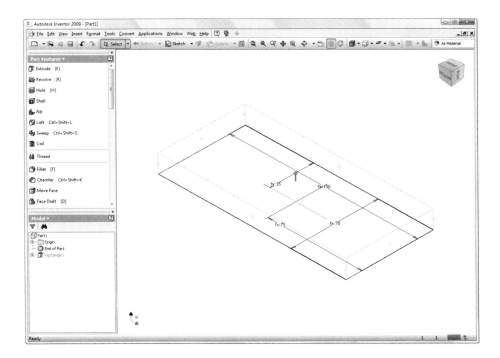

Figure 3.59

Library features are built on fully constained sketches

10. Right-click on the screen and select Done to complete the feature.

11. Set the Material for the part to Aluminum-6061.

12. In the upper right is a pull-down that allows you to change the color of the part. It is displaying As Material. Click the down arrow and select Blue (Sky) from the list. Feel free to choose different colors to see how they display as well. That is all we need for this part—just a basic block.

13. Save the file to the Parts folder, with the filename `Base.ipt`, and close it.

Summary

The part model is the foundation for working in 3D, and the tools that you learned in this chapter are the foundation for nearly all part models. There are many other tools available, and we will cover more of them in Chapter 7.

As we move into assembly modeling, I hope that you have gained confidence that you can create parts easily with Inventor. Assembly modeling will be easier—in fact, I think that as easy as it is, part modeling is far and away the most difficult portion of Inventor or any 3D design application.

Take a deep breath, pat yourself on the back, and now get ready to take the next step.

CHAPTER 4

Putting It All Together with Assemblies

Digital prototyping is a term that you may or not be familiar with. The basic concept is that we should be able not only to build a product on a computer but also to test it completely and validate the design before creating a physical prototype.

Taken to its full potential, the digital model can also be used to build assembly instructions and marketing materials, and even to program the machines that will produce the parts. This trend is gaining popularity with designers who want to get the most out of their work and at the same time make it as painless as possible to share a change with everyone who depends on their data. In this chapter, we will take our next easy step toward this paradigm: creating an assembly model.

Because Inventor LT cannot work with assemblies, the information in this chapter applies only to Inventor.

- **What Is an Assembly?**
- **Applying Constraints**
- **Editing Parts in an Assembly**
- **Representations**
- **Modifying Structure**
- **The Bolted Connection Tool**

The Assembly Modeling Concept

In the previous chapter you created part models. I have always found that in Inventor creating an assembly is a much more direct process than building its parts. A part can be created using a broad variety of tools and techniques based on how you want to edit it. By contrast, the way you build an assembly model is based largely on how you would build the assembly in the real world. In fact, I have found that you can use the assembly model to experiment with different ways of structuring the real assembly and perhaps discover a better way of doing things.

An assembly model can also be used to build variations on a particular design. The ability to swap out parts for alternatives and check fits or test a mechanism's range of motion makes it much easier to detect flaws in a system before spending money on the real thing.

To build an assembly, designers traditionally stack 3D parts together, creating constraints to hold the parts together as they would be in the real world. If you try to create an assembly without using constraints, the parts will not maintain their relationships as they change. Constraints in assembly modeling are different from those in 2D sketching, but the principle of an enduring relationship that limits unexpected behavior is the same.

> Inventor also has the ability to create relationships between 2D parts, and there are techniques that use a 2D sketch to define where parts will be placed in an assembly before they are defined, a topic that is beyond the scope of this book.

Let's get started with the basics: constraining an assembly.

Creating Assembly Constraints

Assembly constraints come in a variety of flavors, but they are all based on the same principle: removing degrees of freedom.

Theoretically, any part has six degrees of freedom (without that pesky gravity). A part can rotate around three axes and translate (move) in three planes. It can also move in any combination of these at the same time. However, as you can imagine, it's difficult for a complex mechanism to work unless parts are attached to one another, and those attachments limit each part's actual degrees of freedom.

By default, the first part that you place will be grounded. The grounded component automatically has all of its degrees of freedom removed, so be careful about what component you place into an assembly first. (However, should you make a mistake or change your mind, you can remove the grounded state and make another component grounded.) It is also possible to have more than one component in a grounded state, but usually one will do the trick. As other components are brought in, they are free to be positioned any way you need them to. Decide which constraint is the best for creating the desired relationship between the parts; you can eventually remove all of the unnecessary degrees of freedom. Also note that you do not have to remove every degree of freedom from every part. When you place a bolt into a hole, for example, the position of the head will be difficult to predict in the real assembly, so it is not normally necessary to define it in the assembly model.

Assembly constraints can also add intelligence to an assembly. For example, you can define constraints between two parts and use their positions to define the size of a third part that will be placed between them in the real world. If you can use assemblies to build parts, think of the possibilities for trying new ideas.

Inventor's assembly tools are only available if you've created an assembly file or if you are editing an existing assembly. Before we begin building an assembly, you need to know your options.

The Place Constraint Tool

You will spend a lot of time in the Place Constraint dialog box when first creating an assembly, so let's start with it. Other tools in the Assembly Panel bar will become more useful as the constraints of the assembly are defined.

The Place Constraint tool has a range of options to handle the many ways you can associate geometry together. Three tabs, Assembly, Motion, and Transitional, allow you to create broadly varied geometric relationships. By this time you are probably becoming good at recognizing the elements of the Inventor dialog boxes and you understand what Inventor is looking for.

The Assembly Tab

The Assembly tab contains most of the tools you will use on a day-to-day basis.

Before looking at the groups of options, notice the checkbox for displaying a preview (the eyeglasses) of the effect that applying the constraint will have. With this option checked, Inventor will move the part or parts as a preview in most cases before you apply the constraint.

Next to that is the Predict Offset And Orientation checkbox. This tool is useful when you have parts moved into an approximate position. When you apply a Mate or Angle constraint, the values of those constraints will automatically be filled in with their current position; otherwise, Inventor would snap the parts tightly together, and you'd then have to experiment with values to return them to the position they are already in.

Also notice the Solution area. As you'll see, the solution you can apply will depend on the type of constraint you are applying.

Let's look at the groups in the dialog box and go through some of the options.

TYPE

The Type group has four primary ways of defining an assembly constraint: Mate, Angle, Tangent, and Insert. Using these tools, you can build any rigid assembly.

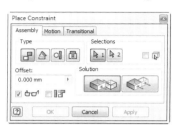

Mate, the first type of constraint (the highlighted box under "Solution") has two solution options. The Mate solution applies an oppositional force. It emulates elements being stuck together. A mate can also be applied between any combination of points, edges (axes), and faces. The other solution, Flush, can only be applied between faces, and it is used to align faces that are parallel to one another.

An Angle constraint defines nonparallel aligned conditions. It can only be placed on edges and faces. There are three solutions for the constraint. The default solution is the

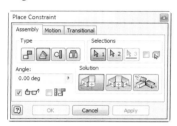

Directed Angle. It applies a positive value clockwise about its axis. The Undirected Angle solution can apply a positive value about the axis in either direction. If parts unpredictably change orientation, try changing the angular constraint used on the parts to this solution. The third solution is Explicit Reference Vector, which allows you to specify the axis directly. This gives

you maximum control and predictability when defining a value. However, in most cases it is not necessary to use this option to get the proper, predictable result, so it is not the default.

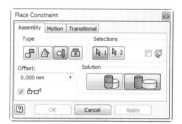

A Tangent constraint can be applied between a curved face and a planar face, a curved face and an edge, or two curved faces. Its two solutions behave much like those in a Mate constraint. The Inside solution will try to align the faces so that the mating face tends to be inside the curved face, and Outside holds the mating face outside the curved face.

The Insert constraint is a specialized Mate constraint. It places a Mate constraint between the axes of two curved faces and, using the Opposed solution, creates a Mate

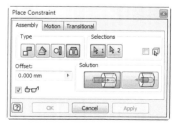

condition between faces adjacent to the curved faces. Using the Aligned solution applies a Flush condition between those faces. As the icon for the type shows, it is perfect for locating bolts into holes. Selections for this constraint will only highlight curved edges that are planar.

SELECTIONS

The Selections group displays the input Inventor needs to create the relationship. As usual, a red arrow indicates that nothing has been selected for that group.

OFFSET

Offset allows you to apply a value to a condition. For example, if you want to leave a space between two faces, you can enter the value for that gap. You can also build an interference condition by using a negative value. In an Angle constraint, this prompt changes to enter the angle value.

The Motion Tab

The Motion tab contains two types of constraint for creating relationships that can be activated to re-create how parts move in a mechanism: Rotation and Rotation-Translation.

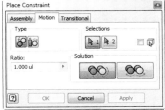

A Rotation constraint can replicate gearing or rollers using the Reverse solution. You can also apply a ratio to the relationship between the two bodies to allow them to turn at different rates. The Forward solution will turn the bodies in the same direction with the option of defining a ratio.

The Rotation-Translation type can emulate a rack-and-pinion joint or the movement of a slide being driven on a threaded shaft by creating a relationship between the rotation of a face and the movement of a body. The Distance value governs how far the second part will move during one revolution of the first part. To emulate a rack and pinion, you would want to set this value to the circumference of the pinion. The Forward and Reverse solutions allow you to select the direction of the linear movement in relation to the rotation.

The Transitional Tab

The Transitional tab only has one tool. It applies a tangency constraint that can follow a curved face such as a cam. The mating faces will remain tangent as long as there is a tangency to follow.

Beginning an Assembly

In this exercise, you will use the parts that you created in the last chapter to build a simple assembly. You will use the assembly to test other tools and approaches as you go through the chapter. Be sure to close any files that you have open in Inventor before you begin.

1. Create a new assembly file based on the Standard (mm).iam file in the Metric tab.

2. Set the position of the empty assembly in the Design window by pressing the F6 key or clicking Home View.

3. In the Assembly panel, select Place Component or press P to use the keyboard shortcut. Select the Parts folder in the Frequently Used Subfolders list to view the parts in the project.

   The Place Component dialog box (Figure 4.1) opens, allowing you to select a single part or several parts to be placed in your assembly. Because this will be the first part placed, you should select only one part to avoid the wrong one being chosen as the base part and grounded.

4. The Place Component dialog box is very similar to the Open dialog box. Select the `Base.ipt` file and click Open.

5. The `Base.ipt` file will be placed at the Origin center point of the assembly. Inventor then allows you to place additional instances of the part; this happens every time you use this tool to place components. Press the Esc key or right-click and choose Done to exit the Place Component tool. It is important to begin thinking of multiple placements as instances of the object rather than copies. In 3D, a copy of a file is a duplicate of the actual file, whereas an instance denotes that there is more than one of the same geometry from the same file shown in the assembly. A change you make to one instance is reflected in all instances. By contrast, if you copy a file and place it in an assembly, it doesn't reflect any changes made to the original.

   Now that the component is placed, look at the Browser. It shows a component Base:1, which means it is the first instance of the Base part. It also displays a thumbtack on the Part icon, which means the part is grounded in the assembly.

Figure 4.1

The Place Component dialog box

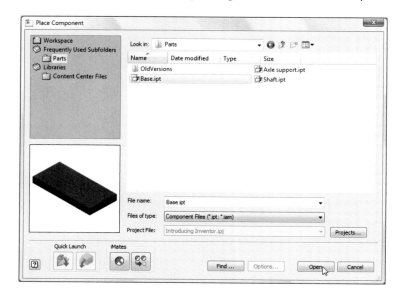

Figure 4.2

Create an Assemblies folder.

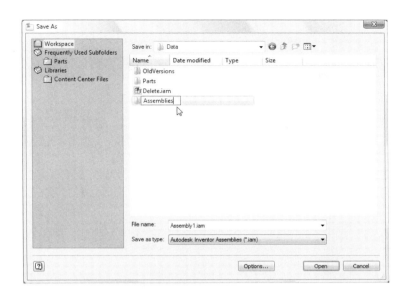

6. Select the Save command. Under the Data folder, create a new folder named **Assemblies** and save the file as `Caster Assembly.iam` in that folder. See Figure 4.2 for reference.

   You can continue to place components in the assembly using the Place Components tool. You can even select more than one component to place at once. As a learning experience, I would like to demonstrate a different approach. In the next steps you will place components into the assembly directly from Windows Explorer.

7. Open Windows Explorer and navigate to your `C:\Data\Parts` folder.

8. Select `Axle support.ipt` and `Shaft.ipt`. Click and drag them into the Design window, as shown in Figure 4.3. A Windows Shortcut icon appears on the cursor when you move over the Design window. Release the mouse button to place an instance of both parts in the assembly at the same time.

9. Click Zoom All to see the result and notice that the Browser has the new components listed.

   Earlier in the chapter I discussed the importance of defining degrees of freedom for parts in the assembly. In the Chapter 2 sketching exercise, you displayed the degrees of freedom (DOF) of a sketch. The same tool exists for the assembly.

10. On the Standard toolbar, select the View pull-down and choose Degrees of Freedom. On your screen you should see Degrees of Freedom glyphs on the Axle support1 and Shaft:1 parts showing that they have freedom in all directions. See Figure 4.4 for comparison.

11. Right-click on Shaft 1 in the Browser or in the Design window and deselect Visibility from the menu. This will hide the shaft. At times it can be useful to turn off the visibility of a part.

Figure 4.3

Select components from Windows Explorer.

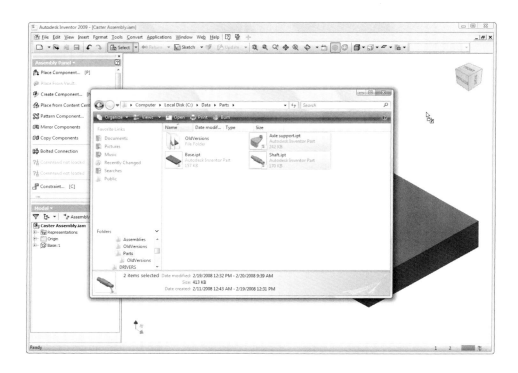

Figure 4.4

Turn on the Degrees of Freedom glyphs.

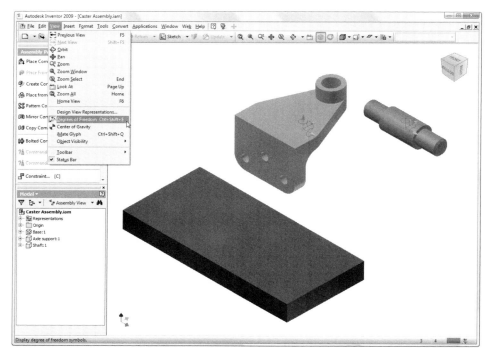

12. Select the Constraint tool from the Panel bar or press the C key.

13. Select the bottom of the Axle support as shown in Figure 4.5; then select the top of the base part. With Preview turned on, the part will snap into place. Click OK to make the constraint permanent and to close the dialog box.

    You have placed your first Assembly constraint. This constraint has removed two degrees of freedom from the part. The DOF symbol shows that the part can move along the X and Y axis and it can rotate about the Z axis.

14. Click on the part and drag it around. The part can pivot (though it may only slide), but it cannot be turned on its side. And even though it can be moved off the base part, its bottom will remain stuck to the plane that the top of the base part represents.

15. For the next constraint you will need to expand the base part. Select the plus icon next to Base:1 in the Browser to expand the part's elements. Note that there is a Mate constraint added under the part, the same way features are added to parts in the Browser.

16. Expand the Origin folder under the base part.

17. Select the Constraint tool, verify that the type is set as a Mate constraint, and for the first selection item hover over the cylinder on the Axle support. When you see the axis highlighted, select it.

Figure 4.5

Place the Mate constraint.

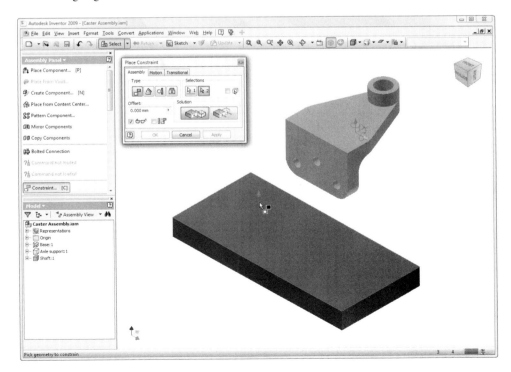

18. For the second selection, click the XZ Plane under the base part's Origin folder. See Figure 4.6 for reference. Select OK to place the constraint, and save the assembly file.

19. Your assembly should look like Figure 4.7. Because you are constraining an axis to a plane, it is possible that it will rotate the part in the opposite direction of the figure. If it the Axle support is facing the opposite direction, step 26 describes how to turn it around without having to redo the constraint.

Figure 4.6

Align the Axle support with the constraint.

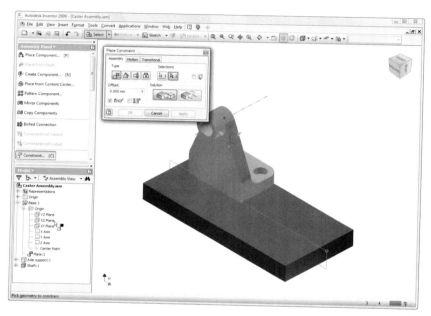

Figure 4.7

Review the remaining Degree of Freedom shown on the screen

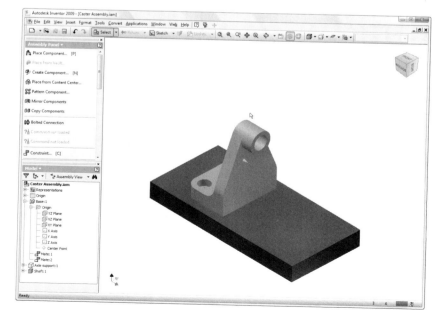

20. Now click and drag the part. It only has one degree of freedom left. It still has its translational degree of freedom along the X axis. Return the part toward the left end of the part when you are done.

21. Make the Shaft:1 part visible again. Turn the DOF symbol visibility on for all parts; you may have to turn it off and then back on again to see the result on the shaft part.

22. Pan and/or zoom to make sure that you can see both parts clearly.

23. Again select the Constraint tool and set your constraint Type to Insert.

24. For the first selection option, click the edge of the large hole on the Axle support. For the second selection, click the edge of the outer diameter of the shaft. See Figure 4.8 for the selection highlighting and Figure 4.9 for the result when finished.

25. The shaft moves into position, but it still has a rotational degree of freedom. For our purposes, we will not need to eliminate it.

Now you need another Axle support. You can use the Place Component tool, but it is easier to just drag another instance into the assembly from the Browser.

26. Click on the Axle support:1 part in the Browser and drag your cursor onto the screen and release. Another instance will appear on the screen and in the Browser.

Figure 4.8

Constraining the shaft

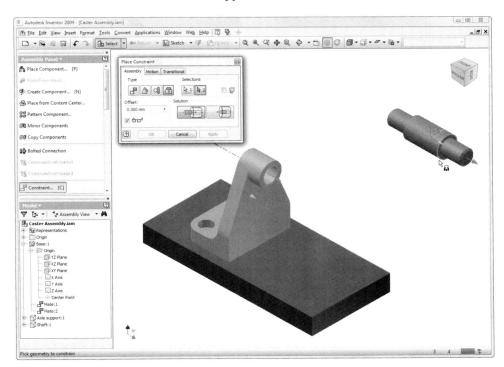

Figure 4.9

The result of applying the Insert constraint

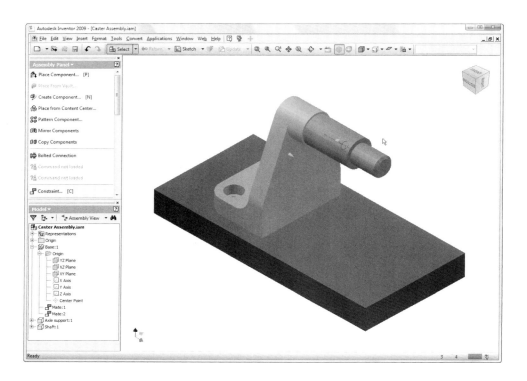

There are times when you may want to rotate a part temporarily in the assembly, perhaps to get a better view of it. You can do this even after a part has been constrained; updating the assembly will restore the effect of the constraints. If a part is constrained in the correct plane but pointing in the wrong direction, you can rotate it to point roughly in the correct direction. When you update the assembly, the part returns to the plane but points in the correct direction.

27. Right-click on the new Axle support, expand the menu next to Component, and select Rotate. You can also click on a part and press the G key. A miniature version of the Reticle that is displayed with the Orbit tool appears. Clicking and dragging inside the Reticle rotates the part.

28. Rotate the part into an odd position, keeping the large hole at the end of the cylinder on the new Axle support visible.

29. Use the Insert constraint to connect the new Axle support to the other end of the shaft. The result should appear similar to Figure 4.10.

There are a couple of different ways to place the final constraint on the second Axle support. Since we haven't used the Angle constraint, now will be a good time.

30. Select the Constrain Component tool and select the Angle type.

Select the faces as shown in Figure 4.11. Accept the change by clicking OK.

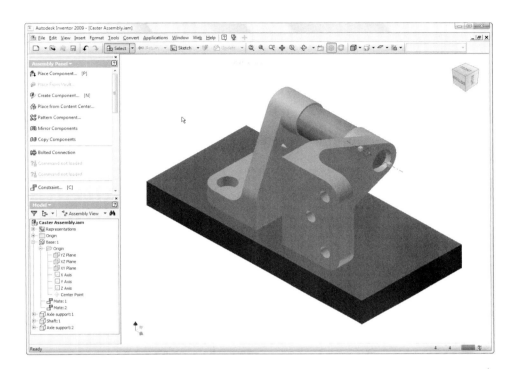

Figure 4.10

Constrain the second Axle support.

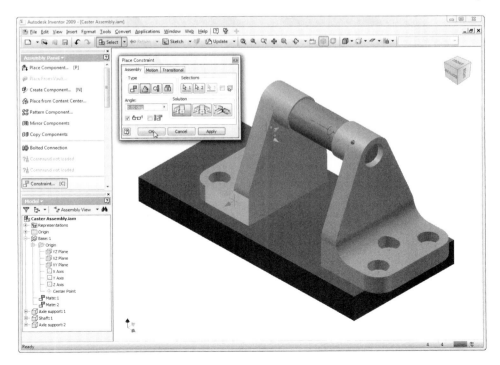

Figure 4.11

Apply an Angular constraint.

This will constrain all of the parts together, but the Axle supports and shaft are still able to move along the X axis. The last thing that you need to do is center the shaft on the base plate.

Editing Parts in an Assembly

In Chapter 3 you learned that when you need a point, edge, or face that doesn't exist, you can create it as a work feature. To complete the assembly you created in the previous exercise, you will need a way to center the length of the shaft on the base plate.

The shaft was not created with a plane or face at the midpoint of its length. Work features can be used for the application of Assembly constraints in the same way that other geometry can, so we need to add a work plane to the Shaft part.

It is not necessary to open a part to edit it. Parts can be edited in the assembly file directly.

1. Double-click the shaft part in the Browser or click the shaft part, right-click, and select Edit.

   When the part becomes active, the other parts in the assembly change to a wireframe display. This is controlled by the application options that you chose in Chapter 1.

2. Zoom in on the shaft part.

3. Select the Work Plane tool and select the circular face of the large diameter of the shaft. A plane preview appears, but you need a plane that bisects the cylinder. Move the cursor near the other end of the large cylinder and the face highlights as shown in Figure 4.12. A preview of a bisecting work plane appears.

Figure 4.12

Create a bisecting work plane.

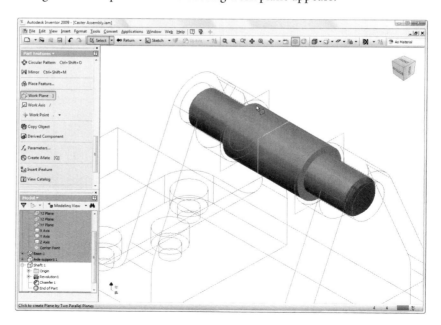

4. Click to create the plane in the middle of the part.

5. Find the new work plane in the Browser. Note that the inactive parts of the assembly are grayed out, as shown in Figure 4.13.

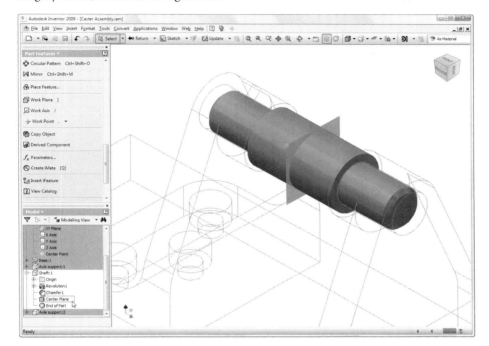

Figure 4.13

The work plane displayed

6. Slowly double-click the name of the work plane and it highlights, allowing you to change the name, much as in Windows Explorer. When it does, change the name to **Center Plane**.

7. Click the Return button to get back to the Assembly environment.

8. Place a Mate constraint between the new center plane of the shaft part and the YZ plane of the base. Rotate the assembly as shown in Figure 4.14. The arrows on the two planes point in the same direction. If you apply the Mate constraint, you may get error messages. Since the arrows should be going in the same direction, change the constraint solution from Mate to Flush.

9. The three parts will move into place, indicating that the constraint will be applied without error. Click OK to accept the constraint.

10. Restore your Home View and save the assembly. Figure 4.15 shows the final result.

Figure 4.14

Apply the Flush constraint.

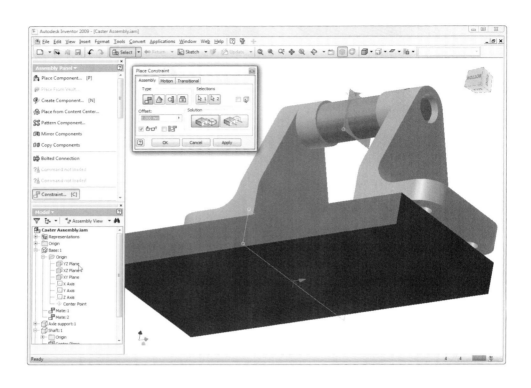

Figure 4.15

The completed assembly

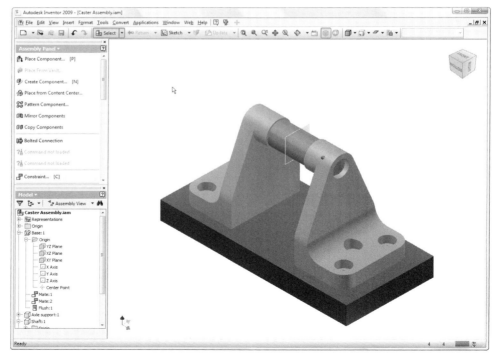

Representations

In the preceding exercise, you were asked to turn off the visibility of a part temporarily, for the sake of clarity. What if you turned off the visibility of several parts? What if you wanted to be able to make parts visible or invisible repeatedly?

In Inventor, one of the least utilized tools in the assembly environment is the representation, which you can use for these purposes and more. Some regard representations as a tool to be used for advanced purposes, but I consider it a fundamental tool that should be understood by everyone. You can find the representations in the Assembly Browser, immediately under the root of the assembly. Expanding the Representations folder will expose the three types available in Inventor: View, Position, and Level of Detail.

View

View representations can be configured to change part visibility and color. You can create as many of them as you like and switch between them with a simple double-click.

Turning off the visibility of parts in a View representation will not reduce the impact the assembly has on system memory, but it can improve graphic performance.

Being able to control visibility is just the beginning. You can also set up a "View rep." to control the color of parts. Views can also be locked using a context menu option so that you can limit how many parts you see; any further parts added to the assembly will not appear in them. Other context menu options will allow you to turn all parts on or off and override any changes to the part colors you may have made.

Position

If you work with mechanisms or assemblies that have elements that can be opened or closed, positional representations can offer you some exciting tools.

Positional representations allow you to override assembly constraints. For example, suppose you place an angular constraint on a door to keep it in its closed state. With a Positional representation, you can override the constraint value when you need to show the door open, and you can display that open state in the drawing using phantom lines to illustrate the range of motion.

You can even create a representation that will turn off a constraint and allow the assembly to be manipulated with a click and drag.

In Chapter 8 you will explore some of the capabilities of Positional representations.

Level of Detail

This type of representation can change the capabilities of Inventor. View representations allow you to turn off the visibility of individual parts in an assembly, but with a Level of Detail (LOD) representation, you can suppress a part or parts from the system memory without interfering with the assembly. This means that when you work with LOD representations, you can manipulate extraordinarily large assemblies without having to use a supercomputer.

You can even replace entire assemblies by fusing the assembly into a single part to simplify things further, and you can replace an entire assembly with a part that will allow the user to still see where the assembly is but only task memory with one part instead of perhaps thousands.

To make it even easier, you can copy an existing View representation to create a new Level of Detail representation by right-clicking and using a context menu option to do so.

Creating a View Representation

This is a simple tool to use, but taking a little time to walk through the process will be well worth the effort.

1. In the Caster Assembly, expand the Representations folder and then the View folder. The folder will display the name View: Default indicating that the active View representation is named Default.

2. Right-click the icon and select New.

3. A new View representation will be created, named View1, and made active.

4. Double-click on the View1 name slowly and rename it **Shaft and Supports**.

5. Make the base invisible. Your screen should look like Figure 4.16.

6. Zoom in closer to the remaining parts and rotate your model to another point of view.

7. Find the center plane of the shaft in the Browser and turn off its visibility using the context menu option.

8. Select Axle support:2 on the screen. When you do, the flyout menu on the end of the Inventor Standard toolbar will show the part's color as As Material. Click the down arrow to display the other options and select Blue (Clear). Compare your screen to Figure 4.17.

9. Change your View representation back to Default by double-clicking it in the View Representations folder in the Browser.

10. Change back to the Shaft and Support View. The colors, visibility, and display should revert to their previous state.

11. Right-click on the Shaft and Supports representation and select Lock from the menu.

12. Activate the Default View representation.

13. Place another instance of Base.ipt into the assembly.

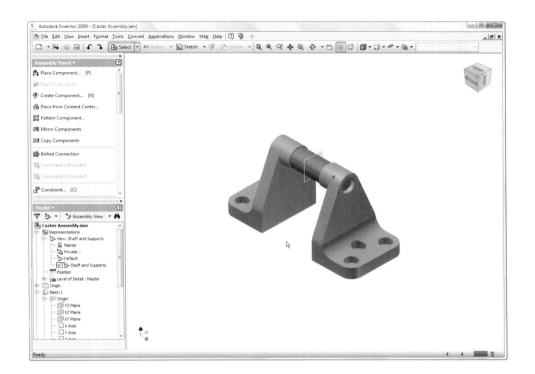

Figure 4.16

The result of creating a new View representation

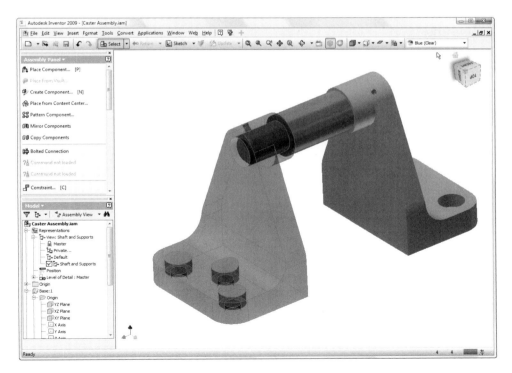

Figure 4.17

Changing the color of the part

14. Change your View Rep. to Shaft and Support once again. Zoom out to see that the new instance of the base part is not visible in this representation.

15. Right-click on the Shaft and Supports representation and choose Copy. A copy will be created but not activated.

16. Change the name of the new View Rep. to **Shaft Only** and activate it.

17. Right-click on the View Rep. and select Remove Color Overrides. The Axle support part should revert back to looking like Steel.

18. Save the assembly file.

Enabled Parts

An *enabled part* in an assembly is one that can be selected as a reference or to be edited. So far, every part that you have worked with in the assembly has been enabled.

Parts that are not enabled will still be visible but may be translucent or in a wireframe state, depending on your settings in the Application Options dialog box. The options that you applied in Chapter 1 did not change the default setting.

A component that is not enabled cannot be selected. This allows you to have a visual reference without having to always select through a part or have it interfere with other parts. Like visibility, whether or not a part is enabled is saved in the View representation, so it can be quickly switched.

Changing the Enabled Part State

Being forced to work through a housing or other parts that are important to visually reference but interfere with the work you need to do can be frustrating. This exercise will help to see how to make things easier.

1. With the Shaft Only View representation active, select both instances of the Axle support.

2. Using the same context menu options you used to access Visibility, deselect Enabled. Note that in the Browser the icons switch from yellow to green. In the Design window, the parts fade. See Figure 4.18.

3. Move your cursor in the Design window. The shaft will still highlight when you pass over it but the Axle supports will not.

4. Switch your View representation to Default.

5. Delete the second Base.ipt instance from the assembly.

6. Cycle between the three View representations and then return to the default.

7. Save your work.

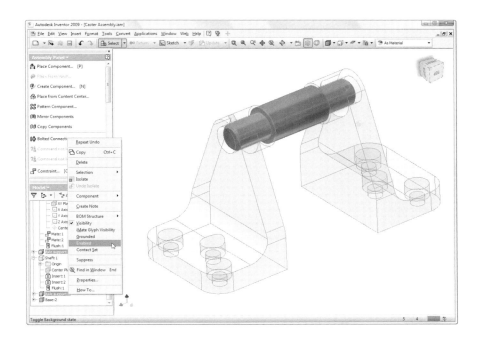

Figure 4.18

Axle supports no longer enabled

Working with Standard Parts

In Chapter 3 you were able to use a standard feature from the Content Center to create a simple part. The Content Center contains standard parts and steel shapes. If you load all of the standards, there are over 700,000 of them. Chances are you will only use a handful, but Inventor allows you to establish your own custom library containing only the content that you will use.

If you did not install Content Center, the following exercise will not work. I cannot recommend strongly enough the importance of installing and understanding the Content Center. Not using it will severely limit many of Inventor's most innovative tools. To better understand how to install and initiate the Content Center, review CC_2009_Install_guide.pdf, which is installed on your hard drive with Inventor automatically. It will guide you through the setup process.

Adding Bolts the Manual Way

In this exercise, you will apply bolts from the Content Center but place them in a more manual fashion. This is the way you would place bolts that you drew yourself.

1. In the Caster Assembly, edit the base part.

2. Create a new sketch on the top of the base part.

Figure 4.19

**Create a sketch on
the base part.**

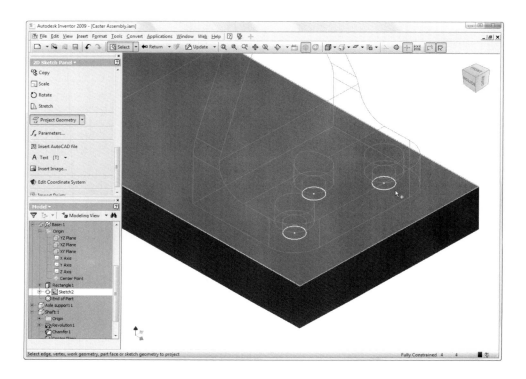

3. Start the Project Geometry tool and select the bottoms of the holes that are in the axle support part, as shown in Figure 4.19. Only project the holes for one end of the base part.

4. Exit the sketch and select the Hole tool.

5. Using the Hole tool, place 6mm, ANSI Metric M Profile, through the entire part with Full Depth threads.

6. By projecting the hole locations, these holes will change location if the holes in the axle part change location.

7. Check the image in Figure 4.20 to see what the holes look like.

8. Return to editing the assembly.

9. Reposition the assembly so that you can see through the holes in the axle support and see the new threaded holes in the base part.

10. In the Assembly Browser, select the Place From Content Center option.

11. When the Place From Content Center dialog box opens, navigate to Fasteners → Bolts → Socket Head. If you loaded all of the content, you will see a pretty amazing array of options, as shown in Figure 4.21.

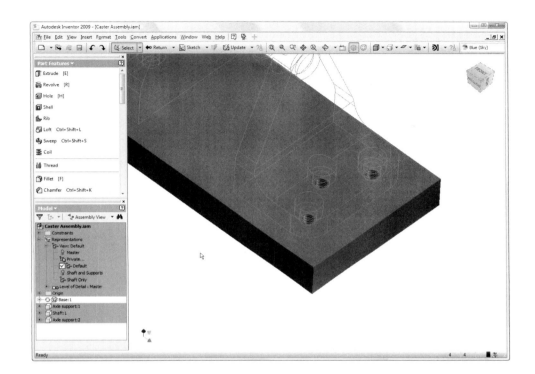

Figure 4.20

Placing Hole features using the sketch

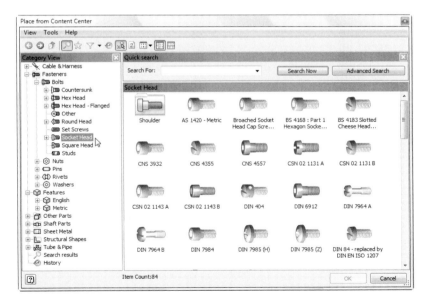

Figure 4.21

Selecting a bolt from the Content Center

12. To simplify the search, click the down arrow next to the Funnel icon. This is actually a filtering tool. Select the ISO standard from the list and it will narrow your options down to only Socket Head Bolts in the ISO standard (Figure 4.22).

Figure 4.22

**Filtering compo-
nents by standard in
the Content Center**

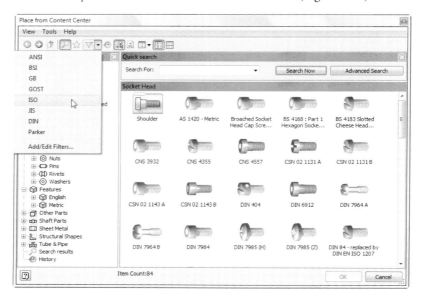

13. Double-click ISO 4762. After a few seconds, a preview of a bolt appears, as shown in Figure 4.23. The size will most likely not be appropriate for the hole in the axle support.

Figure 4.23

**Placing an ISO 4762
bolt in the assembly**

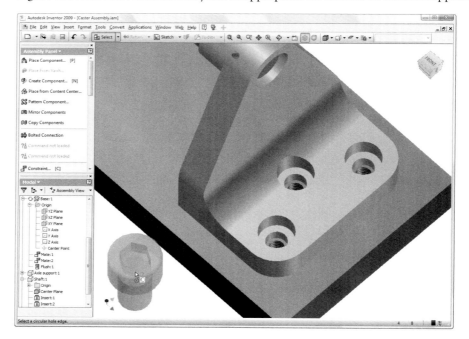

Figure 4.24

The bolt adjusts to fit the hole size.

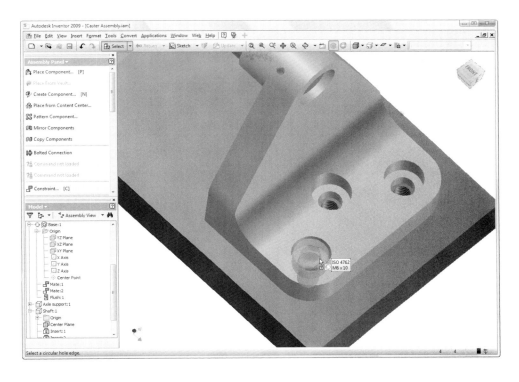

14. Move the bolt preview over the small diameter at the bottom of the counterbore on the axle support part. After you hover it for a second, the bolt will change size and should indicate through a pop-up tooltip that it is an ISO 4762 M6X 10 bolt, as shown in Figure 4.24.

15. Click the hole edge you hovered over to place the bolt temporarily.

    Once this is done, a dialog box appears:

    Here's a summary of its options, from left to right:

    Apply more than one bolt at one time. If Inventor sees the same size and class of hole in a part, it selects all holes in that part using this option.

    Edit the size or length of the previewed fastener. This will be highlighted since there were several holes of the same size placed together on the part.

    Launch a Bolted Connection Design Accelerator. We will explore this tool in the next section.

    The checkmark will place the fasteners and start the tool again to place another fastener.

    Place the fastener and exit the tool.

16. With the bolt preview resized and positioned, a double arrow will appear in red at the bottom of the bolt, as shown in Figure 4.25. Clicking and dragging this arrow allows you to change the length of the bolt. Make the bolt M6X16 and select the last button to place the bolts in the three holes and exit the tool.

17. Look at Figure 4.26 to review.

Figure 4.25
Bolt resizing based on hole size

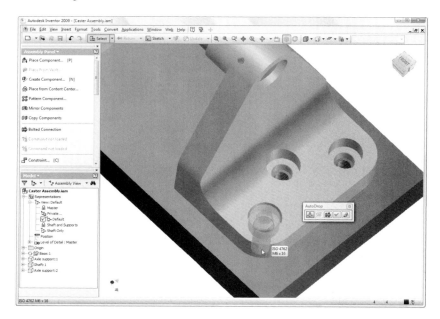

Figure 4.26
Three bolts placed simultaneously

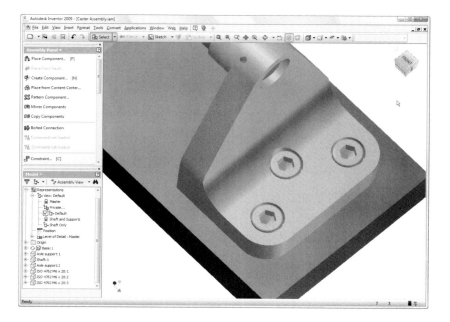

18. Orbit the assembly on the screen so that you can see the bolts in the threaded holes (see Figure 4.27).

19. Restore the Home view and save the assembly.

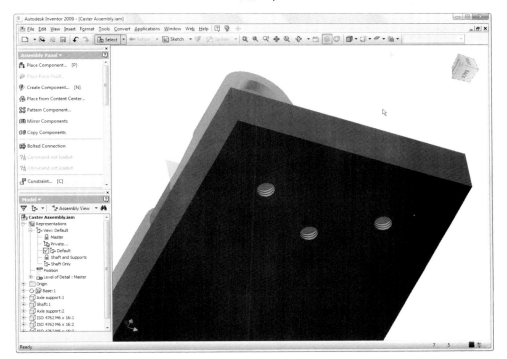

Figure 4.27

Threaded holes added to the base

Using the Bolted Connection Design Accelerator

Another aspect of digital prototyping, along with validating that the assembly will fit properly, is the ability to know and understand the performance of its components.

You can analyze parts and assemblies to understand how they perform, but the performance of some components has been documented for years. Components such as nuts, bolts, bearings, and fittings must perform to a minimum standard to be produced. These standards are documented, and for years designers and engineers have been selecting components based on them.

In Inventor is a collection of tools called Design Accelerators that use these standards to help you select components to be used in your assembly. Instead of looking up the standard specs to determine which bolt (or other item) you need and then selecting it in Inventor, you can use a wizard interface to input the requirements and have Inventor offer you the components that meet the needs of your design.

One of these Design Accelerators is the Bolted Connection tool. In this exercise, you will just scratch the surface of what this tool is capable of, but its value should be apparent even in its most basic form.

1. Position the assembly so that it reflects Figure 4.28. Note that there are no holes in the base part on this end of the assembly.

Figure 4.28

Changing the viewpoint to see no holes in the base

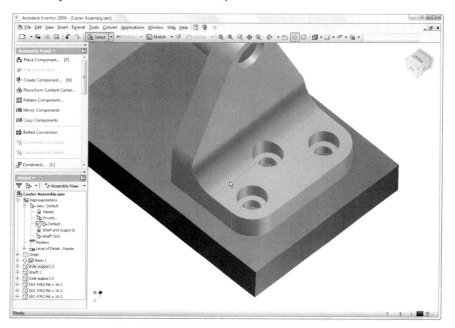

2. Start the Place From Content Center tool. It should open displaying the same fasteners that you placed in the last exercise.

3. Right-click on ISO 4762 and select Add To Favorites.

4. Exit the Place From Content Center tool.

5. Select the down arrow next to the Model header and change your Browser from the Model mode to Favorites (see Figure 4.29).

   Once the Browser mode is changed, you should see a list of the components in the Content Center. This is an alternative to using the Place From Content Center tool.

6. At the bottom of the list of available content categories, you should see the ISO 4762 bolt. This is where your favorites will be listed as you select them.

7. Click the ISO 4762 bolt icon and drag it onto the screen.

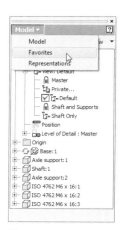

Figure 4.29

Changing the Browser mode from Model to Favorites

8. Place the bolt the same way that you did in the previous exercise.

9. When the AutoDrop menu appears, choose the Bolted Connection icon.

   The Bolted Connection Component Generator dialog box will appear (Figure 4.30). Because you accessed this tool from the AutoDrop menu, some of the options will already be selected.

10. Review the dialog box and you will see that the Termination icon is waiting for input. Hover over the base part as shown in Figure 4.31 and select the bottom of the base part as your terminating face.

Figure 4.30

The Bolted Connection Component Generator dialog box

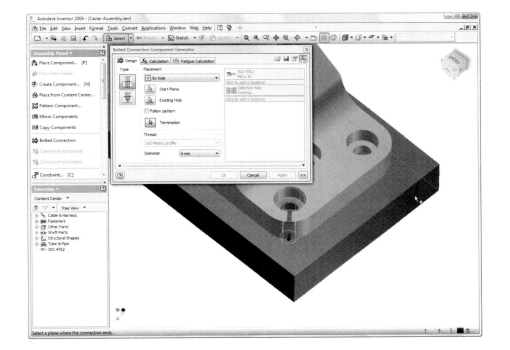

Figure 4.31

Selecting the terminating face for a bolted connection component generator

11. A preview of the hole that will be added through the base part appears in red on the screen, and a hole is added to the graphic on the right of the dialog box that displays the elements of the bolted connection.

    The new hole is listed as a drilled hole; for this design you need a threaded hole.

12. Click the small icon with the ellipsis to open the Modify Hole dialog box. Select Threaded from the dropdown list, as shown in Figure 4.32. Click the icon with the green checkmark to make the change.

13. Drag the length of the bolt to make it an M6X16, as you did in the previous exercise.

14. Just above the Termination icon is a checkbox that if selected will follow a pattern such as a directional or circular pattern. This checkbox is only available if a pattern exists in the part. Select the checkbox and click Apply to place two bolts and create two threaded holes in the base part.

    After the bolts are placed, the dialog box will return but it will be starting over with no information. Now you will use it as though you just wanted to place a bolted connection with an existing hole as your guide.

15. The dialog box asks for a start plane. Position the assembly so that you can see the open hole clearly and, for the start plane, select the upper face on the axle support that you sketched on to place the holes.

16. Select the open hole for the Existing Hole input.

Figure 4.32

Changing the hole type

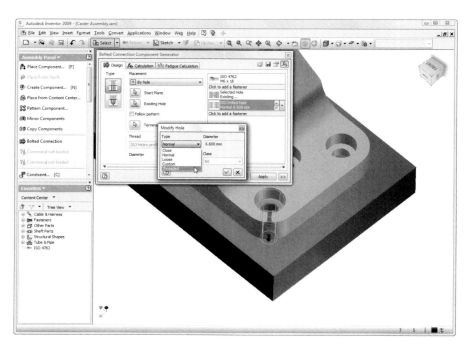

17. Click the bottom of the base part for your Termination plane.

18. Change the drilled hole to a threaded hole as you did with the last bolted connection.

    In the preview in the Design window, you will only see the existing hole and the threaded hole. You need to tell the Bolted Connection tool what type of bolt to place. You can add fasteners before and after holes in cases where you want to apply a washer and nut after a hole.

19. Click to add a fastener at the top of the graphic area.

    A dialog box appears with a listing of the bolts in the Content Center (Figure 4.33).

20. At the top of the dialog box are two filters that allow you to narrow the available options.
    Set the Standard to ISO. In the library's browser select the Socket Head Bolts under the Bolts group. This will greatly simplify the process of finding the ISO 4762 bolt that you need.

Figure 4.33

Adding a bolted connection to an existing hole

21. Click the ISO 4762 and a preview of your bolt is added to the graphic and on the screen.

22. Drag the length to match the others and click OK in the dialog box to place the bolt.

23. Restore the Home view and save the assembly.

The Bolted Connection tool can be accessed directly from the Assembly Panel bar, and there are other placement options similar to the traditional Hole tool that do not require a hole to exist in the assembly.

Other tabs allow you to validate based on loads that the bolt will have to endure, whether or not the bolt is the appropriate one to be used.

Summary

Inventor was created to work extensively in the context of the assembly, including creating parts in the assembly. The reason for this is that most people do not create singular parts; instead, they create assemblies made up of many parts.

Inventor LT is perfect for those in trades that are focused on working with only individual parts, who never need assembly capabilities.

In Chapter 8, you will explore more options that are available in assemblies, but as with the last three chapters the foundational tools you have explored here will allow you to work effectively as you learn even more.

CHAPTER 5

Standards and Styles

The Industrial Revolution would not have been possible if not for the advent of standardization, or the development of interchangeable parts.

Since that time, standards have evolved that allow consistent documentation of how parts are to be made. These standards are so important to maintaining quality and communication that even with the globalization of economies many companies choose to adhere to the national (and in some cases local) standards they have been using instead of adopting international standards. Because standards are so important, the most prevalent standards from around the world are included with Inventor. You can adjust the way Inventor implements these built-in standards to suit the way your office works with them.

In this chapter you will learn how to work with styles and templates, along with Inventor's tools for making those changes and maintaining them for the future.

- **Building Your Standard**

- **Creating a New Standard**

- **Changing Styles**

- **Sharing the New Standard**

- **Templates and Title Blocks**

- **Speeding Up the Drawing Process with a Template**

Styles and Standards

It's often frustrating for people moving from one CAD system to another, or from one company to another, to encounter designers using standards that are different from the ones of the same names they've used before. What's worse is if people within the same company are inconsistent in their interpretation of the standard.

A *style* is a way of defining layer colors and naming, dimension appearance, text fonts, and other elements that nearly every company or designer will define to build a standard with which their drawings must be consistent.

Keeping the standard consistent across your drawings is even more important than how closely you adhere to the version of the standard that was created by the organization that defined it. To build consistency, you must be able to define what your implementation for a given standard will be and you need to be able to manage it.

Inventor will not let you modify its default standards and styles, so changes you make will be added to the options. Also remember that styles can be modified in other types of Inventor files. Drawings have the widest variety of changeable styles, so we'll focus on them in this chapter.

Building Your Standard

If you work with ANSI, ISO, or any other standard, chances are you will flavor it to your taste. Inventor has a simple mechanism that allows you to take one of the included standards and copy it to a new standard, which you can then tailor to suit your needs. Once the new standard is established, it can be shared with others to allow for consistency across multiple users.

There are a lot of style changes that can be made, but I think that it's prudent to start off with the big items, such as layer and dimension styles, and work your way up from there.

If you will be using Inventor in a workgroup, it is also a good idea to have one person control the development of the standard so that changes are kept under control. The exercises that follow in this chapter, which involve building and saving a company standard, assume that the user is this designated standards administrator. If you work in a multiuser environment, it is important to establish a standard to create better-quality drawings with less work.

Creating the new standard is the easy part. You also need to make sure that the changes you make are to the correct standard and that you can save changes.

You can choose among several approaches when creating a new set of styles. I prefer to start with an existing document that contains most of the styles I need, make any necessary changes to the styles, and then save those changes into my new standard.

If you work for a company that has well-documented standards, it is a good idea to match those standards in your Inventor styles before introducing the program. That way, you maintain consistency and limit the reluctance of others who may not understand the capabilities that Inventor offers.

Finally, whether you're an administrator or an individual user, I don't recommend you try to use the following exercises to build standards that you will use going forward. The standards or styles created in this chapter should be considered disposable and for learning purposes only. Once you are comfortable with the exercises and your company standards, you can apply these lessons in production.

Creating a New Standard

In this exercise we'll create our new standard and prepare Inventor to be able to make the changes we want.

1. Close any files that are open in Inventor.

2. Open the Projects editor that you used to create the `Introducing Inventor.ipj` file in Chapter 1.

3. Set Samples to be the active project.

4. Right-click the Use Style Library setting and select Yes, as shown in Figure 5.1.

   By default, Use Style Library is set to Read Only, which means users are allowed to make changes to styles in a drawing or part but they are not able to save those changes back to the standard that is used by others. Selecting No will prevent you from changing the styles. This may be desirable in an organization that wants to prohibit changes to the appearance of their files.

5. Save the change and close the Projects dialog box.

6. Open the `Carb Intake Plate.dwg` file that you created in Chapter 2.

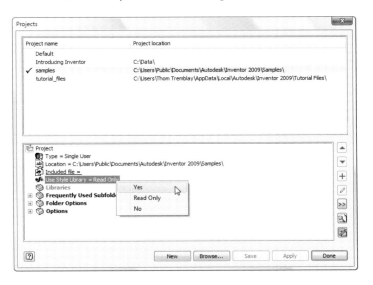

Figure 5.1

Editing the Samples project file

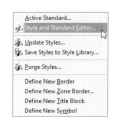

7. On the Inventor Standard toolbar, select Format → Style And Standard Editor.

8. In the editor, right-click on the active standard Default Standard (ANSI) and select New Style, as shown in Figure 5.2.

9. Name your standard in the New Style Name dialog box (Figure 5.3) and select the ANSI Standard to base it on. Clicking OK will create the new standard.

   Notice that I have used the name "Introducing Inventor." Go ahead and use that name for this exercise, substituting something more appropriate if you apply this procedure in a future real application. Even if you will typically be using a standard other than ANSI, you should go through this exercise creating an ANSI-based standard and create your own standard at another time.

10. Right-click on the new standard and choose Active (Figure 5.4); this ensures that changes you make to styles will affect only that standard.

Figure 5.2

Creating a new standard

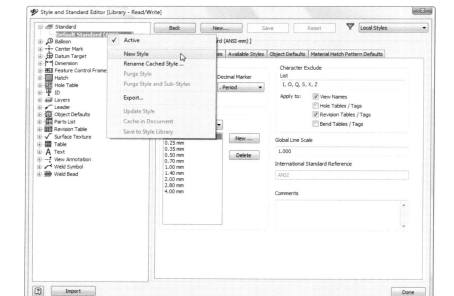

Figure 5.3

Naming the new standard

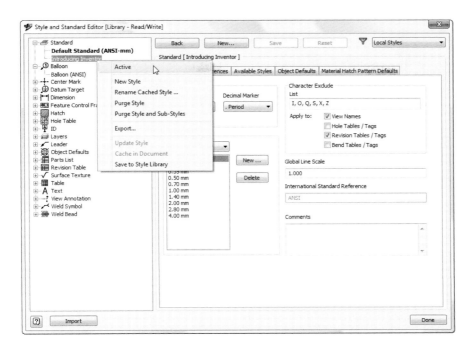

Figure 5.4

**Activating the
new standard**

It is very important to be sure that you are editing the correct standard, or you will
end up having to redo the changes you want and possibly undo the changes that were
mistakenly made to another standard.

The Foundation of the Standard

Now that the standard is active, Inventor will allow you to make changes to it. These
changes can be made using the Style And Standard Editor dialog box or by right-clicking
to invoke various Style settings in the process of creating your drawing. For the sake of
consistency, in the next few exercises you will work with the tabs that occupy the right
two-thirds of the Style And Standard Editor dialog box.

Each one of these tabs plays an important role in defining the standard and making
it suit your needs. As you have seen before, these tabs will also have groups of tools that
control the more detailed settings. We will make changes to some of these settings as we
go through the tabs.

The General Tab

The General tab (Figure 5.5) contains the most foundational elements. For the most
part, these setting are of the "set it and forget it" variety and typically will not need to
be changed once they are established.

Figure 5.5

**The General tab of
the Style And Stan-
dard Editor**

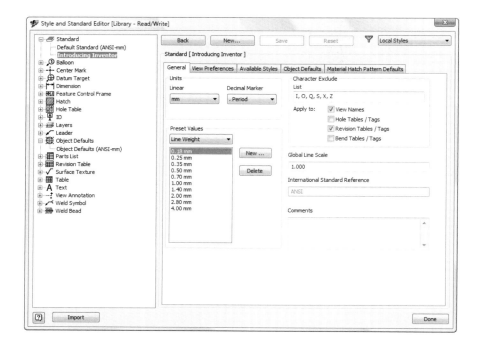

UNITS

Units allow you to choose what units of measurement will be reported in drawings, parts, and assemblies. Here you can also select how the decimal should be displayed: as a period or comma.

PRESET VALUES

Preset Values is a multilevel group. You can select Line Weights to allow in your drawings, as shown here. You can also choose Text Height or Scale from the pull-down to specify what sizes text can appear on your drawing and what standard scales will appear on the list. If you work with very large or very small parts, making adjustments to this list can save you from repeatedly typing in scales manually.

CHARACTER EXCLUDE

To avoid confusing numbers with letters, it is common practice to exclude certain letters from parts of drawings. This group allows you to create a list of those letters and specify up to four types of drawing elements to exclude them from.

The View Preferences Tab

The View Preferences tab (Figure 5.6) offers control over the labeling and calculation of drawing views of all types.

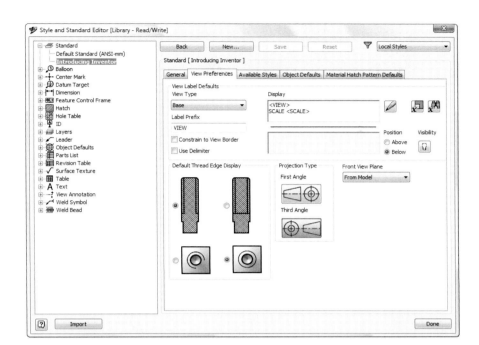

Figure 5.6

**The View Prefer-
ences tab of the
Style And Standard
Editor**

VIEW LABEL DEFAULTS

Working with the Base View dialog box in Chapter 2, you learned how to apply a label to
a drawing view. The View Label Defaults group of tools establishes the default settings for
those labels. The View Type pull-down makes it possible to set options for the Label Prefix and what the view label display will look like for each view type.

This group also includes checkboxes that tie the label to the border
of the view and specify whether to separate portions of the view label
with a delimiter line. You can also quickly add the scale or view identifier using the buttons on the right of the View Preferences tab.

DEFAULT THREAD EDGE DISPLAY

Depending on your standard drawing practice, you may need to change how threads are
displayed. The result of your selection is nicely previewed for you.

PROJECTION TYPE

Much of the world uses First Angle projection for their drawings. Since this new standard
is based on ANSI, Third Angle projection is selected.

FRONT VIEW PLANE

The ViewCube makes it easy to establish what position your parts will maintain as their
front view. This flyout offers you the opportunity to use the Model Front View as the

Drawing Front View selected in the Base View dialog box, or you can instead use one of the three standard planes in the part model.

The Available Styles Tab

The Available Styles tab appears if multiple styles are available and allows you to exclude certain styles from being available to the end user. Thus, you can migrate from an older style (like dimensions or types of text) without removing the older style.

The Object Defaults Tab

If you were wondering how Inventor knew that hidden lines in a drawing view belonged on the Hidden layer, the settings on this tab explain how. The Object Defaults tab (Figure 5.7) tells various objects that appear in drawing views what layers they belong on. If you want to limit the number of layers that you will use in Inventor, you can change objects to appear on different layers.

Figure 5.7

The Object Defaults tab of the Style And Standard Editor

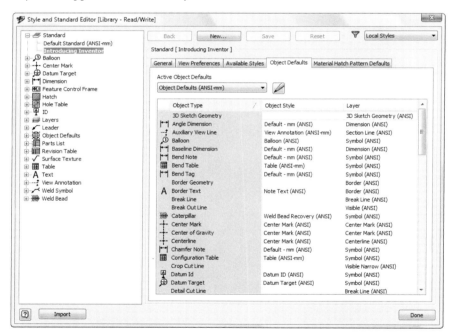

Clicking the icon with the pencil in the Object Defaults tab will switch the tab to editing mode, and Object Defaults will highlight in the column on the left side of the Style And Library Editor dialog box (Figure 5.8). These Object Defaults are carried over from the standard that your standard was created from.

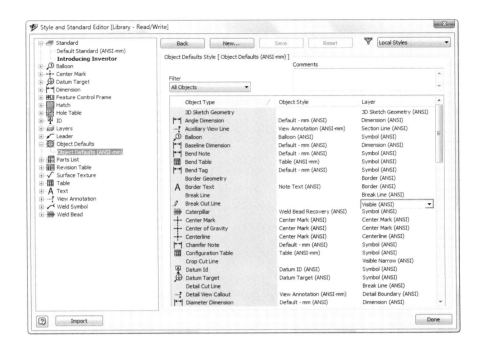

Figure 5.8

Editing Object Defaults in the list

Once you are in editing mode, you can change an Object Style or Layer by clicking on the current value and selecting a new value from the pull-down menu.

You can also filter what Object Types you want to edit using the Filter pull-down menu.

OBJECT STYLE

This column tells Inventor which object style you want to apply by default to a particular object type. For example, this is where you tell the linear dimension which dimension style it will use by default.

The Material Hatch Pattern Defaults Tab

The Material Hatch Pattern Defaults tab (Figure 5.9) enables you to specify the Hatch pattern that is used when sectioning a part based on the part's material.

DEFAULT HATCH STYLE

The pull-down list of standard patterns is accompanied by an Edit button, which will take you to the hatch specification under the object styles. You can also import materials to apply patterns from a file.

The most interesting item to me is From Style Library. This allows you to assign a hatch pattern directly to the materials in the Inventor Style Library. Doing this allows every user to get the correct pattern automatically just by creating a section view; there is no need to manually override anything.

Figure 5.9

**Selecting a
Hatch pattern
for aluminum**

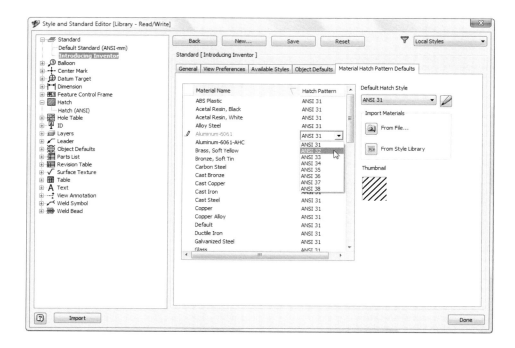

Object Styles

In the column on the left of the Style And Standard Editor, below the standards you can select for editing, are a series of icons that contain object styles that can be edited. The categories are pretty self-explanatory. To expand a category, click the plus sign (+) in the box next to it. To see the individual properties of the object style in that category, just select the name, and the area to the right will change to show properties and tabs that contain more properties. Once you make any change or create a new object style, be sure to save your work.

Working with Object Defaults

You can edit the object defaults as well as duplicate and modify them if you want to avoid overwriting them. Or you can develop an update to a standard for future implementation.

1. In the left column, expand Object Defaults and select Object Defaults (ANSI-mm). Then click the New button at the top of the dialog box to create a new set of object defaults.

2. Give the new set the name **Introducing Inventor Defaults**.

3. Click OK to create the new defaults.

4. Return to the Object Defaults tab under Introducing Inventor Standard and make sure that the new style is listed as the Active Object Default.

5. Save your changes by clicking Save.

Creating a New Dimension Style

In this exercise you will create a new dimension style based on an existing one. If you expand the list of object styles under Dimension, you will see that there is a good variety to begin with. This saves you from having to select all of the options.

1. Expand the Dimension object styles and select the Default - Fraction (ANSI) style.

2. Right-click and select New, or click the New icon at the top of the dialog box to create a new style based on the style you selected.

3. Set the new name to **Diagonal Fraction 1/4 inch precision** in the New Style Name dialog box. Be sure Add To Standard is checked.

   The new style will automatically be highlighted and ready for editing. The right side of the dialog box will display the tabs discussed earlier, where you can make your style changes.

4. On the Units tab, find the Linear Group and on the Format pull-down select the Fraction (Diagonal) option.

5. Under Precision, select 1/4 (see Figure 5.10).

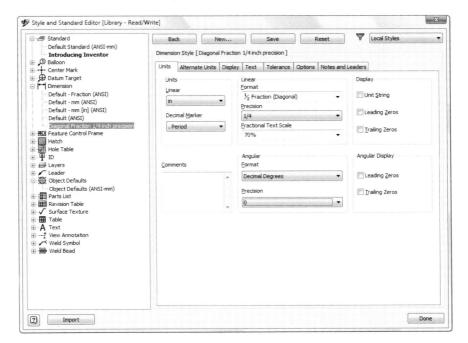

Figure 5.10

Editing the new dimension style

Review the options on other tabs. The options will normally offer previews of how text will be positioned or formatted when the dimension is placed.

6. Select the Options tab. In the upper left under Arrowhead Placement, select the option on the right depicting the arrowhead on the outside of the extension lines.

7. Switch to the Notes And Leaders tab. In Chapter 2 the Hole Note you placed reflected the units in which the part was created rather than the units that you were dimensioning in. Here you can see why that happened. At the top just below the tabs are the four types of leaders; the first is a Hole Note. With that selected, deselect the Part Units checkbox, so that Hole Notes will be placed using the units of the active dimension style.

8. Click Save to keep your changes.

I suspect that when you are preparing to move Inventor into production in your office, you will spend a lot of time perfecting the behavior of your dimension styles. As you clicked through the tabs, I hope that you gained an appreciation for how thorough the options are. Dimensions are so important yet so varied from company to company that you must have a lot of options.

After dimension styles, one of the most common areas of customization is the naming and coloring of the drawing layers. Inventor comes with a fairly long list of layers because in your object defaults there are many different types of objects, and people want to be able to control their display at a very granular level. To do this, they may need a lot of layers with which to establish their display. A layer controls how the objects assigned to it are displayed; the objects themselves do not control how they are displayed by default.

Editing a Layer's Style

In this exercise, you will modify a couple of layers and enable Inventor to purge a layer that you are not using. This is another exercise that is intended purely to demonstrate how to control the various properties. The colors, choice of layers, and other options selected in this exercise are not intended to demonstrate how Inventor should be used; those are your decisions.

1. Under Object Defaults select Introducing Inventor Defaults.

2. Select Model/View Objects from the Filter list.

3. Click the Layer column header twice to sort the object alphabetically (see Figure 5.11).

4. Click on each of the items that list Hidden Narrow (ANSI) as the current layer and change them all to Hidden (ANSI).

A layer that is not used by any object style becomes eligible to be purged from the list. Conversely, if you're trying to purge a layer and Inventor is not offering that option, it means you have not cleared it on this list.

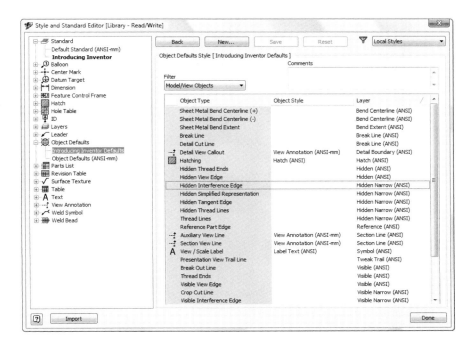

Figure 5.11

Sorting and filtering object types

5. Click Save when you have changed the five layers that needed to be changed.

6. Right-click on Object Defaults (ANSI-mm) and select Replace Style.

7. Make sure Introducing Inventor Defaults is listed as the With style and that Purge Replaced Style is checked.

8. Click OK to remove Object Defaults (ANSI-mm) from the standard.

9. Expand the list of layers.

10. Right-click on the Hidden Narrow (ANSI) layer and select Purge Style.

11. You will be warned that purging the style will affect the Local Standard. Click OK to complete.

You have just removed a layer from the standard. Alternatively, you can also simply rename a layer to suit your existing standards if you prefer. Just be sure that the object type is properly mapped so that everything appears on the correct layer. Now we will continue with our other changes.

12. Click on the Hidden (ANSI) layer in the list of layers on the left. The layer will high-light on the right.

   In the layer's row are columns of options. A lightbulb controls whether the layer is on. There is a block with the color of the layer, along with a column for the Line Type and one for the Line Weight. The Scale By Line Weight option will change the length of line type elements based on the weight. For example, the length of a dash in a hidden line type for a thick line will be different than the length of the dash in a thin line of the same line type. The final option is whether to include the layer in the printer output.

13. Now click on the black block in the Color column. Doing this opens a dialog box where you can select a standard color or define a custom one. Select the color red, as shown in Figure 5.12.

14. Click OK to confirm the selection and the box will turn red.

15. Now click the Line Weight option displayed for the Hidden (ANSI) layer. When you do this, a list of line weights will appear. These are the line weights that you saw listed earlier under Object Defaults. Select .25mm from the list.

Figure 5.12

Changing a layer color

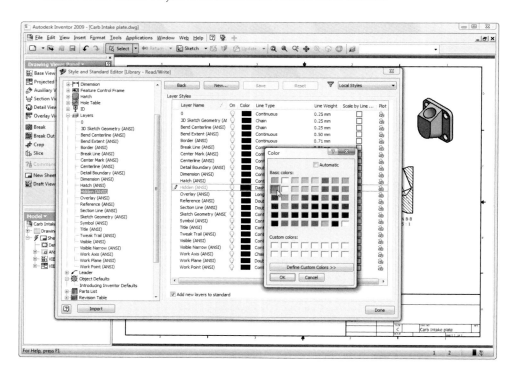

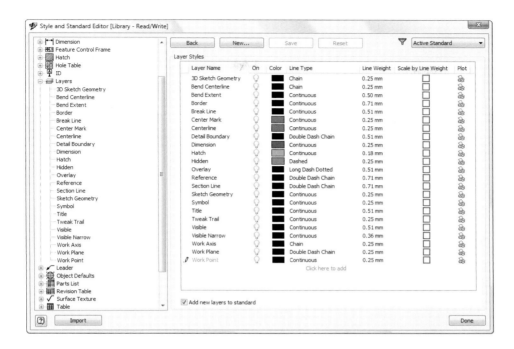

Figure 5.13

**The layer list
after changes**

16. Now change the color of the Centerline and Center Mark Layers to a blue tone of
    your liking.

17. Change the Color or the Hatch (ANSI) Layer to an orange.

18. Click twice slowly on the name Dimension (ANSI) in the Layer Name column
    and change the layer's name to **Dimension**. Change its color to green too.

19. Remove the (ANSI) from all of the remaining layer names.

20. Save your changes. Your layer styles should now appear similar to the list in
    Figure 5.13.

21. Look at the list of object defaults. The layer names have all been updated to reflect
    the new names that you gave to them.

Saving the New Standard for Sharing

All of the changes that you have made are local to this particular drawing. To make the
new standard available to other drawings and other users, you must save the styles and
publish the standard. In the upper right of the dialog box is a Local Styles pull-down for
filtering the view. Typically it displays as Local Styles but it could be showing All Styles
or Active Standard if you have previously selected either of these display modes.

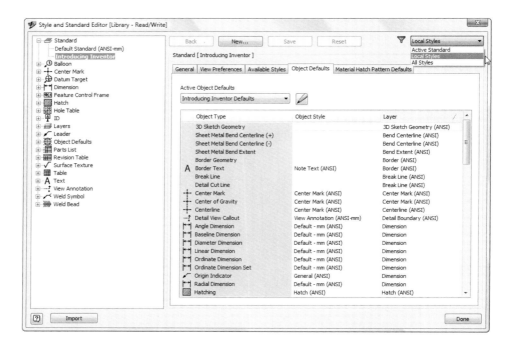

Changing this list to All Styles will show a complete list of standards that are available to Inventor. To make sure our new standard is published into Inventor's list of standards and styles, take the following steps to save the new styles. Chances are you will not change every style associated with your new standard. Because of this, Inventor's Style library does not have to update every part.

1. Right-click on the Introducing Inventor standard and select Save to Style Library.

2. You'll see the dialog shown in Figure 5.14, listing what styles will be saved to the library and what type of style they are.

Figure 5.14

Saving unique Object types and Styles

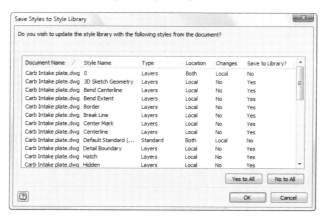

3. For Save to Library, the list that appears will show Yes to all of the unique style data that you have created by modifying the local styles. Click OK to update the Inventor Styles library. The dialog will disappear after the updates are finished.

4. Close the editing dialog and see that your drawing has been updated to reflect the changes to the Layer styles.

5. Save your drawing.

In the rest of the chapter we will use your new standard to create a new drawing template that will use your standard by default. If you want to share your style settings with another user who does not have access to your standards, you can also export an XML file containing your settings. To do this, right-click on your standard in the Style And Standard Editor and select Export. Following the prompts, you will be able to easily create a file that another Inventor user can take advantage of.

Drawing Templates

As you have already seen, Inventor ships with a large number of templates. These templates allow for the various standards to be represented out of the box rather than having you prepare them before you're comfortable with how each element looks. This can help to shorten the process of modifying styles to create your personalized standard.

Templates have a number of uses. The most common for drawings is to make sure that the paper has the correct border, title block, and layers with all of their settings prepared to begin making drawings that match the company's standards. In one exercise in this chapter, you will see how a template can even shorten the drawing process.

Creating a Template and Title Block

You can build a new template from an existing one in a few steps, or you can take a completed drawing and use it to create a template incorporating style changes that have already been made. Creating a title block is also an important part of your documentation.

The title block can carry not just the basic information but also dynamic values that change with your design.

Building a New Template

In this exercise you will take an existing template and use it as a basis to build new template with a modified title block.

1. Create a new drawing using the ANSI (mm).dwg template.

2. In the Browser expand Sheet:1 to see the contents of the drawing.

3. Right-click on the Default Border and delete it from the drawing.

4. Expand the Drawing Resources in the Browser and expand the Borders category.

5. Right-click on Default Border and select Insert Drawing Border.

6. In the resulting dialog box, set the number of Horizontal Zones to 6 and click OK.

    Inventor will place a new border in the drawing, as shown in Figure 5.15.

    There are additional options for setting the spacing between the border and the
    edge of the sheet. For many AutoCAD users,
    templates are also defined for each paper
    size. With this border the Inventor user can
    change the size of the drawing sheet after
    drawing views have been placed and not have
    to worry about changing dimension scales or
    any number of tedious tasks.

7. Right-click on Sheet:1 in the Browser and
    select Edit Sheet.

8. Use the Size pull-down menu to select a D size drawing sheet.

9. Click OK to update the page.

Now we can begin to modify the title block. Inventor's title block is sketch based and
therefore can be modified by specifying dimensions to ensure that its size matches your
existing standard. Editing the title block can be a little confusing, with all of the dimensions and value information displayed in their raw form.

Figure 5.15

**Changing the
drawing border**

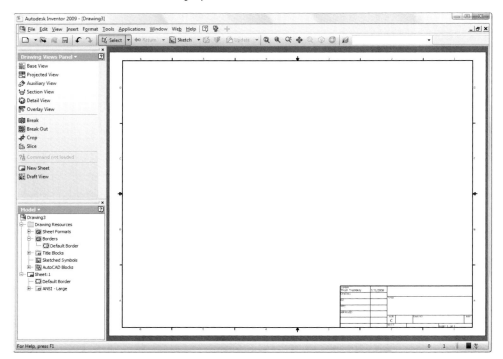

Updating the Standard

To bring together the standard and the template, you first need to set the standard you created to be the active standard in the drawing and make sure everything matches.

1. Go to Format → Active Standard to open the selection dialog box.

2. Set Introducing Inventor as the active standard.

3. Choose Format → Update Styles, and click Yes to update the local style to make sure that everything is in sync (as it should be if you've followed the steps correctly).

Modifying the Title Block

In this exercise we will review the special properties of the existing title block and add one of our own.

1. Check to make sure that one of the elements of Sheet:1 is the ANSI-Large title block.

2. Expand the title block in the Browser and double-click the Field Text element.

The Edit Property Fields dialog (Figure 5.16) will in some cases allow you to modify some values displayed in the title block. In this particular title block, all of the properties that are listed take their values from the iProperties of a part or assembly. You can also add custom properties to the same iProperties that you can modify in this dialog box.

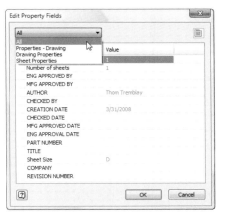

Figure 5.16

Title Block model properties

3. Close the dialog and right-click on ANSI - Large in the Browser.

4. Select Edit Definition.

5. Zoom in on the title block, as shown in Figure 5.17.

6. Edit the dimension with a value of 196.85 above the title block and change its value to 8in.

7. Edit the dimension with a value of 127 above the title block and change its value to 5.25in.

Now you will add some additional information to the title block. Since there is already text in the title block, we will just copy it to maintain the format and then add the special feature. When you are editing a title block, the Panel bar offers the same sketching options that you get when sketching in a part, including the ability to add an image file or even an AutoCAD drawing to your title block.

Figure 5.17

**Editing the
title block**

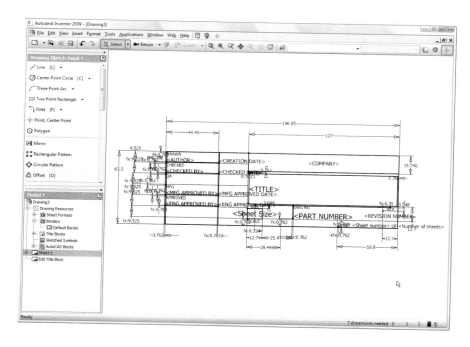

8. Zoom in on the lower-left corner of the title block, as shown in Figure 5.18.

9. Right-click on the text APPROVED and copy it to the clipboard.

Figure 5.18

**Zooming in on
the text we want
to copy**

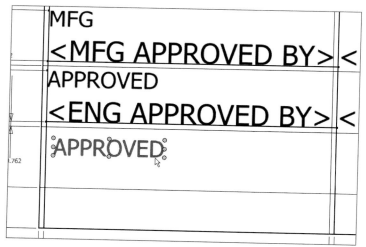

10. Paste the new text onto the screen. It will likely appear on top of the original text. Move it to the open cell below the one that the original APPROVED appeared in.

11. Constrain the text to the vertical line with a coincidence constraint and position it with a dimension of .03 in, as shown in Figure 5.19.

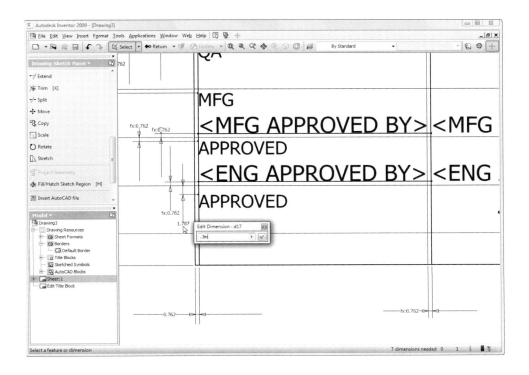

Figure 5.19

**Constraining the
text into place**

12. Right-click on the new text and select Edit Text.

13. Highlight the text in the editing cell and change its value to **MASS**. Click OK to
finish.

14. Now copy and paste the <ENG APPROVED BY> property and move its origin point
to the intersection in the lower-left corner of the cell with the MASS label.

15. Use Edit Text to modify the copied property field.

The Format Text dialog has a huge number of options, from basic font, justification,
and size options for text to the ability to add property values from models. The
property that we copied will put the value that is entered for Approved By in the

iProperties into the title block. We want to change this new property to reflect the mass of the part. This value will update every time the drawing is opened. Text that gets its value from iProperties or other parameters will appear in carets when editing, but the parameter will not appear on the drawing if there is no value.

16. Delete the property value that is in the text window.

17. From the Type pull-down select Physical Properties - Model. Selecting a value here will change what other values are available.

18. Select Mass from the Property pull-down.

19. Leave the precision at two decimal places and click the Add Text Parameter button to the right of the Precision drop-down menu to place the new property in the editing field.

20. Click OK to place the new value into the title block.

21. Select all of the geometry in the title block. From the pull-down at the top, set the layer for all geometry to Title.

22. Right-click on the screen and select Save Title Block.

23. You'll be asked if you want to save. Select the Save As option to create a new title block based on the one you started to edit.

24. In the Title Block dialog box, enter **Introducing Inventor** for the new title block name and save the new title block.

When the title block clears, you will see that nothing has changed on your screen. The changes you made were saved to the Introducing Inventor title block, but the ANSI- Large title block is still used in the drawing.

25. Expand the Title Blocks heading under Drawing Resources. The Introducing Inventor title block has been added to the list.

26. Under Sheet:1, delete the existing title block.

27. Insert the new title block into the drawing. Note that it is slightly longer and that there is now a heading for MASS in the lower left.

28. Click the Zoom All button in your drawing or double-click the middle mouse button.

Now we are ready to create the new template incorporating these changes. The New File button on your Inventor Standard toolbar has a flyout option where you can start a new file from a default part, drawing, or assembly template. If you would like to use your new templates with this feature, you can save them as your Standard file in the folder where the default templates are located. This location can vary between operating systems and between Inventor Suite and Inventor LT.

Creating the Template File

For this exercise I will use the paths for Windows Vista and for an Inventor Suite user. It should be fairly easy to transpose any differences in paths. When you begin a new drawing, you can select templates from several tabs. We will add a tab for your new templates.

1. Select the Save As tool.

2. Using the Navigation tools at the top of the dialog box, navigate to `C:\Users\Public\` `Public Documents\Autodesk\Inventor 2009\Templates` to reach the path in the dialog box you see in Figure 5.20.

3. Once you find your Templates folder, you will see that there are folders with the names English and Metric. This is how Inventor titles the additional tabs for templates. Create a new folder and name it **Personal**.

4. Inventor will switch your Save In folder to your new folder. Save your file with the name `Introducing Inventor.dwg`.

5. You will be warned that the file is outside your path. Click Yes to approve creating the file.

6. Close your drawing.

7. Open a new file. In the dialog box, click the new tab and start a drawing using your newly created template.

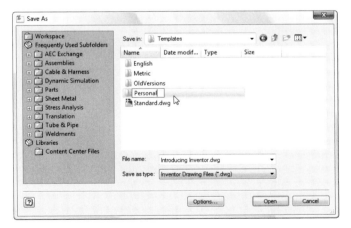

Figure 5.20

Creating a new template path

Creating a "Quick Start" Template File

In the Inventor drawing templates, there is a drawing resource called Sheet Formats that is largely misunderstood and underutilized. It offers users a chance to create multiple drawing views at once by simply double-clicking the sheet format you want to use for a view and then selecting the file that you want to detail.

The limitation of this feature out of the box is that it cannot anticipate what size part you typically work with. In this exercise you will build a new template that is scaled for the size of part you want and will automatically prompt you to choose a part. You can also build several of these templates to establish a variety of view counts and scales.

1. Open the `Carb Intake plate.dwg` file that you have been working with.

2. Make sure that the Introducing Inventor template file that you created is open.

3. In the Drawing Resources → Title Blocks folder, right-click on the Introducing Inventor title block and copy it to the clipboard.

4. Switch to the `Carb Intake plate.dwg` file and expand its drawing resources.

5. Right-click on the Title Blocks folder and paste your new title block into the list of available title blocks (see Figure 5.21).

Figure 5.21

Adding the new title block to a drawing

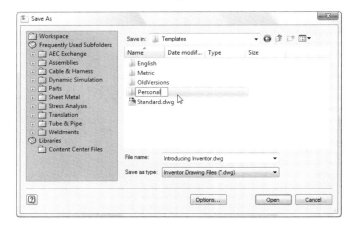

6. As you did before, remove the existing title block from the drawing and replace it with the new one.

7. Select the Save As command and create a file in your Templates → Personal folder named **6 View 5 to 1 scale.dwg**.

8. Start a new drawing with this template.

9. When prompted for a part to use, select the `Carb Shoe - 2.ipt` file from the same directory as `Carb Intake plate.dwg`.

   For Inventor LT users this file is included with your installation so you will not need to download it.

10. The drawing views of the new part will be placed based on the same orientations as the original part (see Figure 5.22).

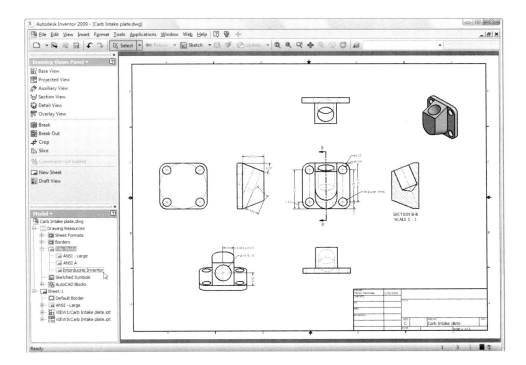

Figure 5.22

Drawing views are placed automatically.

11. Close all of the open files. There's no need to save the drawing of the clutch shoe.

12. Open the Project File editor and change the Use Style Libraries setting to No and save the project file.

Summary

An individual or small workgroup can easily get by working without setting up a standard by simply building well-thought-out templates and sharing them. An organization can also get far more involved in developing standards and styles that we covered in this chapter. But beware of making changes that could cause unwanted problems with drawing consistency.

Also know that there are standards and styles associated with other types of files and that defining templates to incorporate refinements made for those data sources can add just as much productivity as having your drawing templates properly prepared.

The concepts of standards and style became the rule in manufacturing because of the quality, consistency, and time savings they bring. Incorporating them can do all of that for you every day.

CHAPTER 6

Advanced Annotation: Drawing Views and Detailing

In Chapter 2 you learned the basics of creating the 2D drawings that are critical to most people using CAD today.

In this chapter you will move into the advanced annotation that is needed to create complex documents and that offers even more options for creating the views of the 3D geometry. The chapter has two major topics: drawing views and detailing tools.

Some of the tools covered here are not be available in LT, but LT users may be surprised at just how many great tools are available to them.

- **Advanced View Creation**

- **Special Detailing Tools**

- **Assembly Detailing**

Moving Beyond the Basic View

Different software tools and different industries have developed specialized ways of documenting the geometry that they must raise from paper to reality. Going through the process of learning how Inventor defines these views, you will find tools that allow you to document your designs in new ways.

Sketch-Derived Views

Many of the specialized views you will be working with use sketching elements or will require you to create sketches in order to define the construction of the view. Inventor allows you to add sketch elements to the drawing view for the sake of augmenting the view. All of the sketching tools are the same as those used to define 3D models, so everything should be familiar.

One area where users can easily end up with unintended and undesirable results is by accidentally creating sketch elements that aren't associated with the drawing view. It's important to make sure that you have the view that you want to work with highlighted before starting a sketch.

Defining the Break View

The Break tool is useful for creating views in which you need to see details at either end of an object but not what's in the middle. For example, you might use it to detail a long shaft, removing most of the length from the middle. Using the Introducing Inventor template that you created in the previous chapter, you will add a view to the drawing and use the Break tool to remove part of that view. To create the break, you will define two points, the beginning and the endpoints of the portion of your part that will be removed from the view.

Figure 6.1

The Break dialog box

The Break dialog box, shown in Figure 6.1, allows you to define how the break will appear once it has been defined. Similar to the Hole dialog box, it offers the user a preview that is representative of how the view will appear.

Style The Style buttons allow you choose between the Structural style, which is a traditional border line with a single slash representing the break (as in Figure 6.1), and the Rectangular style, which creates a fractured look. The preview on the right will change to reflect your selected style.

Orientation This option establishes whether the break lines will be horizontal or vertical.

Display The slide bar under the preview changes the size of the symbol at the point of the breaks.

Gap The Gap value specifies how far apart the symbols and break lines will be held from each other.

Symbols This option box defines how many symbols will appear on the line with the Structural break style.

Propagate To Parent View This option is only available when the break is applied to a projected drawing view.

CREATING A BREAK VIEW

In this chapter's first exercise, you'll create a break view and work with its display properties.

1. Create a new drawing based on the Introducing Inventor template.

2. Create a base view of the Engine Crank Shaft.ipt file (included with the Inventor LT samples), placing the drawing view of the left side with a 5:1 scale, as shown in Figure 6.2.

3. Zoom into the view so that it fills most of the Design window.

4. Add a linear dimension that covers the length of the entire part.

5. In the Drawing Views Panel bar, select Break View.

6. Select the drawing view to tell Inventor which view you want to break.

7. Click your first point near the left side of the simple cylinder and the second near the right of the simple cylinder.

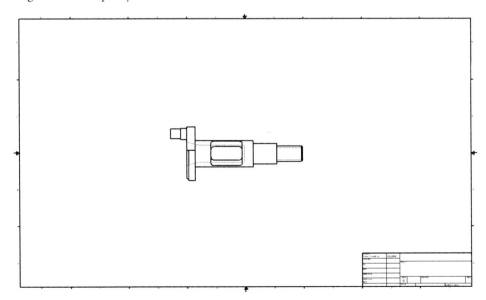

Figure 6.2

Starting a new drawing

8. The shaft will shorten but the dimension will still reflect the original length. A break symbol will appear in the dimension line to show that it is a true length dimension. The completed view should look like Figure 6.3.

Figure 6.3

A broken drawing view

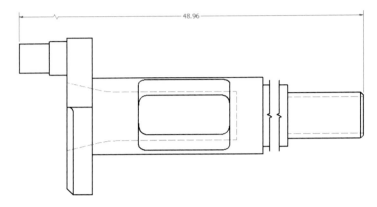

9. Use the Zoom All tool to see the entire page.

10. Create an isometric projected view in the upper-right corner of the page.

11. After the isometric view is placed, edit the view to bring up the Drawing View dialog box.

12. Switch to the Display Options tab.

The Display Options tab allows you to control special features and edges in the view. In earlier examples you saw how certain characteristics of the parent view define the child view. The Cut Inheritance group allows child views of break, break out, and slice views to be projected from those views while being intact views.

13. Deselect the Break checkbox in the Cut Inheritance group, as shown in Figure 6.4.

14. Close the dialog box and note that the isometric view is now a full view, as shown in Figure 6.5.

Figure 6.4

Removing break inheritance from the isometric view

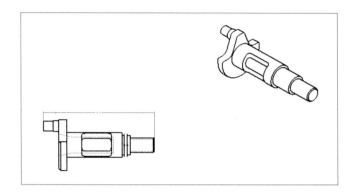

Figure 6.5

The isometric view no longer reflects the view break.

The Slice View

Slice is an interesting view option. It is similar to the section view in that it only displays the geometry that is internal to the part. The slice view is a great way to define a revolved section view.

There are two ways to define a slice. The first is a checkbox in the Section View dialog box that lets you define the geometry to use for the slice in the same way as a section view.

The other way is to use a sketch in the drawing view to define what geometry will be used. This sketch can even pass back and forth through the part or assembly at several points. The other unique feature of this technique is that it is used to modify an existing view. The following steps demonstrate this technique:

1. Create another isometric view in the upper left and suppress the cut inheritance of the break view.

2. To create a sketch in your base view, be sure to click in the area of the view. Then click the Sketch button to start a sketch in the view.

3. Once the sketch tools appear, create a series of vertical lines through the shaft, as shown in Figure 6.6.

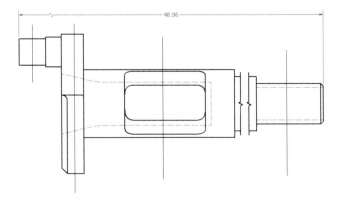

Figure 6.6

Placing lines in the view sketch

4. Using the Project Geometry tool, select the vertical line on the far left of the view so you can dimension to it. After selecting the line, right-click and select Done to complete the projection.

5. Dimension the lines as shown in Figure 6.7.

Figure 6.7

**Dimensioning the
view sketch**

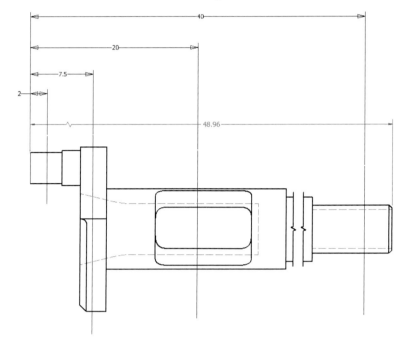

It is not necessary to constrain or dimension the position of the lines in order to use them for a slice, but you can do so if you want to position them relative to the part geometry.

6. Click the Return button to exit the sketch and view the whole drawing. The dimensions will disappear because dimensions created in a view sketch are not visible in the drawing by default.

7. Select the left isometric view and choose the Slice tool.

8. Select one of the lines that you drew in the base view to complete the Slice dialog box requirements and click OK.

The drawing view will be converted to a series of sections of zero-thickness spaces based on the lines that you put into the sketch, as shown in Figure 6.8. One use that I've found for a slice is to place what used to be called a rotated section in the middle of the part. The advantage of the dimensioned sketch is that you can go into the sketch and change the dimensions to move the slice locations.

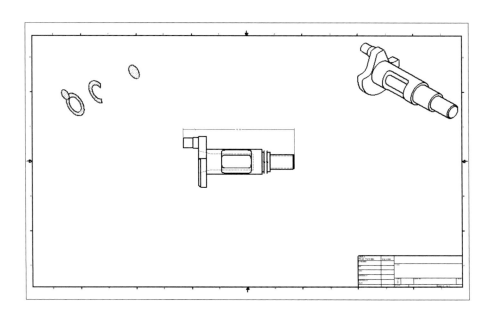

Figure 6.8

Part slices displayed in an isometric view

View Sketching

Beyond defining the locations for a slice view, there are a lot of other uses for sketching in the drawing view. Many users need to define the location of labels or special markings. You can also choose whether sketch elements will eventually appear in the drawing view.

In this exercise we will add geometry to a view and define how it will appear in the drawing view.

1. Create a projected view to the left of the base view.

2. Zoom in on the new view (Figure 6.9).

3. Begin a sketch in the projected view.

4. Draw a rectangle in the view, as shown in Figure 6.10.

5. Project one of the circular edges into the sketch.

6. Draw a line from the midpoint of the top of the rectangle to the center of the projected circle and apply a perpendicular constraint between the rectangle and the line.

7. Dimension the line and the rectangle as shown in Figure 6.11.

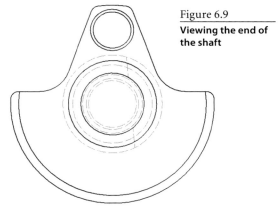

Figure 6.9

Viewing the end of the shaft

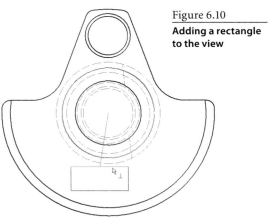

Figure 6.10

Adding a rectangle to the view

Figure 6.11

**Using dimensions to
size the rectangle**

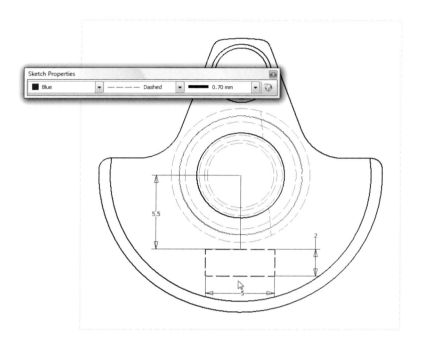

8. You can also change the appearance of the rectangle using the Sketch Properties toolbar, also shown in Figure 6.11. To open this toolbar, select View → Toolbar → Sketch Properties.

9. Select the rectangle's geometry and change its color, linetype, and line weight.

   As a final step you want to be sure that the vertical line that is centering the rectangle does not appear in the drawing view. To do this, you can apply an override to the line. In the upper right is an icon for defining geometry as Sketch Only.

10. Select the vertical line and click the Sketch Only button on the Inventor Standard toolbar.

11. Finish the sketch and check the result in the drawing view.

12. Close the Sketch Properties toolbar.

13. Drag the drawing view to a new location to make sure that the geometry follows the drawing view. If the geometry does not follow, that means the sketch was not associated with the view.

14. Choose Zoom All and save the drawing to the Drawings folder as Alternate views .dwg. Compare your result with Figure 6.12.

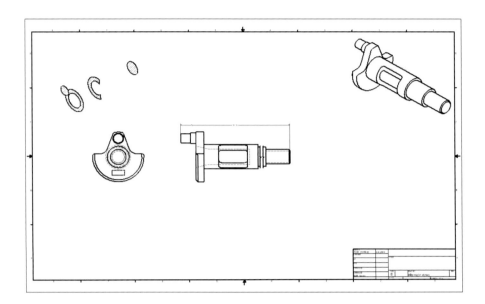

Figure 6.12
The completed drawing

The Break Out View

The break out view has a highly descriptive name, as it allows you to "break out" part of a drawing. It's particularly useful with assemblies but can also be used in the single part model.

The break out view is another view type that relies on a sketch for its definition. You can use any of the sketch tools as long as you create a closed loop for the sketch. To create visually appealing break outs, many people will use a spline to define the boundary.

The workflow is similar to the Slice tool. You create a sketch and then use that sketch to modify an existing view. However, the view that is modified can either be the view that the sketch is defined in or another view that you choose to apply the Break Out to.

The Break Out dialog box (Figure 6.13) will appear once you select the view to be edited. Let's look at each section:

Profile You will only need to select a profile if you have placed more than one closed loop into the view sketch.

Depth The Depth flyout has several options that define where the view will stop passing through the part or assembly. Some options allow you to set a distance.

> **From Point** After selecting a point in the view, you can set a depth from that point to cut. The point you select can be in the view with the cutting profile or another view. Setting a distance of zero stops the cut at the point you select. A positive number will continue the cut past the point you select; a negative number will stop the cut before it reaches the selected point.

Figure 6.13
The Break Out dialog box

To Sketch This option sets the cutting depth to match an open sketch in another drawing view.

To Hole In drafting we commonly want to give a better view of how a part is constructed down to a major feature. Often that feature is either a hole or has a hole centered in it. The To Hole option allows you to use the center axis of a hole selected in the view that is cut or from another view to set the depth.

Through Part Using this option, you select the parts in the assembly view that you want to cut completely through to expose internal parts. Since no depth is specified for the cutting, the parts that are behind the selected parts remain intact.

Display In a drawing view where the hidden lines are removed, it can be difficult to locate points or features that you might want to select. With this button, hidden lines will appear in your selection view to make selection easier.

Section All Parts Standard Content elements such as bolts or shafts are typically not sectioned. The Section All Parts checkbox will section through any part regardless of whether that part would normally be sectioned.

CREATING A BREAK OUT VIEW

In this exercise you will create a break out view in a part and in an assembly. If you're an LT user, you should still read through the assembly portion as it will use different depth options that may also apply to parts.

1. Create a new sketch in the base view that surrounds the conical end of the hole through the shaft in the `Alternate Views.dwg` drawing. See Figure 6.14 for a suggested contour.

2. When your sketch is finished, return to the regular drawing environment.

Figure 6.14

Using a spline as a cutting boundary

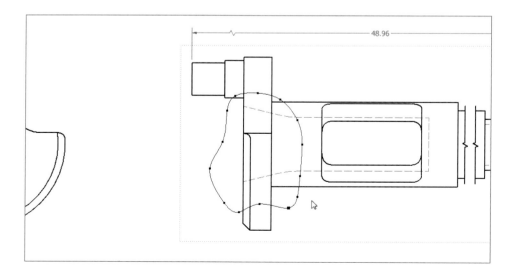

3. Click the Break Out view tool. Before the dialog box opens, you must select the view that you will modify with the break out view.

4. Select the base view.

   Because you have created only one closed profile in the sketch for the base view, you will not have to select a boundary profile. As with several other modeling functions, you would have to choose a boundary profile if you had created more than one closed profile in the sketch.

5. Leave the Depth option set to From Point and move your cursor over the far-left end of the small shaft diameter.

   When you hover the mouse over the middle, the point that appears will be the centerpoint; this shows that Inventor recognizes the line as being the edge of a circle.

6. Select that point and leave the value set to zero.

7. Click OK to execute the command. The result should be similar to that shown in Figure 6.15.

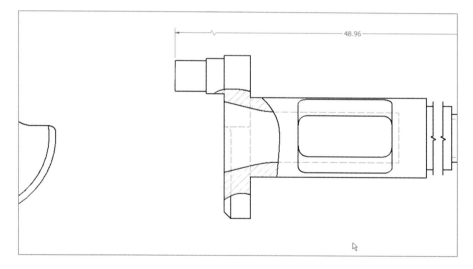

Figure 6.15

The view after creating the break out

CREATING A BREAK OUT VIEW OF AN ASSEMBLY

Now let's create a more elaborate break out in an assembly file. Please keep in mind that none of the Depth options are exclusive to the assembly drawing views.

1. Open the `Assembly Drawing.dwg` file that you created in Chapter 2.

2. Zoom in on the section view and create a spline similar to that in Figure 6.16. (It won't match exactly, because I have used the sketch properties to change the spline's color and line weight to make it easier to see.)

3. Leaving the sketch, zoom into View:1, the largest view.

4. Create a sketch using a circle like that shown in Figure 6.17.

5. Make a break out view for View:1 using the To Sketch termination, incorporating the sketch in the section view, as shown back in Figure 6.16.

The combination of the circle and spline makes a simple but dramatic break out, as you can see in Figure 6.18.

Figure 6.16

A spline placed to define cut depth

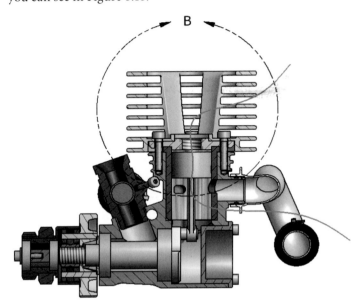

Figure 6.17

Defining the cutting boundary

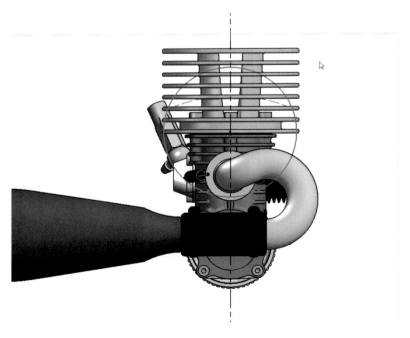

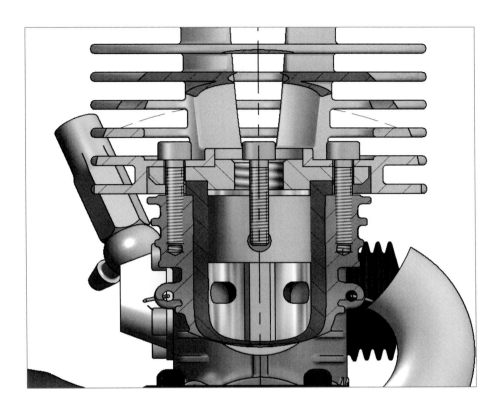

Figure 6.18

**Assembly view
with break out**

Component Overrides

The view in Figure 6.18 looks great, but because the bolts are excluded from the sectioning, a bolt is left in the view, obstructing the view of the hole for the spark plug and the piston. Another anomaly in the drawing view is the way the bolts on either side have no defined edge. With the shaded view we can see where they stop and the engine block starts, but because there is interference between the diameter of the bolts and their holes, no visible edge is created.

Inventor offers options to remedy these situations. Note that none of the changes you make in this exercise will affect that assembly. They are overrides created strictly for the sake of better documentation. First we will remove the bolt from the view.

1. Selecting the filter pull-down (to the left of the Return button) on the Inventor Standard toolbar, set your selection priority to Part Priority.

    Selection filters are a tool that can provide tremendous productivity gains, particularly when you're working in an assembly. Because you can control the types of objects that the mouse highlights as you move around, you can access the correct items more quickly. You

can also access selection filters by holding your Shift key and right-clicking to open a context menu.

With Part Priority selected, individual parts are easy to select.

2. Select the bolt in the middle of the view and turn its visibility off using the context menu. The drawing view will update as soon as you turn off the part.

The other problem with the view, the lack of defined edges, is just as easy to fix.

3. Double-click in the view to open the Drawing View dialog box.

4. Switch to the Display Options tab.

5. Select the Interference Edges checkbox and click OK to close the dialog box.

After the update is done, your view should look like Figure 6.19. These changes may seem subtle, but they make a nice drawing view even better.

Figure 6.19

The view after removing the bolt and repairing the edges

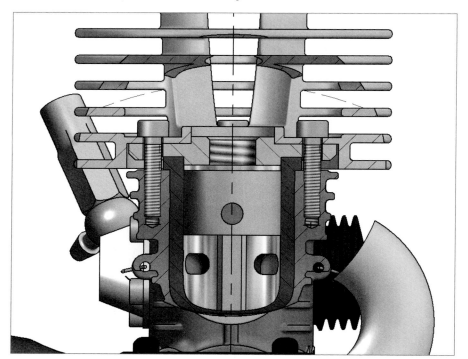

Cropped Views

In AutoCAD, viewports are commonly used to limit the scope of a drawing view when the subject is very large. Similar in concept to a detail view but without the tradition of being an established mechanical view type, these views can be bound by complex shapes—not just by rectangles or circles.

Inventor does not have the viewport feature, but you can create a cropped view in one of two ways. The easier way is to choose the Crop tool, select the view you would like to crop, and drag a rectangle around the portion that you want to remain on the drawing sheet. The other technique is like the other sketch-based views: you define the boundary as a sketch in the view that you want to crop, select the tool, and then select the sketch to use as your boundary. Let's try the second method:

1. Draw a spline similar to the one in Figure 6.20; make sure that the sketch is part of the isometric view in the drawing.

2. Using the Crop tool, select the sketch.

   The resulting view, shown in Figure 6.21, may have to be repositioned, but if you want to limit how much of an assembly or large part is represented in a drawing, this is a nice option within Inventor.

3. Save the changes that you have made to the `Assembly Drawing.dwg` and `Alternate Views.dwg` drawings.

Figure 6.20

Use a spline to define a cropped view boundary

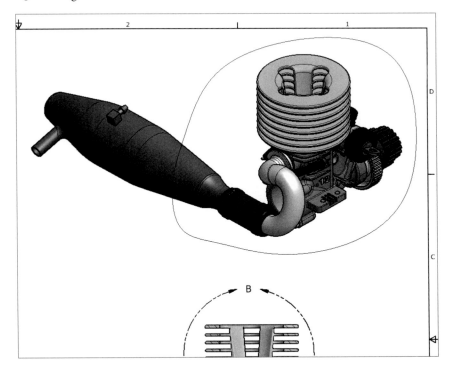

Figure 6.21

**The view after it
has been cropped**

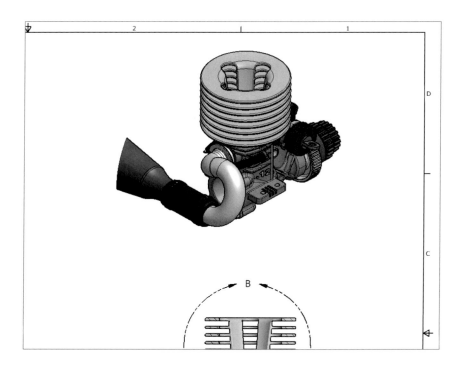

Suppressing a View

On occasion it may be necessary to remove a view from a drawing that is a parent to other views. The trouble is that if you delete the view, not all drawing views are capable of reconstructing themselves as base views.

To solve this, Inventor has the ability to suppress an existing drawing view regardless of whether it is a parent to another view. To demonstrate we will do a very quick exercise.

1. Switch to `Alternate Views.dwg`, which has three views built off the base view.

2. Right-click on the base view on the sheet or in the Browser and select Suppress.

3. Undo the change after verifying that there were no ill effects on the drawing.

Inventor's view creation and modification tools offer a number of advantages in documenting your designs clearly. Experiment with some of them; I think you'll find the people who use your drawings will be impressed.

Expanded Dimensioning Options

In Chapter 2 the focus was to show you the dimensioning tools that are most commonly used. In this chapter we've already extended the types of views you can create, and now it's time to explore other dimensioning and annotation techniques.

Dimension Properties and Annotation

Like the additional view types you've seen in this chapter, Inventor's additional annotation types range from tools that can help you better describe your design to tools that are absolutely critical for documenting certain types of designs completely.

To start out, though, let's take a moment to explore some tools that don't create new dimensions but enhance the dimensions that you've already placed.

Dimension Properties

By using styles and standards, as discussed in Chapter 5, you should be able to place most of the dimensions on your drawing views without having to modify them. However, it's very common for a single drawing view to have dimensions that call out geometry that must be treated differently. For the basics, like a variation in required precision, you can simply change the dimension style used on an individual dimension and on a selection set. In Chapter 2 you even took the properties of a modified dimension and replicated them onto another dimension.

In this exercise we will go beyond precision considerations and focus on adding annotation and tolerancing.

1. Open the `Carb Intake plate.dwg` drawing.
2. Zoom in on the base view in the center of the drawing.
3. Double-click on the text in the 11.9 dimension on the right.
4. In the Edit Dimension dialog box, switch to the Precision And Tolerance tab.
5. From the Tolerance Method list, select Limits - Stacked. As soon as you select one of the methods from the list, the dimension will preview its appearance.
6. Before entering limit values, change the Precision settings of Primary Unit and Primary Tolerance on the right side of the dialog box to three decimal places. Again the dimension on the sheet will preview its new appearance.
7. Set the Upper limit to 11.900 and the Lower limit to 11.870, and click OK.
8. Your view should now look like Figure 6.22.

    If you create a tabulated or "family" part, you may not want a numerical dimension in your view; instead, you want a letter to reference a column in a table.
9. Double-click to edit the 11.9 dimension on the left side of the part. This will open the dialog box for making modifications to the dimension.
10. Select the Text tab.
11. Select the Hide Dimension Value checkbox. This removes the <<>> symbol, which represents the real dimension value.
12. Type a capital **A** in the text area and click OK to close the dialog box. The drawing should now look like Figure 6.23.

Figure 6.22

**Adding a Limits
tolerance**

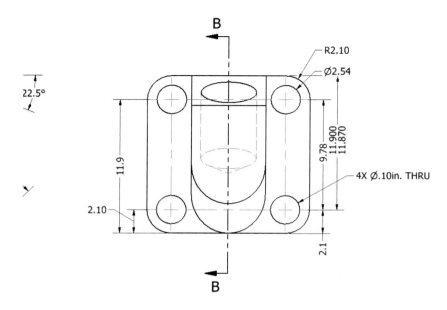

Figure 6.23

**Substituting the
dimension value**

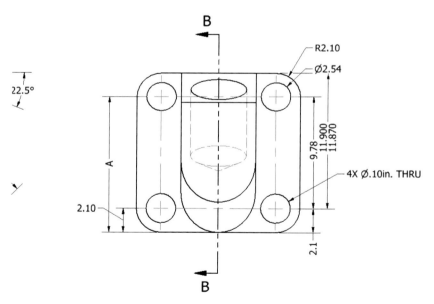

13. Edit the 2.10 radius dimension.

14. In the Text tab, add **TYP** after the dimension value and click OK.

15. Apply a dimension to for the overall height of the part and place the dimension on
the left side of the part.

16. Close the General Dimension tool.

17. Edit the new dimension. Place your cursor in front of the dimension value on the Text tab and from the pull-down on the right side select the square symbol.

With the changes you have made, your view should look like Figure 6.24. There are additional options for changing or even eliminating the arrowhead styles on your dimensions; I encourage you to explore those on your own.

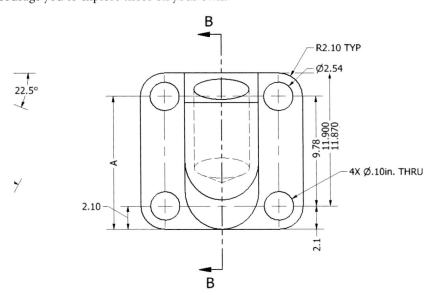

Figure 6.24

Adding a note to a dimension value

The Text Tool

The ability to add notes to a drawing and format them is essential. The Text tool in Inventor is straightforward but it's also feature rich. Not only can you place text on the drawings, but you can also insert parameter values into text entries. If the dialog box in Figure 6.25 looks familiar, it is because it is the same dialog box that you used to add the Mass value to the title block in Chapter 5.

Figure 6.25

The Format Text dialog box

Adding text is easy, but it is important to be comfortable with the process.

1. Zoom to the empty part of the page just above the title block.

2. Select the Text tool.

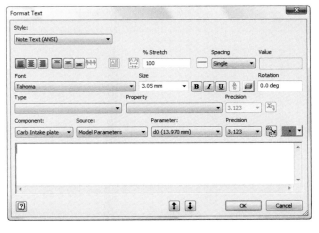

3. Before you can enter text, you have to define where you will place it. Click on the sheet to begin creating a rectangle that will establish the boundary for the text.

4. Continue to hold the mouse button and drag the boundary. When you release the button, the dialog box will appear.

5. Enter any text or properties that you like.

Leader Text

The Leader Text tool will create a leader with any combination of text or property information:

1. Change your view to focus on the side view, View:3.

2. Select a top edge and position a leader above the view.

3. Right-click and choose Create to display the Leader Text dialog box.

    This dialog box is the basic Inventor Text tool and includes tools for inserting model or file properties (like the Mass property you placed into the title block in Chapter 5).

4. Experiment with input of your choice; Figure 6.26 shows one result.

Figure 6.26

The leader placed on the view

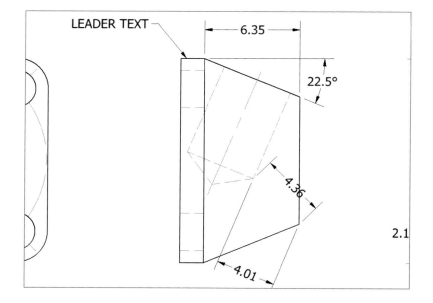

Surface Texture Callouts

The process of placing a surface texture callout is similar to placing a leader, but instead of text you place standard surface texture symbols. In this exercise we will just scratch the surface. Other options that will not be covered include the production method for the surface, surface type, and callouts that define the roughness value.

1. Continue to use the same view as the Leader Text tool.
2. In the Drawing Annotation panel, select the Surface Texture Symbol tool.
3. Click on the left edge, which represents the bottom face of the part.
4. Drag your mouse away from the face, and the symbol will be tied to the leader.
5. Click the placement of the symbol, right-click, and select Continue.
6. The Surface Texture dialog box will appear, allowing you to specify the values of your callout. (You can close the dialog box to use the default finish.)
7. Apply any options that you would like and close the dialog box. Figure 6.27 shows one result.

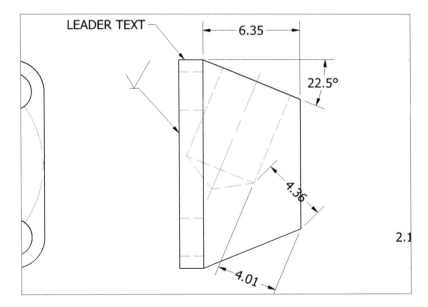

Figure 6.27

The symbol can be placed on the model edge or on a leader.

Revision Table and Tag

Most companies have developed symbols that can be added to drawings to track revisions and build tables. Inventor has a revision tag you can place on the drawing where changes have been made as well as a revision table that will add rows to itself when revisions are made. You can modify the format of the revision table within your standard to refine its appearance and match any existing format.

Let's do a quick exercise to give you an introduction.

1. Select the Revision Table tool from the Drawing Annotation panel.

2. The indexing can be set to be automatic, but in this case set the Start Value to 4 just to prove a point.

3. Place the table near the upper right of the drawing sheet.

4. Click and drag the symbol to the upper right; it will snap to fit into the corner.

5. In the Panel bar use the Revision Table flyout menu to select the Revision Tag tool.

6. To place a symbol near the geometry, click to place the symbol, right-click, and select Continue. Note that the symbol contains the number of the current revision (see Figure 6.28).

7. Close the tool.

8. Double-click on the revision table to edit it, displaying the window shown in Figure 6.29.

Figure 6.28

A revision table placed in the drawing

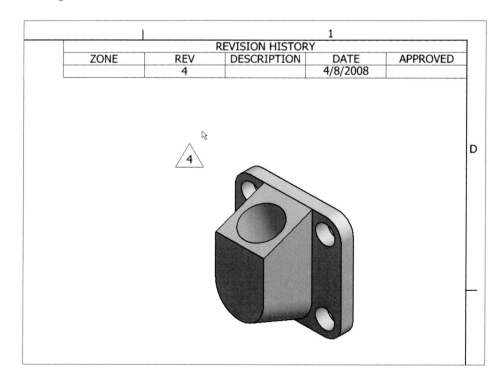

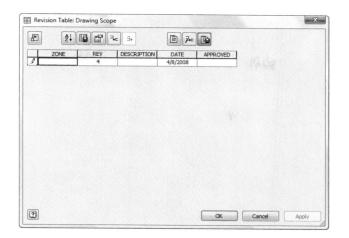

Figure 6.29

Double-clicking on a revision table displays an editing dialog box.

9. Click the Add Revision Row(s) button to add a row and close the dialog box.

10. Add text to the description of one of the revision tables.

11. Add a revision tag to the isometric view on a leader. See Figure 6.30 for an example.

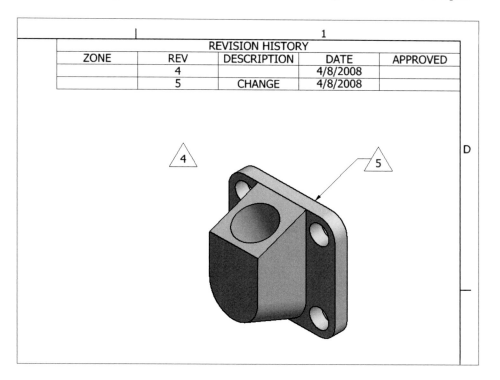

Figure 6.30

Revision tags are associated with the table.

Part Dimensions

Some dimensions and annotation tools are specific to assemblies. The next couple of tools lend themselves to part models. They are more specialized than the General Dimension tools but they work in much the same way.

Ordinate Dimension Set

Depending on the parts you make, you may find ordinate dimensions even more useful than baseline or chain dimensions. Ordinate dimensions are commonly used for machined parts with a large number of features, where having all of the dimension and extension lines would make the view difficult to read. Instead, a single extension line runs between the feature and the dimension that defines its distance from a datum or 0 point.

The Ordinate Dimension Set tool works much like the Baseline Dimension set. Also, like the Baseline Dimension set there is also an Ordinate Dimension tool that separates the dimensions from one another once they are placed.

This exercise doesn't try to completely detail the view. With this and other exercises, please feel free to explore the options once you are comfortable with the basics.

1. Add a sheet to the drawing file.

2. Open the `Vertical Plate.ipt` file, located in the Parts\Plate folder in Inventor Suite (or the Samples folder in LT), and place a Front view with a scale of .8.

3. Place Automated Centerlines with the Hole and Cylindrical Features options selected (see Figure 6.31).

4. Begin the Ordinate Dimension Set tool by selecting it in the Drawing Annotation panel or by pressing the O key.

    The first geometry that you select will be considered your datum point or edge. All other dimensions will be defined by their distance from that point or edge.

5. Start selecting geometry, beginning with the edge in the lower-left corner. Continue selecting hole centerlines and vertical geometry.

6. Place the dimensions below the part, as shown in Figure 6.32. Remember to use Create to place the dimensions.

Most of the options that are available for the Baseline Dimension Set are also available for ordinate dimensions. The ability to reset the origin, rearrange the dimensions, and change the properties as a group can be helpful.

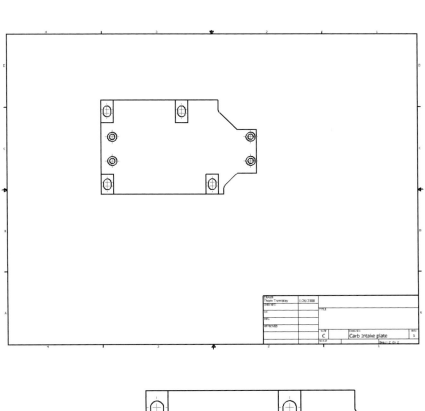

Figure 6.31

Adding centerlines

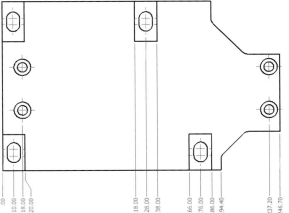

Figure 6.32

Ordinate dimensions added to the vertical plate drawing

Hole Tables

There are three types of Hole table: Selection, View, and Selected Feature. The difference between them boils down to the technique that you use to select the holes you want to document. You can add more than one Hole table if you want to separate them based on size or the function of the hole.

All three types can be found under the same pull-down list in the Panel bar.

Hole Table - Selection The Selection option asks you to click the individual holes that you want to include in the table. You can select them one by one, or use a selection window after selecting the view and the origin for the table.

Hole Table - View The View option only needs you to select what view the holes lie in and then to place the origin; it will include all the holes in that view.

Hole Table - Selected Feature Hole Table - Selected Feature asks you to select a hole in a view and it will select only holes of that size and type; this option makes it easier to tabulate hole types individually.

CREATING A HOLE TABLE

In this exercise, you'll see how simple it is to add a Hole table to our drawing:

1. Select the Hole Table - View tool.
2. Select the drawing view in Sheet:2.
3. Place the origin for the measurement of the Hole table in the lower-left corner.
4. As soon as you select an origin, the outline of the table should appear. Place the table near the drawing view (see Figure 6.33).

Figure 6.33

Adding the Hole table

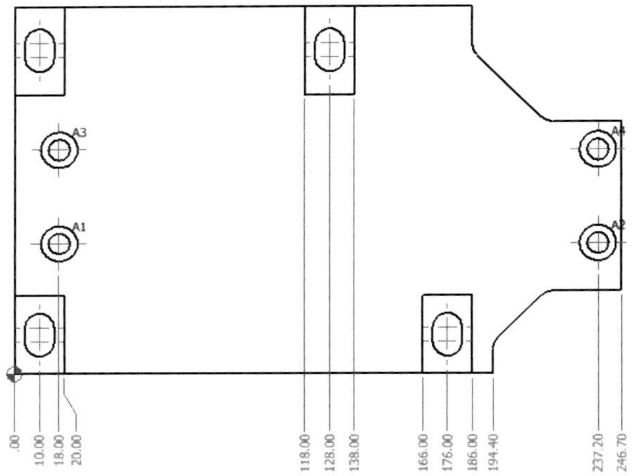

HOLE TABLE			
HOLE	XDIM	YDIM	DESCRIPTION
A1	18.00	54.55	Ø8.80 THRU ⊔ Ø15.00 ▼ 9.00
A2	237.20	54.55	Ø8.80 THRU ⊔ Ø15.00 ▼ 9.00
A3	18.00	93.68	Ø8.80 THRU ⊔ Ø15.00 ▼ 9.00
A4	237.20	93.68	Ø8.80 THRU ⊔ Ø15.00 ▼ 9.00

MODIFYING A HOLE TABLE

Hole Tables, like nearly every type of documentation, are governed by a style within the standard. When you edit the Hole table, you directly access the Options tab of the style. There are some particularly interesting items on the Options tab (see Figure 6.34):

Row Merge Options These options regulate whether or not each hole will be listed in an individual row. With the merge option set to None, each hole will have its own row even if it is the same size as several other holes.

With the Rollup option selected, the table will show only the size of all the holes and label the like holes the same. Combine Notes will list the rows for the individual holes and label the holes individually but group the description for like holes.

View Filters The filters under Included Features allow you to filter out what type of features will automatically be selected. These options include Hole features, Circular Cuts (which allows extruded circles to be detected as a hole), Center marks, and Sheet Metal punch centers.

Included Hole types allow you to exclude types of holes:

Figure 6.34

Options for modifying the Hole table

1. Right-click on the table and select Edit Hole Table.

2. Set the Row Merge Options to Combine Notes.

3. When you close the dialog box, the descriptions will be grouped together, as shown in Figure 6.35.

4. As a final step, try moving one of the hole callouts on the right from their original positions. You can move them and maintain proximity to the hole, or when you move them away from the hole, a leader will appear.

There are other options available to help you document your designs. A complete toolset for geometric dimensioning is also built into the software. You will also find Chamfer notes and Datum targets. Because Inventor's tools work so consistently, with what you've already learned you should find it easy to grasp the basics of any of these tools.

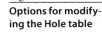

Figure 6.35

**The updated
Hole table with
merged notes**

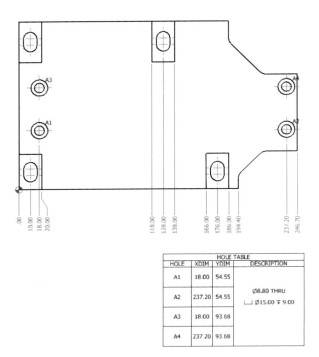

HOLE TABLE			
HOLE	XDIM	YDIM	DESCRIPTION
A1	18.00	54.55	Ø8.80 THRU ⌴ Ø15.00 ⤓ 9.00
A2	237.20	54.55	
A3	18.00	93.68	
A4	237.20	93.68	

Assembly-Oriented Dimensions

Assembly detailing requires additional tools. These types of details do not describe the size or shape of things; they document what is included in the assembly or how that assembly is fused together. For a manufacturer, the parts list is a necessity.

Parts List

Creating a parts list with AutoCAD or most other systems involves a lot of typing and human interaction. With Inventor, the parts list is a representation of the bill of materials database that resides in the assembly file. At the end of this chapter, you'll learn how to edit entries in this database, which is automatically generated as you add parts to the assembly.

Now let's do a quick exercise to show you how easy it is to place a parts list in the drawing.

1. Open Assembly Drawing.dwg and activate Sheet 2.

2. Select the Parts List tool in the Drawing Annotation panel.

3. Select the exploded drawing view and click OK to place the parts list.

4. Place the parts list in the upper right of your drawing.

5. Change the drawing view scale to .8 and relocate the view to an open part of the sheet. Figure 6.36 shows the result.

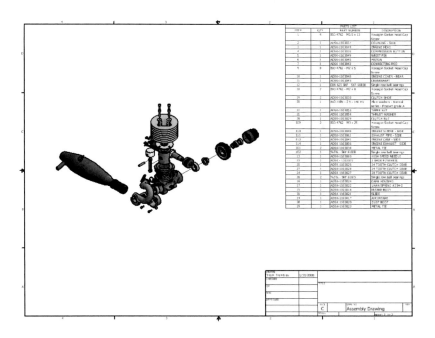

Figure 6.36

Placing a parts list on the drawing

Balloon/Auto Balloon

Having a list of the parts that are included in the assembly is important, but it is also important for the person using the drawings to understand what the parts look like. The Balloon tool creates an annotation that maps parts in the drawing to their descriptions in the parts list. The appearance of this annotation is governed by a style, and like many other things, it has options that can be set to suit your needs.

You can place balloons either individually or as a group. You will do both in this exercise.

1. Zoom in on the Tuned Pipe part on the left side of the view.

2. Select the Balloon tool (not the Auto Balloon) in the Drawing Annotation panel or press the B key.

3. Place the balloon on the sheet. Clicking the first time can place the balloon, or you can continue to click to build a complex leader.

4. You have to tell the tool that you are done to leave the tool by using the right-click menu and selecting Done.

The number that is placed in the balloon is coordinated with the number in the parts list. Both are derived from the bill of materials in the assembly. Keep that in mind.

5. Zoom back so you can see the entire exploded view.

    After selecting a view that you want to base your balloon(s) in, you have to select the components that you want to balloon. You can select components individually, or you can select them with a window. There are different Bill Of Material settings that you can use to alter how parts are selected and displayed as part of the balloons.

    In this portion of the exercise you will use the Auto Balloon tool, but we won't completely explore it.

6. Select the Auto Balloon tool (Figure 6.37). If necessary, select the exploded view.

Figure 6.37

The Auto Balloon dialog box

7. The Add Or Remove Components option will become available to let you select the components and drag a window around the entire view. With the Ignore Multiple Instances options selected, the Tuned Pipe will not highlight since it has already been ballooned, but all other parts visible in the view will.

8. Under Placement, click the Select Placement button. A preview will appear on the screen. Change the Placement options to Around and notice the change in the preview.

9. With the preview active, move your cursor around.

10. Change the Offset Spacing value to 5.

11. Click to place the balloons on the screen.

12. Zoom into the upper-right portion of the view.

    Note that the automatic placement may not be optimal (see Figure 6.38).

13. Click the balloon with the number 26. Click on the green dot in the center of the balloon and drag it to another location.

14. Now click on the tip of the arrow attached to the part that is called out as item 26.

15. Drag that arrow to the clutch housing, which is the gray part labeled 27 in the view.

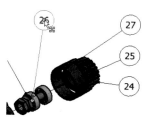

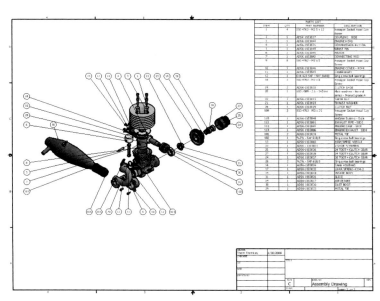

Figure 6.38

**Balloons placed
automatically**

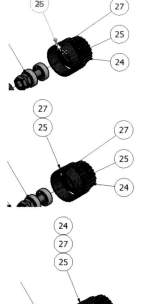

16. When the part highlights, move the balloon over the edge of the part and release.

17. Now right-click on the balloon that you just relocated and select the Attach Balloon option.

18. Inventor will then go into a selection mode, which will allow you to select parts from the drawing view. Select the large gear on the clutch housing.

19. Inventor will add the 27 balloon to the 25 balloon.

20. Move your cursor around to see alternate placements.

21. Click the screen when the 27 balloon appears above 25.

22. Using the Attach Balloon tool, select the small gear.

23. The 24 balloon will position itself inline.

24. Delete the three original balloons for items 24 and 27 on the right.

Capabilities like this make it much easier to help your drawings look great. Many Inventor users don't use these capabilities because they just do not expect it to be so easy.

Bill of Materials

It is important that you understand that the bill of materials is not the same thing as a parts list.

The bill of materials should be thought of as the master document that records what parts are in the assembly. Moreover, it can be used to alter the structure of the assembly without having to reorder how the assembly was built. If you edit the bill of materials from the drawing, you are actually changing the assembly.

A parts list is a representation of all or part of the bill of materials on a drawing. Its appearance can be edited above and beyond the changes to the bill of materials, but it is critical that the bill of materials truly reflect the state of the assembly.

1. Right-click on the parts list and select Bill Of Materials.

2. When the dialog box appears, select the Structured tab.

3. Find the row displaying Item 27, as shown in Figure 6.39.

4. Click on the value of Item 27, and it will highlight for editing.

5. Change the value to 1001 and click Done when you have finished. Figure 6.40 shows the result.

Figure 6.39

The Bill Of Materials dialog box

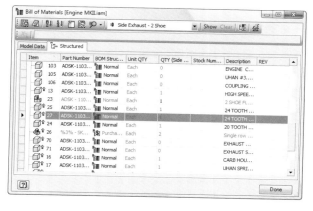

Figure 6.40

Changes to the bill of materials are reflected in balloons and the parts list.

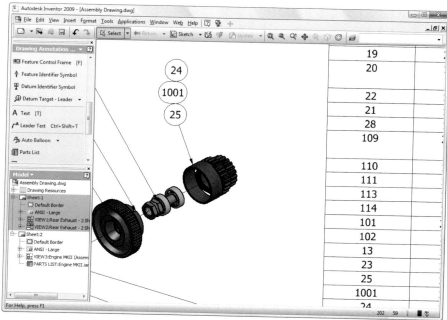

Summary

As I said at the beginning of this book, the best reason to use 3D is 2D. Creating 2D drawings is easy, and properly annotating those drawings should be easy too. Who would have guessed that making 2D drawings just might end up being fun?

Now let's move on and see what else we can do with part modeling.

CHAPTER 7

Getting in Shape:
Advanced Part Modeling

In Chapter 3 you used the most common tools to create parts. In this chapter you'll use additional Inventor features for working with parts, and you'll learn some new sketching techniques to develop more complex parts.

The ways in which you can create parts with Inventor are almost as varied as the different parts you might want to create in various disciplines. There will be times in your work when you'll recognize that there is more than one technique for building a part. In such cases, I recommend going back to the basics and defining as much of the part as possible with the fewest features. With that said, there are times when an extrusion or revolution will not quite cut it and the first feature you create will only set the stage for the prominent feature rather than building it. This chapter shows you more than a dozen of Inventor's advanced part modeling tools, along with iParts, Inventor's tool for creating families of parts.

- **Working with 3D Grips**

- **Advanced Part Modeling**

- **Additional Sketch Geometry**

- **Hybrid Modeling Using Surfaces**

- **iParts: Families of Parts**

A Feature-Rich Application

Extrusions and revolved features will continue to be the most common starting points for your parts, but in this chapter you'll see that lofts can also be used as a sketched base feature. In the following exercises, you'll explore a number of new tools, creating both sketched and placed features, that make Inventor such a strong modeling application.

These exercises will blend many features together; occasionally you'll use a tool in an unexpected way and hopefully find a technique that will help you with your day-to-day work. You'll even explore making more than one version of a part without having to manage multiple files by yourself.

Beginning a New Part

In this exercise, we'll use a number of features to build a trailer hitch ball. Be sure to save your work on this part as it will be used in another exercise.

1. Close any open files and set the project file to `Introducing Inventor`.

2. Start a new part using the `Standard (in).ipt` file on the English tab of the New dialog box.

3. Project the Origin Center Point into the new sketch.

4. Draw a circle centered on that point and give it a diameter of 2 inches.

5. Extrude the circle to create a cylinder 0.25 inches tall.

6. Use the Look At viewing tool and select the XZ plane.

7. Right-click on the ViewCube, which should be showing the Top view as upside-down, and set this current view to be the Front view. (If it doesn't appear upside-down, use the view rotation arrows near the ViewCube to rotate the view on the screen.)

8. Create a new sketch on the XZ plane.

9. Using the Line tool, draw a vertical line (from bottom to top) roughly 2 inches long.

10. Without ending the Line command, position your cursor over the last point that you placed.

11. When a gray dot appears, click and drag your cursor down and to the right. An arc will follow your cursor, as shown in Figure 7.1.

12. Move your cursor to the starting point of the vertical line and release your mouse button when the endpoint constraint glyph appears.

    Many sketches combine arc and lines. The ability to transition from drawing a line to an arc without having to slow down your thought process can be very valuable.

13. Constrain the semicircle to be centered on the part's Z axis. (You'll need to project either the origin center or the Z axis to the sketch to do this.)

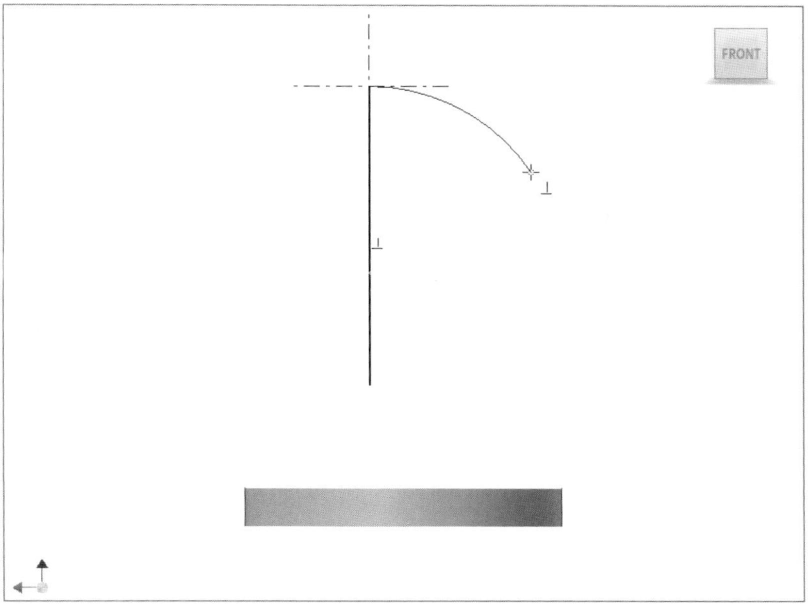

Figure 7.1

**Creating an arc
with the Line tool**

14. Locate the center 2 inches above the bottom of the base.

15. Right-click when placing a dimension and choose the option to place a diameter dimension on the arc of 1 ⅞ inches, as shown in Figure 7.2, instead of the default radial dimension.

Figure 7.2

**Locating the
hitch ball**

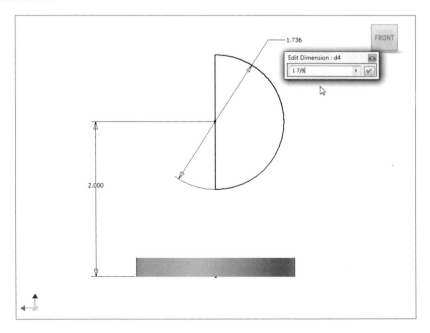

16. Revolve the semicircle into a sphere.

By adding the sphere with no connection to the cylinder, you have created a disjointed feature. This is possible in most design software systems now, but for a long time Inventor was fairly unique in this capability.

17. Create a new sketch on the bottom of the cylinder (opposite the sphere).

18. Draw a 1-inch circle centered on the face.

19. Extrude the 1-inch circle to a height of 2 inches.

20. Save your work as the `Hitch Ball.ipt` file in the Parts folder.

The Thread Tool

Much to the disappointment of the adhesives people, threaded fasteners are still quite popular. Inventor's library of fasteners and threaded holes does not cover everything, though; there are many parts that you need to add external thread to.

As I'm sure you expect by now, the Thread tool works like other placed features; you select geometry and select options in its dialog box. The Thread dialog box has two tabs: Location and Specification.

The Location Tab

In the Location tab, you control the placement of the thread by selecting what Face setting to apply the thread to, whether or not it will be displayed on the model, and the Thread Length value.

When you select the Face setting, you should select the edge that you want the thread to start at. With the Display in Model checkbox selected, a bitmap will display an approximation of the thread on the model. This saves a lot of system resources compared to cutting physical threads. In practice, unless you are putting something into orbit there is little, if any, benefit to putting real threads on a part. The tool previews the thread in the 3D model, but it also calculates the major and minor diameters of the threads in the drawing views.

Thread Length

You can be quite creative when placing threads on a part. The Thread Length group of options gives you complete control:

Full Length This checkbox switches from simply running threads over the complete length to accessing the detailed options.

Offset If you want to hold the thread off from the edge of the part, you can establish the distance with the Offset value.

Length This controls the length of the threaded portion. Like similar values in other dialog boxes, it can also be controlled in the Parameters dialog box.

The Specification Tab

Since there are many standards and classes of threads that can be applied to the same-sized shaft or shank, it is important to have the maximum control over the thread specification.

Thread Type If you have all of the Content Center standards loaded, you'll have 21 different Thread classes available to you—an amazing range.

Size If you want to specify a thread to fit on a slightly larger shaft, you can do so by selecting the size of the major diameter from this flyout. Even if you do that, I still recommend modeling the reduced portion for a better appearance in the drawing.

Designation All of the various thread counts in a given style will be found under this flyout.

Class This flyout allows you to select the quality and fit specification that accompanies the thread designation. Not all classes are available with various designations, as dictated by the standard chosen with the Thread Type.

Right/Left Hand These radio buttons control the direction of the thread.

Adding Detail

In this stage of the exercise, you'll try out the Thread tool by adding a threaded portion to the shaft and completing the design.

1. Open the Thread tool.

2. Start the thread by selecting the far end of the last extrusion.

3. When you select the edge of the cylinder, the thread preview will appear on the face.

4. Deselect the Full Length option.

5. Set the Length to 1.5 inches as shown in Figure 7.3.

6. Review the Specification tab, but do not change the options.

Figure 7.3

**Placing a thread
on the shank**

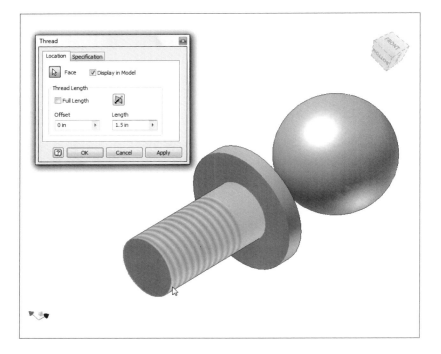

7. Finish placing the thread on the model.

8. Add a 0.05 in chamfer to the end of the shaft where you started the thread.

9. Set your view to the Home view.

10. Save your work.

By selecting a face of a sketched feature and clicking the dot or "handle," you'll access a special editing capability for sketched features in Inventor called *3D grips*.

As you can see in Figure 7.4, the feature will switch to wireframe display; control grip points will appear along with any parametric dimensions that were included in the sketch.

When you hover over the grips that appear on the wireframe, they will display differently based on the geometry they represent, but the capabilities are the same. Hovering over a center or a corner will show a circle with an axis running through it. These grips can be repositioned. Hovering over a grip on a face center or cylindrical quadrant will display an arrow that can be used to drag the face to a different size.

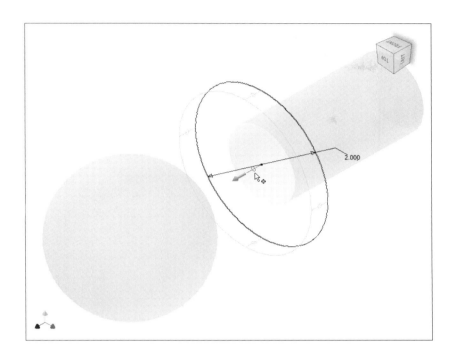

Figure 7.4

Accessing 3D grips

Controlling 3D Grips

While a 3D grip is being edited, you can access different options by right-clicking to display this menu (or one that is similar):

You'll also have to right-click after making a change to keep the change by selecting Done.

Done This option must be used to accept any change made in the 3D grips and then update the model.

Commit And Move This additional option allows you to accept the current size or edits to the size, but then allows you to reposition the feature and even move it to another face on the part, including a curved face.

Edit Extent To modify the overall value for the feature, you use this option.

Edit Offset This option allows you to change the value from its current setting. Entering a negative value will also work to decrease a size.

3D Grip Editing

Let's modify the cylinder using 3D grips to make it larger:

1. Select the top face of the first extruded cylinder.

2. Click the green dot or right-click and choose 3D Grips.

In the center of the cylinder is a circle with an axis running through it. On sketches with sharp corners or tangencies, this grip will appear on the corners. Clicking and dragging on this type of grip will allow you to drag the shape and in most cases the size of the geometry. The Part tab of the Application Options has settings that control whether parametric dimensions can be modified by dragging the grip.

On the top face of the cylinder an arrow is visible that indicates the direction of the extrusion from the sketch. Click and drag it to change the height of the extrusion; a tooltip will show the new value. If you move near the quadrants of the cylindrical face, similar arrows will appear, allowing you to drag the size of the radius of the cylinder as well.

3. Right-click the arrow controlling the extrusion height and use Edit Extent to set the value to 0.3 in.

4. Click and drag one of the arrows on the cylindrical face until the diameter reads 2.500 in, as shown in Figure 7.5.

5. Right-click and select Done to update the model.

6. Open the Fillet tool and choose the Face Fillet option.

7. For the first face, select the sphere.

8. For the second face, select the cylindrical face used for the 3D grips.

Figure 7.5

Dragging a new diameter

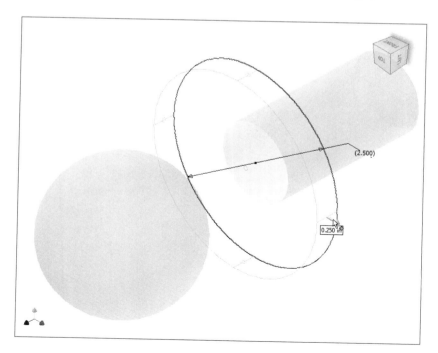

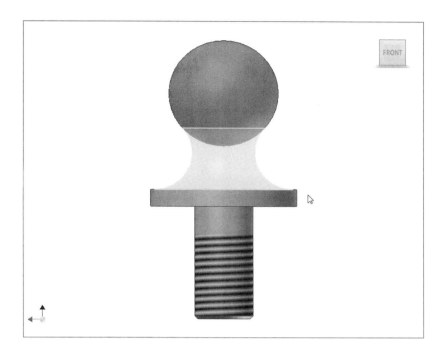

Figure 7.6

Face fillet preview

9. Set your radius to 0.65 and change your view to the Front view to see the preview, as shown in Figure 7.6.

10. Accept the fillet.

Inventor is able to close the gap between the faces. To be honest, this example presented one of the most difficult conditions for this feature to work in, because there is no contact between any portion of the faces that the fillet is being applied to.

If you experiment with different radius values, you'll see that there is a narrow window for the radius.

Sketch Constraints with Circles

In the next stage of the exercise, you'll create wrench flats for holding our hitch ball while tightening it. To do that, you'll use a sketching constraint technique that I like because it limits the number of dimensions needed to create the needed relationship.

1. In the Browser, move the new fillet above Extrusion2.

2. Move the End of Part marker above Extrusion2.

3. Set your view so that you can see the bottom.

4. Create a sketch on the bottom face of the first extrusion.

5. Draw two vertical lines that terminate on the circular edge.

6. Apply an Equal constraint between the two lines. This will automatically create symmetry for centering the next feature on the circle.

7. Place a dimension of 2.2 inches between the two lines.

8. Cut the outer profiles with a To Next termination so the cut does not continue through the sphere (Figure 7.7).

9. Restore the features suppressed below the End of Part marker.

10. Save the part.

As you've just seen, using sketch constraints instead of dimensions can reduce the chances of accidentally changing the geometry in a way that you don't want.

Figure 7.7

Cutting the wrench flats

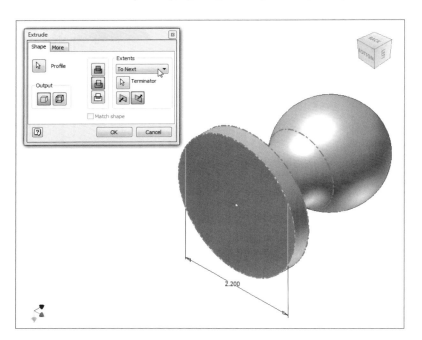

The Split Tool

Many tools in Inventor work differently depending on the options you choose, but the Split tool can work like two different tools depending on the options that you select. It can either remove a portion of the target part or simply split its geometry.

Either way, you can use a sketch or a work plane to split a part or faces of a part by first selecting the tool that you want to cut with and then choosing what elements of the part it will pass through to divide.

Method

Choosing the split method is the big difference in how the tool behaves.

Split Part This option will remove a portion of the target part. With this option, you can also set the direction to choose which portion will be removed.

Split Face This option doesn't remove any geometry from the part, but it will break faces based on the geometry of the tool.

Faces

You can also select whether all or only specific faces will be affected by the tool.

All Any face that the tool passes through will be divided along the tool's geometry.

Select This allows you to select the faces to split. If a face (such as a cylinder) can be passed through more than once, the face will be split more than once.

Squaring the Top of the Part

There are a few ways to put a flat top on the ball; for this part, you'll use the Split tool.

1. Position your part so you can see the underside of the first extrusion.
2. Create a work plane parallel to the bottom of the first extrusion at a distance of –2.8 inches so that it passes through the sphere near the top.
3. Open the Split tool and use the Remove option to cut off the tip of the hitch ball, as shown in Figure 7.8.
4. Shut off the visibility of the work plane.

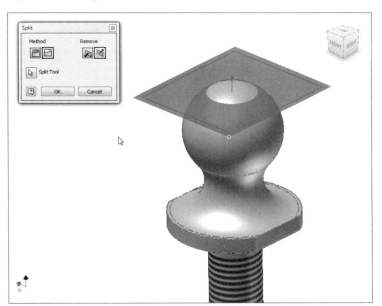

Figure 7.8

Splitting off the top of the hitch ball

5. Set the Physical iProperties of the part to Stainless Steel.

6. Change the color of the part to Chrome.

7. Save your work.

I hope that this exercise has shown you that sometimes you can build around a key feature. This is still not the typical way of doing things, but it's important to know that you have alternatives to explore.

The Emboss Tool

Emboss is a tool that takes the extrusion concept to a completely different level. Rather than simply terminating at a face or a distance from a face, it can incorporate the contour of the face or surface to define the geometry.

In the Emboss dialog box, there are relatively few things Inventor needs to know. Of course, you need to select a profile, and the geometry can either add to the surface (emboss) or subtract from it (engrave), but it can also do both.

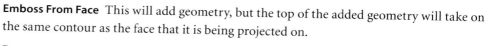

Termination Options

There are three termination methods and two related options.

 Emboss From Face This will add geometry, but the top of the added geometry will take on the same contour as the face that it is being projected on.

 Engrave From Face The cutting version also follows the contour.

 Emboss/Engrave From Plane If the plane that you are sketching from intersects the body, and the sketch extends over portions that are below the plane, this option will add or remove geometry to build a planar surface in the profile's shape.

Wrap To Face When using the Emboss or Engrave termination, the sides of the geometry will be normal to the sketch plane. If you select Wrap To Face, the sides will be normal to the surface that is selected.

Top Face Color There is also a colored square on the dialog box. By setting a color in this square, you ensure that the top face of an embossed feature or the bottom face of an engraved feature takes on this color.

Adding Text to Your Part

In this exercise, you'll add an engraved feature to the part. To do that, you'll use the Text tool, introduced in Chapter 6, to create the text and then use the Emboss tool to add the engraved effect.

1. Position your part so that you are looking at the corner of the Top, Front, and Right view on the Viewcube.

2. Create a work plane tangent to the curved surface on the lower left and parallel to the XZ plane, as shown in Figure 7.9.

3. Create a new sketch on that plane and project the curved face into the sketch.

4. Make the projected edges construction geometry, as shown in Figure 7.10.

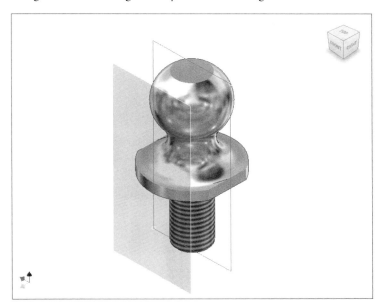

Figure 7.9

Adding a tangent plane

Figure 7.10

New sketch with projected edges

5. Use the Look At view tool and click the work plane or projected geometry to square your view.

6. For clarity, turn off the visibility of the work plane.

Near the end of the Sketch Panel bar is the Text tool. This tool will ask you to specify a rectangle for the text location.

7. Drag the text area to be the same size as the projected rectangle. It will not snap to the corners of the projected rectangle.

The Format Text window is the same one you have used before. You can even include parameters in the text callout if you like.

8. Set your font to Arial.

9. Set the orientation buttons above the font to Center Justification and Middle Justification.

10. In the Text window, enter **TORQUE TO 60 lbs./ft**. Your text should look like Figure 7.11.

Figure 7.11

Text added to sketch

11. Close the Text tool and exit the sketch.

12. Return to the isometric view that you were using before.

13. Select the Emboss tool.

14. Select the text for your profile, set the tool to Engrave From Face, and set the depth to 0.01 inches.

15. Select the Wrap To Face option and select the curved face to wrap to, as shown in Figure 7.12. Then execute the command.

16. Review the result and save the completed part (see Figure 7.13).

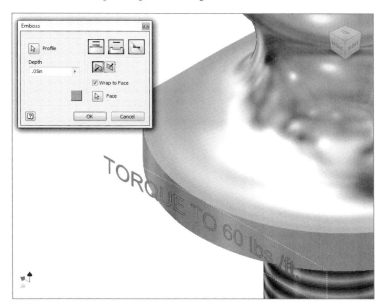

Figure 7.12

Setting up an engraved feature

Figure 7.13

The completed part

Rectangular and Circular Patterns

Inventor has two Pattern functions: Rectangular and Circular. If you are experienced with AutoCAD and its Array command, then you know the main workflow of these tools.

Rectangular

The Rectangular Pattern tool (Figure 7.14 shows its dialog box) does have one special capability in that the two direction values you specify do not need to be perpendicular. You can create rows of geometry in the positive X direction, and the second direction can be the negative X. Setting your direction requires selecting a model edge or axis.

Figure 7.14

The Rectangular Pattern dialog box

Circular

Circular patterns are very simple to create (see the dialog box in Figure 7.15), but it's also easy to overlook a couple of important options:

Pattern The Entire Solid Typically you can select a few features that you want to pattern. The Pattern The Entire Solid option is great if you want to develop a part that has symmetry. This works for either rectangular or circular patterns. Whereas patterning individual features will have Inventor calculate the new pattern members (instances), patterning the entire part calculates more quickly.

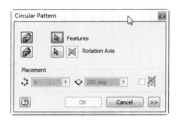

Figure 7.15

The Circular Pattern dialog box

More → Optimized Under the More submenu are additional options. The most important of these is the Optimized option. This option will ignore feature calculations and replicate the body of the features rather than their values.

More → Incremental The default value for Positioning Method is Fitted. This applies the number of features evenly across the angle entered in the main part of the dialog. The Incremental option will cause an angle value to be the angle between instances.

Duplicating Features

To make sure the message in the last feature is seen, we want to duplicate it on the other side of the part:

1. Start the Circular Pattern tool.

2. Select the Embossed feature that you just created either on the screen or from the Browser.

3. Once you have selected the feature to pattern, you'll need to select an axis. Select the curved face that the text was engraved in.

4. You'll see a preview for the number in the Placement value. Change the number to 2.

5. Rotate your part to see a preview of the pattern, as shown in Figure 7.16.

6. Finish the operation.

7. Be sure to save your work. This model will be used for another exercise later in the chapter.

Figure 7.16

Preview of patterned text

More Sketching Tools

Lines, Circles, and Rectangle tools cover a lot of the basics, but unless you create nothing but basic parts you'll find yourself needing more options.

A quick peek at the 2D Sketch panel will show you the Three Point Arc. Note that the first five tools have arrows that indicate further tools underneath the main tool. If you have used any 2D or 3D CAD system, you'll already know how to use the basics of any of these additional sketching tools.

This sections explores some of the sketching tools that we'll use in the upcoming exercises.

Spline

Under the Line tool is the Spline. The Spline tool in Inventor is one of the most capable in any CAD system. To create a spline, you place multiple points and the spline will pass through them. Each point can have its location controlled by dimensions. For advanced control, you can modify how the spline transitions through a point.

Under the Center Point Circle, you'll find two tools:

Tangent Circle This tool will create a circle based on tangency with three line segments.

Ellipse The ellipse is easy to place, but the method of constraining it seems a little odd to some users. When you place the ellipse, you define one axis, and it can inherit constraints such as being horizontal or parallel to an edge. To dimension its size, though, you only dimension half of the overall height and length. That is what some people find odd. It is no less functional; it is just something to be aware of.

Arcs

Rather than attempt to replicate the four thousand types of arcs, Inventor gives you three basic ways of creating an arc:

Three Point Arc This the most common arc. You define it by placing the beginning and endpoint of the arc and then dragging the radius in a real-time representation on the screen. As you drag, the status bar will display the current radius for reference.

Tangent Arc This tool behaves exactly like dragging an arc while in the Line tool. After starting the command, you simply click on any open sketch element near the end you want to place an arc on and drag until the arc is the length and direction that you want it. As a bonus tip, you can do the same thing by starting the Line tool and clicking and dragging from any open-ended sketch element.

Center Point Arc This is an underutilized tool. To place the arc, you begin by placing what will be the center of the radius. You'll then see a circle with the radius to the point you are dragging. To create the arc segment itself, you click once where you want to start the arc. You don't have to worry about whether the endpoint of the arc will be clockwise or counterclockwise, because it will draw the arc segment on the selected radius on either side of the first point that you select.

Thinking Inside the Box

In the exercises so far, we've made only machine parts. Now it's time to make something that shows a bit more of Inventor's potential for consumer products. In the next series of exercises, you'll create a free-form plastic part that could be the housing of a computer mouse or similar shape. This will allow us to explore some alternate construction techniques as well.

On a part where I will use surfaces, I like to build a box around the part to place sketches, rather than using work planes. Unlike work planes, a box can easily and quickly be edited with dimensions. Once your box is built, you can construct your part inside it. This technique will serve us well for a tool you'll use later in the chapter.

Sketching the Layout

For the first feature, you'll define the boundaries of the overall size:

1. Create a new file based on the Standard (mm).ipt template.

2. Draw a rectangle and dimension it to be 120mm wide (X) and 60mm tall (Y).

3. Begin the Extrude tool but change the Output type to Surface.

4. Extrude the surface a Distance of 40 mm.

   When finished, your part should have four surfaces on the perimeter of the rectangle (see Figure 7.17). There is no top, but the bottom could be perceived as the XY plane that your sketch was resting on. Again, this is meant to be a construction feature.

5. Begin a new sketch on the XY plane.

6. Use the Project Geometry tool to add the edges of the box to your current sketch.

7. Change the projected line segments to Construction geometry.

8. Draw an ellipse with its first axis longer and horizontal in the middle of the box.

9. Add a dimension of 45mm to half of the width of the ellipse, as shown in Figure 7.18.

10. Now make the left end, the top, and the bottom tangent to the surrounding projected edges. Use Figure 7.18 for reference.

11. Create a Center Point Arc using the centerpoint of the ellipse as the center for the arc and the arc segment, as shown in Figure 7.19.

    Earlier in this chapter we used the boundary of a circle to contain two line segments that maintained symmetry about the center of the circle. Now you'll reverse that method to establish symmetry on the arc by using a line.

12. As shown in Figure 7.20, draw a vertical line using the construction type through the arc that you created.

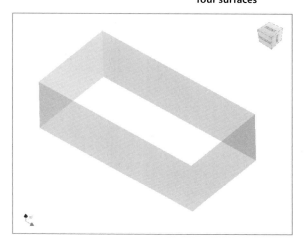

Figure 7.17

A box consisting of four surfaces

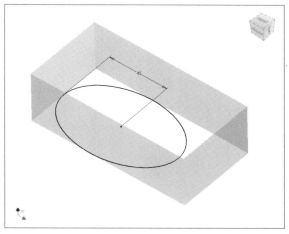

Figure 7.18

Adding the ellipse

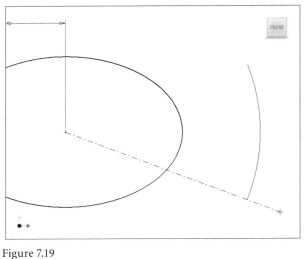

Figure 7.19
Creating a Center Point Arc

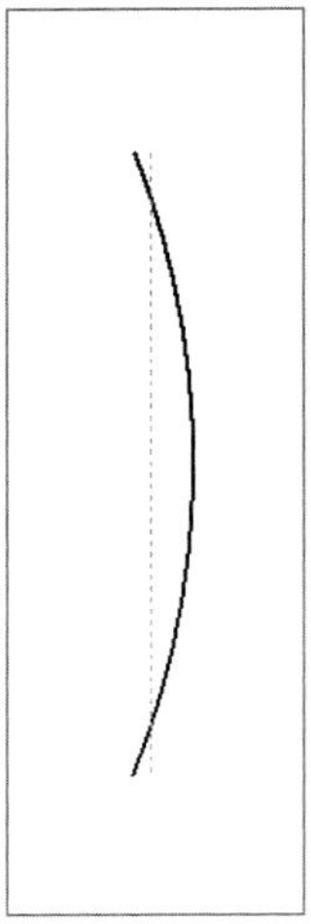

Figure 7.20
Add a vertical construction line through the arc.

13. After creating the line segment, start the Trim command and select the loose ends by clicking them as they highlight as dashed geometry (see Figure 7.21).

14. Dimension the length of the line to be 45mm.

15. Add two arcs between the ellipse and the ends of the Center Point Arc, as shown in Figure 7.22. Be sure to put your line class back to Normal.

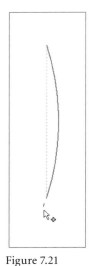

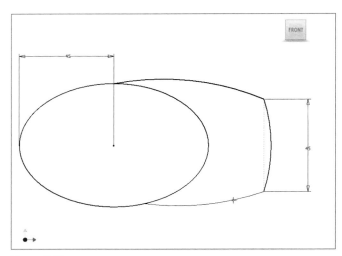

Figure 7.21
Trim the arc and line to form corners

Figure 7.22
Adding new arcs

16. Make the new arcs tangent to the ellipse and the horizontal lines that were projected from the box.

17. Trim the portion of the ellipse from between the new arcs, as shown in Figure 7.23.

    Normally I don't trim a sketch to the point where it is just a perimeter, but for this part we are exploring using surfaces to build a solid, and perimeter sketches are more effective for this purpose. This part could be created using a solid and using the Split tool as well, but my goal is to expose you to a technique that many overlook, so you'll have it for times where a simple split wouldn't be effective.

18. Extrude the profile as a surface. Use the Show Dimensions option to link the height of the new extrusion to the height of the box and set the Taper to –2 on the More tab, as shown in Figure 7.24.

19. Save the file to the Parts folder with the name `Plastic Part.ipt`.

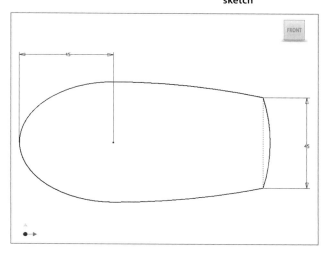

Figure 7.23

The completed sketch

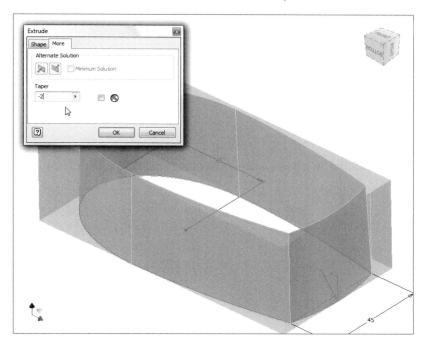

Figure 7.24

Adding a draft to an extruded surface

The Loft Tool

To create the complex surfaces that are sought for many modern designs, extrusions and revolved features can fall short. Lofted features create solids and surfaces by calculating the shapes that transition between sketches.

The dialog box used by the Loft tool has quite a few options. The tool itself uses several techniques to construct how the loft will be created. These techniques are reflected in the grouping of options on three tabs: Curves, Conditions, and Transition.

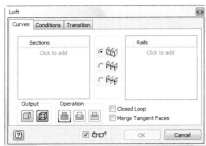

The Curves Tab

This tab is where you define what curves and profiles will be used to construct the loft. You also select what method will be used for the definition of the feature.

Sections As noted, a loft is built based on sections, which can be sketches or model edges. As you select what sections you want to build with, the selections will appear as a list in the Sections area of the tab.

Loft Types Between the Sections and Rails lists are three options for the type of loft solution that will be applied:

> **Rails** To use this solution, you have to have at least two sections and a third curve that you'll select as a rail. This rail must come in contact with geometry in each of the sections.

> **Center Line** This works just like the Rails definition, but the centerline does not have to contact the sections.

> **Area Loft** This is a useful option for those building manifolds or who need to control flow. It works like the Center Line option but allows you to calculate the area of the shape as it transitions down the centerline.

Rails/Center Line/Placed Sections This list will change names based on the construction technique, but it displays the options used to guide your sections to form the lofted shape.

Closed Loop Selecting this option will cause the end section to transition back into the beginning section.

Merge Tangent Faces As Inventor develops a loft, it will generate separate surfaces for each segment in a section sketch. If you select this option, it will merge those separate surfaces together if they are tangent to one another.

The Conditions Tab

Each section selected (sketched or part edge) will be listed on this tab with a transition condition applied. There are several types of transitions that can either be applied by the program automatically or selected from the pull-down list. Not all conditions will be available for all sections.

Free Condition This is typical of using open sketches and offers no additional control or capability. It just takes the shape the way it is.

Direction Using this condition, you can control the angle that the loft transitions from the sketch plane. This is only available for a sketched section.

Tangent This option allows you to guide the lofted surface based on an existing surface or face that is adjacent to the selected section sketch or selected face edges.

Smooth The Smooth option is similar to Tangent but is enhanced by focusing on the overall curvature of the original and resulting faces to maintain continuous curvature.

Sharp Point This option allows you to loft from a loop (open or closed) to a single point.

Tangent (To Point) When transitioning from a loop to a point, you can add curvature to the surface by bringing the surface tangent to the sketch plane of the point.

Tangent To Plane This option is similar to Tangent but also offers the ability to specify what plane the surface is tangent to as it approaches the point.

As you use some of these options, you may be presented with prompts for additional modification:

Angle When using the Direction condition, you can specify the angle that the shape begins to transition along as it moves to the next curve.

Weight Use this value to control how quickly the shape of one section begins to transition to the shape of another. This is a value that is referred to as "unitless," meaning that it is an arbitrary value that you can change until the effect is appropriate.

The Transition Tab

Inventor automatically maps how a surface will transition between edges on the various sections. You can override these selections on this tab and specify how a surface will be defined by selecting beginning and ending points for the surfaces of the loft. With care, you can even introduce twist into the shape.

A lot of the options are selected for you automatically, and very often the automatic result will give you the look and shape that you need.

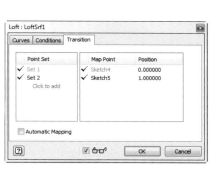

Setting Up the Next Feature

For the complex top that is desired for our plastic part, we'll need to build the boundaries for the Loft feature:

1. Set your part's view orientation to match Figure 7.25.

2. Create a new sketch on the face closest to you.

3. Change the projected edges to Construction geometry. If the edges don't project automatically, project all of the edges by clicking the face.

4. Create a spline using four points beginning and ending on the vertical edges that were projected. Position and dimension the points as shown in Figure 7.26.

Figure 7.25

Orientation for the new sketch

Figure 7.26

Defining the spline

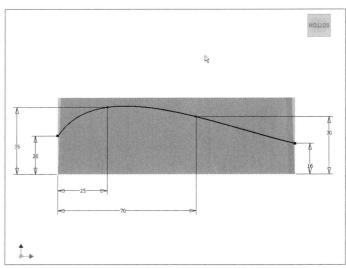

Using Parametric dimensions, you'll find it easy to position the points and create a basic control for the curvature of the spline. To develop more control, you can use constraints to other geometry.

5. Draw a Construction line from the left end of the spline and dimension its angle as 35 degrees from vertical, as shown in Figure 7.27.

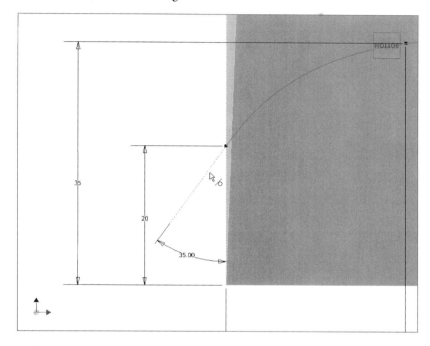

Figure 7.27

Controlling the curvature using a line segment

6. Add a tangency constraint to associate the curvature of the spline to the angle of the line.

7. Add the same control with a different value to the other end of the spline, as shown in Figure 7.28.

8. Finish editing the sketch and save your work.

To create our top surface, you'll need to add two more sketches. The basic process will be the same. Although it's not completely necessary to change the projected edges to construction geometry, it does make it easier to select the geometry for our loft. What is necessary for our loft to work is to project the endpoint of the spline into our new sketches and to attach the arcs you'll create to that projected point on the appropriate end.

9. Create a new sketch on the left end of the part.

Figure 7.28

Define the transition for the other end of the spline.

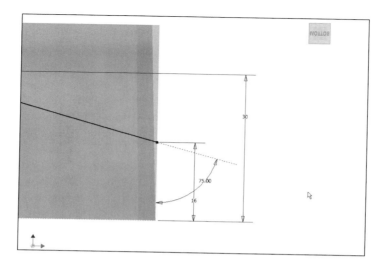

10. Draw an arc that is connected to the projected edge on one side and the projected point mentioned previously.

11. Dimension as shown in Figure 7.29.

Figure 7.29

Creating the beginning shape

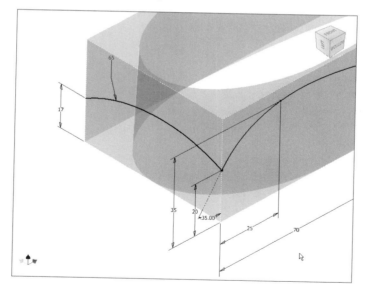

12. Finish that sketch and define a new one on the opposite end of the part.

13. Include the required projections and use an arc to approximate the sketch, as shown in Figure 7.30.

14. Leave the sketch environment and start the Loft command. For this model, you'll use the Rails solution, which is the default.

15. Inventor will first look for your choices for sections. Select the last two sketches you created.

    A preview will appear of a simple loft between those curves.

16. Click the Click To Add prompt in the Rails area and click the spline.

    The preview will update to show the two shapes transitioning as they follow the path of the rail, as shown in Figure 7.31.

17. Finish creating the loft. Your model should look similar to Figure 7.32.

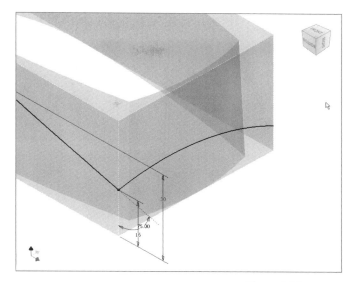

Figure 7.30

Place an undercon-strained sketch on the opposite end.

In most 3D solid modeling systems, you can develop a solid model by constructing surfaces as you have just done. In other systems there would be additional steps to trim the surfaces so that their edges met. Even when you think that you had it perfect, they often failed to be able to stitch the surface properly.

Autodesk Inventor has a functionality that skips the part of the process that is the least pleasant to get to the solid more easily.

Figure 7.31

The geometry of the new loft is previewed before creation.

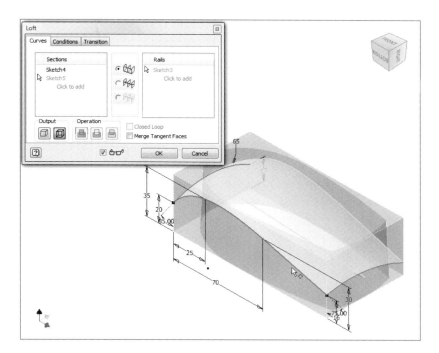

Figure 7.32

The finished boundary of the part

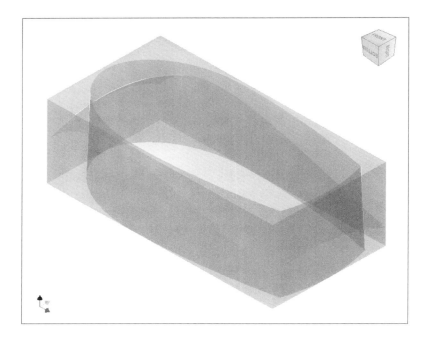

The Sculpt Tool

In previous jobs I've frequently worked with surface modeling tools. If you've never worked with a dedicated surface modeler, don't bother. There are relatively few product types that require it, and typically the workflow to create parts is considerably more complex than should be necessary. I wish I'd had access to Inventor's Sculpt tool years ago. It would've saved me many hours per week.

Using the tool is a straightforward process. First, you do what you have already done: you construct a collection of overlapping surfaces. Then you start the Sculpt tool and click those surfaces (or planes); Sculpt then finds the void between the surfaces and fills it with a solid model. There is only one primary option. When you select surfaces, a double-ended arrow will appear, indicating the direction that you want to favor. This can switch Inventor from ignoring a surface that passes through the body to using it to create another void contour that acts like a part has been cut out. Sculpt can also be used to modify an existing solid body similar to the Split tool but with more flexibility.

The Sculpt tool's dialog box is very simple. If you have an existing body, you can select whether you'll be adding or subtracting geometry as the default. You select the planes and surfaces. Expanding the dialog box will display the list of selected surfaces so you can choose the surface direction in the dialog box instead of clicking the arrows on the surfaces themselves.

Creating a Solid from Space

To try out the Sculpt tool, here's a short exercise to fill the space in your plastic part model.

1. Turn off the visibility of ExtrusionSrf1 in the Browser.

2. Start the Sculpt tool.

3. Select the XY Plane from the Browser.

4. Select the extruded surface made from the ellipse and arcs.

5. Select the top lofted surface.

After you've selected enough surfaces for Inventor to find a body, a preview will appear, as shown in Figure 7.33.

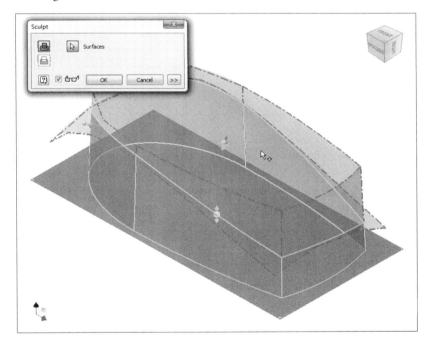

Figure 7.33

Preview of the body

6. Click OK once the surfaces are selected to create the solid model. Figure 7.34 shows the result.

   The solid that is created is still associated with the surface that defined it. The surfaces are associated with the sketches that defined them. This means that you can edit the solid by modifying the sketches, just as with any other sketched feature.

7. Expand the Sculpt1 feature. Under it you'll see the planes and surfaces that constructed it.

8. Expand the LoftSrf1 feature. Moving your cursor over the sketches will display them in the Design window.

Figure 7.34

**The resulting
solid model**

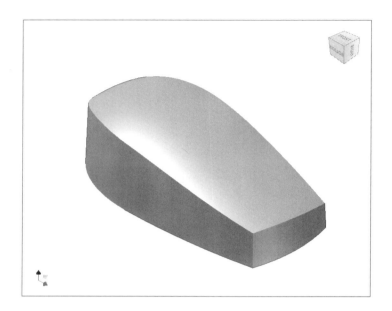

9. Make visible the sketch that contains the spline.

10. Edit the 70mm dimension and make it 75mm.

11. Edit the 30mm dimension and set its value to 25mm.

12. Update the model and see the solid change. Figure 7.35 shows the result.

13. Turn off the visibility of the sketch that you edited and save the file.

Figure 7.35

**The modified
solid model**

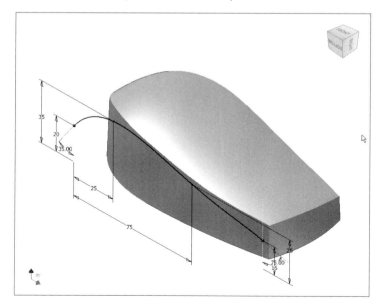

Adding Advanced Fillets

The Sculpt and Loft tools are wonderful, but when you need to round an edge, it is still usually easier to use a fillet. In many designs these rounded edges can be complex, and a simple fillet or round just won't do.

With this exercise you'll explore every major option of the Fillet tool. To make the results of the fillets easier to see, you should first make a change to the Application Options:

1. Open Application Options.

2. In the Display tab, turn on Edges under Shaded Display Modes for the active part.

3. Open the Fillet tool.

   All of the fillets you'll create will be added as one feature, using three different techniques. (Please pay close attention to the figures for each step.)

4. Set the first radius to 6 (mm) and click the top edge on the right end of the part, as shown in Figure 7.36.

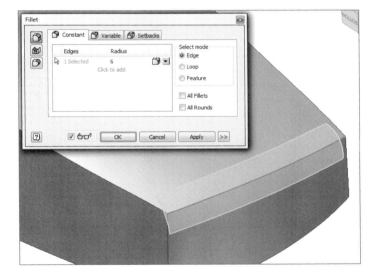

Figure 7.36

Selecting the first edge

5. Use the Click To Add option to add a second radius. Set the radius to 12 and select the two vertical edges adjacent to the first fillet selection, as shown in Figure 7.37.

6. Switch to the Variable tab and select the curved edge at the top of the part. Set the Start and End radius to 4. Click below the listed points and then move your cursor to the middle of the elliptical curve and click when you see the green point highlight.

This will indicate the middle of the curve length, and the position will be listed as .5000 to show that it is the middle.

7. Set the radius to 16, and if the Position Value is anything but 0.5000, edit the value to reposition the point to the middle of the curve (see Figure 7.38).

8. Select the Setbacks tab in the Fillet tool.

9. Hover over one of the corners at the intersection of the three previously placed fillets and click the vertex when you see the small circle.

Figure 7.37

Selecting the two vertical edges

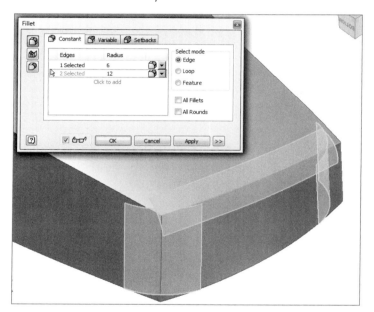

Figure 7.38

With a Variable radius, you can add fillet points with different radii.

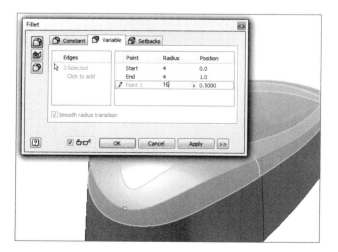

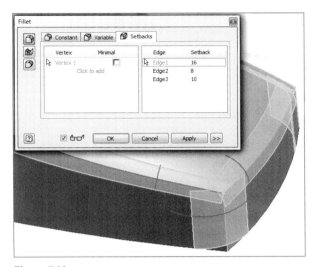

Figure 7.39

Fillet setbacks can be added to revise how corners are constructed.

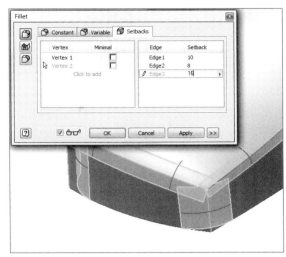

Figure 7.40

Repeat the setbacks for the opposite corner.

10. Set the value of the setback along the long, curved edge to 16, set the value for the vertical edge to 8, and set the value along the arc edge to 10 (see Figure 7.39).

11. In the Vertex list. use Click To Add and select the other corner (see Figure 7.40).

12. Set the values for each edge setback the same as the other corner. The order of the edges may be different, but the edge will highlight in the Design window when you click it on the list in the dialog box.

13. Click OK to apply all of the fillets as one feature. Compare your model to Figure 7.41.

Figure 7.41

The finished fillets

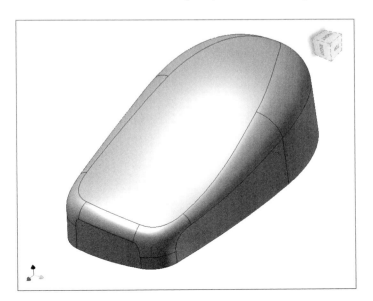

The Shell Tool

When you need a part to be hollow and (usually) with a consistent remaining wall thickness, you can use the Shell command to remove a large portion of the body rather than modeling the walls of a model individually. To do this, you select a face or faces to be removed. The faces that you do not select will be thickened and remain a solid.

The Shell dialog box has relatively few options, but a few of them are worthy of more explanation.

The Shell Tab

In most cases, the Shell tab will give you all the tools you need to create a shell feature.

Shell Types

 Inside Shell This will remove material from the interior of the part, leaving the body that you created intact.

 Outside Shell The outside adds material beginning at the surface of the body that you created. In essence, you create a model of the void and add material to it.

 Both Option Using this option will use the surface of your model as the mid-surface, adding thickness in both directions simultaneously.

Automatic Face Chain

The Automatic Face Chain option is checked by default. Deselecting it will enable you to select faces for removal without automatically selecting tangent faces as well.

Unique Face Thickness

 The Shell dialog box has a More button at the bottom to expand the dialog box. Doing this will expose the additional option of adding a Unique Face Thickness setting.

By default, selecting a face for removal applies the thickness to all of the remaining faces. If you want a different thickness applied to a specific face, you can use the Click To Add function and add the special face and a unique thickness for it to the list. You can add multiple faces and, in theory, hollow out a part and give each remaining face a different thickness.

The More Tab

There may be times when you have difficulty getting a shell to calculate. The More tab offers several workflows that should allow you get the part to shell.

Allow Approximation

This option is on by default. Optimized shelling will create the shell quickly but in order to do so will allow infinitesimally small variations in the thickness. In all but a handful of cases, this shell is more accurate than most people need. If you require extreme accuracy, you can deselect this option.

Mean This approximation will allow the thickness to vary, being either slightly thinner or thicker than the Thickness value.

Never Too Thin If the shell thickness is critical, this option will allow the variation to be thicker than the specification but never thinner than it.

Never Too Thick With this option, the shell can be thinner than the callout but not thicker.

Specify Tolerance To allow deviation but limit to a tolerance, you can specify a value along with the solution. Doing so can add time to creating the shell, but in cases where you must be sure, this is the way.

Shelling the Part

For this stage of the plastic part exercise, we only need to add a basic thickness to the faces that will remain.

1. Orbit the part so that the flat surface is visible.
2. Using the Shell tool, select the flat face.
3. Click OK to create the shelled part, as shown in Figure 7.42.
4. Save your work.

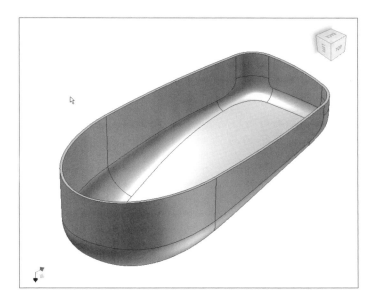

Figure 7.42

The shelled part

A New Sketch for the Next Step

In this stage of the exercise, you'll reuse a technique from Chapter 3 that is so useful it should be repeated.

1. With the shelled portion of the plastic part still visible, open the Sketch tool.

2. Carefully move the mouse over the newly created edge until it highlights.

3. Click and drag the mouse into the part and set the value for the offset of the new work plane to −3mm. The result should look like Figure 7.43.

Figure 7.43

A new work plane

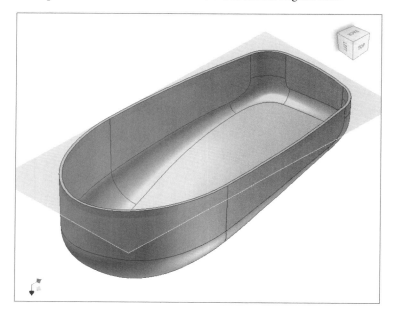

This will create a new work plane and simultaneously start a new sketch on that plane. This is a technique that you may use hundreds of times in the future.

4. Draw a rectangle the fits between the shelled walls, as shown in Figure 7.44. Include the lines from the midpoints to make four sections.

5. In the 2D Sketch panel find the Scale tool and start it.

The Scale, Stretch, and Rotate tools were added to Inventor's sketching environment in response to customer requests for more flexibility.

From the outset I have stressed that it is important to create your sketches close to the correct size. If you accidentally miss that goal, these tools will allow you to modify the sketch elements until they are closer. If you're an experienced AutoCAD user, these tools behave very much like their counterparts in that system.

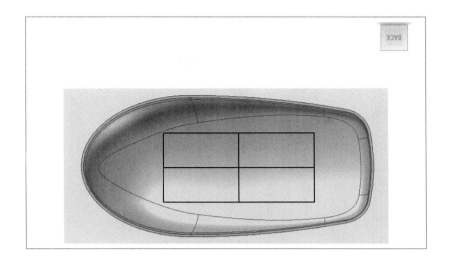

Figure 7.44
**Sketching the
path for ribs**

6. Select the short line on the left. The Scale tool will allow you to keep selecting geometry, but this is all we want at the moment.

7. Click the Base Point option and select the middle of the line as the base point for scaling.

8. You'll be asked if you want to break constraints to other geometry in order to change the selected line. Click OK to do this.

9. Drag the mouse so that the line becomes slightly longer than it was (see Figure 7.45), and then click to set the new length.

10. Repeat this for the other side, but as you are typing note that the scale appears in real time in the dialog box. Type **1.3** while dragging and press the Enter key. This will give you a precise scale.

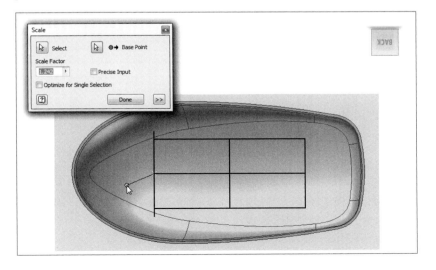

Figure 7.45
**Extending sketch
elements**

11. Click Done to leave the dialog box.

12. Exit the sketch and save your work.

The Rib and Web Tools

For plastic or cast-metal parts, reinforcement ribs are a common need. Drawing ribs individually can be very time-consuming, and creating the parametric relationships to maintain consistency across all of the ribs can add a great deal of complexity to the part. Similar to ribs are webs. Unlike ribs, which typically terminate on a face and have their geometry blend into the part, webs begin on a plane but stop at a distance from that plane.

The process of creating both features is quite direct. Select the sketch elements that you want to use and then click the Direction button. Drag your mouse on the screen to determine the direction the ribs (or web) will be built in. The dialog box also presents a few options:

Extents   This is where you select whether to create a rib or a web. If you select Web, a field will appear below the Extents buttons so you can enter the depth of the web from the sketch plane.

Thickness   This option controls the width of the web or rib as it goes to its termination. Buttons below the value control whether the width is offset to one side or the other, or split in the middle of the sketch element.

Extend Profile   When this is checked, a sketch element that is not closed will continue in its path until it finds a boundary on the existing geometry. If this is not selected, the rib will stop at the end of the sketch element.

Taper   This option will add a draft angle as the rib is created. Unlike when adding taper to an extrusion, you need not worry about a positive or negative angle.

Adding the Ribs

Now you'll put the Rib tool to use on our plastic part.

1. Turn off the visibility of the work plane.

2. Open the Rib tool.

3. Select each of the line segments that you created.

4. Click the Direction button and move it around until the direction is going into the body of the part, as shown in Figure 7.46. You'll need to click in the Design window to set the direction.

5. Set the Thickness to 2 and the Taper to 2 as well; then click OK to create the ribs.

6. For a final touch, open the Fillet tool and click the All Fillets checkbox in the lower right. Note the number of edges selected.

7. Set the Radius to 0.5 and finish placing the fillets. If this fails, experiment with different radius sizes.

8. Save your great work and compare it to Figure 7.47.

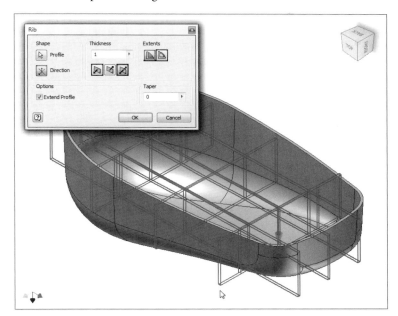

Figure 7.46

Setting the direction for the ribs

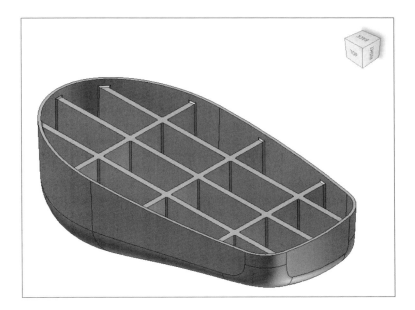

Figure 7.47

The completed ribs

The Sweep Tool

An extrusion builds a body based on projecting a profile so that it's normal to its sketch plane. Sometimes you need that sketch to follow a path but you do not need it to change shape, so a loft isn't appropriate. This is what the Sweep tool is for.

Because the concept is similar to extrusion, the Sweep dialog box has a lot of the same elements as Extrude. There are some features that are genuinely unique and demonstrate some truly spectacular capabilities.

Type

The basic idea for having a profile follow a path is powerful. But there are additional ways to define the feature that can be selected from the Type pull-down list:

Path The simplest and most common type, this option only needs a profile and a path to follow. The path does not need to intersect the profile.

Path & Guide Rail Along with the profile and a path to follow, this option requires the selection of a second rail that will modify the transition of the profile along the selected path.

Path & Guide Surface Rather than using a basic sketch to modify the profile transition, this option takes into account the normal of a surface to control the profile. If you need to create a shape that transitions across a complex surface yet maintains its position, this is your tool. Think about running a machine tool bit across a surface and keeping the bit normal to the face; this will allow you to emulate that.

Orientation

For the Path option, you have the ability to define how the profile will follow the path without using a guide rail or surface:

Path This option will keep the profile normal to the path as it transitions.

Parallel While the profile moves along the path, this setting will keep the profile parallel with its sketch plane.

Creating a Lip Using Sweep

In this stage of the exercise, you'll try out the Sweep tool by putting a recessed lip on the part.

1. Start a new sketch on the remaining flat edge of the part bottom, as shown in Figure 7.48.

2. Close the new sketch.

3. Using the Work Plane tool, create a plane based on the point where the fillet meets the long arc edge and use the arc edge of the part to define the plane, as shown in Figure 7.49.

4. Create a sketch on the new plane.

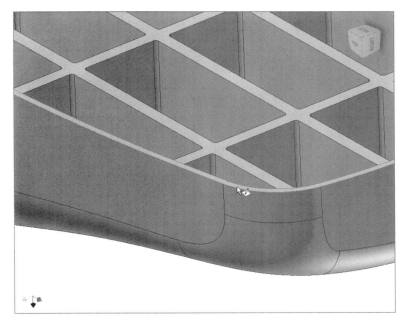

Figure 7.48

Creating the sketch for the path

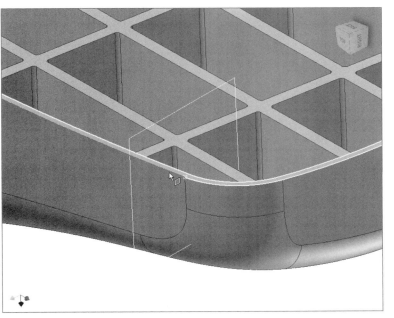

Figure 7.49

Defining a plane for the profile sketch

Figure 7.50

Placing the Coincident constraint

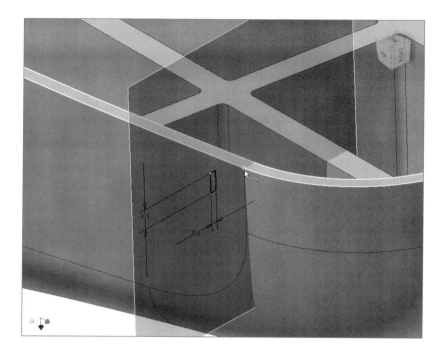

5. Create a rectangle 1.5mm tall and 0.5mm wide. Create the sketch away from the part; then place a Coincident constraint between a corner of the sketch and the point on the part that the plane was based on. When this constraint is placed, the sketch should pretty much disappear into the part, as Figure 7.50 shows.

6. Finish the sketch.

7. Turn off the visibility of the recently created work plane.

8. Using the Sweep tool, select the rectangle for the profile.

9. Select the outer perimeter of the sketch placed on the part edge.

10. Set the Sweep option to Cut and leave the Type of sweep set to Path and use a Path orientation.

11. Finish the sweep; see Figure 7.51.

12. Turn the edge visibility off again if you like.

13. Try changing your part color to Chrome or Black Chrome to see how the surfaces look.

14. Be sure to save the part. It will be reused in another exercise.

   This was a fairly complex part, and it could have been done using a different combination of tools that might have been a little quicker, but I think the learning opportunity was well worth it. Using tools like Loft and Sculpt, you'll be hard-pressed to find a part that is impossible to create in Inventor.

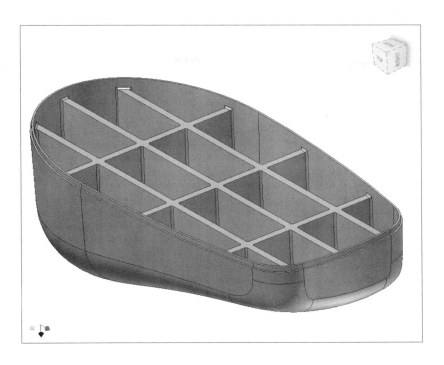

Figure 7.51

The finished lip

Loft as the Primary Feature

So far you've used the Loft tool for building a portion of the part. But for most users who need the Loft tool, it will be used to build the main portion of the body. So in the next brief exercise, you'll use the Loft tool in its normal role.

Creating a Nose Cone

In this exercise, you'll use the Loft tool as the primary tool—and in a novel way.

1. Begin a new file based on the Standard (mm).ipt template.

2. Project the Origin Center Point into the sketch.

3. Open the Polygon tool, set it for three sides, and place the triangle centered on the projected point, as shown in Figure 7.52.

4. Constrain the bottom line to be horizontal and dimension its width to 0.3m (this is m for meters).

Figure 7.52

Drawing a
triangle with the
Polygon tool

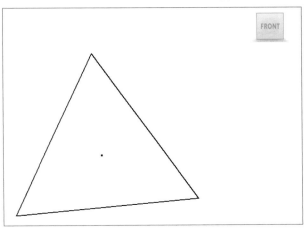

5. Switch to the Home view.

   The Fillet tool in the Sketch environment will ask you to define a radius and then select pairs of edges to fillet the corners of. You'll need to use Esc or right-click Done to exit the tool.

6. Use the sketch Fillet tool to round all three corners to 40mm.

7. Finish the sketch and make the XY plane visible.

8. Create a new sketch .5m (500mm) above the XY plane.

9. Project the Origin Center Point into the new sketch (see Figure 7.53).

Figure 7.53

Adding a second sketch and center point

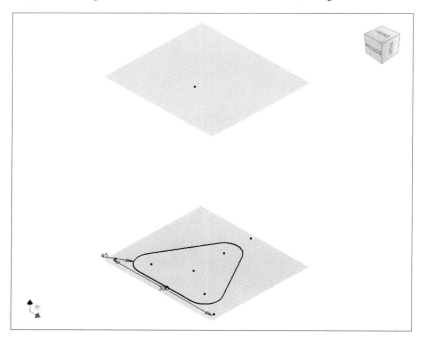

10. Finish the Sketch and open the Loft tool.

11. First select the triangular sketch, then select the point in the second sketch. Compare your preview with Figure 7.54.

12. Switch to the Conditions tab in the Loft dialog box.

13. Change the Condition setting on the point to Tangent and set the Weight option to 0.7, as shown in Figure 7.55.

14. Complete the Loft tool and turn off the visibility of the work planes.

15. Save the file to your Parts folder as **Nose Cone**.

You can experiment with this model to try different weighting or to modify its other components. Shelling the model will give you a nice part. Again, this exercise was meant as an extra look at the Loft capabilities.

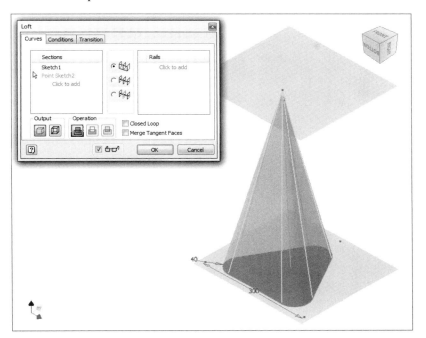

Figure 7.54

The initial loft preview

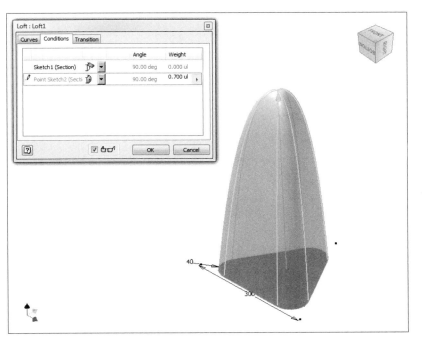

Figure 7.55

Adjustments to the loft

The Coil Tool

In its assembly environment, you can access a large suite of tools called the Design Accelerators. Among the phenomenal tools included in that category is a Spring design tool. If you intend to build a spring or a worm gear, I recommend that you use those tools.

For other spiraled shapes, the Coil tool works very well. If you want to make a spring using it, I'm sure it won't mind at all.

The Coil tool is an adaptation of the Sweep tool. Instead of selecting a profile and a path, you select a profile and an axis that the tool will create a helical path along for you. Since you have used the other tools, I will skip over familiar parts of its dialog box and focus on what's new.

If you want to learn more about the Design Accelerators, *Mastering Autodesk Inventor 2009 and Autodesk Inventor LT 2009*, by Curtis Waguespack, et al. (Wiley, 2008), covers all the Design Accelerator tools. In addition, Chapter 8 of this book covers several of these tools in the context of advanced assembly design.

The Coil Shape Tab

The Add, Cut, and Intersect options will not be available if the Coil is the first feature in the part.

Rotation

This pair of buttons provides you with a quick direction switch.

The Coil Size Tab

This tab establishes the size and length values for the coil using different methodologies.

Type

There are four definitions for the type of coil that you want to create, and you select them from the Type pull-down list. As you select a type, the input area below the pull-down list will change to suit the required information:

Pitch And Revolution This type will look for the pitch (distance between coils) and how many coils you want to create.

Revolution And Height This option defines how many coils you would like to fit into a space and adjusts the pitch to suit.

Pitch And Height The first two options will work to put the coil in loops of 360 degrees. With this option, it will use a combination of the pitch and height, and the resulting coil may not have its ends align.

Spiral This option works off of Pitch And Revolution but only in the plane that is perpendicular to the axis and the profile.

The Coil Ends Tab

The values established on this tab will determine how the ends of the coil will be constructed.

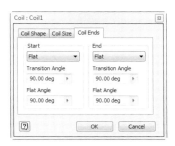

Start/End

This pull-down list allows you to select between the Natural Start/End condition (in which the profile terminates at the end of the helical path) and the Flat option. The Flat option offers two values, which alter the way the coil appears:

Transition Angle This variable controls how quickly the coil transitions from the coiled body to the Flat portion.

Flat Angle This variable establishes how far the coil continues to be developed after it has flattened.

The Flat condition should not be confused with a ground ending. Many springs are ground flat at the ends to ensure that they have consistent engagement with the parts they contact. That is not the same as having the coil flattened in its transition. You can achieve a ground appearance by cutting or splitting the end of the coil.

Making a Spring

As I mentioned earlier, Inventor has the ability to generate springs based on engineering data. This exercise will use the old-fashioned way to draw one using the Coil tool.

1. Start a new file based on the Standard (mm).ipt template.

2. Draw a horizontal line. The length doesn't really matter.

3. Draw a circle above the left end and dimension it as shown in Figure 7.56.

4. Open the Coil tool.

5. Select the horizontal line as the axis for the coil.

6. In the Coil Size tab, set the Coil Size option to Pitch And Revolution with a Pitch value of 10 and a Revolution value of 6 (see Figure 7.57).

Figure 7.56

Create the circle for the coil profile.

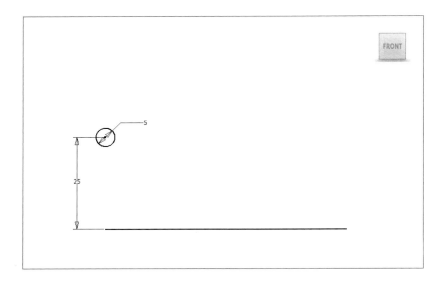

Figure 7.56

Create the circle for the coil profile.

Figure 7.57

Setting the coil values

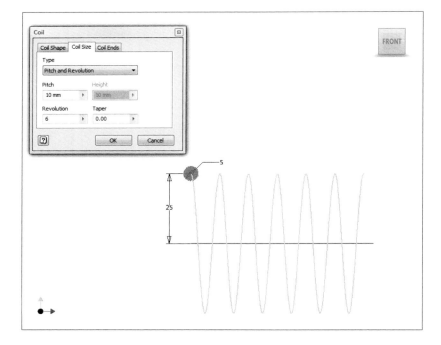

Figure 7.57

Setting the coil values

7. Create the coil. It should look like the example in Figure 7.58.

8. Expand the Coil1 feature in the Browser and edit the sketch.

9. Draw a rectangle over the circle, as shown in Figure 7.59.

Figure 7.58

The finished coil

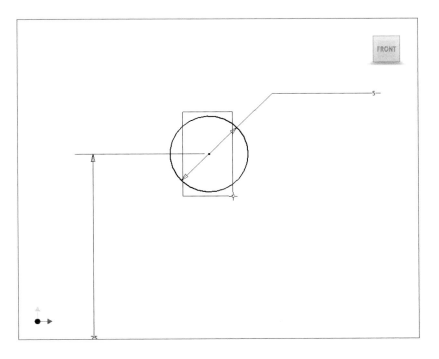

Figure 7.59

Changing the coil profile

10. Delete the circle from the sketch and finish editing the sketch.

   The coil should regenerate using the only closed profile. In this case, it will generate using the rectangle, as shown in Figure 7.60.

11. Edit the Coil feature.

Figure 7.60

The finished coil with flat ends

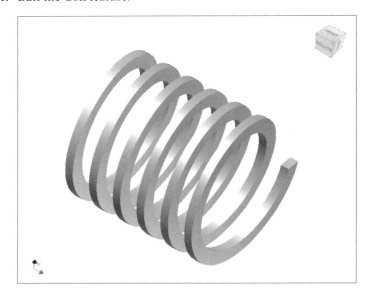

12. Change the Start and End conditions to Flat with values of 90 in all areas.

13. Update the model and save if you would like. You won't use this coil with any other parts you're modeling.

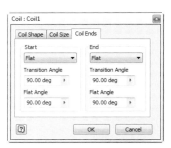

The Mirror Tool

Like the Patterns we reviewed earlier, the Mirror tool closely follows the workflow of an AutoCAD command— in this case, Mirror. And like the Pattern dialog boxes, the Mirror tool gives you a lot of the same options for selecting individual features, mirroring the entire part, and even using optimized calculations to improve performance.

Mirroring Features

Symmetrical parts are obvious candidates for using the Mirror tool. You can also create conditions that you can use to construct other features.

1. Start a new file based on the Standard (mm).ipt template.

2. Create a sketch as shown in Figure 7.61.

3. Extrude the rectangle to 15mm.

4. Switch to the Home view and create a work plane 20mm from the right side of the extrusion, as shown in Figure 7.62.

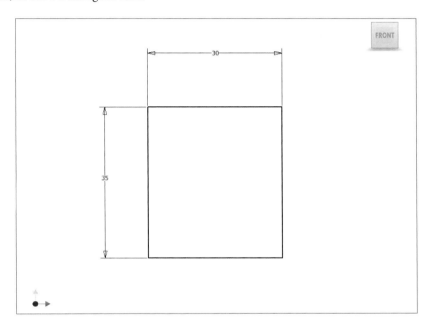

Figure 7.61

The sketch for mirroring

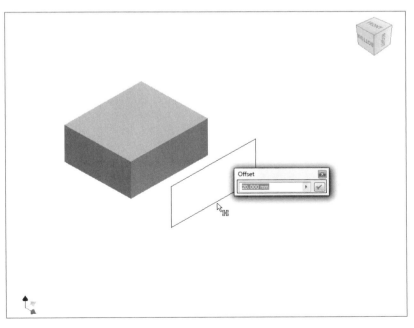

Figure 7.62

Defining the mirror plane

5. Using the Mirror tool, choose to mirror the Entire body.

6. Select the work plane that you created to be the mirror plane and create the new mirror feature.

   It's important to note that any planar face or existing plane can be used for a mirror plane. It's also important to keep in mind that Inventor can work in conditions where there are gaps in the part. This means you can create symmetrical sides using Mirror and then develop asymmetrical geometry to fill the space between them.

7. Set the work plane to Invisible.

8. Using the Loft tool, select the faces nearest to each other on the two halves of the part. The preview will look like Figure 7.63.

Figure 7.63

The Loft preview

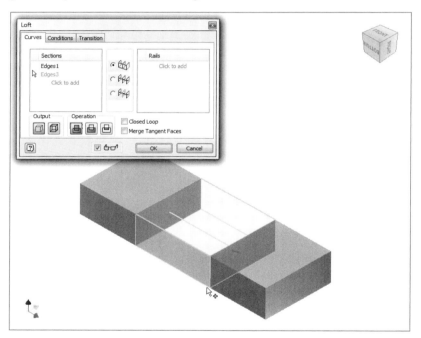

9. In the Transition tab, deselect the Automatic Mapping option.

10. When the point sets appear, delete them.

11. Select the Click To Add option under Point Set, and click the two corners, as shown in Figure 7.64.

12. Select Click To Add again to define a second point set using the next set of corners, as shown in Figure 7.65.

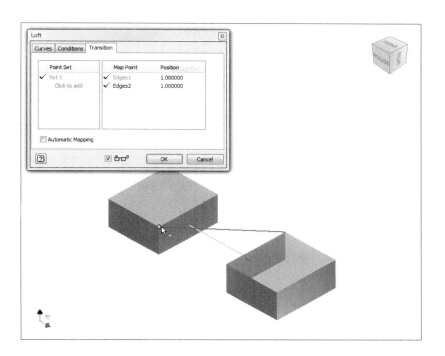

Figure 7.64

Creating a new angled point set

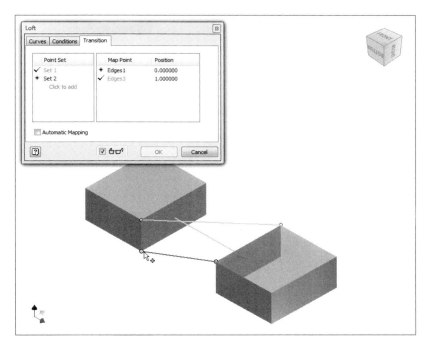

Figure 7.65

Building a twist using another point set

13. Repeat this for the last two point sets, and the preview should resemble Figure 7.66.

14. Switch to the Conditions tab and set the conditions for both profiles to Tangent Condition (see Figure 7.67).

Figure 7.66

All four point sets defined

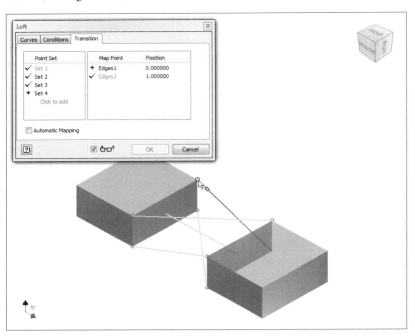

Figure 7.67

Use conditions to control the transition of the loft.

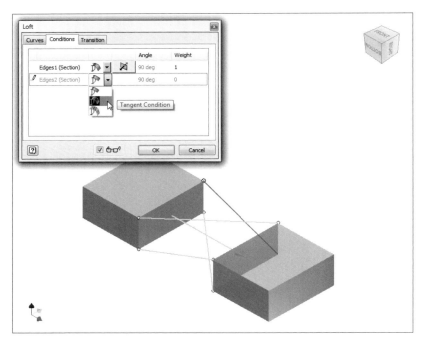

15. Close the Loft tool. Your completed part should look like Figure 7.68.

16. Edit the Extrude:1 feature using grip edits so that it's 45mm wide, and then change the extrusion height to 20mm (see Figure 7.69). Remember to eight-click and select Done to save the changes you made while using 3D grips.

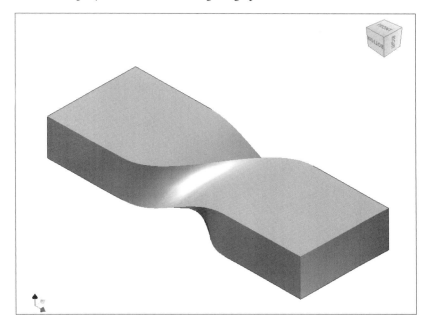

Figure 7.68

The Loft tool is used to create a twist in the part.

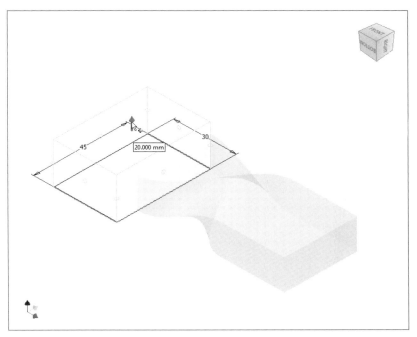

Figure 7.69

Grip-editing the original block

17. Double-click on the work plane used to mirror the part in the Browser.

18. Change its value to 30mm and update the part. The finished part should look like Figure 7.70.

The advantage of using a mirror rather than just drawing a second block is that the size of both ends of the twisted part remain the same without having to point back and forth between dimensions.

Figure 7.70

The updated part after additional editing

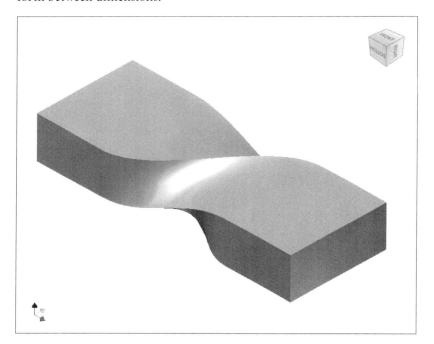

The Thicken/Offset Tool

If you need to build a feature that has a basic shape or a complex contour, and you want to have a consistent thickness but do not want to use the Shell tool to remove all but one side, you can use Thicken/Offset.

It is two features in one. Thicken will develop a solid body from an existing face or surface. Offset will take an existing face or surface and create another surface with a space between it and the original.

The dialog box for the tool has one unique feature that you haven't encountered yet. You can select either a face (or several faces) or a quilt. A quilt is a number of surfaces that are tangent to one another and that form a continuous surface.

Thickening a Surface into a Solid

This exercise will show one use for the Thicken tool as well as explore the reuse of files.

1. Open the `Plastic Part.ipt` file that you created earlier.

2. Use the File → Save As command to create a new part in the Parts folder; call it `Contour Solid.ipt`.

   Be sure to use Save As, not Save Copy As. Using Save As will create a new file based on a source file and make the new file the active file. Save Copy As will create a new duplicate file but leave the source file active, which means you might accidentally modify the original file instead of the copy.

3. In the Browser, move the End Of Part marker to just below the Sculpt1 feature.

4. Right-click on the End Of Part marker and select Delete All Features Below EOP to delete all the features that you no longer need.

5. Right-click on the Sculpt1 feature and select Delete.

   This will bring up the Delete Features dialog box. When a feature is created using other features or sketches, the new feature will consume those other elements into it. If you later decide to remove that feature, Inventor will ask you whether you want to remove the elements that were used to construct the feature. Since we want to reuse some of these items, you won't have Inventor delete them along with the Sculpt1 feature.

6. Deselect the Consumed Sketches And Features option.

7. Using the Thicken/Offset tool, select the LoftSrf1 feature.

8. Set the direction so the new solid will go downward and set the Distance option to 3, as shown in Figure 7.71.

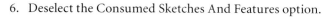

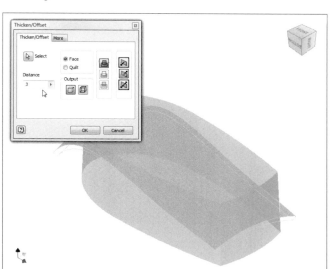

Figure 7.71

Set the direction to thicken the surface into a solid.

9. Create the new solid body.

10. Open the Sculpt tool.

11. Select the ExtrusionSrf2 feature that is visible.

12. Set the Sculpt operation to Remove.

13. Initially the outer edges of your Thickened solid will highlight, indicating that they will be removed. Click on the body that is inside the extruded surface to remove it instead. See Figure 7.72 for a preview.

14. Click OK to create the modified solid.

15. Save the part if you would like it for future reference, though it will not be used in another exercise.

Figure 7.72

Select the portion of the solid to be removed.

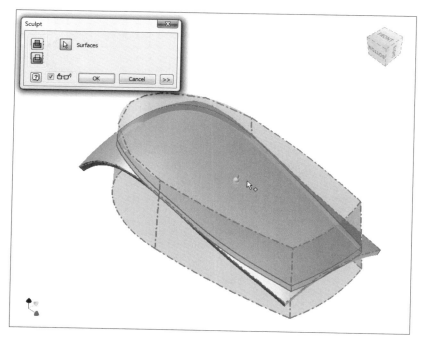

iParts

Suppose you need a collection of parts that are essentially similar but with small variations. A process of creating a part, copying it, and modifying the copy will work. However, it will be time-consuming and difficult to remember to update all of the parts if you have to make a change common to all of them.

In the glory days of hand CAD (board drafting), we often used a part family or tabulated part to deal with this. The process consisted of creating the geometry once in a

2D drawing and then listing the size differences or other unique properties. This worked well for 2D, but in 3D you need to be able to insert different members into assemblies, or sometimes multiple versions into the same assembly, and they all must exhibit the characteristics that make them unique.

To make this possible, Inventor uses the iPart. Creating an iPart is no different than any other part until you finish creating the geometry of the initial part. That's when you take the one part and convert it into many parts. You do this by generating a table in which you define almost anything that will make one member unique compared to the other members. The iPart table can control size, material, or whether or not certain features will be present in a particular member of the family.

In the following exercises, we'll touch on the basics of the iPart concept. iPart offers a phenomenal opportunity if you need to create this type of component. Creating variations like those we'll do here typically requires the use of parameters and an understanding of how they work.

Parameters

As you create a part, every value that you enter or don't enter is stored in the part in a table as a parameter.

Each parameter has a name. In a part file, these names are automatically generated, beginning with d0 and going up from there. Each parameter has a number of elements and ways you can work with it. For example, in Chapter 3 you created an association between two dimensions by selecting one dimension to be the value of another dimension. As you'll see in the next exercise, you can do the same thing in the Parameters dialog box by entering values in cells as you would in a spreadsheet. Each value has a unit associated with it that can be changed in the table. You can even share a parameter with other parts by selecting a checkbox to export the parameter.

Converting an Existing Part to an iPart

In this exercise, you'll take the first steps in moving into iParts, converting the hitch ball from the beginning of this chapter into an iPart.

1. Open the `Hitch Ball.ipt` file that you created earlier.

2. For clarity, set your view so that you are looking at the corner of Top, Front, and Right on the ViewCube.

3. Make this your Home view.

4. Under the Tools pull-down menu, select Create iPart.

   The iPart Author dialog box (Figure 7.73) will appear. In the bottom section you'll see two columns: Member and Part Number. By default, a −01 has been added to the existing filename, and since we did not declare a part number in the file's iProperties, it has adopted the member name as the part number. This dialog box will automatically propagate with other columns if there are named parameters present in the part.

5. Close the iPart Author dialog box.

6. Find the Parameters tool in the Part Features panel and open it. You'll see the Parameters dialog box shown in Figure 7.74.

Figure 7.73

The iPart Author dialog box

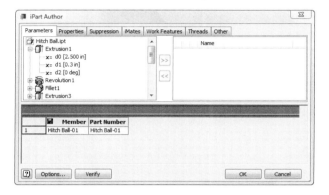

Figure 7.74

The Parameters dialog box

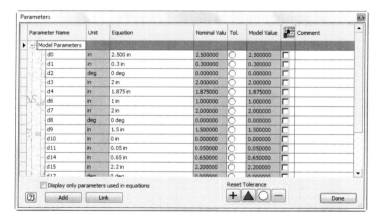

7. Find the Parameter with the Equation value of 1.875 in. This is the value that you entered for the diameter of the ball.

8. Change the Parameter name by clicking in its cell and changing the name to **Ball_Dia**. Note that spaces are not allowed and parameter names are case sensitive.

9. Find the parameter with the value of 0.65 in. This was the radius of the fillet between the ball and the plate. Set this parameter's name to Fillet.

10. Click Done to complete the changes.

11. Open the iPart creation tool again.

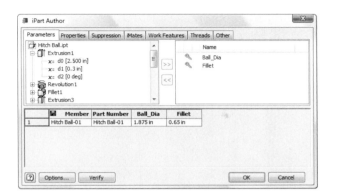

Figure 7.75

**New columns added
to the part table**

12. As you can see in Figure 7.75, the new columns have been added. Change the Part Number in Row 1 to 1.875–HB.

13. Right-click in the row and select Insert Row.

14. In the Part Number column on the new row, enter **2.000–HB**.

15. In the Ball_Dia column, set the value to 2 in.

16. In the Fillet column, set the Value to 0.60 in.

17. Close the dialog box to save the changes.

    In the Browser just below the part icon, a Table icon and label will appear. If you expand the Table icon, you'll see a listing of the Member names for this new iPart.

18. In the Browser, double-click on the Hitch Ball-02 to calculate the larger ball size.

19. Click back and forth between the items and note the changes that occur.

20. Return to the Parameters dialog box and find the value –2.8. Set its Parameter name to **Slice**.

21. Open the iPart table by double-clicking on it in the Browser.

22. On the Parameters tab, find the work plane1 feature and expand it.

23. Under that feature, you'll see the renamed parameter Slice.

24. Double-click on the parameter to add it to the columns of parameters in the part rows.

25. Set the value for Slice on Row 2 to –75mm.

In addition to changing physical values, you can add special parameters using the Other tab. Any value can be made a Key parameter. Inventor refers to key parameters for selecting which member of the family you want to insert into an assembly. If you added a key only to the part number, users would select which part number they wanted to insert. If you instead added the first key as the ball diameter and a second key to a material change, the user could choose what ball size and which material to use.

There is another way of editing members that you should try. It works more directly in the window and is most effective when adding members to an existing family or editing an existing family member.

There are two modes that can be used to modify the part members on screen:

Edit Factory Scope This is the default. If you add a feature to any member part, all of the members of the part family will also have that feature calculated.

Edit Member Scope This mode will only calculate a new feature on the active part family member. The feature will be added to the other family members, but it will automatically be suppressed. You can have the feature calculated on other members by editing their row in the iPart and changing the word Suppress in the feature's column to Calculate, Yes, or 1.

To change what mode you are working in, you need to make a toolbar visible. To access the toolbar, select Tools → Customize, select the Toolbars tab, select the iPart/iAssembly toolbar, and click Show in the upper right portion of the dialog box.

When you click Show, the dialog box shown in Figure 7.76 will appear. Switch modes by using the pull-down menu on the left side.

There are also buttons that will open the iPart table or open the table in a spreadsheet format:

Figure 7.76

Toolbar list in the Customization dialog box

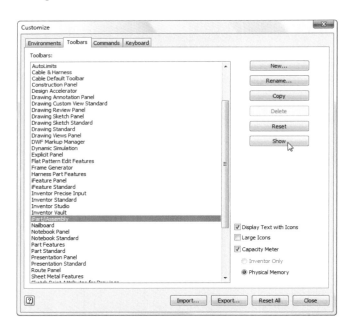

Editing One Member of an iPart Family

Using the Edit Member scope option, you'll change one member.

1. Display the iPart/iAssembly toolbar.

2. Make the Hitch Ball-02 member the active member.

3. Set Edit Member Scope as the active iPart editing state.

4. As shown in Figure 7.77, add 0.05 in chamfers to the curved edges at the top of the base.

5. Finish adding the chamfer.

6. Switch the active member to the Hitch Ball-01 member. Note that the chamfer is not on the edges in the -01 member.

7. Change the part color on the -01 member to Blue Chrome.

8. Open the iPart table and see that the feature has been added to the part as a column and that Color has been added as a column (Figure 7.78).

Figure 7.77

Using Member Scope makes it possible to add features to a single family member

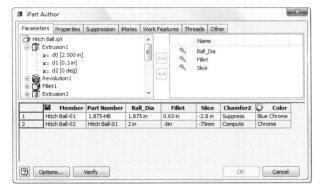

Figure 7.78

The iPart Author dialog box shows part values in a table.

Using the Member scope editing is a great way to modify the individual members. It's a shame that many Inventor users aren't fully aware of the availability of the tool. But you are.

Summary

This book is meant to be an introduction to Inventor. The trouble with writing an introductory book is that it is too easy to start using advanced features because they are usually one click or dialog box tab away. As many tools as you have already learned (and there are a lot), there are even more to explore as you go forward.

Now let's move on to the next phase and increase your understanding of the potential to be found in the Assembly environment.

CHAPTER 8

Advanced Assembly Tools

As with part modeling, the basics will take you far in your day-to-day work with assembly modeling. In this chapter you will find that many of the advanced tools in the assembly environment are used to create parts or modify them using the constraints that were covered in Chapter 4.

In Chapter 2 you created a drawing view of a presentation file. These files are great for making exploded views, which depend on the existence of an assembly file, so we will also discuss them briefly in this chapter.

There are other ways of working with assemblies that can greatly expand their uses, including the ability to define a family of assemblies driven by a table called an iAssembly.

You can also take an assembly and change it to a special type of assembly called a *weldment*. We won't do an exercise with weldments, but I will give you more information on this very useful tool.

- ■ **Design Accelerators**

- ■ **Tabulated Assemblies**

- ■ **Animating Assemblies**

- ■ **Creating Assembly Instructions**

An Assembly-centric Application

When Inventor was created, there were already many other 3D mechanical design packages on the market, including Autodesk's very successful Mechanical Desktop. So why did Autodesk create Inventor?

All of the packages in the late 1990s had the same basic framework and architecture. They were part modelers that you could also create drawings and assemblies with. For the purpose of this introductory book, I'll confess, I have presented Inventor primarily in that light, but it really does work best in the context of an assembly. In fact, there are even part modeling techniques that can be prepared in a part model but only incorporated from the assembly. You will use a simple version of this approach in one of the exercises in this chapter.

When I design in Inventor, I know that I am going to be creating an assembly, so I will usually start out that way and build my parts in their proper context. In this chapter we will do a quick experiment with that, but we will also use the assembly environment to try out other advanced tools, similar to the Bolted Connection tool that you used in Chapter 4.

In this chapter you will be using not only assembly tools, but also tools that work in the assembly environment to build members of the assembly following the philosophy that I discussed before. You will also use tools that modify members of the assembly. The key is that all of these tools require the ability to work freely in the assembly and require the underlying technology that Inventor has in the assembly that make it unique.

The exercises in this chapter will use tools in ways that they would most commonly be used in day-to-day work. In some ways that makes it a little difficult to sort them nicely by the type of tools, but I think that using them in context makes them more relevant and you can more easily understand their value.

Design Accelerators

The Design Accelerators exist for one reason: design. As powerful as Inventor is, what you have been doing to this point is modeling, and any 3D system should be able to model parts. Design is a different issue. Design is using engineering calculations to determine the correct component for the job rather than hoping that you have it right.

The geometry of a part is the solution, not the question; so while tools like finite element analysis are still the best solution for creating custom parts, using time-tested data to find which standard components meet your requirements is the more intelligent approach when working with common parts of a typical machine design.

You've already tried an example of this approach, when you worked with the Bolted Connection Design Accelerator in Chapter 4. Bolted Connection is a great tool that follows the design approach I've just described, and I highly encourage you to explore it in full. There are many more Design Accelerators (see Figure 8.1) than I have room to cover in this chapter, so I'll focus on demonstrating a few that are particularly useful in assembly design: the Bearing Generator, the Shaft Generator, the Spur Gears Component Generator, and the Engineer's Handbook. Along the way, you'll also get experience with the related assembly techniques of adaptive modeling and mirroring. To learn more about the Design Accelerators, see *Mastering Autodesk Inventor 2009 and Autodesk Inventor LT 2009 Autodesk Inventor 2009*, by Curtis Waguespack, et al. (Wiley, 2008).

Figure 8.1

The Design Accelerator Panel bar

Design Accelerator Dialog Boxes

Like other Inventor tools, the Design Accelerator dialog boxes generally all work in the same way: the Design tab handles modeling considerations such as size and shape, and the Calculation tab will focus on engineering or product design considerations.

I know that this may be a little confusing, because I just finished saying that design was more than just modeling—but the concept is intact even if the tab names can be a bit confusing.

Starting a New Assembly

This exercise will require you to download the `Chapter 8 Components.zip` file from `www.sybex.com/go/introducinginventor2009`. This file contains two part files that will be the foundation of the assembly. Copy the two files into the `C:\Data\Parts` folder with the other files that you have created from scratch.

Figure 8.2

The first part placed into the assembly

1. Make sure your project file is set to Introducing Inventor.

2. Create a new assembly file using the `Standard (in).iam` file in the English templates tab.

3. Place the `Gearbox Machined.ipt` file into the assembly. Place only one instance in the assembly.

4. Save the assembly to the Assemblies folder as `Gearbox.iam` (see Figure 8.2).

The Bearing Generator

The first Design Accelerator you will use is the Bearing Generator. Like most design accelerators, it can be used two ways. You can use it to place geometry based on the size that you want

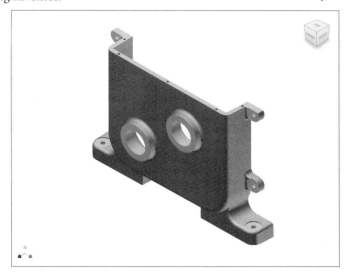

or to calculate what geometry is needed to fulfill the engineering requirements. Again, the first one is the approach we've taken so far; the second is a capability we'll begin to explore here. In practice, you'll often combine the techniques.

One thing that is unique to this tool is that the dialog box can present a list of suitable bearings based on a query. In Figure 8.3, the bearings that match the criteria listed in the dimensions appear in the upper-right portion of the dialog box.

The two tabs can be used back and forth to help limit the list based on what standards are searched and what engineering requirements are placed on the design.

Figure 8.3

The Bearing Generator dialog box's Design tab

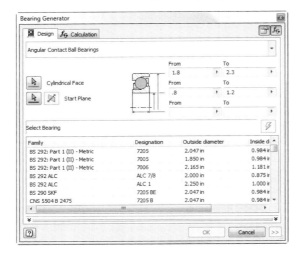

The Design Tab

This tab has some straightforward inputs, but don't let the simplicity fool you—there is a huge amount of data that can be located quickly using this tab.

The pull-down list on the top will launch a dialog box similar to the one used for placing components from the Content Center. The dialog box includes two pull-down lists that allow you to filter based on the Standard or the Category of bearing. Once the filters are set, the list of bearing standards will be displayed as icons, as shown in Figure 8.4.

Figure 8.4

Bearings for selection in the Content Center

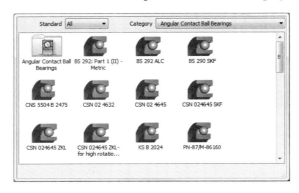

Back in the Bearing Generator dialog box, the dimensional range in the upper right will limit the selection of bearings based on space consideration.

The selection arrows on the left will allow you to select geometry directly in the assembly for the diameter and starting plane for placing a bearing.

Once you have selected your search criteria, click the Update button to have Inventor search the Content Center for the matching items. The list will appear in the Select Bearing area in the lower half of the window.

The Calculation Tab

Looking at Figure 8.5 you can immediately see that the Calculation tab is intended to be used quite differently than the Design tab. You'll input your requirements and Inventor will calculate which standard bearings meet your needs.

Discussing every option here would lead us into engineering topics that are beyond the scope of this book. The bottom line is that if you want to be absolutely certain that the bearing you select will do the job, this is where to find out. There are a couple of key elements that every user should be aware of.

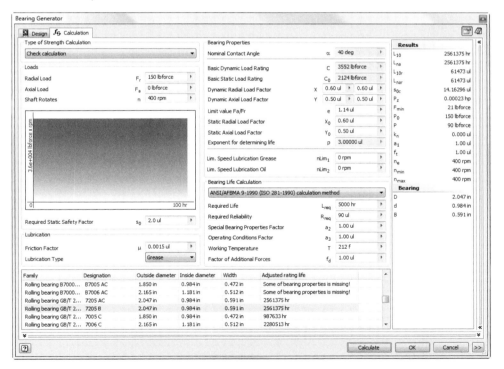

Figure 8.5

The Calculation tab of the Bearing Generator dialog box. On the right are the results calculated from the input.

TYPE OF STRENGTH CALCULATION

The first pull-down option is located in the upper-left of the dialog box and controls which method will be used to evaluate the bearings:

Check Calculation When you select a bearing from the list at the bottom of the tab, its properties will be displayed based on the loads specified in the Loads group.

Bearing Design By also calculating the effect the loads will have on the life of the bearing, this option will filter the list further and make it easier for you to select the proper bearing.

LOADS

It is critical that you enter the appropriate Radial and Axial loads as well as the number of shaft rotations per minute that will occur, in order to validate the bearings for selection.

BEARING LIFE CALCULATION

This pull-down list will select which ANSI or other standard method will be used to calculate the life of the bearing. Be sure to use the appropriate methodology to ensure the results that you need.

MESSAGES

At the very bottom and on the right side of most Design Accelerator dialog boxes are double arrows that will expand the dialog box to show messages relating to the calculation. If the bottom or right edge of a Design Accelerator dialog box turns red after a calculation, expand this area to see what the error message is.

Selecting the Bearings

In this exercise you'll use the Bearing Generator to find what bearings will work properly for the design requirements:

1. Change your Panel bar from Assembly tools to the Design Accelerator panel.

2. Open the Bearing Generator tool from the Panel bar.

3. Enter the size values from Figure 8.5 into the dialog box and update the list. The list should narrow to display only four bearings, as shown in Figure 8.6.

4. Using the selection filters, find the STN 02 4670 N class of bearing under the Cylindrical Roller category and click the Update button.

5. Switch to the Calculation tab and enter **400 lbforce** for the Radial Load, **50 lbforce** for the Axial Load, and **350 rpm** for the Shaft Rotates values.

6. Click Calculate to update.

The list of bearings on the bottom should display the Outer Diameter (OD), the Inner Diameter (ID), the sectional width of the bearing, and now the Adjusted Life Rating. The values that are calculated are more than satisfactory, and we can use any of these bearings with confidence.

7. Return to the Design tab.

8. Select the N1006 designation and click OK to generate the geometry for the selected bearing.

   A dialog box will appear displaying the name and path of the file that will be created for the new bearing. You can click the button to the right of the displayed name to modify the name and path. You can also deselect the checkbox on the lower left to skip these confirmation dialog boxes in the future.

9. Click OK to accept the name and place the bearing into the assembly by clicking in the Design window (see Figure 8.7).

10. Save the assembly file.

Figure 8.7

Place the bearing in the assembly near the upper hole.

Adaptive Modeling

Working with the Bearing Generator has given you a good introduction to the Design Accelerators and the flexibility you need to design or select parts that fit the needs of a complex assembly. We'll continue to explore this toolset shortly, but we've now reached an appropriate stage in our ongoing example—that is, in the assembly design process itself—to try out two Inventor techniques that are extremely useful with assemblies: adaptive modeling and mirroring.

As an extension of Inventor's focus on the assembly, adaptive modeling uses the constraints in an assembly to modify part features. Rather than always modeling everything to fit perfectly, it's possible to define fits between parts in the environment where it makes the most sense: the assembly.

To create an adaptive relationship, you must designate a feature in a part as adaptive, and to be adaptive the part must have flexibility in its sketch that will allow it to change size. If you want to change a part's length, its length value must be dimensioned either with a driven dimension or not at all.

Once you've made the feature adaptive, you have to make the part adaptive within the assembly. For the sake of security, a part can only be adaptive to one assembly's constraints; this way, you avoid the risk of an adaptive "tug of war" scenario.

This technology was the hallmark of Inventor's early days, but the addition of dozens of other capabilities has made it less important. I think it's a great way to bring a design into focus, but I do recommend disabling the adaptive relationship to enhance performance once the sizes are understood. Inventor's safety check and validation of the constraints is run every time you make a change to the models, even if the adaptive relationship isn't updated, so it can save you some processor time to disable the feature when you're not making modifications to the relevant parts. Adaptability can always be restored and updated whenever you like.

Using Adaptive Modeling

In this exercise you will use your selected bearing to size its own location hole:

1. Activate the Gearbox Machined part in the assembly by double-clicking it.

2. Find the Hole6 - Make Adaptive feature in the Browser (see Figure 8.8).

Figure 8.8

Right-click on a feature to make it adaptive.

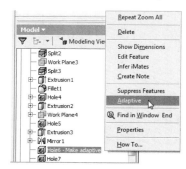

3. Right-click on the feature and select Adaptive from the context menu.

After you turn on the Adaptive capability of a feature or part, a symbol will appear next to its normal icon in the Browser to serve as a visual cue of its special status.

4. Return to the assembly.

In the following steps, you'll see that because you modified the adaptive status of the feature while working in an assembly, the part was also made adaptive to the assembly that you are working in.

5. Switch your Panel bar back to the Assembly tools and select the Constraint tool, or press the C key from the Design Accelerator environment to start placing a constraint.

6. Hover over the outer surface of the bearing until the Select Other icon appears. Use the selection arrows or the mouse wheel to cycle options until just the outer surface is highlighted. The axis of the bearing should *not* be visible or highlighted.

7. Click to select the outer surface when it's available (see Figure 8.9).

Now that you've selected the cylindrical face, Inventor will automatically be looking for other faces rather than an axis.

8. Select the surface of the upper hole as shown in Figure 8.6 earlier.

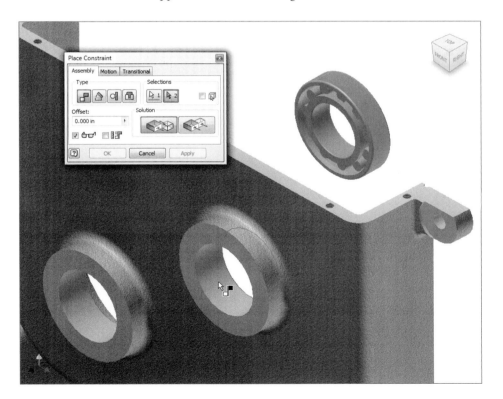

Figure 8.9

Selecting only the surface of one part makes selecting another surface easy.

9. Click OK to create the constraint.

The bearing will move to be centered in the hole, but the hole will resize to fit the bearing. Using the offset value in the Place Constraint dialog box will even allow you to establish a fit between the two surfaces. This technology is still a fantastic tool for constructing a design when you have unknowns.

You have centered the part but it can still slide in the hole. Let's fix it in place.

10. Create a Mate constraint with a Flush solution between the faces, as shown in Figure 8.10.

Figure 8.10

Use a flush solution to align the bearing and the inside of the gearbox housing.

11. Now select your bearing and press Ctrl+C to copy the bearing to the Windows Clipboard.

Pressing Ctrl+V will paste a copy of the bearing wherever you cursor is in the Design window. You can do this repeatedly to place several instances.

12. Place one additional instance of the bearing into the assembly.

13. Constrain the new bearing using an Insert constraint with the Aligned solution, as shown in Figure 8.11. Be careful of the chamfer on the hole.

You've now built one side of the Gearbox housing. The housing is symmetrical, so rather than building a second half we will let Inventor and the computer do the work.

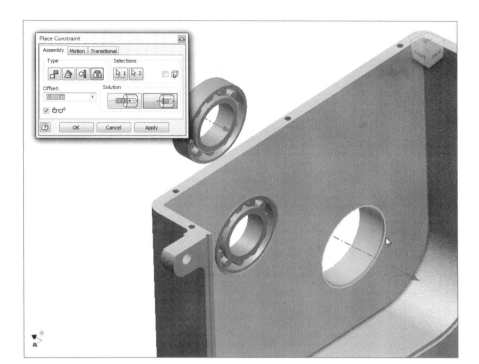

Figure 8.11
Position the second bearing using Insert.

Mirroring Components

In a case such as this, where you have identical components that are mirror images of each other, there's no need to model both components. You can create one and then mirror it. For components in an assembly, Inventor provides the Mirror Components tool, similar to the Mirror tool for features you worked with in Chapter 7.

It's important to note that the mirrored part will be dependent on the original part, and so changes that are made to the original will appear in the second. If one part needs a unique feature, you should make it the mirrored part so that you can add the unique feature without having it appear in the second part.

You can break the link between the two parts, but the mirrored part will not become a fully featured model. If only a small number of features will be consistent, it would be better to model the second part individually and create relationships between the two parts so that they reflect one another.

The Mirror Components: Status dialog box (Figure 8.12) is quite simple, and the process of using it is, too. You select components that you want to create mirror images of and then select a plane to mirror them about.

Figure 8.12
The Mirror Components: Status dialog box

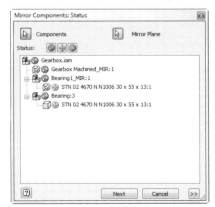

There are three options that can make quite a difference, though. After you select a component, icons will appear next to it in the Status area of the dialog box. Clicking an icon can change the behavior of the mirroring:

 This icon indicates that the selected component will be mirrored, creating a new file.

 This icon indicates that the geometry will be copied and repositioned to appear mirrored. By default, Content Center components will have this option automatically as it is uncommon to need a mirrored bolt or bearing.

 This icon allows a component to be ignored for mirroring. If there are several instances in a pattern, you can use this option to omit some of them.

The >> (More) icon at the bottom expands the dialog box so you can set defaults for whether to reuse standard content and whether to preview components when using the Mirror Components tool.

Mirroring the Assembly

Let's complete the housing by mirroring the main component.

1. Select the Mirror Components tool from the Assembly Panel bar.

2. Select the housing and both bearings.

3. In the dialog box click the Mirror Plane button and select the large machined surface on the Gearbox Machined part. See Figure 8.13 for the preview that will appear.

   Once again Inventor is able to color-code the onscreen feedback. The icon that tells Inventor to mirror components is green, and therefore mirrored components preview in green. The reuse icon is yellow, and reused components preview in yellow.

Figure 8.13

Preview of the mirrored components

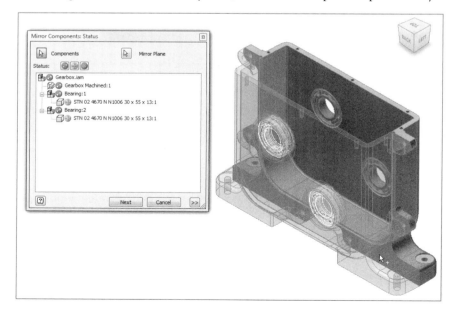

4. Click the reuse icon for Bearing:2 to switch it to Ignore. Notice that the preview disappears.

5. Click the icon for Bearing:2 again to return it to the preview.

6. Click the Next button to move forward.

The Mirror Components: File Names dialog box will now appear, listing the files that need to be created to add the parts to the assembly. In the dialog box (shown in Figure 8.14), you can add a suffix or prefix to create a unique filename. You can also create a specific name by selecting the filename in its cell under the New Name column. The Component Destination option gives you the choice of creating components in individual files without placing them in the assembly or creating the files and dropping them into the assembly as previewed.

7. Click OK to create the new components. See Figure 8.15 for the final result.

Figure 8.14

The Mirror Components: File Names dialog box

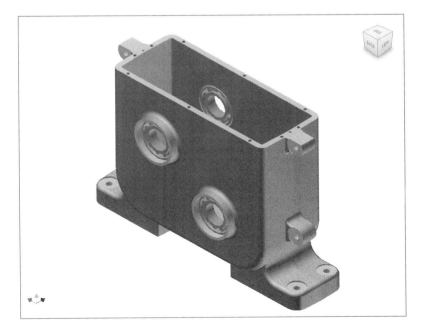

Figure 8.15

The completed Gearbox housing

Now we need to add components to the gearbox. You won't be modeling any of them. Instead, you will use additional Design Accelerators to specify what you need and then have the tool build the component.

The Shaft Generator

This tool builds round things. It's especially adept at spinning round things, so there are some great features for rotating shafts.

Like all Design Accelerators, the Shaft Generator could be used simply as a quick way to draw the shaft, but in the next stage of our example we will use a combination of tools to build a shaft in the context of the assembly and validate it based on what we need for performance.

In the upper-right corner are icons that allow you to save the shaft configuration to a template file for future use. You can also generate a report of the results for review. See Figure 8.16 for a partial preview.

The Shaft Component Generator dialog box's Design tab, shown in Figure 8.17, uses a list of shaft elements and special treatments to develop the geometry of the shaft. Let's go over a few of the special items in the dialog box.

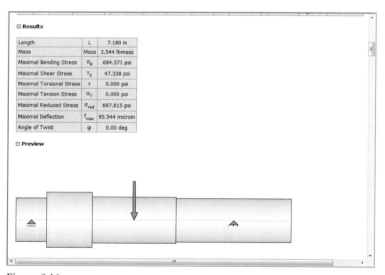

Figure 8.16

One portion of the extensive calculation report

Figure 8.17

Shaft Component Generator's Design tab

The Design Tab

As with the other Design Accelerators, you'll use the Design tab when you want to start by defining the initial geometry rather than by calculating the geometry from the engineering requirements.

PLACEMENT

This group of tools allows you to select the geometry the shaft will be centered on, where it will start, and what direction it will be developed in. The Mate checkbox will even place a constraint between the new shaft and its location as you define it.

SECTIONS

This flyout menu controls which geometry is being placed in the shaft at any given time:

Sections In this mode, geometry that you add will constitute the exterior of the shaft.

Bore On The Left/Right The other two modes will remove geometry from the interior of the shaft starting either on the left or right end.

The buttons to the right of the pull-down list will add segments to the shaft or control the display of its elements.

The Calculation Tab

The Calculation tab for the Shaft Component Generator features a graphical display of the shaft geometry that you can use to position the loads and supports that the shaft will have.

Material You can specify a material or use by selecting it from the pull-down list or entering the physical values directly, or you can simply accept the material that is set for the part in its iProperties.

Loads & Supports You can add as many loads or supports as the shaft will encounter in real use to validate the design. Some loads, such as Torque, must have a countering load to be properly defined.

The Graphs Tab

In the Graphs tab you can select which calculation result graph you want to display. With the Shaft Generator, graphs you can display include Shear force, Bending Moment, Bending Stress, and several other critical measurements. The graph will appear under the profile of the shaft to provide visual feedback on the behavior of the shaft. You can also move the load and support positions for a better understanding of how they affect the result.

Creating a Shaft

In this exercise you will use a "middle-out" approach to building the shaft by using existing components to define the geometry of the shaft and engineering data to validate it.

1. Switch to the Design Accelerator panel and select the Shaft tool.

2. In the Sections group, click the Specify Shaft By Picking Geometry In Assembly button (see Figure 8.18).

Figure 8.18

Shafts can be placed by entering values or selecting existing geometry to assist in their definition.

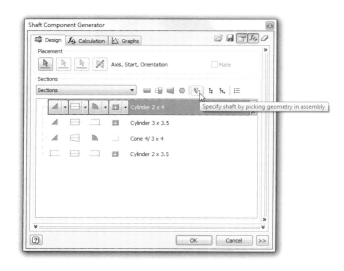

3. When the Geometry Definition dialog box appears, click the cylindrical face holding the bearing, as shown in Figure 8.19.

   Selecting the face will fill the length and diameter of the face with the new shaft.

4. Click OK to accept the new shaft segment.

Figure 8.19

Select the hole face to orient the new shaft.

The Shaft Component Generator dialog box will reappear with the new shaft segment displayed. In each row representing a segment are four icons and a display of the characteristics, and at the right end are two buttons. Clicking the top one launches an editing dialog box, and clicking the bottom button deletes the segment. However, you cannot remove all of the segments.

The four icons represent options. The first on the left offers the ability to place optional end treatments on the left end of the segment. The next allows you to form the segment as a cylinder, a cone, or a polygon. The third applies end treatments to the right end. The fourth icon has a list of elements that can be added to the face of the segment, such as axial holes, grooves, or wrench flats.

In the preview you will notice direction arrows, a double-ended arrow that you can click and drag to change the segment length, and four points at the quadrants that you can click to change the diameter.

5. Click the icon to modify the left end of the shaft and select Chamfer, as shown in Figure 8.20.

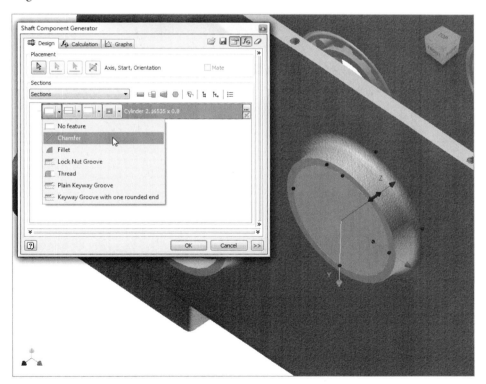

Figure 8.20

Adding a chamfer to the end of a shaft segment

6. Selecting the Chamfer option launches a second dialog box where you can specify the chamfer distance. Enter **.05** in the Distance value and click the checkmark icon to add the chamfer to the segment.

7. Click on one of the quadrants and drag the diameter of the shaft down to 0.875 inches, as shown in Figure 8.21. You must click a second time to accept the value.

Figure 8.21

Drag-editing the shaft diameter

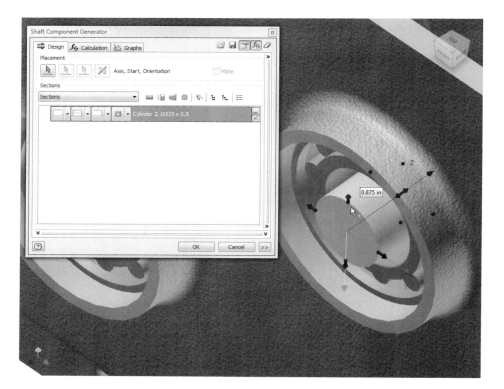

You will need an accurate sizing, so click the Edit icon on the segment row, or double-click the description of the segment, to launch a dialog box showing the size of the segment.

8. Click on the diameter, and an arrow will appear for more options. Select the Measure option and measure the inside diameter of the bearing, as shown in Figure 8.22. Click when the inside diameter is highlighted.

9. When you click, the shaft will update immediately. Click OK in the Cylinder dialog box to accept the new values.

Figure 8.22

**Measuring the
required diameter
for the shaft**

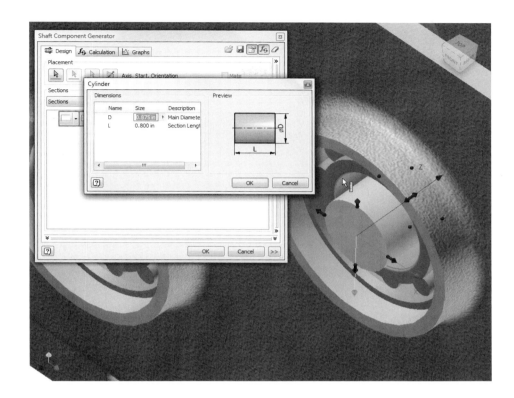

10. Rotate the model so you can see the other end of the shaft on the interior of the gearbox.

11. Click the Cylinder icon in the Shaft Component Generator dialog box to add a new segment to the shaft. Note that the new segment is automatically sized to be the same as the previous segment.

12. Double-click the description of the new segment and set its diameter to 1.5 inch. Set the length to 3.38 inches (the measured distance to the next bearing) and click OK to accept these values.

13. Click OK to create the shaft and exit the dialog box.

    If you are prompted to save the shaft, accept the defaults by clicking OK. The shaft will then need to be placed. Click to place it in an open part of the screen.

14. Use an Insert constraint to place it back into the bearing, as shown in Figure 8.23.

The shaft is not yet complete, but at this point you have an opportunity to try editing a component created with a Design Accelerator.

Figure 8.23

**Constraining the
shaft into position**

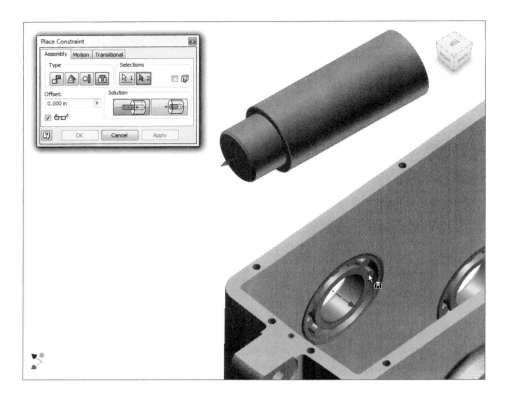

Editing a Shaft

You don't use the typical Edit feature to modify a Design Accelerator–generated component. Instead, there is a special right-click option specific to Design Accelerators for this purpose.

1. Right-click on the newly created shaft and select Edit Using Design Accelerator from the menu.

2. Click on the second shaft segment to highlight it.

3. In the Sections group, locate the Split Selected Section tool and click it.

4. In the Cylinder dialog box, set the value of L1 to 1.19 inch and set the value of D2 to 1.25.

5. Click OK to accept.

    This will split the previous segment into two segments that equal the same total length as the original. With this technique, you'll never have to calculate a series of stepped segments.

6. Activate the last segment in the shaft.

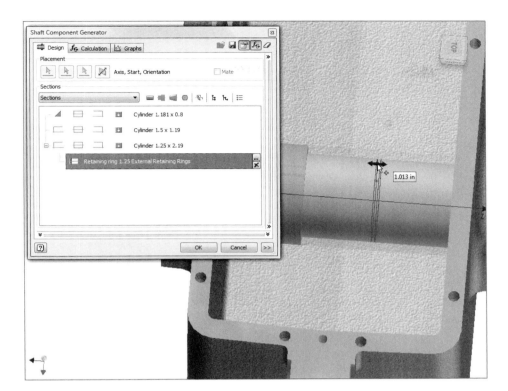

Figure 8.24

Placing the retaining ring groove

7. Click the icon on the right to get a fly out list of options and select Add Retaining Ring.

8. Drag the arrow on the ring groove preview until it displays that the ring is just over one inch from the shaft split (see Figure 8.24).

9. Click to place the groove in its location.

10. Select the first shaft segment.

11. While it is highlighted, click the Cylinder button in the Sections group. This will create a duplicate of the first segment as a second segment, moving the others out of the way.

12. When the duplicate section is created, it will be next to the original. To move it into its proper location, click and drag the new segment to the end. Note that it's easier to click the modification buttons to get the segment to relocate.

13. Add a 0.05-inch chamfer to the right end of the new shaft segment.

14. Set the length of the last segment to 3 inches.

   Before closing the Shaft Component Generator dialog box, you should switch to the Calculation tab and then the Graphs tab to see how the shaft can be tested.

15. Once you've finished the testing, click OK to complete the shaft.

16. Locate the Shaft:1 component in the Browser.

17. Click on the icon for the component and drag it onto the screen. When you release the mouse button, a new instance will appear.

18. Use an Insert constraint to install the new shaft into the lower set of bearings facing the opposite direction (see Figure 8.25).

19. Save the assembly.

Figure 8.25

Gearbox assembly with shafts constrained

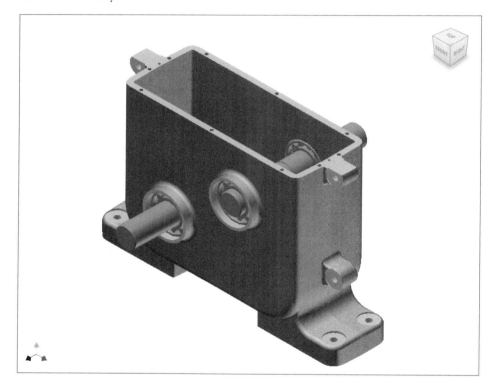

Spur Gears

There are three types of Gear generators among the Inventor Design Accelerators: Worm, Bevel, and Spur. We won't explore the first two types, but we will include Spur gears in our design.

The Spur Gears Component Generator dialog box (Figure 8.26) follows the same workflow as the others. Gears require more information to define than many of the other components you can generate with the Accelerator tools because even simple gear relationships are relatively complex. To begin using the Gear generator, you will need to have either the shafts or the holes where the shafts will go in place.

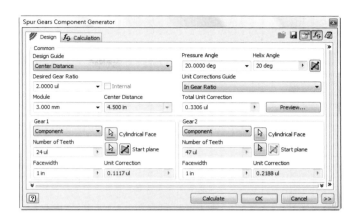

Figure 8.26

The Spur Gear Component Generator dialog box

Because so many companies and so many different products approach gear design differently, this tool offers many options. Before trying it out in the next stage of our exercise, you should first read the following basic overview of the dialog box.

The Design Tab

There is a lot of detail in this tab, and depending on the Design Guide you select, some of the items will have their values calculated automatically.

DESIGN GUIDE

This pull-down menu allows you to choose among five different types of missing information. The guides define what information you need to provide and what information will be calculated for you. For example, searching for the Number Of Teeth will result in Inventor calculating the number of teeth needed on each gear based on their spacing, gear ratio, and other inputs. Searching for the Center Distance will use different inputs to calculate from.

GEAR1/GEAR2

The two groups that occupy the bottom of the dialog box are for locating where the gears will be placed and defining some of the inputs for the Design Guide calculation.

Immediately under the group label (Gear 1, Gear 2) is a pull-down menu with three options that determine how the selections and calculations will be used:

Component This option develops a model of a gear that will be independent of the geometry it's located on and saved in its own file.

Feature If you plan to build the gear as part of a shaft, the Feature option will edit a Design Accelerator shaft and add the gear geometry to it.

No Feature The third option allows you to develop the design requirements and keep them as a part of the assembly without developing the geometry. If you purchase gears and plan to use them in your design, you can use this tool to verify that they'll work and also be able to revalidate should something change in the assembly.

MORE (>>)

For constructing a gear set, be sure to pay attention to the items that are exposed using the More (>>) button in the lower right. These options can greatly affect the calculation both in the Design and Calculation tabs.

The Calculation Tab

Depending on the method that you rely on to validate your gear design, the contents of this tab (Figure 8.27) will vary greatly:

Method Of Strength Calculation The seven calculation standards available from this pull-down menu range from highly complex input options to the relatively simple.

More - Type of Load Calculation This variable controls what type of input will be used to calculate the load capacities of a gear.

Figure 8.27

The Spur Gear Generator dialog box showing additional options

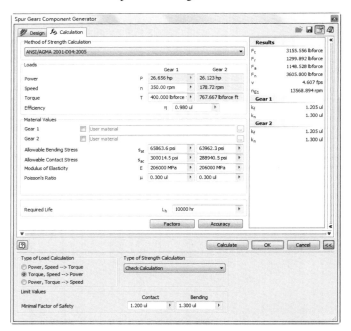

Adding the Gears

In this stage of the exercise we'll use the Spur Gear Component Generator to create a gear set:

1. Remove the Enabled state of the Gearbox Machined parts so that they can be seen through.

2. Select the Spur Gears tool from the Design Accelerator panel.

3. Set the Design Guide to Module and Number Of Teeth. See Figure 8.28 for the Design tab settings.

4. For the Gear1 Cylindrical Face, select the middle cylindrical surface (between the retaining ring groove and then step up to the 1.5-inch diameter segment) of the lower shaft.

5. Click the selection icon for the Start Plane for Gear1 and select the face between the 1.5-inch and the 1.25-inch diameter sections. See Figure 8.29 for the highlighted face.

   Selecting this face will cause a preview of the gear to appear in place.

6. Select the same face on the upper shaft for the Cylindrical Face of Gear 2.

7. Click the Calculate button to update the Module and Teeth numbers for the gears.

8. Click OK to generate the gears on the shafts.

Figure 8.28

Design tab settings

Figure 8.29

Select the Start Plane face on the lower shaft.

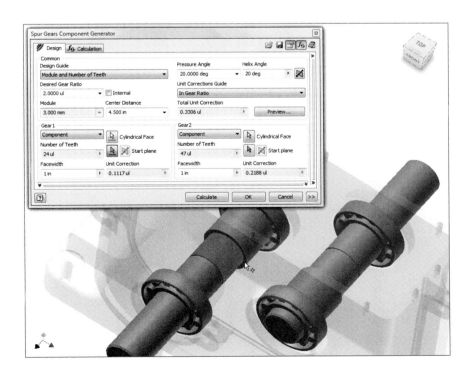

9. Click OK again to save the generated files. Your assembly should look like Figure 8.30.

10. Save the assembly.

There are a number of other Design Accelerators that could be used to continue developing this design. For example, I encourage you to explore the Key Connection generator, which you can use to properly connect the gears to the shafts. You can find it under the Shaft tool in the Design Accelerator panel.

Figure 8.30

Spur gears developed on shafts

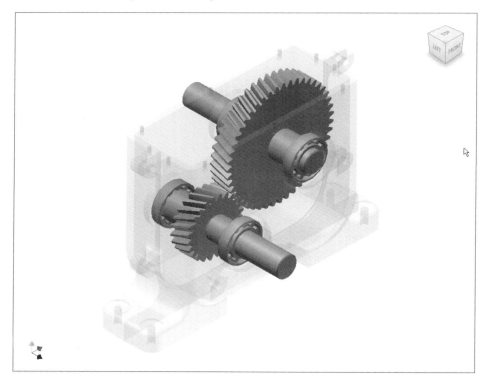

The Engineer's Handbook

Of all of the icons in the Design Accelerators panel, the most important may be the last one.

The Engineer's Handbook is a guide to the formulas and methodologies used by the Design Accelerator tools to make their calculations and validations. It is constructed like a help file, categorized and sorted by the tool and the units that you work with. Figure 8.31 shows an example.

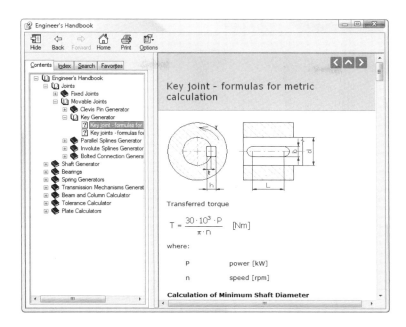

Derived Parts

Inventor's Derived Parts technology is primarily a tool for part modeling, but it can be used in many ways, including complex assembly designs.

The most common use for Derived Parts is to create one part model based on another and keep the resulting model associated with the original. Another use is to be able to fuse the parts of an assembly into a single part file. A third, very powerful option is to extract dimension values and parameter values from one part for reuse in another part. This is a great way to build enduring relationships between parts without using adaptive modeling. This method even allows you to draw model values from several parts into one so that it responds to changes from multiple sources.

In our model the Gearbox Machined part is derived from the `Gearbox Casting.ipt` file. Changes to the Casting file will be reflected in the Machined part. Let's take a closer look at our assembly and make modifications where needed.

Modifying the Assembly

After adding the gears, it's important to review the design to make sure there are proper clearances for the parts.

1. Select the Front view on the ViewCube. Your view should look like Figure 8.32.

Figure 8.32

**Gears interfere
with the housing.**

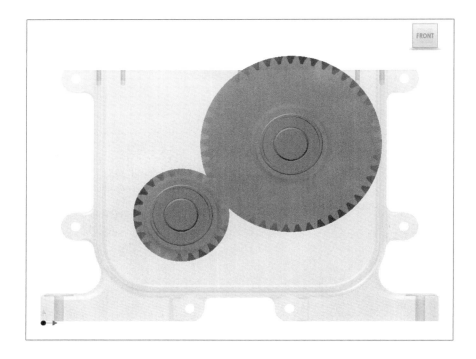

Notice that the large gear interferes with the side of the gearbox housing. Normally you would just change where the holes that locate the shafts are drilled. However, in this case the housing is a casting, so you have to move the bosses in the casting to relocate the holes.

2. In the Browser, locate the Gearbox Machined:1 part.

3. Double-click on the part to make it the active file.

4. In the Browser, locate the derived part icon with the name Gearbox Casting. This is the link to the source part. Double-click on the Gearbox Casting to open that file.

5. Click on the flat face of the lower boss. When the 3D Grips glyph appears, click on it to activate 3D Grips (see Figure 8.33).

6. With the parametric dimension exposed, change the 3.000-inch dimension to 2.5 inches.

7. Change the 5.300-inch dimension to 5.5 inches.

8. Right-click and select Done to complete the change.

9. Close the casting file and save the changes.

10. After you close the casting part, you will return to the machined part. Update the part to show the changes.

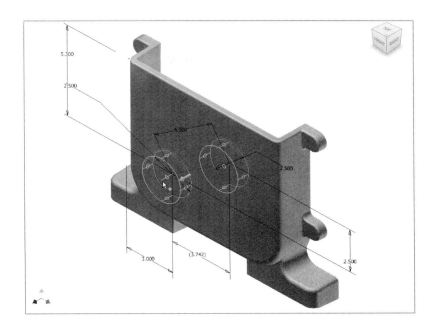

Figure 8.33
3D Grip editing exposes the parametric dimension.

11. Return to the assembly and update it to reposition the shafts and gears.

12. Change the state of the other half of the assembly to Enabled.

13. Review your design. It should look like Figure 8.34.

14. Save your design.

Figure 8.34
The completed gearbox

Component Move and Rotate

Being able to see the geometry underlying an assembly you are trying to build can be tricky at times. Perhaps you've inserted a part and need to constrain geometry on the opposite side. Rotating the view of the model helps, but sometimes with axial relationships the part can be facing the opposite direction that you need. We looked briefly at this potential problem and possible solutions in Chapter 4 (when you placed the first Axle support part), but here I'd like to do more.

Being able to move or rotate components after they have been partially or fully constrained can be frustrating. The solution is simple—but as with many things, finding the solution may not be so simple.

Moving Constrained Parts

Though it seems like a minor thing, understanding that you are able to move temporarily is useful.

1. Make sure the Gearbox assembly is open.

2. Find the Move Component tool in the Assembly panel and select it. (Note that the V key is a shortcut for the tool.)

3. Click and drag the lower shaft outside of the housing, as shown in Figure 8.35.

Figure 8.35

Move the shaft out of the assembly, temporarily suspending its constraints.

4. Click on the shaft that you moved, and either press the G key to start the Rotate Component tool or select it in the Panel bar.

5. When the Reticle appears, rotate the part in the same way that you can rotate the view with the Orbit tool (see Figure 8.36).

6. Click the Update button in the Inventor Standard toolbar to restore the assembly constraints.

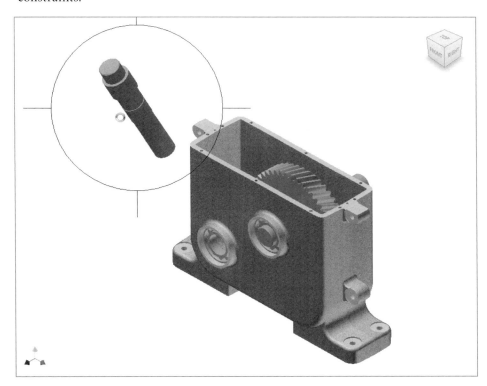

Figure 8.36

The Rotate Component tool allows you to rotate the component even if it is constrained.

iAssembly

I still grumble when I think of the hours of work I could've saved if I'd had iParts in previous jobs, but the idea of having iAssemblies *really* makes me think about creating that time machine.

An iAssembly is the same concept as an iPart but at the assembly level. Some people refer to the concept as "configurations," a name that sells the concept short.

iAssemblies can change out parts and can even change out constraint systems or the values of individual constraints. They are a remarkable tool if you have used tables to define assemblies in the past.

Creating a Simple iAssembly

If you create table-driven assemblies, a basic exercise should be enough to get you going in the right direction.

1. Open the `Caster Assembly.iam` file that you created in Chapter 4.

2. Right-click on the Shaft part and open it in its own window.

3. Using the Save As command (not Save Copy As), create a new file named **`Shaft - large.ipt`**.

4. Change the 0.7-inch diameter to 1.2 inch.

5. Change the part color to Red and save the file to update the Caster Assembly file.

6. Switch to the Caster Assembly.

7. Use the Place Component tool to place an instance of the Shaft - large part in the assembly.

8. Use an Insert constraint to place it into the assembly in the same way the current shaft is located (see Figure 8.37).

9. Go to the Tools pull-down list and click Create iAssembly.

10. Insert a new row by right-clicking on row 1.

    The iAssembly Author dialog box has seven tabs you can use to access and modify different elements for the individual iAssembly members.

Figure 8.37

Constrain the new large shaft into the same position as the old shaft.

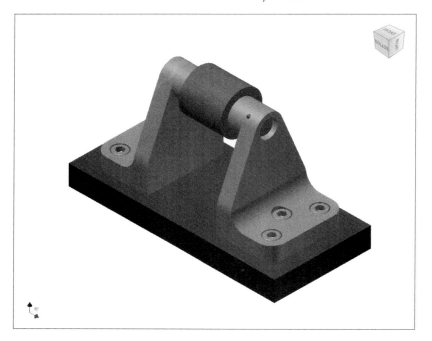

The Components tab shows a listing of the parts that are in the assembly. In each component there are subelements that you can manage, specifying such things as whether the part will be included in the row, whether the component will be grounded, whether it will be adaptive.

11. In the Components tab, find the Shaft:1 part and expand its list of subelements.

12. Double-click on the Include/Exclude element of the Shaft:1 component.

This will add a column where you can select whether or not Shaft:1 will be included in the child assembly. The default Include value in the cell is actually a pull-down that you can switch to Exclude.

13. In Row 2, switch the Shaft:1 part to Exclude.

14. Locate the Shaft - Large part and add its Include/Exclude value to the table.

15. Exclude Shaft - large:1 from Row 1 but Include it in Row 2. Figure 8.38 shows how your table should appear.

This will create two assemblies that share the same parts—except the shaft, which will be different in each assembly.

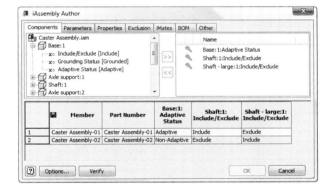

Figure 8.38

The iAssembly Author dialog box showing the edits to create two unique assemblies

16. Click OK to create the two member assemblies.

17. In the Browser, expand the table and click back and forth between the two assembly versions.

When Inventor creates an iPart or an iAssembly, it will create a folder that stores versions of the individual members. To make sure that all team members have quick access to versions, it's good practice to generate the files of the individual child assemblies. This is true for both iAssemblies and iParts.

18. Right-click on the Caster Assembly-02 table member in the Browser and select Generate Files. Click Yes when prompted to save new files.

19. Save the main assembly file.

Documenting an iAssembly

Since many people create tabulated assemblies by simply creating a parts list that swaps out the different parts, Inventor needs to be able to do the same thing. The following steps demonstrate how:

1. Create a new drawing based on the ANSI (mm).dwg template.

2. Create a Base view of the assembly. Use the Change View Orientation button under the list of view Orientations to set up a view that looks like Figure 8.39.

3. Using the Drawing Annotation panel, create a parts list of the assembly and place it above the title block.

4. Double-click on the parts list to open its editing dialog box (see Figure 8.40).

Figure 8.39

The drawing of an iAssembly can display any member of the family.

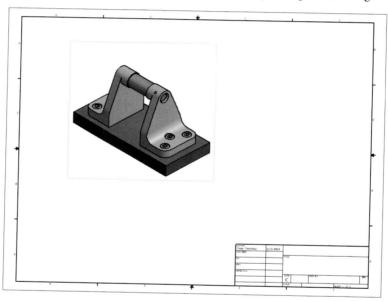

Figure 8.40

The editing dialog box for the parts list will indicate nondisplayed parts in gray.

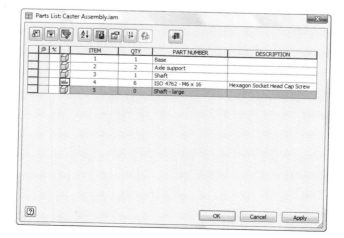

5. At the top of the dialog box click the Member Selection icon.

6. The Select Member dialog box shown in Figure 8.41 opens. Click to add a checkmark next to Caster Assembly-02.

7. Click OK to accept the change and close the Select Member dialog box, and click OK again to close the editing dialog box.

8. A new QTY column will be added to the parts list. Dragging the width of the columns reveals that these are parts counts for the versions of the assembly (see Figure 8.42).

9. Double-click on the drawing view to open the editing dialog box.

10. In the Model State tab, select Caster Assembly-02 in the iAssembly Member group and click OK to update the drawing view. See Figure 8.43 for the result.

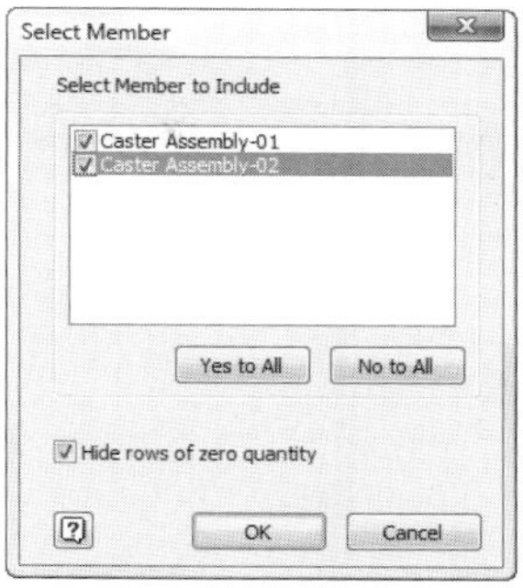

Figure 8.41

You can select any combination of iAssembly members to display in the parts list.

Figure 8.42

The parts list can display the part quantities of the various member assemblies.

Figure 8.43

Updated drawing view showing a different member

PARTS LIST				
ITEM	QTY Caster Assembly-01	QTY Caster Assembly-02	PART NUMBER	DESCRIPTION
1	1	1	Base	
2	2	2	Axle support	
3	1	0	Shaft	
4	6	6	ISO 4762 - M6 x 16	Hexagon Socket Head Cap Screw
5	0	1	Shaft - large	

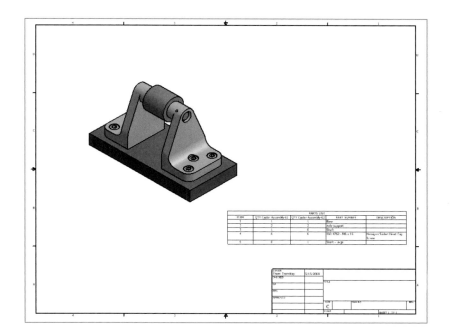

The drawing will not be reused in the future. You can save it for your own reference if you like.

The way Inventor works with iParts and iAssemblies allows for consistent document management, so not only do you get the benefit of easily creating tabulated assemblies, you can also work with them in a group environment.

Animation within the Assembly

In Chapter 4 you learned that parts can be moved when there are existing degrees of freedom. With the Move and Rotate Component tools, you can move parts regardless of whether they are constrained. This movement is not very well controlled, though, and it cannot reasonably represent the action of a mechanism.

To meet the need for this kind of representation, Inventor has several levels of animation. At the most basic, you can just drag a partially free part to see its range of motion. A more advanced tool you can use for creating presentations to clients and other stakeholders is the animation and rendering environment called Inventor Studio; Chapter 10 provides an overview. Inventor Professional has the ability to simulate the physics of a mechanism, but before most people use that extraordinary capability they will usually put an assembly constraint through a range of motion.

Any assembly constraint can be animated, but you won't necessarily get impressive results in every situation. Driving the value of an axis-to-axis mate may not seem to do anything. There are even times where you may want to create constraints for the sake of driving them to animate an assembly.

Preparing the Assembly

In our Gearbox the gears are free to move (yes, they're automatically meshed), but there's no purpose in constraining that movement for the design. To show someone how it works is a different matter, and you will set up an animation to do that.

1. Open or switch to the Gearbox.iam file.

2. Orient you view of the assembly so that you can see both gears, as in Figure 8.44.

3. Click on the larger gear and drag it to show that there is a relationship between the gears that reflects the ratio.

4. Locate the Spur Gears:1 Design Accelerator item in the Browser.

5. Expand the Spur Gears and then expand the Spur Gear:1 component.

6. Create an angular Constraint of 0 degrees between the YZ Origin Plane of Spur Gear:1 and the top of the housing, as shown in Figure 8.45.

Figure 8.44

Set your view so you can see the gears clearly.

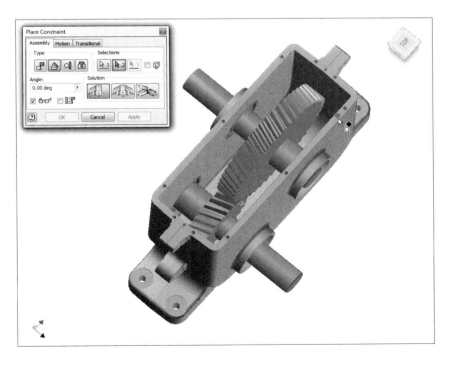

Figure 8.45

Create an angular constraint aligning the gear to the housing.

When you create the constraint, the gears should shift into position. The constraint will also prevent you from being able to drag the motion of the gears. That limitation may not be desirable, so it's important to know that you can drive a constraint through a range of motion even if the constraint is suppressed.

7. Locate the Angle:1 constraint at the end of the Browser list.

8. Right-click on the constraint and select Suppress.

9. Drag your gears again to see that they are free to move.

Drive Constraint

The Drive Constraint dialog box (see Figure 8.46) is used to define the values that will establish a range of motion for the assembly constraint. To access this dialog box, right-click on a constraint in the Browser and select Drive Constraint from the context menu.

Figure 8.46

The Drive Constraint dialog box expanded to show additional options

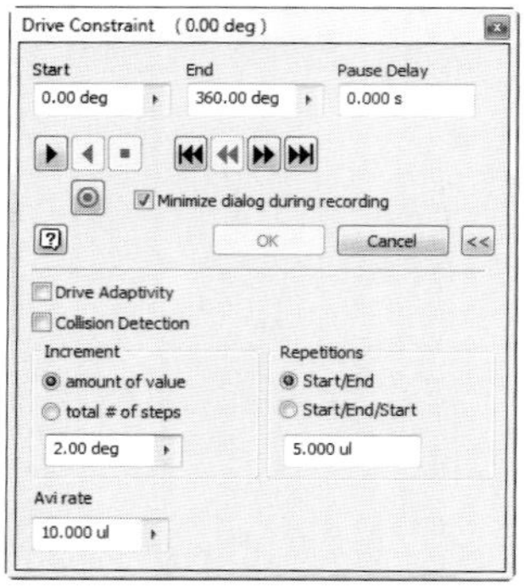

The values are sensitive to the type of constraint that will be driven. A mate constraint will show values of the range in the units of the assembly. An angular constraint will be shown in degrees.

The elements of the dialog box are for the most part self-explanatory, but they're worth reviewing. Some of the most valuable items are only visible with the >> option expanding the dialog box.

Start/End These values establish the beginning and end positions for the parts included in the constraint and the parts attached to them. It is not necessary to start the range at zero. You can have the components jump to a position of your choice.

Controls You can play Forward or Backward or stop. You can skip to the Minimum or Maximum of the timeline. You can also step Forward or Backward in increments.

Record In several dialog boxes in Inventor you will find a button with a red "target." This indicates that you want the action of the dialog box to be recorded as an animation. The movement of the assembly can be recorded to an AVI or WMV file with controls over the codec to be used and quality settings.

Drive Adaptivity Since adaptivity depends on assembly constraints, the size of an adaptive component can be changed during the animation. If a spring's length is determined by two planes, for example, driving the distance between those planes will change the length of the spring as part of the animation process.

Collision Detection As an assembly transitions through a range of motion, it will stop if it detects a collision with this option turned on.

Increment This value defines how quickly the assembly transitions through its range of motion. You can define these steps based the value of the constraint or the number of total steps that you want to take from beginning to end.

Repetitions If you want the animation to repeat, you can enter the number of times in the value box, but you can also control whether the animation starts over from the beginning or transitions back and forth between the beginning and end.

Animating the Assembly

Let's drive the range of motion in our gearbox to create an animation.

1. Right-click on the suppressed Angle:1 constraint and select Drive Constraint from the context menu.

2. Set the End value to 360 degrees to get a full revolution.

3. Set Increment to 2 degrees to make the transition faster.

4. Because this is a revolving motion, we will want to use the Start/End value. To get it to go through the action multiple times, set the value to 5.

5. Click the Forward icon to put the animation through its range of motion.

6. Close the dialog box when you are finished and save the assembly to keep the values that you used.

That's really all there is to it. This is a simple thing to do, but it makes communicating an idea to other people much easier—especially when you're working with nonengineers to get them to understand how the process will work.

Presentation Files

The ability to animate the action of an Inventor assembly quickly and easily can communicate the function of the assembly well, but manufacturing a design requires very different information. One tool for communicating this information is the presentation file, which you briefly worked with in Chapter 2.

A presentation file creates an exploded version of the assembly so that you can animate the assembly process without harming the assembly file. This is primarily used for creating the exploded drawing views that you worked with in the drawing chapters.

The process is quite direct. You link an assembly to the presentation file and use tools to separate the parts and animate their rejoining. We will go over the dialog boxes for the tools, but it's better to explore those dialogs when they come up.

Creating an Exploded View

This is one of those tools that is easier to use than to explain, so let's get to it:

1. Create a new presentation file using the Standard (in).ipn template on the English tab.

2. In the Presentation panel, select the only available option, Create View.

3. As shown in Figure 8.47, select the Gearbox assembly as the source file for the presentation using the Manual explosion method.

Below the file selection window is the Explosion Method. Here you choose whether Inventor will separate the parts or you will use manual tools to do so. If your assembly is a stacked series of components using Mate or Insert constraints, then the Automatic mode may work well. For most complex assemblies, the Manual method will be the most effective.

Figure 8.47

The Select Assembly dialog box for choosing a source assembly

4. Click OK to import the assembly data.

5. In the Presentation panel, select the Tweak Components tool.

The Tweak Component dialog box is used to establish what parts will be moved, what direction they will be moved in, and how far they will be moved. There is a checkbox that controls whether or not a trail will be created to show the travel of the component. The process is the same whether tweaking components in a linear transition or rotating the part.

6. As you can see in the dialog box, the first requirement is to set the direction. Click on the face of the gearbox housing to set the direction. The direction will be highlighted (see Figure 8.48).

7. Once the direction is set, Inventor will need to know what component(s) you want to tweak. Select the side of the housing near you.

Figure 8.48

The Z axis will be the highlighted direction axis by default.

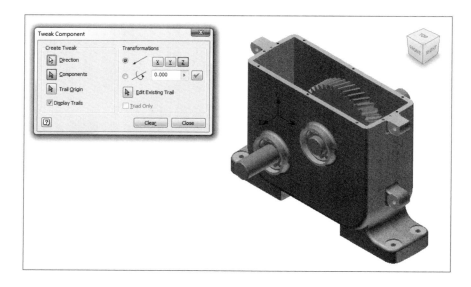

Inventor will now offer the option of selecting a specific point to the trail origin. Instead, we will just move the part that you have selected.

8. Click a location on the screen and drag to the left until the display under the Transformations group reads approximately 10 inches.

9. Highlight the value of the transformation, enter **12** for the value, and click the checkmark button to change the transformation. Figure 8.49 shows the result.

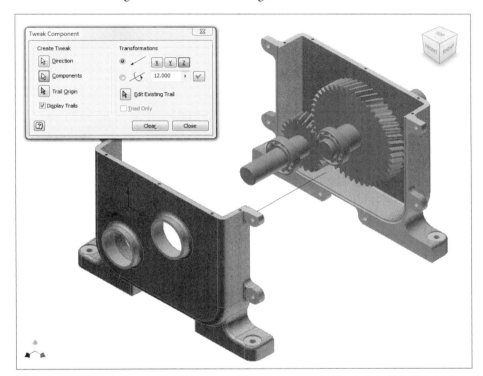

Figure 8.49

Drag the housing away from the rest of the assembly.

10. Click the Clear button to reset the selections that you made in the previous steps.

11. Reselect the same Direction, and while holding the Ctrl key, select the same side of the housing and select the two bearings that were in that housing.

12. Click and drag the three components out roughly 8 inches, as shown in Figure 8.50.

13. Click Close to keep the changes to the exploded assembly.

14. Zoom all to see the entire assembly.

15. Click the Animate tool in the Panel bar.

The Animation dialog box has many of the same controls as you used in driving the assembly constraint. Another similarity to the Drive Constraint tool is the importance of items that are typically concealed with the >> option (see Figure 8.51).

Figure 8.50

Drag the bearings and housing to create more separation.

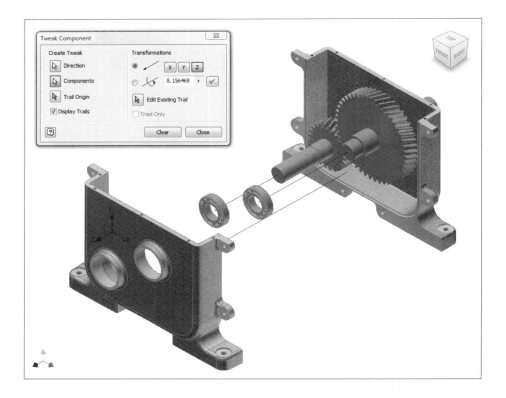

Figure 8.51

The Animation dialog box controls the motion of the presentation file.

16. Click the Play Forward icon to see the presentation file animate.

17. When the animation is finished, click Play Reverse to see the assembly explode again.

    The recording function will work in either direction for creating assembly or maintenance instructions. You can also use the Auto Reverse button to show both directions with a single click.

18. Click the Reset button to return the exploded assembly to its beginning state.

19. Click the >> button in the lower right to expand the dialog box.

20. Click Sequence 2 and click the Move Up button to make it the first sequence.

21. Click the Apply button and click the >> button to reduce the dialog box.

22. Click Play Forward to review the change to the assembly animation process.

    Making changes to the sequence of the expansion offers a great deal of flexibility in how you show the assembly of the design. It also opens up the opportunity to move components without having to worry too much about what order you do things.

    Changing the order is powerful, but you can also combine steps.

23. Click Reset to move the components back into starting position.

24. Click >> to expand the dialog box again.

25. Holding the Shift key, select all of the sequence steps in the Animation Sequence list.

26. Click the Group button to combine the two separate steps that you created into one step.

27. Replay the animation to see the new movement.

    You can use the Tweak Components dialog to modify the tweaks that have been applied to the presentation. If you are displaying trails, you can also edit the tweak directly.

28. Click on the trail that leads to the housing part and drag it to the right to narrow the gap.

29. Replay the animation to show that it respects the change and incorporates it into the animation (see Figure 8.52).

30. Save your presentation file as Gearbox.ipn in the Assemblies folder.

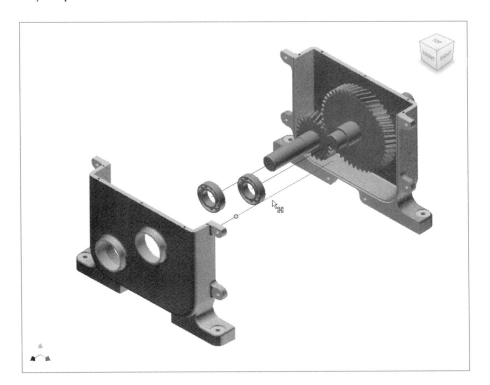

Figure 8.52

Dragging a trail edits the tweak directly.

Presentation files can be used to greatly improve the quality of products by sharing the intent of the designer or engineer with the people responsible for building the product or even the end customer.

There are a number of more creative uses for the simple tools as well. For example, you can combine a linear tweak with a rotational tweak to show a fastener being screwed onto the machine. What's more, all of the work that is done in the presentation file is not lost if there's a change to the assembly. Changes to the assembly components will automatically appear in the presentation file.

Explore this tool; it has so much to offer. Setting camera views and part visibility to sequences will allow you to create truly custom animations that will save you a lot of time when your designs go into production.

Positional Representation

In Chapter 4 you were given a brief overview of the Positional representation tool, which allows you to create alternate positions for the components in your assembly. It is most often used to show mechanisms or moving parts in their minimum and maximum range of motion positions.

This is one of those tools that I think you need to use in order to see its potential.

Creating a Positional Representation

When you put the components from the `Chapter 8 Components.zip` file into your Parts folder, it contained the files necessary for this exercise.

1. Open the `Door.iam` file in the Parts folder (see Figure 8.53).

Figure 8.53

In its initial position, the door is open.

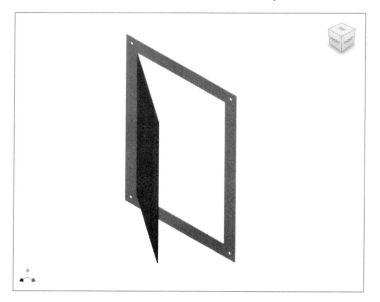

2. In the Browser, expand the Representations list if it isn't expanded already, navigate to Position, and expand that folder as well.

   This assembly already has two position representations included: Master and Closed.

3. Double-click the icon next to Closed.

   A double-click on a representation updates the assembly to display the properties of that representation. In this case, the door moves to a closed position.

4. Expand the Door part in the Browser (if collapsed) and note that the value of the Angle:1 constraint is 0.00 degrees and the constraint and its value are in a bold font.

5. Double-click on the Master positional representation and look at the behavior of the Angle:1 constraint as it is restored.

6. Right-click on Position: Master and select New from the context menu.

   A new positional representation named Position1 will be created and made active.

7. Slowly double-click on the word Position1 and rename it to **Open**, as shown in Figure 8.54.

8. Right-click on the Angle:1 constraint and select Override from the context menu.

   This launches the Override Object dialog box (Figure 8.55). This dialog box will, depending on the constraint or feature that you select, allow you to change the value, suppression, or adaptivity of a part. For this exercise we will only work with the Constraint override tools.

9. Click the checkbox next to value to be able to apply a new value to the constraint and set its value to 120.

10. Click OK to accept the new override.

    The door will swing to a 120-degree position for the Angle:1 constraint. Now let's create an override where the assembly can be flexible.

11. Right-click on the Open position representation and select Copy from the context menu. This will create a duplicate of the Open representation called Open1.

12. Rename Open1 as **Free**.

13. Activate Free.

14. Override the Angle:1 constraint again. This time deselect the Value checkbox.

Figure 8.54

Rename the new position representation in the Browser.

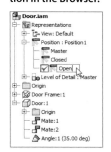

Figure 8.55

The Override Object dialog box allows you to experiment with different positions in an assembly.

15. Select the checkbox next to Suppression and select Suppress from the pull-down list that becomes available (see Figure 8.56).

16. Click OK to accept the changes and return to the assembly

    The Angle:1 value now displays (Suppress) instead of a numerical value. This is because the constraint is suppressed just as it would be had you suppressed it in the Browser, but in this case it's only suppressed in this position representation.

17. Click and drag the door to make sure that it is able to move through a full range of motion.

18. Save the changes that you've made to the assembly. Inventor will inform you that the assembly cannot be saved in a positional representation. Accept the change back to the Master representation and save.

Figure 8.56

You can also suppress constraints as an override.

Creating positional representations is very easy. They also have a purpose beyond just visualizing in 3D—they can enhance our 2D drawings as well.

Detailing Using a Positional Representation

The representations that you created can be used in a special type of drawing view called an Overlay view.

1. Create a new drawing using the ANSI (mm).dwg template.

2. Create a Base view of the drawing by using the Iso Top Right view and selecting the Closed position (found in the list of Position options in the center of the Drawing View dialog box, as shown in Figure 8.57).

Figure 8.57

You can create drawing views based on position representations.

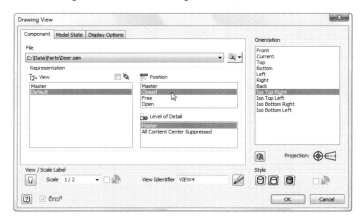

3. Place the view near the center of the sheet.

4. With the view placed, select Overlay View from the Drawing Views Panel bar. If the dialog box doesn't immediately appear, click on the base view that you created.

5. Select Open from the list of position representations in the upper left of the Overlay View dialog box, as shown in Figure 8.58.

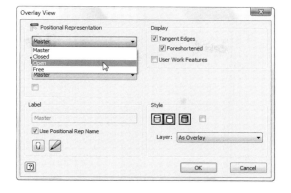

Figure 8.58

The Overlay View dialog box gives you a list of available overrides.

6. Click OK to place the overlay onto the original drawing view.

The new geometry will be in a Phantom linetype and will reflect the values of the active positional representations, as shown in Figure 8.59.

7. Save your drawing to the Drawings folder for future reference.

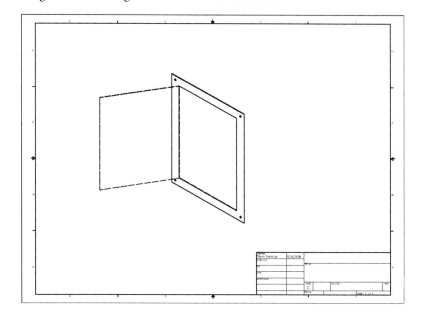

Figure 8.59

Multiple positions of a mechanism are easily shown with Overlay views based on position representations.

Weldments

The tools that are part of the Design Accelerators should be a huge help for machine designers in particular. Another challenge for machine designers is properly organizing the structure of the assembly and documenting the manufacturing process when components are welded together. We won't do an exercise on this advanced feature, but I think it's important that you are aware of its capability.

In Inventor, a weldment is a specialized assembly. To enable the weldment tools, you will need to convert a saved assembly to a weldment. To make the conversion, open the

Figure 8.60

Multiple positions of a mechanism are easily shown with Overlay views based on positional representations.

pull-down menu and select Convert → Weldment. This will open the Convert To Weldment dialog box (see Figure 8.60), where you will set your welding standard, the bead material, and bill of material structure that will be used.

Once you convert your assembly to a weldment, you can perform specialized tasks on it. Operations such as adding beveled edges to the parts to prepare them to be welded together can be done in a weldment. What is important about this is the beveled edge (created with the Chamfer tool) is generated as a feature in the weldment assembly. The individual part does not show this feature. This follows the traditional workflow used by most manufacturers.

Preparation features (as well as Weld and Machining features that are added to the assembly after it's welded) are placed in the Browser above the parts of the assembly. This keeps things organized as these features are all part of the assembly.

A final feature of a weldment is the ability to have weld annotations generated in the 3D model that can be reused in the 2D drawing. Either way, if you work with weldments there is still more to gain from Inventor.

Summary

Inventor's focus on the assembly rather than just the part yields fantastic benefits for the majority of users.

Not only can you generate multiple versions of essentially similar assemblies, but being able to directly communicate the vision of the designer to manufacturing, and properly represent the structure of an assembly where components are welded together, should save many hours of confusion, frustration, and lost productivity.

CHAPTER 9

Introducing Sheet Metal Parts

A common material used in machine building is sheet metal. It comes in myriad thicknesses and materials, and it requires a completely different approach to manufacturing.

To design a sheet metal part properly, you have to take into account its manufacturing process. Inventor has tools that allow for the design of sheet metal parts that are folded. Stamped parts or parts fabricated through a deformation process can be modeled, but it will not be possible to obtain the flat pattern of the part that is so critical for its accurate production.

Inventor also offers a completely different set of tools to define the features of these sheet metal parts. These tools carry names that will be familiar to designers who work with sheet metal.

- **The Unique Approach to Defining Sheet Metal Parts**

- **Defining Sheet Metal Styles**

- **Using Sheet Metal Features**

- **Creating a Flat Pattern**

- **Special Sheet Metal Detailing Tools**

A Manufacturing-Focused Toolset

Because the process to create a sheet metal part is so closely related to the limitations of the design, the sheet metal tools in Inventor are more closely related to a set of standards than the traditional part models are.

Most people build their sheet metal parts from readily available sheets that have predefined thickness and material properties. Based on the tooling, you can even predict how the material will stretch as it is processed. For years engineers and designers have developed tables that they use to calculate what shape and size they need to cut into the sheet to be able to bend the part into the proper finished size. Now they can let the computer do the work for them by creating their parts using Inventor. Unfortunately, sheet metal capabilities are not available in Inventor 2009 LT, because of its solid modeling focus.

Sheet Metal Rules

Sheet metal rules are essentially styles in the vein of layer styles or dimension styles. They are meant to be quickly established within the standard and selected for use in the part. A sheet metal rule is a name given to a set of properties for the sheet metal that will be used for a part. It consists of three elements: a thickness, a material, and an unfolding method. You define a style through the Sheet Metal Defaults and Style And Standard Editor dialog boxes. Once a sheet metal style is defined, it can be shared through the style libraries. In this section you'll work with all three of those tools.

The Sheet Metal Defaults Dialog Box

The Sheet Metal Defaults dialog box (Figure 9.1) works a little differently than most dialog boxes in Inventor. Instead of being the source of the feature that will be created, or where the edits are performed, it is simply a front-end for making quick changes. You don't establish the rules of your sheet metal components here (you'll do that in the Style And Standard Editor); you select which rule will be used and, if you like, you can choose to override portions of the rule. Here's an overview:

Sheet Metal Rule This flyout lets you select which existing sheet metal rule you want to use.

If you're creating a new rule, click the pencil icon to launch the Style And Standard Editor.

Figure 9.1

The Sheet Metal Defaults dialog box

Use Thickness From Rule Deselect this checkbox, and you'll be able to override the default thickness of the selected sheet metal rule.

Material Style This pull-down shows a list of the materials available in the standard and allows you to select one that is different from the material specified in the sheet metal rule.

Unfolding Rule As with the Material Style pull-down, Unfolding Rule is an override option to the active rule and allows you to switch the unfold method from the default.

Creating a New Sheet Metal Rule

In this exercise you will create a new sheet metal rule that will be modified later:

1. Make sure that your active project file is `Introducing Inventor.ipj`.

2. Create a new part using the `Sheet Metal (in).ipt` template on the English tab.

3. The new part will open in the Sketch mode. Press Return to finish the sketch.

   In Figure 9.2 you will see the first new Panel bar that you've seen in a while. In some of the previous Panel bars you may have noticed a few icons grayed out and unavailable. When you first start a sheet metal, you will see that most of the sheet metal tools are placed features. Since you have just started a part and have not created a sketched feature, a majority of the tools will be unavailable.

   These tools will have different names, but the workflows should be easy to work through.

   An important thing to note is that you can still access traditional solid modeling tools by switching the Panel bar to the Part Features panel if you want to use tools like Emboss.

4. Click the Sheet Metal Defaults tool in the Panel bar.

5. You can explore the options of the dialog box, but there won't be much available. Click the pencil (Edit) icon next to Sheet Metal Rule.

6. The Style And Standard Editor opens with the sheet metal rule that was active. Click the New icon to create a new style with the settings shown in Figure 9.3.

7. Give the new style the name **16 ga. Steel**.

8. Click OK to create the new style.

Figure 9.2

The Sheet Metal Features Panel bar

Figure 9.3

**Creating a new
sheet metal rule**

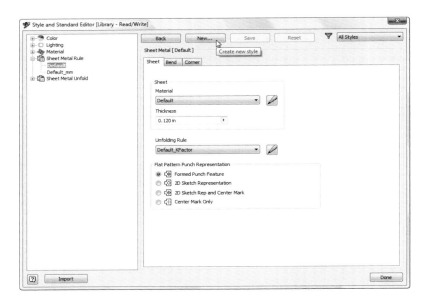

9. The new sheet metal rule will appear on the list on the left side of the dialog box. Right-click on the new style and select Active from the menu to make it the style that will be edited.

10. Click the Save button at the top of the dialog box to save the style.

In the next stage of the exercise, you'll use the Style And Standard Editor to define new values for the rule. First, let's examine this tool.

The Style And Standard Editor

On the right side of the Style And Standard Editor dialog are three tabs, which establish the conditions for the active rule and let you create the properties of the rule.

The Sheet Tab

The Sheet tab (Figure 9.3) controls the properties of the raw material and how it will deform when you begin to bend it.

SHEET

The Sheet group is used to establish the material that will be used in the part:

Material Use this pull-down list to select the default material for the rule.

Thickness Enter the value of the material for the rule here. For production use I suggest checking with your suppliers and perhaps your Manufacturing department to verify the thickness of the material that you use for a particular gauge.

UNFOLDING RULE

One of the most important things to discuss with Manufacturing is the method they use to calculate the flat pattern. Based on that method, you may need to modify the formulas for calculating a K Factor unfold or establish some different bend tables for your material. Working with Manufacturing may get you access to existing data that they use, which will make things go much smoother when it's time to get the parts produced.

Once you've established the range of options for calculating the flat pattern, you can use the Unfolding Rule pull-down to set the default method for this rule.

FLAT PATTERN PUNCH REPRESENTATION

This is another area where it is beneficial to work with Manufacturing if you haven't been previously responsible for generating flat patterns.

Depending on your organization, you may have to include detailed representations of features that will be punched into your part, or only a simple center mark for where the punch should strike, or something in between.

Inventor offers four methods, and selecting the appropriate one is very important:

Formed Punch Feature Even though the part will be flat, the punched features will continue to display in 3D with this option, and a center mark will be displayed at the placement origin for the punch feature.

2D Sketch Representation When you define a punch tool (as discussed later in this chapter), Inventor will allow you to specify a 2D sketch to use as a representation. This sketch may be the perimeter of the feature or it can be a symbol that an automated programming system might use for tool selection.

2D Sketch Rep And Center Mark This will display the 2D sketch and a center mark for where the strike will be programmed to occur.

Center Mark Only If you plan to use a table to list what punches will be used, you can just show where the punches need to be placed on the flat part.

The Bend Tab

The Bend tab (Figure 9.4) controls the default radius of bends that will be applied and specifies how to treat bends that are less than the full width of another face.

BEND RELIEF

Before you create a bend, it is sometimes necessary to cut a notch into the metal to limit the distortion of the unbent portion. This is called a Bend Relief.

Figure 9.4

The Bend tab of the Style And Standard Editor

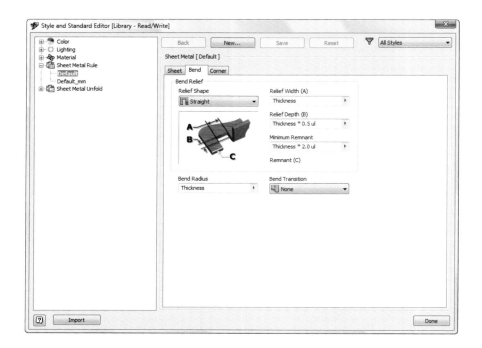

RELIEF SHAPE

This pull-down list lets you select the default relief shape for the rule. The standard shapes are as follows:

Straight Straight creates a rectangular shape.

Round With this option enabled, the interior edge of the relief is rounded.

Tear With this option enabled, there is no predefined relief and the metal is allowed to shear during the bending process.

Along with the shape there will be a preview of the bend shape with dimensions, whose values can be entered on the right to size the default bend relief.

BEND RADIUS

The default radius can be an absolute value or a factor such as the thickness of the material divided by 2.

BEND TRANSITION

When a bend occurs that doesn't require a relief but the edges do not align, you can use this pull-down list to establish the shape of the material at the edge of the bend. The differences between the options are easiest to see in the flat pattern.

The Corner Tab

The Corner tab (Figure 9.5) tells Inventor how you want the edges of bends to relate when they are next to one another in a corner.

TWO-BEND INTERSECTION

There are six methods for defining how a two-bend intersection will be calculated. Two of them (Round and Square) also offer a size for the intersection. The others calculate the intersection based on the size of the bends included in the corner and the process that will be used in manufacturing.

The method you choose will be reflected in the 3D model and the flat pattern.

THREE-BEND INTERSECTION

A corner where three bends meet is extraordinarily difficult to calculate. In all reality, as long as the faces and major bends are correct, the geometry of the corner is only relevant in the flat pattern that the part will be formed from.

For this reason, the value that you select for the 3 Bend Intersection option only modifies the way the corner is calculated in the flat pattern. If you look at the corner in the folded part, it will show a notch in the corner and display the gaps between the edges. The corner will construct properly when the physical part is made from the accurate flat pattern—and that is far more important.

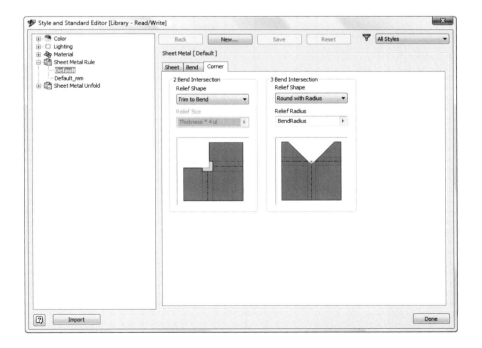

Figure 9.5

The Corner tab of the Style And Standard Editor

Defining Sheet Metal Rules

Now let's modify the new rule to give it meaning in how we define our new part. In this exercise you will also create other rules for another thickness and material.

1. On the Sheet tab, set Steel as the Material.

2. Enter **0.0598** (inches) as the Thickness.

3. Leave the Formed Punch Feature setting as the Flat Pattern Punch Representation.

4. On the Bend tab, set Relief Shape to Round.

5. Change Bend Radius to Thickness/2.

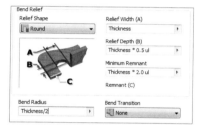

6. Switch to the Corner tab and use Linear Weld as the 2 Bend Intersection method.

7. Set the 3 Bend Intersection value to Full Round.

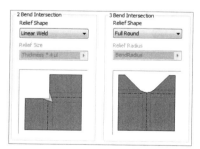

8. Save the changes that you've made to the 16 ga. Steel rule.

9. Right-click on the 16 ga. Steel rule and select New from the context menu to create a new rule.

10. In the resulting dialog box, enter **12 ga. Steel** for the name of the new sheet metal rule.

11. Make the new rule active.

12. On the Sheet tab, enter **0.1046** for the Thickness value.

13. On the Bend tab, select Thickness/3 for the Bend Radius setting.

14. Save the changes to the new style.

With this method you can easily take values from one existing rule and with minor tweaks create a new rule. Let's make one more new rule.

15. Right-click on the 16 ga. Steel rule and use it again as the template for a new style named **.062 Aluminum**.

16. Activate the new style by double-clicking on it.

17. Set Material to Aluminum-6061 and Thickness to **0.062**.

18   Change the Flat Pattern Punch Representation to Center Mark Only.

19. Save this last sheet metal rule and set the active rule back to the 16 ga. Steel rule.

20. Click Done to close the dialog box and return to the Sheet Metal Defaults dialog box.

When you return to the Sheet Metal Defaults dialog box, it reflects that you set the active rule to 16 ga. Steel.

21. Close the defaults dialog box. Do not close the sheet metal part file.

While it is easy to build sheet metal rules, there's no reason for colleagues in an office to re-create the same ones over and over. You can add your styles to the style library so that you can establish the standard and have it available to everyone.

Publishing the Sheet Metal Rules

To be able to share the rules that you've created, you have to save them to the style library, which you first worked with in Chapter 5.

1. Choose Format → Save Styles To Style Library.

2. By default, the dialog box will show No in the Save to Library? column. Click the Yes To All button to change all those column entries to Yes, as shown in Figure 9.6.

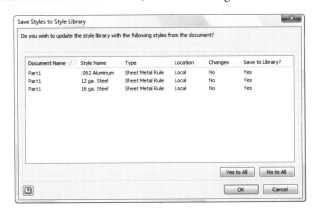

Figure 9.6

Saving the sheet metal rules to the style library

3. Click OK to save your updated style library.

4. You will be warned that changes to the library cannot be undone (it doesn't mention that you can purge the styles from the library); agree to the update of the library.

Now you should verify that the new rules are part of the style library.

5. Create a new file using the same default `Sheet Metal (in.).ipt` file that you used before.

6. Exit the sketch and click the Sheet Metal Defaults icon.

7. Expand the list to see that the three rules you created are available in the new part without creating a specific template to store the styles (see Figure 9.7).

8. Set the active rule to 16 ga. Steel and close the dialog box.

Figure 9.7

The new sheet metal rules are available to any sheet metal template.

The ability to make the styles readily available to everyone should greatly improve the consistency across multiple users. As long as you've got a new file, let's finally make some sheet metal.

Making Sheet Metal Parts

As I mentioned briefly earlier, most of the sheet metal tools are placed features. To begin a sheet metal part, you need to create a sketched feature just as you would in a conventional solid model.

Two sheet metal sketched feature tools are available: Face and Contour Flange. These are the two tools that will start all of your conventional sheet metal parts, but they have completely different approaches. The tools can also be used after the first feature is placed and used in conjunction with each another.

The exercises in this chapter will introduce placed features such as the Flange, Hem, Cut, and Punch tools.

The Face Tool

The Face tool is like Extrude but with it you don't have to set a distance. The distance is determined by the thickness of the material. The only other rule is that you have to have at least one closed loop in the sketch. Figure 9.8 shows the dialog box.

Figure 9.8

The Face dialog box

Both dialog boxes have additional tabs such as Unfold Options and Bends. These tabs provide access to override tools for the individual feature. The tabs contain the same properties as the sheet metal rule definition tabs, but changes will only affect the current feature, not the active rule. This gives you the ability to take one feature and give it a special bend radius or change the bend relief. You can even go back and change a feature after it has been placed using Edit Feature.

Creating a Basic Part

Let's start out with a basic sheet metal part:

1. Double-click to edit Sketch1.

2. Sketch and dimension two rectangles as shown in Figure 9.9.

3. Press Return to leave the sketch.

4. Turn on the edges for your active part in the Application Options Display tab as you did with the plastic part in Chapter 7. This can help to see the part edges easier.

5. Open the Face tool and select both rectangles.

6. Click OK to create the face. Figure 9.10 shows the result.

7. Save your part into the Parts folder as Shield.ipt.

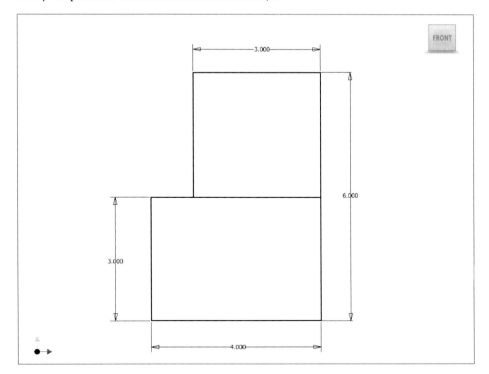

Figure 9.9

Developing the sketch for the Face feature

Figure 9.10

**Creating the
Face feature**

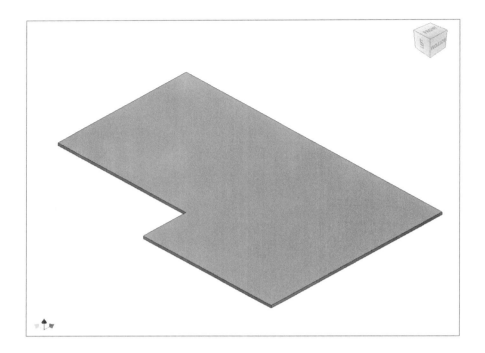

The Flange Tool

After you create a base feature in sheet metal, chances are you will use the Flange tool next. Figure 9.11 shows its dialog box.

A flange is a placed feature with a lot of options. It and the Face tool have the same tabs that allow individual override, so we'll focus on the Shape tab.

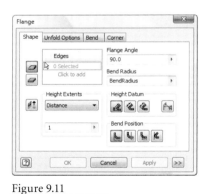

Figure 9.11

The Flange dialog box

The Shape Tab

You place a flange by selecting an edge to add a bend and adjacent face to. The upper-left portion of the Shape tab (Figure 9.11) is where you select those edges. The Edges list will display the number of edges that have been selected.

You can select edges in two ways:

Edge Select Mode This option lets you select individual edges to place flanges on. You can select multiple edges, but you have to select them with individual clicks of the mouse.

Loop Select Mode This option lets you select all the perimeter edges of a face with a single click.

These selection options also work with the Contour Flange tool when it is placed after the initial feature is placed.

Addition options on the Shape tab are as follows:

Flange Angle This option establishes the angle at which the flange will be developed once you've located it by selecting the edge.

Height Extents You can set the height of a flange by value using Distance or until it meets a face using the To option. You select these options from a pull-down list.

You can also flip the direction of the flange by clicking the Flip Direction button.

Height Datum The three buttons illustrate the options that you can use to define whether the height of a flange is measured aligned to the length of the flange or orthogonal to the face plane.

Bend Position Four modes are available to define how the bend will be started from the selected edge. The icons illustrate clearly how the bend will be developed.

More (>>) Expanding the dialog box exposes an option to create flanges that are narrower than the selected edge using different types of selections.

Adding Flanges

Now let's continue developing our part:

1. Start the Flange tool from the Panel bar.

2. Set Height to 1 (inch).

3. Using Single Select Mode, select the three top edges of the face, as shown in Figure 9.12.

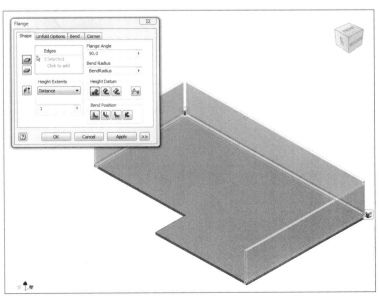

Figure 9.12

Select the edges to place flanges.

4. Click Apply to create the three flanges.

5. Change the flange height to 0.6 (inch).

6. Select the three additional edges, as shown in Figure 9.13.

7. Click OK to create the new flanges and close the dialog box. Compare your result to Figure 9.14.

Figure 9.13

Select the inside edges to place more flanges.

Figure 9.14

Flanges are created with mitred corners.

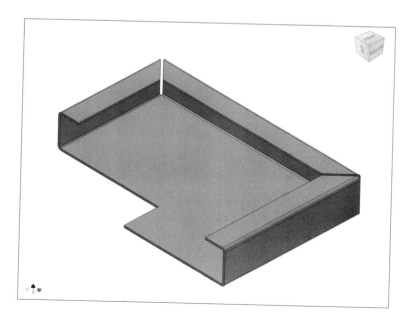

Look closely at the finished part. The corners have consistent spacing between the flanges, even though the edges that are closest together change as the flanges transition.

Re-creating this part using traditional solid modeling tools would be difficult and time-consuming—maybe even impossible. Even if you could endure the building process using traditional solids, that is only half of the problem. A sheet metal part is only complete if you can show both the folded and flat state.

8. Click the Flat Pattern tool in the Panel bar to display the dialog box shown in Figure 9.15.

Figure 9.15

The Flat pattern is calculated to include allowances for the stretching during folding.

9. Double-click the Folded Model icon in the Browser to return to the folded part.

Now we will create a disjointed face to build on. When you're adding a face feature to something other than the first feature, it's possible to build bent portions automatically to connect the face to the rest of the part.

10. Create a new sketch, selecting the top face of the last flange added.

11. Project the short edge from the first face to the sketch (see Figure 9.16).

12. Draw a rectangle starting on the outside end of the projected line.

13. Set the length of the rectangle to 0.8 (inch).

14. Use a dimension between the other end of the projected line and the side of the rectangle with a value of BendReliefWidth to create a space for the flange to unfold (see Figure 9.17).

Figure 9.16

Starting a new sketch for a face

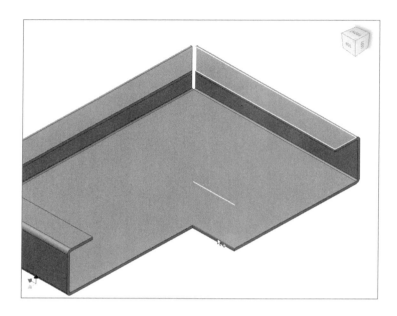

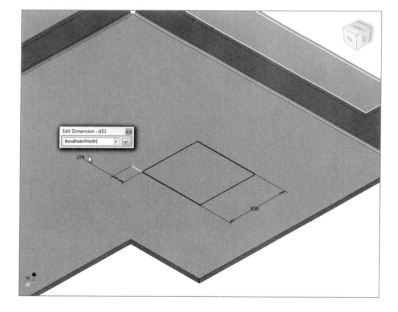

15. Open the Face tool.

    Make sure that the material of the new face is being added back toward the main body of the part.

16. Click the Edges button and then select the top edge below the new face, as shown in Figure 9.18.

17. Click OK to create the new features. See Figure 9.19 for the correct result.

18. Select the Corner Round tool from the Panel bar.

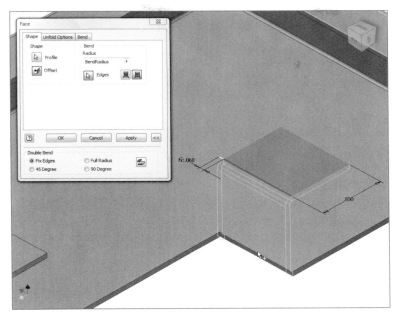

Figure 9.18

Creating the new face and connecting it to the rest of the part

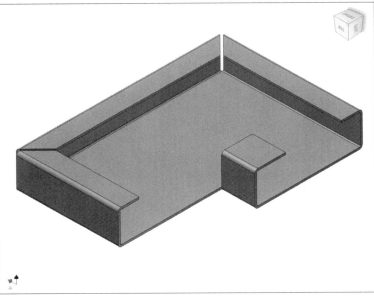

Figure 9.19

The new features have been added to the part.

19. Select the edges shown in Figure 9.20 using a 0.25-inch radius. Note that passing over long edges does not highlight them for selection; you can only select edges that can be rounded during the creation of the flat pattern.

Figure 9.20

Adding corner rounds

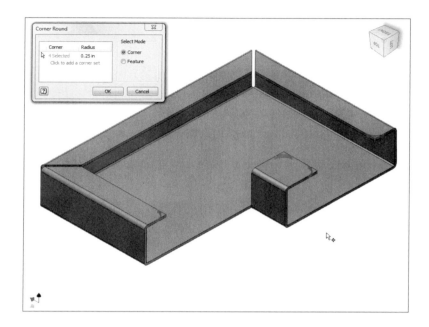

20. Double-click on the flat pattern to see the result, shown in Figure 9.21.

21. Return to the folded state of the part to make the next change.

22. Open the Sheet Metal Defaults dialog box.

Figure 9.21

The updated flat pattern showing the new face unfolded

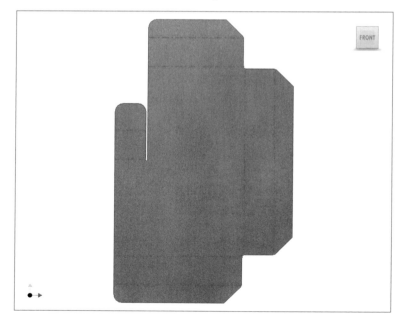

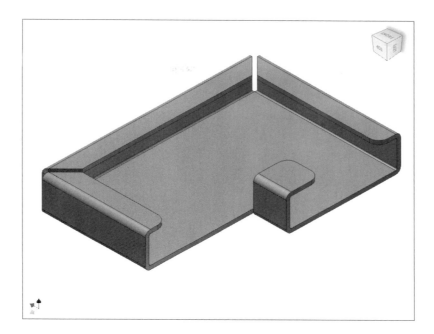

Figure 9.22

The model rebuilds using the new sheet metal rule.

23. Change the Sheet Metal Rule to 12 ga. Steel; Figure 9.22 shows the result.

    Changing the active rule will cause the model to update, reflecting changes to any properties that are different between the new rule and the previous one.

    If you need to create a family of parts with the same basic geometry made from different materials, you can also define an iPart with sheet metal using the same techniques you used in Chapter 7.

24. Save the part file.

The Contour Flange Tool

There are times where you need to create a part with a lot of bends but they're all the same width. Think of a drainage gutter. It's cut to consistent length, but it has bends that flip from one side to the other. If you were to sketch the basic shape, thicken it, and have it extend to a length, the part would be done. That is the inspiration for the Contour Flange tool; its dialog box is shown in Figure 9.23.

Figure 9.23

The Contour Flange dialog box

Starting a New Part with Contour Flange

Let's use the Contour Flange to save some steps in defining a new part:

1. Create a new part using `Sheet Metal (in).ipt`.

2. Duplicate the sketch shown in Figure 9.24.

3. When the sketch is complete, close it and change the Sheet Metal Rule to 16 ga. Aluminum.

4. Open the Contour Flange tool.

5. Select the sketch. Once the profile is selected, a preview of the length and thickness will appear.

6. Flip the contour direction to the apparent top of the sketch.

7. Set the length of the part to 8 (inches). See Figure 9.25.

8. Click OK to create the new feature (see Figure 9.26).

9. Save the part into the Parts folder as `Gutter.ipt`.

Figure 9.24

Replicate the gutter profile sketch

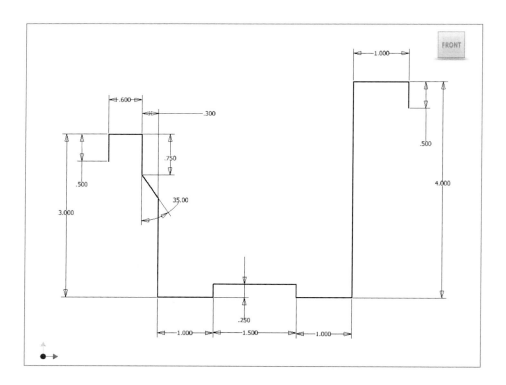

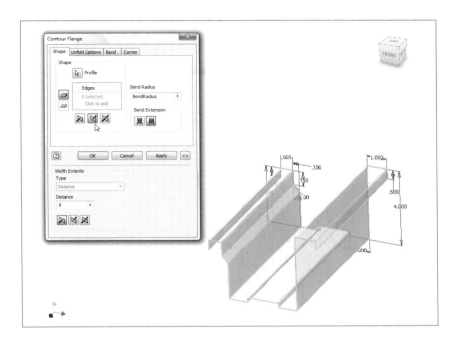

Figure 9.25

The preview of the contour flange

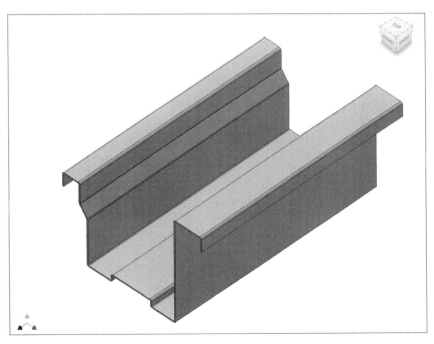

Figure 9.26

The completed feature

The Hem Tool

There are four types of hem that can be added to reinforce an edge. They can all be selected from the Hem dialog box's Type pull-down list (Figure 9.27), and each has its own unique sizing values that you can enter.

After selecting the type of hem that you want to apply, you can set the direction as well as values for the gap between faces, length, angle, and bend radius of the hem.

Adding a Hem Feature

Placing a hem is much like placing a flange. In this exercise, you will place a special hem on the part:

1. Open the Hem tool.

2. Click on the outer edge, as shown in Figure 9.28.

3. Set the Hem options as shown in Figure 9.28.

4. Click OK to place the hem.

5. Place a new sketch on the back, inside face, as shown highlighted in Figure 9.29.

   Once the new sketch is defined, you will use an adaptation of the Project Geometry tool to preview the flat pattern in the sketch. This is a unique and powerful way to use the information on the flat pattern in the folded part.

6. Under the Project Geometry tool is a tool called Project Flat Pattern. Select this tool.

   The tool will want you to select a face on the folded part. It will then create sketch elements projected from that face, which you can use to define the shape's placement.

Figure 9.27

The Hem dialog box

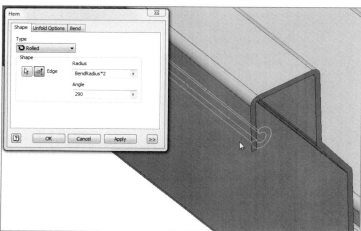

Figure 9.28

Place a Rolled hem on the outer edge.

7. Use the Select Other tool to project the 0.5-inch flange that is the farthest back.

8. Create a rectangle in the sketch and position it as shown in Figure 9.30.

   Why did we project the flat? You'll see that with the next tool you will use: Cut.

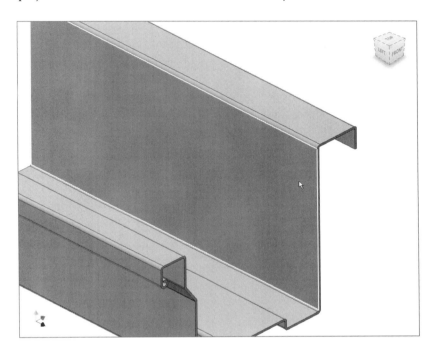

Figure 9.29

Place the new sketch for locating a new feature.

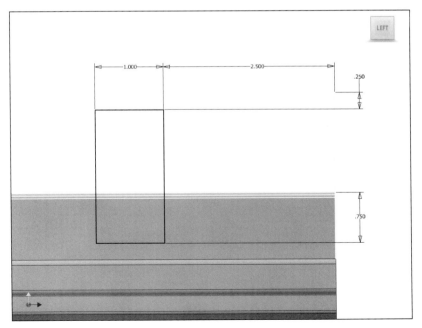

Figure 9.30

The rectangle is dimensioned to geometry on the back of the part.

The Cut Tool

The Cut tool (Figure 9.31) is similar to the Emboss feature. Normally the cutting feature will be set to Thickness and the selected shape will pass through the entire part. It can, however, be set to a depth that will cut into, but not through, the part.

Where it really resembles the Emboss tool is its ability to wrap around a face. The Cut tool can transition over bends when the Cut Across Bend option is selected.

Figure 9.31

The Cut dialog box

When you're placing a cut, it is not necessary to cut all the way through. You can also set a distance in the Cut dialog box that will still be able to wrap around a face but will only cut to a specified depth. This is similar to the Emboss tool.

Cutting Across Bends

Because you have dimensioned the sketch that was projected, you can control how much material will be left between the cut and the edge.

1. Open the Cut tool.

2. Select the rectangle that you drew.

3. Click the Cut Across Bend checkbox to enable it.

4. Click OK to create the new feature and compare your results to Figure 9.32.

5. Save the part.

Figure 9.32

The completed cut across the bends

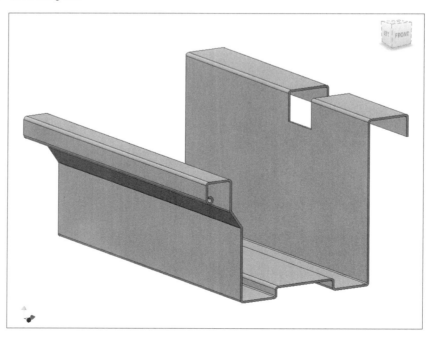

The Punch Tool

The Punch tool is a specialized feature that creates deformations or custom-shaped holes in the part. The location points of these features can be extracted for detailing in the drawing or for programming production machinery. Figure 9.33 shows the PunchTool dialog box.

When you open the tool, you will be shown a list of included sample punch tools. There is also a dialog box where you can access special geometry or size the tool if it has optional sizes.

The Geometry Tab

The Geometry tab (Figure 9.34) lets you select placement points for the Punch tool and set its placement angle.

The Size Tab

When an iFeature or Punch tool is defined, its size values can be set to unlimited, within a range, or with only certain sizes selectable from a list. Use the Size tab (Figure 9.35) to set those size values by entering a value or selecting it from the Name pull-down next to Value.

Adding Punch Tools

Punch tools are placed on sketch geometry. In this exercise you will place two features on the part:

1. Create a new sketch on the inside back face of the part. This is the same plane you had created the sketch on for the Cut feature.

2. Draw two points and dimension them from the top edge and sides, as shown in Figure 9.36.

3. Close the sketch and open the Punch tool.

4. A browse dialog box will appear. Click Cancel to skip this step.

5. When the PunchTool dialog box appears, select Round Emboss.ide from the list.

6. Click Finish to place the punch features (see Figure 9.37).

Figure 9.33

The PunchTool dialog box

Figure 9.34

The PunchTool dialog box's Geometry tab

Figure 9.35

The PunchTool dialog box's Size tab

Figure 9.36

Place two points to locate the Punch tools.

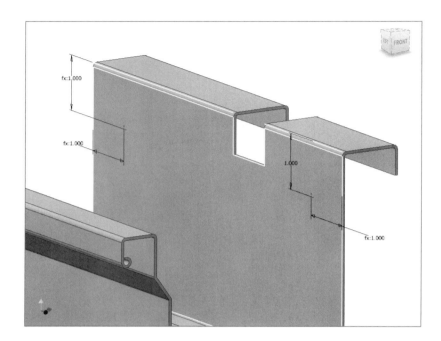

Figure 9.37

The completed Punch features

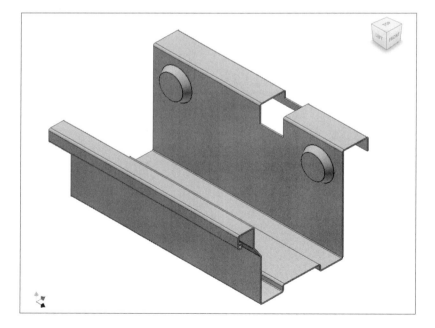

7. Create a flat pattern for the part.

8. Save the part.

Sheet Metal Detailing

To complete the manufacturing focus of the sheet metal tools, Inventor offers special capabilities for detailing the parts that will make it easier for manufacturing personnel to develop the part.

The most prominent of these tools is the ability to add bend notes and even bend tables to the part. You can also add punch tables for parts that have Punch tools applied to them. Punch locations will be represented based on the settings of the sheet metal rule that the part was created from.

Creating a Sheet Metal Drawing

Sheet metal parts can be shown folded, flat, or both in the drawing.

1. Create a new drawing file using the ANSI (in).dwg template.

2. Create a base view of the Flat Pattern for gutter.ipt with a 1:1 scale, as shown in Figure 9.38.

3. In the Drawing Annotation panel, locate and open the Bend Notes tool.

4. Click on two of the bend lines on the drawing.

   This will add a note listing the bend direction, angle, and radius. These notes can be dragged out on a leader as well.

   For a large number of bends, it can be easier to use a table.

5. Delete the bend notes that you added.

6. Locate the Table tool in the Drawing Annotation panel and open it.

Figure 9.38

Place a flat pattern view in the drawing.

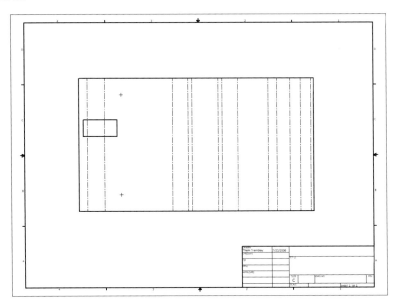

7. Select the drawing view if it did not select automatically.

   The Table dialog box will display in the Selected Columns list box the columns that will be placed in the table (see Figure 9.39).

8. Click OK and locate the Bend table on the sheet (See Figure 9.40).

   Callouts that correlate to the table rows will be added to the drawing.

Traditional dimensioning tools can also be used to document the size of the flat pattern and establish the location of the bend lines, penetrations, and Punch tools.

Flat pattern data can also be exported directly from the 3D model to DWG or DXF files for use with manufacturing software.

Figure 9.39

The Table dialog box displaying Sheet Metal properties

Figure 9.40

The completed drawing with Bend Table added

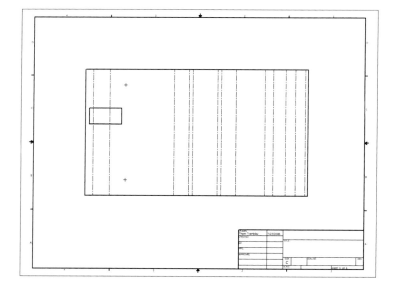

Summary

If you need to create sheet metal parts, the tools in Inventor should make it easy. Setting up your rules and validating your unfold method to make sure that it works with your production equipment and practices is a critical step as you incorporate Inventor into your workflow.

Hopefully you'll get a chance to use the sheet metal tools; they are a lot of fun.

CHAPTER 10

Introducing Inventor Studio

In this book, you have learned how to create drawings, build all sorts of parts, construct assemblies, and even use automated tools to calculate complex relationships between parts. Now it's time to make things look really cool.

- The Inventor Studio Environment
- Creating Still Renderings
- Creating an Animation

Enhancing Your Design

The Inventor Studio tools are not meant to replace dedicated, professional rendering systems like Autodesk 3ds Max or Maya, but they will allow you to create great-looking renderings and animations of your parts and assemblies with relatively little work.

Using these tools, you can spend many hours experimenting with different lighting scenes, cameras, and so forth, but it is also possible to make attractive images in just a few seconds with only a couple of mouse clicks. In this chapter we'll explore the basics of Inventor Studio, but there will be many great options left for you and your imagination to explore.

There are dedicated rendering tools such as Autodesk Maya and 3ds Max that would give you the highest quality rendering, but the Inventor Studio tools do a very nice job and maintain associativity with the CAD model.

Creating a Rendering

Inventor Studio is not just another tool that is used in the assembly or part file; it is actually a separate environment that runs in parallel with the part and assembly file.

To change your working environment from the part and assembly tools, you go to the pull-down menus and select Applications → Inventor Studio.

Entering the new environment won't just change the Panel bar as you're now accustomed to; it will also change the Browser. Having this environment inside the part and assembly files also keeps it in line with any changes made to the model data. Once you set up rendering conditions, any changes to the model will be reflected in the rendering environment without the need to modify settings that you made previously.

Starting the Render Image tool in the Inventor Studio Panel bar will open the Render Image dialog box, which contains three tabs: General, Output, and Style. Along with the dialog box, a red rectangle will appear in the Design window that shows the frame of the rendering that will be created.

The General Tab

You've probably noticed that in Inventor's tool dialog boxes, the basic and most important settings are typically on the first tab, and the same holds true with Inventor Studio's General tab (Figure 10.1). This is where you tell Inventor Studio how to view, light, and surround the model as well as where you set the type of rendering and the resolution for the image:

Width and Height The values for the width and height of the rendered image can be entered individually, or you can select common screen resolutions from the pop-up menu that appears after you click the Select Output Size icon to the right.

A Lock Aspect Ratio checkbox allows you to enter either the width or height and have Inventor automatically calculate the other value to maintain the 4:3 ratio.

Camera A camera can be created on the screen by clicking the Camera tool in the Panel bar and establishing a target and position. You can also copy an existing camera. My favorite technique is to establish a view in the Design window, right-click in the window, and select Create Camera From View on the screen menu. After creating your cameras, you can select which one will be used for the rendering using the Camera pull-down list.

You can create a list of cameras, each of which will save a particular view position and size of the model. When you create a rendering, you can pick between cameras to quickly create a different look while reusing other elements like lighting and scene styles.

Lighting Style Inventor comes with a collection of default lighting styles that you can use for the rendering or as a template for a new style. Use this pull-down list to select which style you want to use.

Scene Style For a theatrical touch, Inventor Studio has the ability to change the surroundings that your models are in. Scenes create an environment for the rendering by setting background colors or applying images to simulate a location for the model to be rendered in. Inventor comes with a few scenes, but the greatest impact on your renderings can be created with a good scene style.

Render Type Inventor allows two types of rendering: Realistic and Illustration. Realistic rendering is the type that people most commonly want to create. Illustration style will create renderings that are great for technical documentation and assembly instructions. This style has its own options that you can modify on the Style tab.

The Output Tab

The quality of the image is controlled by the Output tab (Figure 10.2). Here's a look at its most important settings:

Save Rendered Image Selecting this checkbox will launch the File Explorer dialog box, where you can define the name of the rendering that will be saved. You also can create your rendering and then define the file after the fact.

Antialiasing Unless you are running at a very low screen resolution, the rendering of your model will

Figure 10.1

The Render Image dialog box's General tab

Figure 10.2

The Output tab

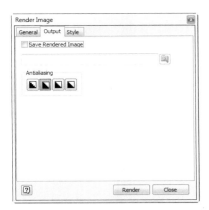

be at a lower resolution than the source model. In order to keep the edges smooth, Inventor Studio has to calculate a smooth edge. How this is done depends on the quality settings under Antialiasing. It's important to note that the higher the quality, the longer the rendering will take.

The Style Tab (Realistic Rendering)

Options controlling the way the model works with its environment are set on the Style tab. Figure 10.3 shows the Style tab when Realistic has been chosen as the Render Type on the General tab:

True Reflection If this option is selected, a rendering with multiple parts will have the parts in the scene reflect off one another and other faces of the same part. Not selecting this option will cause the parts to reflect the elements set in the scene style but not the other parts. Figures 10.4 and 10.5 illustrate the difference.

Figure 10.3

The Style tab options for Realistic rendering

Figure 10.4

Rendering with True Reflection set to Off

Figure 10.5

Rendering with True Reflection set to On

The Style Tab (Illustration Rendering)

Many more options appear when the Illustration is selected as the Rendering Style (Figure 10.6).

Color Fill

There are three source options for Color Fill; these determine what (if any) color is included in the rendering. There is also a slide bar for the quantity of colors in the rendering and an option to display highlights:

No Color This option removes any reference to the part's color(s) in the rendering. The resulting appearance has a line art quality.

Surface Style Applying a surface style or color to your part can still have value in the Illustration rendering using this option. The Levels slide bar will set the number of colors from none, when the value is 1, to multiple color steps when set to 10.

Figure 10.6

The Style tab options for Illustration rendering

Specify Setting a color using Specify will override the colors of all the parts in the rendering. The Levels slide bar will set the number of colors representing the curvature in the same way that it does with Surface Style selected.

Show Shiny Highlights With this box selected, areas that would be highlighted in a realistic rendering will still highlight to accentuate curvature.

Edges

Careful selection of how or whether to display edges in the rendering can create very dramatic results:

Show Outline Edges This selection defines whether you want to calculate the profile edges of the model or just show a shape that is colored.

Show Interior Edges Choose this option to display the tangent or other sharp edges of the model's interior.

Thickness The Thickness value is a sliding scale that controls the thickness of the edges that are selected to be displayed. While there's no specific width value offered, the effect is very noticeable and the range of line widths (thickness) is dramatic.

Color Clicking the color sample will bring up the Inventor color selection dialog box, which lets you choose a color for the displayed edges.

Setting Up a Basic Rendering

In this exercise you will create a simple rendering of a part that you created earlier.

1. Open the `Hitch Ball.ipt` file that you created in Chapter 7.

2. Change the active member of that iPart to Hitch Ball - 02.

3. Switch to the Inventor Studio environment by going to the Applications pull-down and selecting Inventor Studio.

4. Use your mouse wheel to enlarge the Hitch Ball to fill most of the Design window.

5. Click the Render Image tool in the Panel bar.

6. Without changing any of the rendering options, click the Render button at the bottom of the dialog box. See Figure 10.7 for the result.

Figure 10.7

A realistic rendering in the Render Output window

7. Close the Render Output window without saving the image.

   The Render Image tool will still be active, enabling you to make modifications and regenerate the rendering quickly.

8. In the Render Image dialog box, select XY Ground Plane from the Scene Style pull-down list.

9. Click the Render button again to generate the image. Figure 10.8 shows the result.

   Notice that the threaded shaft disappears. This is because the XY plane of the model is directly under the circular base, and using this scene style cuts off anything on the other side of the plane from the rendering.

10. Close the Render Output window without saving.

11. Change the Scene Style setting to XY Reflective GP and rerun the rendering. See Figure 10.9 for the result.

12. For a final quick rendering, change the Lighting Style setting to Desktop with the XY Reflective GP still set as Scene Style (see Figure 10.10).

13. Close the Render Output window.

Figure 10.8

The rendering with a scene style of XY Ground Plane

Figure 10.9

The rendering with a scene style of XY Reflective GP

Figure 10.10

Using a different lighting style changes the shadows and the appearance of the part.

Creating an Illustration Rendering

There are times when photorealism can be confusing or when your communication medium won't allow the complexity. The Illustration rendering type will offer a whole new set of options for those situations. In this exercise you will create a rendering using the Illustration style. This will create a more pictoral image.

1. Change all of the style settings on the Render Image dialog back to default.

2. Change the Rendering Type setting to Illustration.

3. Switch to the Style tab.

4. Set the value for the Source group to Surface Style.

5. Make sure that the slide bar for Levels is 2. You can check it by clicking it and holding it. A tooltip will appear with its current value.

6. Change the Line Thickness value to 1.7.

7. Click Render. Figure 10.11 shows the result.

8. Close the Render Output window and the Render Image dialog box.

Simply using the styles and options that are included with Inventor can offer a great deal of potential in making your designs easy to present. Now let's make a few changes and see how a handful of mouse clicks can really change things.

Figure 10.11

The Illustration rendering offers an interesting alternative.

Scene Styles

An easy way to make a dramatic impact on a rendering is to customize the scene that you are working in. You can open the Scene Styles dialog box (Figure 10.12) from the Inventor Studio Panel bar. This dialog box lets you modify existing styles or copy them to create something new.

Figure 10.12

The Scene Styles dialog box with the Background tab active

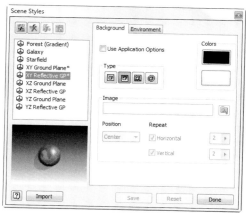

The Scene Styles dialog box has a list of existing styles in the upper left. Selecting one of the styles will cause the preview in the lower left to update, giving a general preview of how a rendering in the scene would appear. Above the list of styles are buttons that will create, purge, update, or save styles to the library for use by others.

The dialog box has two tabs that control the properties of the scene style.

The Background Tab

This tab tells Inventor Studio what will be seen behind or around the model.

Use Application Options

Selecting the Use Application Options checkbox bypasses other background options in favor of using the settings in the Application Options Color tab that are used in your Design window.

Colors

Depending on the type of scene, you are able to click on the color preview boxes and change what colors will be present in the rendering through the standard Inventor color selection dialog box.

Selecting one of the four types of scene will quickly change the look of the rendering:

Solid This option will use a single color for the background of the scene and for the color of a plane that might pass around or through the part. When it's activated, there will only be one color selection in the Colors group.

Color Gradient In some of the renderings that you have already created, the background transitions from black on the top to white at the bottom. The scene style that you selected used a Color Gradient type and used the two colors defined in the Colors area. The box on top specifies the color at the top edge of the screen, and the lower color box is used to select the color at the bottom of the screen.

Image Clicking the Image option will launch an Open dialog box where you can select an image file to use as the background for the rendering scene. Once an image is selected, additional options appear in the Image group for managing the appearance of the background.

Image Sphere Similar to the Image type, Image Sphere will wrap an image around the part rather than just applying an image behind the model. This enables the reflection of a different part of the environment on the front of the model than is shown behind the model. To use this scene, I think it's necessary to use a spherical or hemispherical image. There are resources on the Web for this type of image. Later in the chapter you'll learn another technique that can simulate the result.

Image

When either of the Image types is selected, these tools become available:

Position The options in this pull-down list work in the same way that applying an image to your Windows desktop would. There are three options for the position of the image:

> **Centered** Uses the image's true resolution to fill as much of the background as possible.
>
> **Tile** Tile will repeat the image to fill the background. You can limit the number of repetitions using the Repeat options to the right of the Position pull-down list.
>
> **Stretch** This option allows the image to be distorted in order to fill the background of the rendering scene.

Tile When the Tile Position option is used, you can specify how many repetitions of the image will appear or whether the image will be repeated, using the checkbox next to Horizontal and Vertical.

The Environment Tab

You control the position of the reflection plane relative to its origin in the model and how shadows and reflections are shown on it using the Environment tab (Figure 10.13).

Figure 10.13

The Scene Styles dialog box's Environment tab

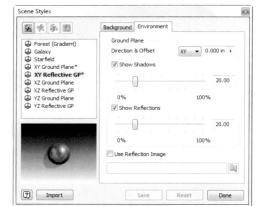

Ground Plane

As mentioned before, your previous renderings used a Ground Plane to cut off part of the model. You can change that effect using the options in the Ground Plane group:

Direction & Offset Using the pull-down list, you can select the primary plane to use in the scene style and then enter positive or negative values to reposition the plane relative to its model source.

Show Shadows This checkbox controls whether shadows will be cast on the ground plane or other parts of the model. The slider beneath it lets you set the opacity of the shadow. Moving the bar all the way to the right or entering the value 100 will create a completely black shadow. A value of 30–60 is usually optimal.

Show Reflections Show Reflections works like Show Shadows. Having the value at 100 will make the reflection appear to be very bright, almost luminous. A value of 30–60 is usually optimal.

Use Reflection Image When you select the color scheme that you will work in (using Application Options), you also select a reflection that will appear in your model. This option allows you to select a different image to reflect in your part along with other components.

Earlier I mentioned another workflow that could yield similar results to a spherical image environment. The image of the Helicopter Rotor Head on this book's cover was created by using a flat image of a cloudy sky and then reflecting a different image of a cloudy sky to simulate the effect of having different portions of the same sky in the rendering. Let's get back to experimenting with the rendering by creating our own scene style.

Building a New Scene Style

Scene styles can easily be constructed from scratch, but I will often build one based on another. This not only saves a few clicks, it also lets me quickly iterate from a style that I like to a new one that I can experiment with while keeping the last one intact.

1. Open the Scene Styles dialog box.

2. Right-click on the XY Reflective GP style and select Copy Scene Style.

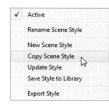

3. A New Style Name dialog box will appear. Type **Introducing Inventor - Black** as the name and click OK to create the new style.

4. On the Background tab, set the type to Single Color. Make sure that the color preview is black.

5. Switch to the Environment tab.

6. Set the value of the XY plane in Direction & Offset to –2.

7. Click the Save button to keep the changes and click Done to exit the dialog box.

8. Make your part smaller in the Design window and use Pan to move it near the top of the screen.

9. Open the Render Image tool.

10. Set Lighting to Desktop, Scene Style to Introducing Inventor - Black, and Render Type to Realistic (see Figure 10.14).

11. Click Render to create the new image. See Figure 10.15 for the result.

    Moving the ground plane allows you to change how much of the model is reflected. Let's create another style and see a different look.

Figure 10.14

Reposition the model and set the values for the rendering.

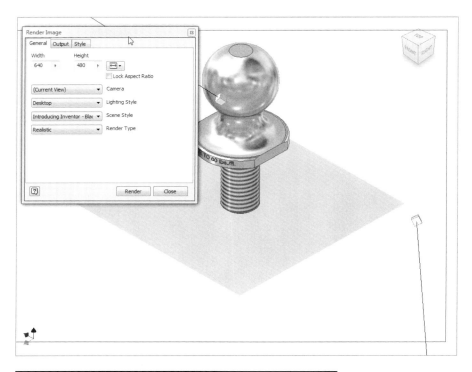

Figure 10.15

Rendering using the new scene style

12. Close the Render Output window but without closing the Render Image dialog box, click on Scene Styles in the Panel bar.

    In the Inventor Studio environment (as elsewhere in Inventor), you can cancel the running tool by selecting another tool.

13. Copy the Introducing Inventor - Black style to a new one that you will name **Introducing Inventor - White**.

14. Change the color from Black to White on the Background tab of the Scene Styles dialog box.

15. Save the new style and return to the Render Image tool.

16. Set the Lighting style to Global Lighting [1lt], and switch Scene Style to the newly created style.

17. Run the Render tool to get the image shown in Figure 10.16.

    In this case, the only portion of the reflection that you see is where the shadow is on the ground plane.

18. Close the rendering window.

Figure 10.16

In a white environment, reflections are only visible in the shadows.

Surface Styles

Along with lighting, scene, and render styles, Inventor offers surface styles. Surface styles will typically carry the same name as a color that you can select for your part from the Inventor Standard toolbar list. The difference is you can modify the surface style to carry additional information and properties that control how the surface will appear in the rendering. You can give a surface different reflection levels, change its opacity, apply a different texture, and even use a bump map to make the rendered version of the part appear to have an uneven surface texture.

In this introduction to Inventor Studio, we won't explore the full capabilities of surface styles, but one brief exercise will, I hope, pique your interest in learning more about them.

Rendering with a Surface Style

Some of the color selections that come with Inventor are already associated with surface styles that have a bump map enabled. In this exercise you will do a rendering with and without a bump map to see the difference.

1. Zoom in on the upper portion of the Hitch Ball model.

2. From the Color pull-down list on the Inventor Standard toolbar, select Plastic (Black) as the color of the part.

3. Create a rendering of the part using the Shop Lighting style and XY Reflective GP as the scene style. The image should look like Figure 10.17.

   The rendering using a surface style without a bump map should just appear as an improvement on the part that was on the screen. Now let's switch to a new color that has a bump map.

Figure 10.17

Rendering using the Plastic (Black) color

4. Close the image.

5. Now change the color of the part to Plastic (Texture).

6. Run the rendering again using the same properties. See Figure 10.18.

Figure 10.18

**Rendering using
the Plastic
(Texture) color**

In this rendering you should be able to see apparent peaks and valleys on the texture. As you move away from the brightest part of the surface, the high points on the surface should also be highlighted by the light. You should be able to see a marked difference between the appearance of the rendered model and the model in the Design window.

7. Click the Save Rendered Image icon in the upper right of the Render Output window.

8. Set the Save In folder to Parts, enter the filename **Hitch Ball**, and select the PNG format from the Save As Type pull-down list, as shown in Figure 10.19.

9. Save the image by clicking the Save button.

Figure 10.19

**Saving a
rendered image**

10. Close the Render Image tool.

11. Switch Inventor back to Part mode by using the Applications pull-down and selecting Part.

12. Save your part. Inventor will ask if you want to update your part table to have Plastic (Texture) as the new color for your part. Click Yes.

13. Close the file.

The rendering tools in Inventor Studio have much more to offer. Explore these tools, and as always, don't be afraid to try something just to see what happens.

In addition to rendering still images, you can use Inventor Studio to animate a model or the items around it; this can take your creativity to new levels.

Working with Animation

Presentation files, which you explored in Chapter 8, are wonderful tools for creating technical documentation. When you need to go beyond that and build truly amazing animations, Inventor Studio is the place to be. Animations can be built using combinations of a number of techniques. You can animate nearly anything in parts and assemblies. You can drive an assembly constraint (even showing acceleration), you can change the value of a parameter over time, and you can even control parts fading in and out.

After building the animation, you can apply the same rendering properties to components to create a great-looking movie of your work. By switching rendering styles, you can use the same animation steps to create materials for many different applications. The steps and activities within the animation are displayed on a timeline (see Figure 10.20), which makes editing easy.

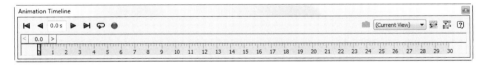

Figure 10.20

The Animation Timeline (collapsed)

In collapsed mode, all you will see are the main controls and the timeline. In expanded mode, you will see the individual actions that take place, with their positions and durations displayed as colored bars along the timeline.

Clicking and dragging on the slider in the timeline will move you through the timeline. As you drag any animation, actions will play out on the screen. This is a fantastic way to see your animation coming together.

Let's do some basic hands-on work to see a little bit of what is possible by animating in Inventor Studio. As we go through the exercise, you will be introduced to the tools as needed.

You can see the animation that I created at the book's website, www.sybex.com/go/ introducinginventor2009.

Setting the Timeline

Using a small number of tools, you can build a dramatic animation that you will want to show off.

1. Open the Gearbox.iam file that you created in Chapter 8.

2. Switch to the Inventor Studio environment.

3. Switch to your perspective view; you'll find the option on the Inventor Standard toolbar.

4. Zoom into the assembly so that your view resembles Figure 10.21.

Figure 10.21

Setting up a view of the Gearbox assembly

5. In the Inventor Studio Panel bar, click the Animation Timeline tool.

6. Click OK when prompted to move to be able to use the animation commands. This will allow the Animation Timeline window to open.

7. Click the Animation Options icon in the Animation Timeline toolbar.

   This opens the Animation Options dialog box, shown in Figure 10.22. In this dialog box, you set how long your animation will last. You can also use two options to control the velocity of events, or a third option that has the animation move at a constant speed. These values can be set in absolute time or as a percentage of the overall timeline.

8. In the Animation Options dialog box, set the Length value to 4 (seconds).

9. Click the Specify Velocity option, and make the ramp-up value (on the left) 30% and the ramp-down value (on the right) 5%. Inventor will calculate the middle value.

10. Click OK to accept these settings. The timeline will change from showing 30 seconds to showing 4.

Now let's begin our animation by animating our point of view.

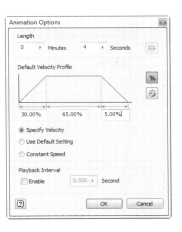

Figure 10.22

The Animation Options dialog box controls the time and tempo of the animation.

Animating a Camera

Your renderings can be created using your current point of view or cameras, but for animations to be truly effective it's best to use at least one camera.

1. Right-click in an empty part of the screen and select Create Camera From View to have Inventor Studio create a new camera with the name Camera1.

2. Select Camera1 from the pull-down list in the Animation Timeline toolbar.

3. Drag the slider in the timeline to 3.0 seconds.

4. Click on the corner of the ViewCube to show the Top, Left, and Front views in an isometric view and zoom in on the gearbox so that your screen looks like Figure 10.23.

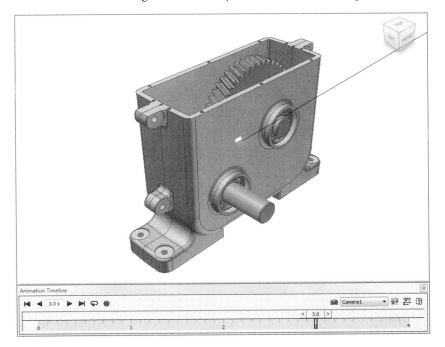

Figure 10.23

Setting how the assembly will look at 3 seconds

5. When the view is set up, click the Add Camera Action icon in the Animation Time-line toolbar.

   This enables Inventor Studio to transition the position of the camera through the animation by setting a view for the beginning point in time and at various points in time during the animation.

6. Drag the timeline slider back and forth between 0 and 3 seconds and see how the preview changes.

7. Click the Go To Start icon to return the animation to 0.

8. Save your work.

   Cameras can be as advanced or simple as you like. Not only can you set up actions that reposition the camera, but you can also animate the camera's focal point or depth of focus through the timeline.

Animating a Part Fade

Changing the visibility of a component can add clarity to your animation:

1. Click the Animate Fade tool in the Panel bar.

   The Animate Fade dialog box will require you to select one or more components to

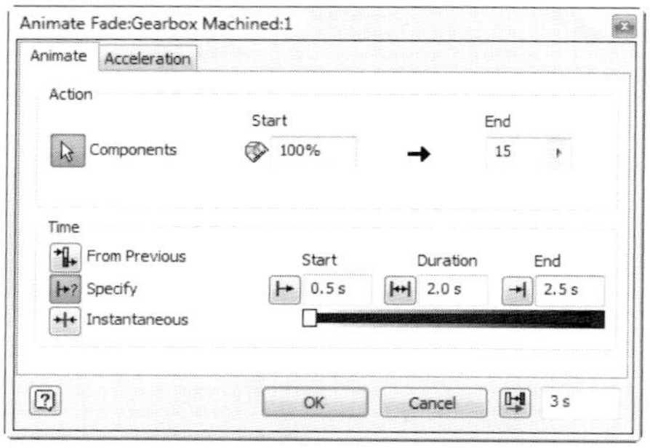

Figure 10.24

The Animate Fade dialog box controls the visibility of parts in the animation.

be faded over time. After selecting the components, you set the Start and End percentages of opacity along a length of time.

The length of time is defined from a previous event, by specifying a start time and duration, or you can make a part instantaneously change its fade level (see Figure 10.24).

2. Select the Gearbox Machined:1 part from the Browser.

3. In the Time group, use the Specify option to start the fade at 0.5 seconds and end it at 2.5 seconds.

4. Set the End opacity level at 15%.

5. Click OK to accept.

6. Click the Expand Action Editor button to see the full timeline shown in Figure 10.25.

   When your timeline is expanded, you will see icons on the left of the action that you specified. Aligned with the action will be a blue bar showing the start and end of the action. You can change the position and duration of events by clicking and dragging the bars that are in the timeline. You can also edit the event by double-clicking the bar to open the dialog box.

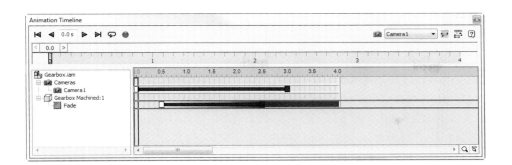

Figure 10.25

Expanding the timeline shows the actions in place

7. Drag the timeline slider to see the camera action occurring with the fade of the housing part.

8. Click Go To Start to return the animation to the beginning.

9. Save the file.

Animating an Assembly Constraint

In the assembly environment you can create an animation of a constraint by driving its value. That same technique can be employed in the Inventor Studio environment.

1. Click the Animate Constraints tool in the Panel bar.

2. Expand the Spur Gears: 1 component in the Browser and click on the suppressed Angle:1 constraint.

   The Animate Constraints dialog box (Figure 10.26) will show that the constraint is suppressed, because the constraint was suppressed in the assembly, but it is still possible to drive the constraint.

3. In the Action group, click the Constraint icon and set the End value to 360 degrees.

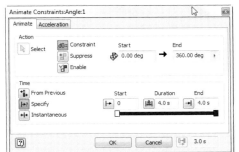

Figure 10.26

You can drive the value of an assembly constraint in an animation.

4. In the Time group, click the Specify option and set the animation Start at 0 and End at 4 seconds.

5. Click OK to save the settings. This will add the Angle:1 action to the timeline.

6. Click Go To Start and then Play Animation to see your work in motion.

7. Click and drag the camera from the beginning of the timeline to the right so it ends at the 4-second mark.

8. Move the Slider to the beginning and click Play Animation to see the change.

9. Put the Camera action back to its original position in the timeline.

10. Click the Collapse Action Editor button to reduce the timeline.

    Note that the motion of the gears accelerates slowly and then slows again at the very end. This is controlled by the values that you entered in the Animation Options dialog box at the beginning of the process.

11. Click the red Record Animation button to save the animation to a file. This will open the Render Animation dialog box.

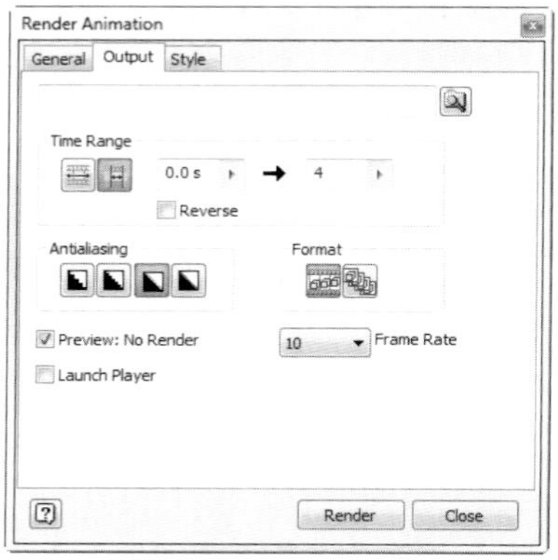

Figure 10.27

The Render Animation dialog box's Output tab controls the quality and duration of the animation.

The Render Animation and Render Image dialog boxes are similar with the exception of the Output tab, shown in Figure 10.27.

On this tab you will specify the time range to be recorded. It is not necessary to record the entire length of an animation to a file. You can use this option to record separate portions of a single animation.

You can also adjust the Frame Rate of the animation and whether it will be created as a single file or a series of images.

12. Click the Output tab of the Render Animation dialog box.

13. Set the end of the time range to 4. Initially it shows 30 seconds in red because it exceeds the timeline.

14. Click the Preview: No Render option. This will allow you to create a file without the high-quality rendering for test purposes.

15. Change the frame rate to 10.

16. Click Render to create the file.

17. When the Save dialog box appears, set the folder to Data, give it the filename of **Gearbox**, and change the type of file to AVI, as shown in Figure 10.28.

Figure 10.28

Creating the test animation file

18. Click Save to add the filename and path to the Render Animation dialog box.

19. Click Render again to select an animation codec (a standard that defines video compression and performance).

20. Select Microsoft Video 1 from the list and click OK to create the AVI.

    If you like, you can open the AVI file to see what Inventor created. The model is still shown in basic colors with edges showing (if you left this option active from the sheet metal exercises), and the fading of the housing part is not completely smooth. This is good enough for a test and may even be good enough to show your idea to another person.

    Now let's take the last step and create a rendered version.

21. Close the Render Output window.

22. On the Output tab, deselect the Preview option.

23. Give your file the name **Gearbox - Rendered** and start the rendering process.

24. When the AVI is finished, close the Output window, return to the Assembly environment, and save the file. All of the animation work will be saved with the file.

Gearbox.avi took 11 seconds to be generated on my computer. In comparison, Gearbox - Rendered.avi took 4 minutes and 25 seconds. That was with the most basic lighting and scene available.

The true value of the preview animation is that you can check your camera placement, timing, and other elements before you spend perhaps hours generating a fully rendered animation.

Summary

This chapter was intended to be a basic introduction to Inventor Studio. There is so much in this tool that it could be a book of its own.

With some time and experimentation, the only limitation for using this tool will be your imagination. Having the ability to create the quality of rendering and animation, combined with the ability to reuse assembly constraints and having the rendering associative to changes to the model, is almost too good to be true.

Appendices and Reference

APPENDIX A ■ Keyboard Shortcut Guide

APPENDIX B ■ Import and Export File Formats

APPENDIX C ■ Additional Resources

Keyboard Shortcut Guide

I have found Inventor's keyboard shortcuts to be priceless. Although I included the relevant shortcuts in the exercises, there are many more that weren't used you should know about.

This appendix lists the default shortcuts included with Inventor, but it's worth mentioning that you can also add or reassign shortcuts to whatever you like by using the Tools → Customize → Keyboard tab, and you can even export shortcuts to share with others. Before you do, take a look at the available shortcuts and be sure to keep in mind that the same keystroke can be used for different shortcuts based on the environment that you're in. A few shortcuts can even change the environment. For example, hitting the S key in a sketch will finish the sketch, or pressing E will automatically start the Extrude tool if you are working in a new, unconsumed sketch.

If you decide to make changes, you may want to incrementally export the changes to allow you to restore the changes to a point. If you decide to abandon your changes, you can click the Reset All Keys button to restore Inventor's keyboard shortcuts to the default.

Tables A.1 through A.8 list Inventor's default keyboard shortcuts, sorted by the environment in which you would access them.

Table A.1

Function Keys

KEYSTROKE	FUNCTION
F1	Help Topics
F2	Pan
F3	Zoom
F4	Orbit
F5	Previous View
Shift+F5	Next View
F6	Home View
F7	Slice Graphics in Sketch
F8	Show All Constraints
Alt+F8	Open Macros dialog box
F9	Hide All Constraints
F10	Unconsumed Sketch visibility toggle
Alt+F11	Open Visual Basic Editor

Table A.2

General Environment and Viewing Shortcuts

KEYSTROKE	FUNCTION
Ctrl+C	Copy to Clipboard
Ctrl+Shift+E	Assembly Degrees of Freedom visibility toggle
M	Measure Distance
Ctrl+N	New File
Ctrl+O	Open File
Ctrl+P	Print
Ctrl+Shift+Q	iMate Glyph visibility toggle
Ctrl+S	Save file
Ctrl+V	Paste from Clipboard
Ctrl+W	SteeringWheels
Ctrl+Shift+W	Weld Symbols visibility toggle
Ctrl+X	Cut to Clipboard
Ctrl+Y	Redo
Z	Zoom Window
Ctrl+Z	Undo
Esc	Ends Active Command
Home	Zoom All
Page Up	Look At
Delete	Deletes selected object
End	Zoom Select
Ctrl+/	Origin Axes visibility toggle
Ctrl+]	Origin Planes visibility toggle
Ctrl+.	Origin Points visibility toggle
Alt+/	User Work Axes visibility toggle
Alt+]	User Work Planes visibility toggle
Alt+.	User Work Points visibility toggle

KEYSTROKE	FUNCTION
Ctrl+Shift+N	Create New Sheet

Table A.3

Drawing View Shortcut

KEYSTROKE	FUNCTION
A	Baseline Dimension Set
B	Balloon
D	General Dimension
F	Feature Control Frame
O	Ordinate Dimension Set
T	Text
Ctrl+Shift+T	Leader Text

Table A.4

Drawing Annotation Shortcuts

KEYSTROKE	FUNCTION
A	Center Point Arc
C	Center Point Circle
D	General Dimension
F	Fillet
H	Fill/Hatch Sketch Region
I	Vertical
L	Line
O	Offset
T	Text
X	Trim
=	Equal

Table A.5

Sketching Shortcuts

KEYSTROKE	FUNCTION	FEATURE TYPE
D	Face Draft	Placed
E	Extrude	Sketched
F	Fillet	Placed
H	Hole	Sketched
Ctrl+Shift+K	Chamfer	Placed
Ctrl+Shift+L	Loft	Sketched
Ctrl+Shift+M	Mirror	Placed
Ctrl+Shift+O	Circular Pattern	Placed
Q	Create iMate	Placed
R	Revolve	Sketched
Ctrl+Shift+R	Rectangular Pattern	Placed
S	2D Sketch	Placed
Ctrl+Shift+S	Sweep	Sketched
;	Grounded Work Point	Work
/	Work Axis	Work
]	Work Plane	Work
.	Work Point	Work

Table A.6

Part Modeling Shortcuts

Table A.7

Assembly Modeling Shortcuts

KEYSTROKE	FUNCTION
A	Analyze Interference
C	Constraint (Assembly)
Ctrl+Shift+E	Degrees of Freedom visibility toggle
G	Rotate Component
Ctrl+H	Replace
Ctrl+Shift+H	Replace All
N	Create Component in Assembly
P	Place Component in Assembly
V	Move Component
W	Fillet Weld (Weldment environment)
Tab	Demote
Shift+Tab	Promote
Ctrl+Enter	Return
/	Work Axis
]	Work Plane
.	Work Point
Ctrl+=	Parent
Ctrl+-	Top

Table A.8

Presentation Shortcut

KEYSTROKE	FUNCTION
T	Tweak Components

Import and Export File Formats

Inventor has the ability to communicate with many computer-aided design (CAD) and non-CAD software applications.

The reasons for exporting or importing data are widely varied. You may want to import an old AutoCAD file to convert to 3D, or you may need to export a file to a rapid prototyping and computer-aided manufacturing (CAM) application.

Regardless of the reason, you'll need flexibility. This appendix lists the available formats for exchange between other applications and Inventor.

Import File Formats

Inventor stores its data in several formats depending on the type of file that you're creating. You can also import a number of neutral file formats as well as data directly from other 3D CAD systems. Here is a list of file extensions and the source that the data may come from:

FORMAT	PURPOSE
.idw	Inventor 2D drawing file format
.dwg	Inventor and AutoCAD 2D drawing file format
.ipt	Inventor part file format
.iam	Inventor assembly file format
.ipn	Inventor presentation file
.ide	Inventor library feature format
.dxf	Neutral 2D file format
.sat	ACIS kernel-neutral exchange format
.igs, .ige, iges	Neutral 3D surface file formats
.stp, .ste, .step	Neutral 3D solid file formats
.x_b, .x_t	Parasolids binary and text-based exchange formats
.prt, .asm	Pro/ENGINEER part and assembly file formats
.g, .neu	Pro/ENGINEER kernel-based exchange format
.prt,.sldprt, .asm, .sldasm	SolidWorks part and assembly formats
.prt	Unigraphics part and assembly formats

Inventor can also share 2D and 3D data with many types of application. Here is a list of the supported file types for export:

FORMAT	PURPOSE
.idw	Inventor 2D drawing file format
.dwg	Inventor and AutoCAD 2D drawing file format
.ipt	Inventor part file format
.iam	Inventor assembly file format
.dxf	Neutral 2D file format
.sat	ACIS kernel-neutral exchange format
.igs, .ige, iges	Neutral 3D surface file formats
.stp, .ste, .step	Neutral 3D solid file formats
.stl	Stereolithography 3D-neutral format
.x_b, .x_t	Parasolids binary and text-based exchange formats
.g, .neu	Pro/ENGINEER kernel-based exchange format
.dwf	Autodesk 2D/3D Drawing Web format
.pdf	Adobe Acrobat file
.png	Adobe Portable Network Graphics file
.jt	Compressed format file used by Siemens/PLM data management applications
.bmp	Windows bitmap file
.gif	Graphic Information file
.jpg	Common graphic file (Joint Photographic Experts Group)
.tif	Tagged image file
.xgl, zgl	Neutral 3D graphic viewing format

Additional Resources

Inventor has sold nearly 800,000 licenses. This means that you are not alone in learning Inventor. Accessing additional information, applications, and the assistance of other users can help shorten the learning curve and present new possibilities as you explore the work that others have done.

This appendix lists some resources for you to expand your knowledge of Inventor and perhaps even expand the capabilities of Inventor itself.

Autodesk Labs

Autodesk Labs is website where Autodesk posts free technology previews for many of its applications, including Inventor.

Inventor LT users should already be familiar with Labs because that's where you are able to access the software, but for non-LT users I cannot recommend strongly enough that you visit and explore the technology available at http://labs.autodesk.com. You can also access the site by choosing Web → Autodesk Labs in Inventor.

The ability to import Pro/ENGINEER, Unigraphics, and SolidWorks data was first tested for Inventor 2008 users through the Autodesk Labs website. New applications are posted there on a regular basis, and you're bound to find something exciting.

Autodesk Manufacturing Community

Having support from others and being able to share your success is a great thing. Autodesk hosts a Manufacturing Community, where you can ask questions, download data, and see what others have done. You can also access this site from Inventor; simply choose Web → Manufacturing Community, or type http://mfgcommunity.autodesk.com in your browser.

The popularity of Inventor continues to make it easier to find other information and users on the Web. In the Manufacturing Community you will find a listing of upcoming events, discussion groups, and access to excellent blogs hosted by Autodesk personnel. You can also set up a network where you can search for and communicate with other users in your area or in your industry.

Autodesk Education Community

If you are a student or educator, or you know someone you think would be interested in Inventor, Autodesk has a website that I hope you will visit or pass along: http://www.autodesk.com/educommunity.

This site is a resource for students and teachers at the secondary and postsecondary levels. On the site you will find free software downloads for over 15 of Autodesk's top applications, job postings, a question-and-answer area, and excellent tutorials.

The software is for learning purposes only, and most of the titles have all the functionality of the commercial versions, with the only limitation being that printing from the application applies an "Education version" label to the drawings.

Autodesk User Group International (AUGI)

AUGI is a well-known resource for AutoCAD users. While its support for Inventor is not as strong as I would like to see, there is a healthy discussion group, an Inventor wish list, and a way to locate local users groups where you can meet others with similar interests.

To join AUGI at no cost and access the available resources, go to http://www.augi.com.

Autodesk Vault

Very few things are as important in day-to-day engineering work as knowing what version of a part is the one that is being built, and controlling the data that defines it.

Autodesk Vault is a free workgroup level CAD data management system that allows you to control and keep multiple versions (not revisions) of the file for future reference. This is not a release and revision control system. Autodesk Productstream is for that, but Vault will give you the basic elements plus some great additional tools.

Some of those additional tools include basic check in/check out so others can't change a file that you're editing. This still allows others to use files that you're editing in their drawings or assemblies, and the changes you make will appear in those files.

There's a phenomenal tool called Copy Design which can not only copy a part or assembly, but any drawings or presentation files associated with them to new files and in the case of an assembly it allows you to pick and choose what files will be reused from the original and what files will be unique to the new assembly.

You can purchase Productstream from your Autodesk reseller if you want Release, Revision, and ECO control, but Vault is free. While I recommend you consult with a reseller to set it up, it can be done by an individual. Be sure to read the documentation that comes with your Inventor installation.

Index

Note to Reader: **Bolded** page numbers refer to definitions and main discussions of a topic. *Italicized* page numbers refer to illustrations.

#

2D (two-dimensional) drawings, from 3D data, 37–79
  adding dimensions. *see* dimensions
  assembly drawings, **74–75**, *75*
  associativity, **71–74**, *72–73*
  creating auxiliary view, **48–50**
  creating base views, *40–41*, **40–44**, *43–44*
  creating projected views, **44–48**, *45–48*
  creating section views, **53–55**, *54–55*
  detail views, **75–77**, *76–77*
  detailing drawing views, *55–59*, **55–59**
  drawing views of a part, *38–40*, **38–40**
  Hole/Thread Notes, **68–69**, *68–69*
  presentation views, **77–78**
  Retrieve Dimensions, **70–71**
  rotating view, **50–53**
3D display modes, *15–16*
3D (three-dimensional) Grip
  controlling, **235**
  defined, **234**
  editing, *235–237*, **235–237**, **320–321**, *321*
3D (three-dimensional) models, making, **104–108**, *105–108*

A

Absolute Angle, rotate view, **50–51**, *51*
adaptive modeling, *300–303*, **300–303**
Add button, project files, **31**
advanced part modeling. *see* part modeling, advanced
Angular constraint, assemblies, *140*, **140**, **148–149**, *149*
angular dimensions, 60, **62**, *62*, **127**, *127*
Animate Constraints dialog box, **387–389**
Animate Fade tool, *386*, **386–387**
Animate tool, 333–334
animation, Inventor Studio, 383–389
  assembly constraints, *387–388*, **387–389**
  cameras, **385**, *385–386*
  overview of, **383**, *383*

part fades, *386–387*, **386–387**
  timeline settings, *384*, **384–385**
animation, of assemblies
  constraints, *387–388*, **387–389**
  overview of, **328**
  preparing for, **328–330**, *329*
  using Drive Constraint dialog, *330*, **330–331**
  working with, **331**
Animation Options dialog box, 384–385
Animation Timeline tool
  animating cameras, *385*, **386**
  overview of, *383*, **383**
  setting, *384–385*, **384–385**
annotation
  expanded dimensioning. *see* dimensioning, expanded
  keyboard shortcuts, **395**
  sketch-derived views. *see* sketch-derived views
  weldment tool features, 340
antialiasing, renderings, **371–372**
Application Options dialog box, 19
  Assembly tab, **25**
  Colors tab, *21*, **21**
  creating new work environment, **25–28**, *27–28*
  Display tab, **21–23**, *22*
  Drawing tab, **23**
  General tab, *19*, **20**
  Hardware tab, **23**
  Help button, **20**
  Import and Export buttons, **20**
  overview of, *19*, **19–20**
  Part tab, **25**
  Sketch tab, **23–25**, *24*
Apply button, **2**
arcs
  creating, **246**
  creating bolt circles with Centerline tool, **58**
  creating holes, 113
  creating lip using Sweep tool, 269
  creating with Line tool, **230–231**, *231*

radius dimensions using, 63
sketch constraints for, **87**
using Hole feature, **115–120**
arrow buttons, **2**, 31
aspect ratio, renderings, 370
assembly constraints, creating, 138–152
    animating assemblies, **328–330**
    beginning assembly, **141–150**
    editing parts, *150–152*, **150–152**
    overview of, **138–139**
    Place Constraint tool, **139–141**, *139–141*
assembly modeling, 137–167
    concept of, **138**
    constraints. *see* assembly constraints, creating
    creating breakout view, **205–207**, *206–207*
    creating simple drawing, **74–75**, *75*
    keyboard shortcuts, **396**
    using Bolted Connection Design Accelerator, **163–167**, *164–167*
    using enabled parts, **156–157**, *157*
    using representations, **153–156**, *155*
    using standard parts, **157–163**, *158–163*
assembly modeling, advanced, 293–340
    animation within assembly, **328–331**
    Derived Parts, **319–321**, *320*
    Design Accelerators. *see* Design Accelerators
    iAssembly, **323–328**, *324–327*
    Move and Rotate Component tools, **322–323**
    overview of, **294**
    positional representations, *336–338*, **336–339**
    presentation files, **331–336**, *332–335*
    weldments, **339–340**, *340*
assembly-oriented dimensions, 222–226
    bill of materials, **225–226**, *226*
    placing parts list in drawing, **222–223**, *223*
    using Auto-Balloon tool, *223–226*, **224–225**
    using Balloon tool, **223–224**
Assembly tab, Application Options dialog box, **25**
Assembly tab, Place Constraint tool, **139–141**, *140*
associativity, **71–74**, *72–73*
Attach Balloon tool, **225**
AUGI (Autodesk User Group International), **400**

Auto Balloon tool, *223–226*, **224–225**
AutoCAD_Related_Options.xml file, 20
Autodesk Labs, **399**
Autodesk Manufacturing Community, **399**
Autodesk Vault. *see* Vault
auxiliary views, creating, **48–50**, *48–50*
Available Styles tab, Style and Standard Editor, **176**
Axle support
    changing enabled part state, 156–157, *157*
    creating 3D model, 104–106
    creating assembly constraints, 143, *145–149*, 145–150
    creating View representation, 154–156

B

background
    color options, **21**, **25**
    images, 26
    wireframe display modes, 22
Background tab, Scene Style dialog box, **377–378**
Balloon tool, **223–224**, *223–226*
Base View dialog box, **74**, **175**
Base View tool
    creating assembly drawing, **74**
    creating base views, *40–41*, **40–43**, *43*
    saving drawing file, **43–44**, *44*
Baseline Dimension Set tool, **64–65**, *65*
Baseline Dimension tool, **64–65**, *65*
Bearing Generator
    Calculation tab, *297*, **297–298**
    Design tab, *296*, **296–297**
    overview of, **295–296**, *296*
    selecting bearings, **298–299**, *299*
Bend Notes tool, **367–368**, *367–368*
Bend tab, Style and Standard Editor, **345–346**, *346*
bill of materials, **225–226**, *226*
bolt circles, creating, *58*, 58
Bolted Connection Design Accelerator, **163–167**, *164–167*
borders, template, 185–186, *186*
Break dialog box, *196*, **196–197**
break out view
    creating, **204–205**, *204–205*
    creating for assembly, **205–207**, *206–207*
    Hole feature, *203–205*
    overview of, *203*, **203–204**

Break tool, *196*, *196–197*
break view, *196–199*, **196–199**
Browse for Folder dialog box, 32
Browser bar, **17**, 27–28, *28*
buttons, Project File manager, *31*
buttons, using, **2**, *2*

C

Calculation tab, Bearing Generator, *297*,
  297–298
Calculation tab, Shaft Component Generator,
  307, 313
Calculation tab, Spur Gear Component
  Generator, *316*, **316**
Camera tool, **371**
cameras, animating, *385*, **385–386**
Cancel button, **2**
Cancel setting, Open dialog box, **6**
Center Mark tool, **55–56**, *56*
Center Point Arc tool, **246–248**, *247–248*
Center Point Circle, **246**
Center Point option
  Hole feature, 113, **123**
  Origin Center Point. *see* Origin
    Center Point
  sketch dimensions, 95
Centerline Bisector tool, **58–59**, *59*
Centerline setting
  using Ordinate Dimension Set tool,
    218–219, *219*
  using Revolve tool, 131–132
  using sketch dimensions, 95
Centerline tool
  creating bolt circle with, **58**, *58*
  creating centerline bisector with,
    58–59, *59*
  placing centerline in view, **56–57**, *57*
Chamfer Notes, 221
Chamfer tool
  adding beveled edges in weldment, 340
  adding chamfer to end of shaft, 309–310
  creating turned part, 134
Change View Orientation icon, **41**
Character Exclude settings, Style and
  Standard Editor, 174
child views, 40, 82
circles, sketch constraints with, **237–238**, *238*
Circular Pattern tool, *244–245*, **244–245**
Clearance Hole, Hole dialog box, 114–115

click-sensitivity, General Dimension tool, 60
Coil tool
  generating springs, **275–278**, *276–278*
  overview of, **274**
  tabs, *274–275*, **274–275**
Coincident constraint
  defined, **87**
  editing title block text, 188–189
  viewing in existing sketch, 89
Collinear constraint, **87**, 132
color settings
  Illustration rendering styles, **373**, *373*
  layer styles, *182–183*, **182–183**
  scene styles, background, 377
  View representation, **154–156**, *155*
Colors tab, Application Options dialog box,
  21, *21*, **25**
commands, restarting, **46**
Communication Center, **18**
Component Opacity, *16*, **16**
component overrides, *207–208*, **207–208**
Component tab, Drawing View dialog box, 41
Components tab, iAssembly Author
  dialog box, 325
Concentric constraint, **87**
Concentric placement, Hole dialog box, 113
Conditions tab, Loft tool, **251**, *251*
Constrain Component tool, **148**
Constrained Orbit tool, **13**
Constraint Inference, **96**
Constraint Persistence, **96**
constraints
  adaptive modeling using, **301–302**
  animated assemblies using, **328–330**
  assembly. *see* assembly constraints,
    creating
  moving or rotating parts after applying,
    322–323, *322–323*
  sketch. *see* sketch constraints
Construction geometry
  sketch constraints and, **96–98**, *97*
  sketching layout, **247–248**, *248*
Content Center
  assembly modeling, **157–163**, *158–163*
  importance of installing, 157
  overview of, **31**
context menus
  creating projected view, **44–45**, *45*
  options for baseline dimensions, *65*, **65–66**
  overview of, 3

Contour Flange tool, *359–361*, **359–361**
Convert to Weldment dialog box, **340**
Corner Round tool, **357–358**, *358*
Corner tab, Style and Standard Editor, **347**, *347*
Counterbore, Hole dialog box, 114
Countersink, Hole dialog box, 114
Create New Folder icon, 4
Create New Folder tool, **43–44**
cropped views, **209–210**, *209–210*
Curves tab, Loft tool, 250, *250*
Customization dialog box, **290**
Cut tool, *364*, **364**, *364*
Cutout Shape, Detail View tool, 76

D

Default Hatch Style, **177–178**, *178*
Default Thread Edge Display tool, 175
Definition in Base View option, **48**
degrees of freedom. *see* DOF (degrees of freedom)
Delete Features dialog box, *285*, **285**
Depth option, Break Out dialog box, 203–204
Derived Parts, **319–321**, *320*
Design Accelerators, 294–319
　　Bearing Generator, *295–297*, **295–299**
　　Bolted Connection, *164–167*, **164–167**
　　dialog boxes, **295**
　　Engineer's Handbook, **318–319**, *319*
　　Key Connection generator, **318**
　　Mirror Components, *303–305*, **303–306**
　　overview of, **163**, **294–295**, *295*
　　resources for, **274**
　　Shaft Generator. *see* Shaft Component Generator
　　Spur Gears Component Generator, **314–318**, *315–318*
　　starting new assembly, *295*, **295**
　　using adaptive modeling, **300–303**, *300–303*
Design Doctor, Help system, **34–35**, *35*
Design tab, Bearing Generator, *296*, **296–297**, *299*
Design tab, Shaft Component Generator, *306*, **306–307**
Design tab, Spur Gear Component Generator, **315**
Design window, *7*, **17**
detail views, **75–77**, *76–77*

dialog boxes
　　Design Accelerator, **295**
　　learning to use, *2*, **2–3**
diameter dimensions, **62–63**, *63*
digital prototyping, 137. *see also* assembly modeling
dimensioning, expanded, 210–226
　　assembly-oriented dimensions, **222–226**, *223*
　　keyboard shortcuts, **395**
　　Leader Text tool, **214**
　　part dimensions, **217–222**, *219–222*
　　properties, **211–213**, *212–213*
　　revision tables and tags, **215–217**, *216–217*
　　surface texture callouts, **215**, *215*
　　Text tool, **213–214**
dimensions, 59–67. *see also* dimensioning, expanded
　　adding, **59–63**, *60–63*
　　adding sketch, **89–94**, *91–92*, *94*
　　assembly-oriented, **222–226**, *223–226*
　　with Baseline Dimension tool, **64–65**, *65*
　　creating new style, *179*, **179–180**
　　creating slice view, 200
　　editing tools, **65–67**, *67*
　　with Hole tool, 117
　　modifying title block, **187**
　　overview of, 59
　　with Retrieve Dimensions tool, **70–71**, *70–71*
　　with Revolve tool, 132–133
Display options
　　Break dialog box, 196
　　Break Out dialog, 204
　　Detail View tool, 76
　　Inventor Standard toolbar, **14–17**, *15–16*
　　Sketch tab, **24**
Display Options tab, Drawing View dialog box
　　assembly drawings, 74
　　base views, 41
　　break views, 198
　　component overrides, 208
　　presentation views, 78
Display tab, Application Options dialog box
　　adding advanced fillets, 259
　　creating basic part, *351*, **351**
　　creating work environment, **26–27**, *27*
　　overview of, **21–23**, *22*
Distance, Hole dialog box, 114

documenting, iAssembly, **326–328**
DOF (degrees of freedom)
    adding dimensions to sketches, **90–91**, *91*
    construction geometry, **96–98**, *97*
    displaying for sketch, **89**
    removing for assembly constraints,
        138–139
    turning on for assembly constraints,
        143–144, *144*
    viewing, *146–147*, **146–147**
draft, adding to extruded surface, 249
drag-selection, **131**
Drawing Annotation panel, **55**, 367–368
Drawing tab, Application Options dialog
    box, **23**
Drawing View dialog box, **40–42**, *41*, 77–78
drawing views
    detailing, *55–59*, **55–59**
    Drawing Views panel for, 39, *40*
    keyboard shortcuts, **395**
Drill Point, Hole dialog box, 114
Drilled, Hole dialog box, 114
Drive Constraint dialog box, *330*, **330–331**
driven dimensions, **95**

E

Edge Fillet, Fillet dialog box
    adding edge fillet, **110–113**, *111–112*
    overview of, **108–110**
Edge option, Rotate View dialog box,
    50–51, *51*
edges
    adding flanges to. *see* Flange tool
    adding hems to, *362–363*, **362–363**
    autoprojecting, Sketch tab, **24**
    Style tab options for Illustration
        rendering, 373, *373*
Edit button, project files, **31**
Edit Dimension dialog box, **66**, 211–213
editing
    3D grips, **235–237**, *235–237*
    adding Hole/Thread Notes, *68–69*, **68–69**
    dimensions, **24**, **65–67**, *67*, 211
    Hole Tables, **221–222**
    one member of iPart family, **291–292**
    parts in assemblies, **150–152**, *150–152*
    project files, 29
    properties, 187
    shafts, **312–314**, *313–314*

title blocks, **187–190**, *187–190*
    using Baseline Dimension Set tool, **65–66**
    using degrees of freedom, **89**
    using Design Accelerator, **312–314**
education community, Autodesk, **400**
Ellipse tool, **246**, *247*
Emboss tool, *240–243*, **240–243**, 364
Enabled display, Application Options
    dialog box, 22
enabled parts, **156–157**, *157*
End of Part icon, **127**, *127*
Engineer's Handbook, **318–319**, *319*
English template folder, **191**
environment, keyboard shortcuts, **394–395**
Environment tab, Scene Style dialog box, *378*,
    378–381
Equal constraint, **87**, 132
exploded views, **77**, **331–336**
Export button, Application Options
    dialog box, **20**
exporting
    file formats, **397**
    flat pattern data, 368
Extents options, Revolve tool, **129–130**
Extrude tool
    making 3D model, **103–107**, *105–107*
    modifying part with parametric
        dimensions, **107–108**, *108*
    overview of, **103**, *103*
    Revolve tool vs., 129
    sketching layout, 247

F

Face Fillet, Fillet dialog box, 108–109
Face tool
    adding flanges, **356**
    creating basic sheet metal part, *351–352*,
        351–352
    overview of, *350*, **350–351**
feature libraries, **134–136**, *135*
features
    deleting, **285**
    parametric modeling revolving around, **82**
Fence Shape, Detail View tool, 76
File display, Open dialog box, *5–6*, **5–6**
file formats, import and export, **396–397**
File List, Open dialog box, **4**, *5*
File Name, display by, **5–6**
File Names dialog box, **305**

Files of Type, display by, **5–6**
Fillet tool
    adding advanced fillets, **259–261**
    adding edge fillet, **110–113**, *111–112*
    applying work features, **125–126**, *126*
    creating nose cone, **272–273**
    overview of, *108*, **108–110**
filters, 160
Filters list, **10**
Find tool dialog box, *6*, **6**
Fix constraint, **87**, 92
Flange tool
    adding flanges, **353–359**, *354–359*
    Contour Flange tool, *359–361*, **359–361**
    overview of, *352*, **352**
    Shape tab, **352–353**
Flat Pattern tool, *355*, **355**
Flush constraint, assemblies
    adaptive modeling, 302
    applying, **151–152**, *152*
    defined, **140**
Folder Options, project files, **30**
folders
    creating assembly, **142–143**, *143*
    creating for project file, **32**, *32*
    iAssembly, 325
Format Text dialog box, **189–190**, *213*, **213–214**
Free Orbit tool, **12–13**
Frequently Used Subfolders, *4*, **4**, **29–30**, 33
From Sketch placement, Hole dialog box, 113
Front View Plane tool, 175–176
Full Round, Fillet dialog box, 108–109
function keys, keyboard shortcuts, **394**
functional design, 116
Funnel icon, Place From Content Center tool, 160

G

Gap options, Break dialog box, 197
General Dimension tool
    adding angular dimensions, **62**, *62*
    adding basic dimensions, **60**, *60*
    adding diameter and radius dimensions, **62–63**, *63*
    adding dimensions to sketches, **90**, **92–93**, *102–103*, **102–104**
    applying work features, **123**, **127**

    dimensioning with complex selections, *61*, **61**
    overview of, **59–60**
General tab, Application Options dialog box, *19*, **20–21**
General tab, Render Image dialog box, **370–371**, *371*
General tab, Style and Standard Editor, **173–174**, *174*
geometry
    parametric modeling concepts, **82–83**
    placing constraints on, **84–86**
    sketch dimensions simplifying, **90**
    viewing existing constraints, *88*, **88–89**
Geometry tab, Punch tool, *365*, **365**
gesturing, **85**
Go To Last Folder Visited icon, **4**
graphical user interface. *see* user interface
Graphs tab, Shaft Component Generator, **307**, 313
Ground Plane setting, scene styles, 378
Ground Shadow, **15–16**
grounded state, assembly constraints, 138
GUI (graphical user interface). *see* user interface

H

Hardware tab, Application Options dialog box, **23**
Hatch pattern, **177–178**, *178*, 183
Height setting, renderings, 370
Help button, Application Options dialog box, **20**
Help system, **34–35**, *35*
Hem tool, *362–363*, **362–363**
Hidden Edge Display option, **15**
Hide All Degrees Of Freedom, sketch constraints, 96
Hole dialog box, *113–115*, **113–115**
Hole tables
    creating, **220**, *220*
    modifying, **221–222**, *221–222*
    overview of, **219–220**
Hole/Thread Notes, *68–69*, **68–69**, 180
Hole tool
    adding bolts manually, *158–163*, **158–163**
    applying work features, **123–124**
    using, **115–120**, *116–120*
    using Hole dialog box, *113–115*, **113–115**
holes, adding with Punch tool, 365–366
Horizontal constraint, **87**

I

iAssembly, 323–328
  creating simple, *324–325*, **324–325**
  documenting, *326–327*, **326–328**
  overview of, *322–323*, **323**
iAssembly Author dialog box, **324–325**, *325*
Illustration rendering
  creating, *376*, **376**
  defined, **371**
  Style tab options for, **372–373**, *372–373*
Image Sphere setting, scene style
  background, 377
images, background
  overview of, **26**
  scene styles, **377–379**
Import button, Application Options
  dialog box, **20**
importing, file formats, **397**
inference lines, section views, 54–55
Insert constraint, assemblies
  adaptive modeling, **302–303**
  applying, **147–148**, *148*
  creating simple iAssembly, 324
  editing shafts, 314
  overview of, **140**, *140*
intelligence, with assembly constraints, 138
Inventor LT, 3
Inventor, overview of
  customizing. *see* Application Options
    dialog box
  dialog boxes, *2*, **2–3**
  Help system, **34–35**, *35*
  New File dialog box, **7–8**, *8*
  Open dialog box, **3–7**, *3–7*
  project files. *see* project files
  user interface. *see* user interface
Inventor Project wizard, **31–32**, *32*
Inventor Standard toolbar
  Display options, **14–17**
  Style and Standard Editor, **172–173**
  tools of, **8–13**
Inventor Studio, 369–389
  creating animation in, 328, **383–389**
  creating rendering, **370–376**
  overview of, 370
  scene styles, *376*, **376–381**
  surface styles, *381–382*, **381–383**
Inventor_Default_Options.xml file, 20
iPart Author dialog box, **287–288**, 291

iParts, 286–292
  converting existing part to, **287–290**,
    288–290
  editing one member of iPart family, *291*,
    291–292
  overview of, **286–287**
  parameters, **287**
isometric view
  adding dimensions in, **103**
  creating, *46*
  creating slice view, **199–201**
  editing, 52–53
  removing break inheritance from, 198–199

J

Join tool, **103**

K

Key Connection generator, **318**
keyboard shortcuts
  accessing Help system, **34**
  guide to, **393–396**
  on Inventor Standard toolbar, **12**

L

Labs, Autodesk, **399**
layers, editing style, *181–183*
layers, editing style of, **180–183**
layout, sketching, **247–248**, *247–249*
Leader Text tool, *214*, **214**, *214*
libraries
  feature, **134–136**, *135*
  project file, **30**
Lighting Style setting, renderings, **371**, *375*
Limits tolerance, 211–212
Line tool, **230–231**, *231*
Line Weight option, layer styles, 182
Linear placement, Hole dialog box, 113
linetypes, specialized, **95–96**
lips, creating recessed, **268–271**, *268–271*
Local Styles, **183–185**
Location setting, project files, **30**
Location tab, Thread tool, **232–233**
Lock Aspect Ratio checkbox, renderings, 370
LOD (Level of Detail) representations,
  assembly modeling, **153–154**

Loft command, 254
Loft tool, 250–256
    Conditions tab, **251**, *251*
    Curves tab, **250**, *250*
    overview of, *250*, **250**
    setting up for next feature, **252–256**, *252–256*
    Transition tab, *251*, **251**, *251*
    using as primary feature, *271–273*, **271–273**
    using with Mirror tool, 280–283
Look At tool, **13**, 230
Look In field, Open dialog box, 4

M

manager buttons, project files, **30–31**
manual override, radius and diameter dimensions, 63
Manufacturing Community, Autodesk, **399**
manufacturing-focused toolset, **342**
Mastering Autodesk Inventor 2009 and Autodesk Inventor LT 2009 (Waguespack, et al.), 10–12, 274
Mate constraint, assemblies, **140**, *140*, 145
Material Hatch Pattern Defaults tab, Style and Standard Editor, **177–178**, *178*
Member Scope, iPart, **291–292**
menu bar, *8*, **8–9**
merge options, Hole table, 221
Messages, Bearing Generator, 298
Metric template folder, **191**
Mirror Components tool, *303–305*, **303–306**
Mirror tool, *278–284*, **278–284**
Model State tab, Drawing View dialog box, 41, 77
More button, **2**
More tab, Shell tool, **262–263**
Motion tab, Place Constraint tool, *141*, **141**
Move Component tool, **322–323**

N

naming
    mirroring assembly, *305*, **305**
    new standards, **172**
    renderings, 371
navigation controls, 4
    Open dialog box, *5*

New File dialog box, **7–8**, *8*
New Style Name dialog box, **172–173**, **179**
nose cone, creating, *271–273*, **271–273**

O

Object Defaults tab, Style and Standard Editor
    editing layer's style, **180–183**
    overview of, **176–177**, *176–177*
    working with object defaults, *178*, **178–179**
object styles, 177, 178, *178*
Offset setting, assembly constraints, 141
OK button, **2**
OldVersions directory, project files, **30–31**
On Point placement, Hole dialog box, 113
Open dialog box
    beginning new drawing from template, **38–40**
    file display, **5–6**, *5–6*
    navigation controls, **4–5**, *5*
    opening file, **6–7**, *7*
    other controls, 6
    overview of, **3**
    shortcuts and File List, **4–5**, *5*
Open Documents in Session, status bar, **18**
Open From Vault tool, **10**
Open setting, Open dialog box, **6**
Options setting, Baseline Dimension Set tool, 65
Options setting, Open dialog box, **6**
Options setting, project files, 30
Orbit tool, **12–13**
Ordinate Dimension Set tool, **218–219**, *219*
Orientation group, Drawing View dialog box, 41
Orientation options, Break dialog box, 196
Orientation options, Sweep tool, **268**
Origin Center Point
    Loft tool, **271–272**
    sketch constraints, 98–100
    using Place Constraint tool, 142
    using Revolve to create turned part, 130
osnap options, AutoCAD, 84
Output tab, Render Animation dialog box, *388*, **388**
Output tab, Render Image dialog box, *371*, **371–372**
Overconstrained dimensions, Sketch tab, **23**
Overlay views, 339

P

Pan command, **10**
Panel bars
    creating new work environment, **26–28**, *28*
    for new drawing, 39
    using, **17**
paper size, defining templates for, 186
Parallel constraint, **87–89**
parameters, iPart, **287–289**
parametric modeling
    concept of, **82–83**
    defined, **81**
    introduction to sketching, **83–84**, *84–86*
    modifying part with dimensions, **107–108**
parent views
    adding features, 82
    creating auxiliary views, **48–49**
    creating projected views, 44–45
    defined, 40
part dimensions
    Hole tables, **219–222**, *220–222*
    Ordinate Dimension Set tool, **218–219**, *219*
part fade, animating, *386–387*, **386–387**
Part Features tools
    applying work features, **121**
    Chamfer tool, 134
    drawing view associativity, **72**
    Hole feature, 115
    Parameters tool, **288**
    Revolve tool, 132
part modeling
    adding sketch dimensions, **89–94**, *91–92*, *94*
    applying Hole feature, **113–120**, *116–120*
    applying work features, **120–129**, *122–128*
    introduction to sketching, **83–86**, *84–86*
    keyboard shortcuts, **395**
    overview of, 81
    parametric modeling concept, **82–83**
    sketch constraints. *see* sketch constraints
    sketching, *84–86*
    using Extrude tool, **103**
    using feature libraries, **134–136**, *135*
    using Fillet tool, **108–113**, *111–112*
    using Revolve tool, *129–134*, **129–134**
part modeling, advanced, 229–292
    beginning new part, **230–232**, *231*
    Coil tool, *274–278*, **274–278**
    Emboss tool, *240–243*, **240–243**
    iParts, **286–292**, *288–291*
    Loft tool. *see* Loft tool

    Mirror tool, **278–284**, *278–284*
    rectangular and circular patterns, *244–245*,
        244–245
    Rib and Web tools, *266–267*, **266–267**
    Sculpt tool, *256–261*, **256–261**
    Shell tool, *262–265*, **262–266**
    Spline tool, **245–246**
    Split tool, *238–239*, **238–240**
    Sweep tool, *268–271*, **268–271**
    Thicken/Offset tool, **284–286**, *284–286*
    Thread tool. *see* Thread tool
Part tab, Application Options dialog, **25**
parts. *see* sheet metal parts
parts list
    changes reflected in, 226
    documenting iAssembly, 326–327
    placing in drawing, **222–223**, *223*
Perpendicular constraint, **87**, 92
perspective, **15–16**, 384
Place Component tool, 142–143, *142–143*, 324
Place Constraint tool, *139–141*, **139–141**
Place Feature tool, **135–136**
Place From Content Center tool, 158–160, 164
placed features, **82**
Placement options, Hole dialog box, 113
Placement tools, Shaft Component
    Generator, 307
Positional representation tool
    creating positional representation, *336–338*,
        336–338
    defined, **336**
    detailing using, **338–339**, *338–339*
    overview of, **153**
Precision setting, Baseline Dimension Set
    tool, 65
Predict Offset and Orientation checkbox,
    Place Constraint tool, 139
preferences, Style and Standard Editor,
    174–176, *175*
presentations
    creating, **77–78**, *78*
    creating exploded view, **331–336**, *332–335*
    keyboard shortcut, **396**
    overview of, **78**, 331
Preserve All Features, Fillet dialog box, 110
Preset Value settings, Style and Standard
    Editor, 174
previewing, assembly constraints, 139, 145
Profile option, Break Out dialog, 203
Project File, display by, **5–6**

Project File editor, 29, *29*
project files
    creating, **31–34**, *32–33*
    manager buttons, **30–31**
    overview of, **28–29**, *29*
    rules for, **29**
    settings, **30**
    types of, **29–30**, *32*
Project Flat Pattern tool, **362–363**
Project Geometry tool
    adding bolts manually, 158
    adding hem, 362–363
    applying work features, **123**
    creating slice view, 200
    sketching layout, 247
projected view
    creating, **44–48**, *45–47*
    creating assembly drawing, **74**
    removing break inheritance from
        isometric, 198–199
Projection Type tool, 175
Projects dialog box, 171
Propagate to Parent View option, Break
    dialog box, 197
properties
    applying to work features, 128–129
    dimension, **211–213**, *212–213*
    editing title block text, **189–190**
    view sketching, 202
publishing, sheet metal rules, *349–350*,
    349–350
Punch tool, *365–366*, **365–366**

R

radius dimensions, **62–63**, *63*
Realistic rendering
    defined, **371**
    setting up basic, **373–374**, *374–375*
    Style tab options for, *372*, **372**
Record Animation button, 387–389
Recover, Help system, **34**
Rectangular Pattern tool, **244–245**, *244–245*
Redo, **10**
Reflection Environment, Colors tab, 21
reflection, scene styles, **379**
Relative Angle, rotate view by, **50–51**, *51*
Render Animation dialog box, *388*, **388**
Render Image dialog box, 388

Render Image tool. *see* renderings, creating
renderings, creating, 370–376
    of animations. *see* animation, Inventor
        Studio
    General tab, **370–371**, *371*
    Illustration, **376**, *376*
    Output tab, *371*, **371–372**
    scene styles, **376–381**
    setting up basic, **373–375**, *374–375*
    Style tab, *372–373*, **372–373**
    surface styles, *381–382*, **381–383**
representations
    assembly modeling using, **153–156**, *155*
    creating View, **154–156**, *155*
    types of, **153–154**
resizing, dialog boxes, *3*, *3*
resources
    animation, **383**
    Autodesk, **399–400**
    Autodesk Labs, **399**
    Design Accelerators, **274**
Retrieve Dimensions tool, **70–71**, *70–71*
Return button, **10**
Revision Table tool and Tag, **215–217**,
    216–217
Revolve tool, **129–134**
    creating turned part with, *130–134*,
        130–134
    Extents options, **129–130**
    overview of, 129, *129*
Rewind tool, **14**, *14*
Rib tool, *266–267*, **266–267**
Rotate Component tool, **319–320**, **323**
Rotation assembly constraint, **141**, 148
Rotation-Translation assembly constraint, **141**
rotation, view, **50–53**, *51–53*
rules. *see* sheet metal rules

S

scale
    creating auxiliary views, 48
    creating base views, **41–42**
    creating break view, 197
    creating detail views, 75–76
    creating quick start template file, 192
    creating sheet metal drawings using, 367
    creating simple assembly drawing, 74
    editing layer style, 182

General tab, Style and Standard Editor, 174
placing parts list in drawing, 222
presentation views, 78
rotating views, 52
Scale tool, **264–265**
scene styles, 376–381
    Background tab, *377*, **377–378**
    building, **379–381**, *380–381*
    defined, **371**
    Environment tab, *378*, **378–379**
    overview of, *376*, **376–377**
    setting up basic rendering with, *374–375*,
        374–375
Sculpt tool, 256–261
    adding advanced fillets, *259–261*, **259–261**
    creating solid from space, *257–258*,
        257–258
    overview of, *256*, **256**
section lines, **53–55**
Section View dialog, 199
section views
    assembly drawing with, 75
    centerline bisector for, 59
    creating, **53–55**, *54–55*
    slice view vs., **199**
    specifying hatch pattern using,
        177–178, *178*
    view associativity with, 73
Sections menu, Shaft Component
    Generator, 307
Select Member dialog box, 327
Select Other tool, 363
selected views, 44
Selection, Application Options dialog box, 20
Selections group, Place Constraint tool, 141
Shaded Display modes, Application Options
    dialog box, 22
Shaded Display option, **15**
shadows
    creating, **15–16**
    scene styles, **379**
Shaft Component Generator, 306–314
    creating shaft, **307–312**, *308–312*
    Design tab, *306*, **306–307**
    editing shaft, **312–314**, *313–314*
    Graphs tab, **307**
    overview of, **306**
Shape tab, Flange tool, **352–353**
Sheet Formats, **191–192**

Sheet Metal Default dialog box, *342*, **342–343**
sheet metal parts, 341–368
    with Contour Flange tool, **359–361**,
        359–361
    Cut tool, *364*
    with Cut tool, *364*
    Cut tool, **364**
    Flange tool, **352–359**
    Hem tool, **362–363**, *362–363*
    with Hem tool, *362–363*
    making with Face tool, *350*, **350–351**
    making with Punch tool, *365–366*
    manufacturing-focused toolset, **342**
    with Punch tool, **365–366**
    rules for. *see* sheet metal rules
    special detailing tools, **367–368**, *367–368*
sheet metal rules, 342–350
    creating new rule, *343–344*, **343–344**
    defining, *348*, **348–349**
    overview of, **342**
    publishing, **349–350**, *349–350*
    Sheet Metal Default dialog box, *342*,
        342–343
    Style and Standard Editor, **344–347**, *347*
Sheet tab, Style and Standard Editor, 344–345
Shell tab, Shell tool, *262*, **262**
Shell tool, 262–266
    More tab, **262–263**
    new sketch for next step, *264–265*,
        264–266
    Shell tab, **262**, *262*, *262–265*
    shelling of part, **263**, *263*
Show Reflections, scene styles, 379
Show Shadows, scene styles, 379
Simple Drill, Hole dialog box, 114
Single User project file, **29**
Size tab, Punch tool, *365*, **365**
sketch constraints, *87*, 87–104, *91–92*
    adding dimensions, **89–94**, *91–92*, *94*,
        102–103, **102–104**
    building complex part model, **98–102**,
        99–101
    with circles, **237–238**, *238*
    construction geometry, **96–98**, *97*
    overview of, **87–88**
    specialized linetypes, **95–96**
    using Revolve tool to create turned part, 132
    viewing existing, *88*, **88–89**
    working with, **84–86**

Sketch Constraints menu, **87**, *87*
sketch-derived views, 196–210
   break out view, **203–207**
   component overrides, *207–208*, **207–208**
   creating break view, **197–199**
   cropped views, *209–210*, **209–210**
   defining break view, *196*, **196–197**
   expanding dimensions. *see* dimensioning,
     expanded
   overview of, 196
   sketching, *201–203*, **201–203**
   slice view, *199–201*, **199–201**
   suppressing view, **210**
Sketch Properties toolbar, **202**
Sketch tab, Application Options dialog box,
   23–25, *24*
sketched features, **82**
sketching, 113–120
   adding bolts manually, 158–159
   adding constraints. *see* constraints
   adding dimensions, **89–94**, *91–92*, *94*,
     102–103, **102–104**
   adding text to part, **240–243**
   creating slice view, *199*, **199–201**
   with Fillet tool, *108*, **108–113**, *111–112*
   with Hole feature, **113–120**
   keyboard shortcuts, **395**
   layout, **247–248**
   parametric models, **82–83**
   part models, **83–86**, *84–86*
   views, **201–203**, *201–203*
slice views, **199–201**, *199–201*
Smooth constraint, **87**
Snap Settings, General Dimension tool, 62
Specification tab, Thread tool, **233**, *233*
Spline tool, **245–246**
Split tool, *238–239*, **238–240**
Spotface, Hole dialog box, 114
Spur Gear Component Generator, 314–318
   adding gears, **316–318**, *317–318*
   Calculation tab, **315–316**, *316*
   Design tab, **315–316**
   overview of, 314–315, *315*
standard parts
   adding bolts manually, **157–163**, *158–163*
   using Bolted Connection Design
     Accelerator, **163–167**, *164–167*
   working with, **157**
Standard toolbar. *see* Inventor Standard
   toolbar

standards and styles
   changing style settings. *see* Style and
     Standard Editor dialog box
   creating new standard, **170–173**, *171–173*
   drawing templates. *see* templates, drawing
   overview of, **169–170**
   saving new standard for sharing, **183–185**, *184*
Start-up Action, Application Options
   dialog box, 20
Start-up, Application Options dialog, 20
status bar, *18*, **18**
Status dialog box, **303–304**
Steering Wheels, Inventor Standard toolbar,
   13–14
Style and Standard Editor dialog box
   Available Styles tab, 176
   Bend tab, **345–346**, *346*
   Corner tab, *347*, **347**
   creating new dimension style, *179*,
     179–180
   creating new standard, **172–173**
   editing layer's style, **180–183**, *181–183*
   General tab, **173–174**, *174*
   Material Hatch Pattern Defaults tab,
     177–178, *178*
   Object Defaults tab, *176–177*, **176–177**
   sheet metal rules, **344–347**, *347*
   Sheet tab, **344–345**
   View Preferences tab, **174–176**, *175*
   working with object defaults, *178*, **178–179**
style settings. *see also* Style and Standard
  Editor dialog box
   assembly drawings, **74**
   base views, **42**
   break views, **196–197**
   dimensions, 65, 71
   folder options for, **30**
   Hole tables, **221**
   presentation views, **78**
   Rewind tool, **14**
   rotating views, **51–52**
   scene, **376–381**
   sheet metal rules as. *see* sheet metal rules
   style library, **30**, 184
   surface, *381–382*, **381–383**
Style tab, Render Image dialog box, **372–373**,
   372–373
styles, defined, 170
suppressing views, **210**
surface styles, *381–382*, **381–383**

surface texture callouts, *215*, **215**
Surface Texture Symbol tool, 222–226
Sweep tool, **268–271**, *268–271*, 274
Symbols options, Break dialog box, 197
Symmetric constraint, **87**

T

Table tool, 367–368
tabs, dialog box, *2*, **2**
Tangent Arc tool, **246**
Tangent Circle tool, **246**
Tangent constraint, **87**, *140*, **140**
Taper Tapped, Hole dialog box, 115
Tapped Hole, Hole dialog box, 114
templates
    beginning new drawings from, *38–40*,
        38–40
    New File dialog box, **7–8**, *8*
templates, drawing, 184–193
    building new template, **185–186**, *186*
    creating quick start template file, **191–193**,
        191–193
    creating template file, *191*, **191**
    modifying title block, *187–190*, **187–190**
    overview of, 184
    updating standard, **187**
termination options, Emboss tool, **240**
text
    describing revision tables, 217
    dimension, 62–63
    dimension editing tools, **65–67**
    previewing patterned, **245**
text, standards and styles settings
    Available Styles tab, **176**
    creating new dimension style, 180
    modifying title block, **187–190**, *187–190*
    Preset Value, 174
Text tab, Edit Dimension dialog box, 211–213
Text tool
    adding text to part with, **240–242**
    Leader Text tool, *214*, **214**
    overview of, *213*, **213–214**
Termination Group, Hole dialog box, 114
Thicken/Offset tool, **284–286**, *284–286*
Thread tool, 232–238
    3D grip editing, *235–237*, **235–237**
    adding detail, **233–234**, *234*
    controlling 3D grips, **235**
    Location tab, **232–233**

sketching constraints with circles,
    237–238, *238*
    Specification tab, **233**, *233*
three-dimensional Grip
    controlling, **235**
    defined, **234**
    editing, **235–237**, *235–237*, **320–321**, *321*
three-dimensional models, making, **104–108**,
    105–108
Three Point Arc tool, **246**
Through All, Hole dialog box, 114
timeline, animation, **383–385**, *383–385*
title bar, *8*, **8–9**
title block
    creating quick start template file, *192*, **192**
    defined, **185**
    modifying, **187–190**, *187–190*
To option, Hole dialog box, 114
Tolerance Method list, dimensions, 211–212
Toolbar list, Customization dialog, 290
ToolTip Appearance, Application Options
    dialog box, 20
Transition tab, Loft tool, *251*, **251**, *251*
Transitional tab, Place Constraint tool, **141**, *141*
Trim command, 248
True Reflection option, Realistic rendering,
    372, **372**
Tweak Components tool, 332, 335
two-dimensional drawings, from 3D data.
    see 2D (two-dimensional) drawings, from
    3D data

U

Undo, **10**
Units settings, Style and Standard Editor, 174,
    179–180
Up One Level icon, **4**
Update Styles, 187
Use Reflection Image, scene styles, 379
Use Style Library setting, Project File Editor
    creating new standard, 171
    creating quick start template file, 193
    defined, 30
user interface
    Browser bar, **17**
    Design window, **17**
    Display options, **14–17**, *15–16*
    overview of, *8–13*, **8–13**
    Panel bars, **17**

Rewind tool, **14**, *14*
status bar, **18**, *18*
Steering Wheels, **13–14**
ViewCube, *13*, **13**

V

Vault
    opening from files from, **6**
    project file, **29**, 31
    resources for Autodesk, **400**
Vertical constraint, **87**, 123
View Filters, Edit Hole Table dialog, 221
View Label Defaults tools, Style and Standard
    Editor, 175
View menu icon, **4**
View Preferences tab, Style and Standard
    Editor, **174–176**, *175*
View representations, **153–156**, *155*
ViewCube
    adding dimensions, 103
    animating cameras, 385–386
    beginning new part, 230
    Inventor Standard toolbar, **13**, *13*
views
    existing constraints, *88*, **88–89**
    keyboard shortcut for drawing, **395**
    overlay, 339
    sketch-derived. *see* sketch-derived views
views, creating, *38–40*
    adding dimensions. *see* dimensions
    adding Hole/Thread Notes, *68–69*, **68–69**
    auxiliary, **48–50**
    base, *40–41*, **40–44**, *43–44*
    detailing, **55–59**
    drawing associativity, *72–73*, **72–74**
    drawing of a part, **38–40**
    presentation, **77–78**, *78*

projected, **44–48**
retrieving dimensions from, **70–71**, *71*
rotating, **50–53**
section, **53–55**
Visual Syllabus, Help system, **34–35**, *35*

W

Web tool, **266–267**, *266–267*
weldments, **339–340**, *340*
Width setting, renderings, 370
Windows Explorer, **143–144**, *144*
Wireframe display, **15**, **22**
work axis
    applying, **121–122**, **125–126**
    defined, **113**, **121**
work environment, creating new, **25–28**,
    27–28
work features
    applying, **121–128**, *122–128*
    overview of, **120–121**
work plane
    applying, **121–124**, *122–123*, **127–128**, *128*
    editing parts in assemblies with, 150–152,
    150–152
    overview of, **120**
work point, **121–123**, *122*

X

X-Ray Ground Shadow tool, **15–16**
XML files, saving settings as, 20

Z

Zoom All command, **10**, 73
Zoom command, **10**, *11*
Zoom Selected tool, **12**
Zoom Window tool, **10**